Share the Gift
teaches you the dynamic
Seven-Layer Healing Process
that empowers you
to teach your Inner Child
the Laws of the Universe
that Attract Success!

Cathryn L. Taylor, MA, MFT, LADC

ISBN-13: 978-1542365260
ISBN-10: 1542365260

"You don't attract what you want—you attract what you feel about what you want—and that feeling is based on the vibration of emotion associated with your sense of self-worth.
That vibration is established in childhood.
It follows you into adulthood and becomes the vibrational beacon which is transmitted to the Universe with respect to your heart's desires. Your manifestations mirror the vibration of what you most fragile self feels he or she deserves.
That part of you is longing to feel safe enough to dream.
That part of you is waiting for you to care enough to protect and love. He or she is waiting for you to say, *I am the one you have been waiting for—I am here to love you—to keep you safe.*
This *Seven-Layer Healing Process* teaches you all you need to know in order to have that conversation."

A quote by Cathryn from a Seminar offered at
Echo Bodine's Center for Living
In Minneapolis, Minnesota March 7th, 2007

Share the Gift teaches you how to build the loving relationship that invites your Inner Child to feel safe. The exercises, meditations, and tapping sequences equip you to heal his or her pain, to transform fear into faith, betrayal into trust, shame into unconditional love. Once done, you truly can teach your Inner Child the law of attraction and bring his or her Divine energy to the manifestation table!

PRINTED BOOKS BY CATHRYN

Cathryn's bestselling *The Inner Child Workbook*
(Available at Barnes and Noble, amazon.com)

Life Beyond Confusion and Fear
… an overview of the four stages of addiction and recovery…

Maximized
… a shamanic tale about a road trip with her dog named Max…

Which Lifetime Is This Anyway?
… a metaphysical bible for multidimensional healing…

Soul Steps
… an innovative 90-day Program integrating body, mind, heart, and Soul … and introducing "conscious aerobic exercise."

Share the Gift
Introducing Cathryn's *Seven-layer Healing Process* featuring her signature "Interactive Tapping™".This Process is applied to Attracting Intimate Relationships; Attracting Abundance; Attracting Right Livelihood and Developing Reciprocal Partnerships with Inner Child Work and EFT.

Beyond Compassion
… a program which teaches you how to *"Access your Point of Power in Response to Loss …* "(Inspired by the author's personal losses)

Accept Who You Are! Get What You Want!
… a seven-layer healing formula that takes you into self-acceptance and depicts the connection between this acceptance and the ability to attract all that you desire. Includes a 30-day EFT/Inner Child video program!

All books are available through Cathryn's website-
www.EFTForYourInnerChild.com

In addition, her YouTube channel, which can be accessed at: https://www.youtube.com/user/ctinnerchildwork, has over 100 Educational videos demonstrating her unique style of energy therapy she calls, Interactive Tapping™ Also you can tune into Cathryn's Internet-based Radio show on EFT Radio called, EFT for Your Inner Child and Soul, and on BBM Radio entitled, EFT for Spiritual Fitness.

Dedication — June 9th, 2018

This book is dedicated to my God-child,
Lillian Audrey King Berger
No one has taught me more profound lessons
about "sharing the gift", than my
Lily-girl. You truly are a little, Illuminating Angel.

Then   Now

The picture on the front cover entitled, "Sharing the Gift," was created by Charles Frizzell of Colorado. (http://frizzellstudios.com/)

I first saw this picture on a greeting card in New Leaf bookstore in San Rafael, California on December 1st, 1989. I stopped there on my way home from the hospital. My God-child had just been born. The minute I saw this picture I knew it embodied the relationship I hoped to develop with Lily. I instantly bought and framed two copies—one for her and one for me.

For the first two years of Lillian's life, I was blessed to be able to spend two to three nights a week with her. I was indeed an auxiliary parent. In that first year, I was also completing the manuscript for The *Inner Child Workbook*. I'd write all week and then get to relax and cuddle up with Lily on the weekends. There were many "firsts" that year, but the one I most remember was the moment Lily looked up at me with a great big smile and said, "Bama". Those first two years were precious indeed. But in the few years that followed, circumstances changed … addresses changed … our time together changed.

Yet, even though we were apart, we stayed connected … our bond remained strong. We grew together and shared our gifts together … our gifts for passion … for "processing" … for creativity … honesty …for laughter. And, we established traditions. Sharing our annual birth-minute became one of my favorites. Every year on December 1st, at 5:40 AM and on June 9th, at 9:40 PM we get on the phone and mark our birth-minute with a meditation of affirmation and intention. We have not missed a birthday in over twenty years.

Yes, we have had many exchanges during Lillian's twenty-eight years on this planet …most of them by phone. Once she had turned eighteen it became most common for our conversations to begin with, "Bama, will you open my records?" Often we consulted her Akashic Records as Lillian inquired about what school would be most beneficial to enroll in, or what to do about her latest passion, her latest love. And often these talks concluded with our neutralizing/reinforcing the current situation with tapping. But no conversation was more heart-wrenching and transforming than the day we were talking on the phone and the subject evolved into the one about my leaving California … about my leaving her.

This conversation was different. It was not just about her challenges. It was about OUR challenge. It was the "elephant in the room." The subject we had both done a great job of avoiding. It was personal. It was raw. It was honest. But together, while tapping on our endpoints, we walked through the tumultuous feelings of our separation. Amongst tears and apologies, the truth of the pain … hers and mine … was spoken and heard.

I do not believe there is any other single moment in my life that has been so full of raw intimacy. That exchange gave an entirely new meaning to this painting and to the words, "sharing the gift." Shortly thereafter, I contacted Charles Frizzell and purchased the rights to this painting. I knew that one day I would write a book about the process of using tapping to heal old wounds. I knew that book would be called, *Share the Gift*. And I knew it would be dedicated to my God-child, Lillian.

Contents

SECTION ONE:
WHAT YOU CAN EXPECT

**Preface:
The Inspiration for the *Seven-Layer Healing
Process*!
What's Not Working?
Where Did It Begin?
How Can It Be Healed?**

What You Can Expect

Share the Gift, originally developed in 2007, was inspired by the *Teachings of Abraham* and the laws of the Universe. The material also introduced, for the first time, my signature, multilayered interactive tapping™ process which integrated the context of my Inner Child/Soul work with the concepts of the laws of the Universe and the energy psychology of Gary Craig's *"Emotional Freedom Techniques."* This tapping technique was further enhanced over the next decade by my interest in the new brain science.

What ultimately evolved was my *Seven-Layer Healing Process* became my working model for helping others heal by addressing and resolving core issues such as addiction, abandonment, betrayal, and shame. The process itself has been applied to systematically bring clarity and resolution to core desires such as establishing intimate relationships, attracting abundance and right livelihood, and creating reciprocal partnerships. Through meditations and journal exercises, you will learn how to give form to your Adult Self, vision to your future self, and support to your wounded self. You will be taught how to neutralize the emotional disturbances of your Inner Child, empower your inner adult, rewire your brain, and reprogram the DNA of your physical and etheric forms.

Using interactive tapping™ sequences and imagery, you will infuse every fiber and every cell with the divine essence of your Higher Self. You will be equipped with the tools to evolve into and enhance the new you. A state of magic and self-confidence will return. I recommend you purchase a special journal you can use to record the exercises and to comment on your thoughts and feelings throughout this process. It will serve a diary of your experience and may be useful as a useful reference of your progress because, by the time you have finished this book, you will have a viable formula for implementing this process into your daily life.

PLEASE NOTE: You will notice throughout this material whenever I reference a part of you, be it the Inner Child, Adult Self, Higher Self etc., I use capital letters. I do this to emphasize the fact that these are separate parts—a clarification that needs to be acknowledged in order to reinforce the need for the interaction between the different parts of you if a Healing is going to take place.

Preface:
The Inspiration For The Birth Of My Seven-Layer Healing Process

L ike most things, the "mother of intervention" is need. This model is no exception. Below is a letter written and emailed to the founder of EFT, Gary Craig, on 11/17/06. It was written after my first organic tapping experience which became the foundation for the merger of my Inner Child expertise with the innovative techniques of the new energy therapy called EFT. It further evolved into my signature method of energy therapy I then coined, Interactive Tapping™. This technique ultimately wove into my *Seven-Layer Healing Process* that became the cornerstone of every consult I conduct.

Dear Gary,

I just had the most profound experience with EFT. My name is Cathryn Taylor. I am the author of *The Inner Child Workbook*, which was first published in 1991 and is considered one of the classics in the "inner child" field. For the past twenty years, I have been working with this concept and instructing others on how to identify and resolve their Inner Child's conflicts. Several years ago I came across your EFT techniques. Since then I have been applying them to addictive behaviors and teaching clients how to use EFT to mitigate their anxieties.

But today was a real milestone.

For the past several months, I have been facilitating a new series called *teaching your Inner Child the Law of Attraction*. The series was inspired by the movie, *The Secret*. As is usually the case, we teach what we need to learn. When we attract more Light, we illuminate that shadow self who vibrates at a lower frequency. The very act of teaching this subject uncovered my last "cherished saboteur™" (my coined phrase for the part of us whose actions are intended to keep us safe, but whose impact keeps us from getting what we want).

"She" had been acting up ever since I taught my first class. I came to discover that this little one is my inner 17-year-old that is stuck in a moment of time when, just as she was ready to leave for college, her hero (my father) had a nervous breakdown. That part of me has been frozen and held captive at that moment ever since. It became apparent today that according to the belief system of my inner adolescent, any time I truly wanted to step into my mastery and manifest abundance, she assumed it would require "leaving" my father. This perceived reality triggered her fear which compelled her to addictively act out or compulsively distract. Her "perceived" threat eclipsed my passion and sabotaged my ability to succeed. No matter how healthy I got in all areas of my life, there always remained this shadow part of me that sabotaged my success. This distraction sustained her loyalty to her father but resulted in my experiencing an underlying and uniden-tified state of anxiety and despair.

Today is the day that I finally put it all together. I simply taught this inner adolescent how to do EFT; I brought her into my mind's eye and invited her not only to learn the principles of *The Secret* but to also learn how to use tapping to cope with her grief over Dad's breakdown. I had used EFT to deal with emotional disturbances, but I had never combined tapping with my Inner Child meditations to go back in time to actually teach that frozen part of me how to tackle the gut-wrenching emotions of helplessness, fear, anger, embarrassment, and utter despair. That part of me was never able to cope with the fact that she could not save her father from his emotional demise. His breakdown had somehow become her failure and that failure translated into her not being able to fully succeed without feeling as though she were abandoning him. It is amazing to me how a part of us can stay so incredibly loyal to the parent who does not cope with his or her own life. Afraid to surpass and abandon that parent, many of us sustain one area of our lives that remains dysfunctional.

Inner child work is based on externalizing the old wound, giving it a face, and then interacting with that part to make him or her feel safe. The model is a magical way of empowering our most competent Adult Self while simultaneously being able to acknowledge and respond to our more frightened parts. It is a way to "repairent" ourselves. It is a way to "right" old wrongs, to retrain the brain to expect something new—something healthy and life-giving.

So today, a miraculous shift occurred when I actually stepped back in time and taught my inner teen how to neutralize the frightening feelings of the time. By combining EFT and guided Inner Child meditations I was able to go back to that frozen time in math class when she looked at the clock and knew that, at that exact moment, her father was getting electric shock treatments to eradicate his pain. Having identified with him to such a degree she wondered how long it would be before the same would be necessary for her. She had no idea how she could possibly deal with her life any differently. If he couldn't cope then how could she?

I had been running from that moment, and that question, ever since.

But today I was finally able to help her find relief. Today I was able to set her, as well as myself, free. Faith was restored, and I am now able to step into the mastery I have worked so hard to achieve. I had done many meditations, but nothing had completed, dissolved, or neutralized, the pain of that moment. This combination finally did just that. EFT is a brilliant method to neutralize the pain of our Inner Child's past. Thank you for bringing it to the world and for being so dedicated to teaching others how to use this tool to heal.

CATHRYN TAYLOR, MA, MFT, LADC
November 17th, 2006

This particular experience inspired me to officially integrate EFT into my Inner Child work because I found that this combination offered one of the most comprehensive and effective methods to heal. Again, what evolved was my signature method of energy therapy I call Interactive tapping™. This then became the foundation for the dynamic model of healing I offer which I came to call, the *Seven Layer Healing Process. Share the Gift* systematically escorts you through these seven layers of healing that need to be addressed if you are to bring those wounded aspects back into the vibration of love and Light to feel safe. Through the process, you learn how to determine what's not working, understand where it began, and master the methods to heal.

So, What's Not Working?

Many of us have issues from our past that just won't go away—that stop us from achieving our goals? Whether it's a career that never gets off the ground, a relationship that never appears, or an exercise program to which we can never quite commit, it is easy to give up when we do not succeed. Many of us lose hope in our ability to manifest what we desire. We set our intentions; say our prayers and affirmations, and yet, continue to experience struggle in attaining our goals. So what exactly is it that is not working?

Whether remembered or not, there was that moment in your life when you first felt a loss of safety. The circumstances may not be the same as another, but the impact was the same—you froze. That moment in time is what Hal Bennett in his book, Follow your Bliss, refers to as the *essential wound*. It was at that exact moment when you first feared you would be unable to cope. You feared you might not survive. It was then that your life, even if you did not know it, began to *not* work. That moment followed you into adulthood and has been sabotaging your efforts to succeed ever since.

To understand the mechanics of this self-sabotage you have to adjust your kaleidoscopic lens a bit to grasp that we do not get what we want through wishes, intentions, prayers, or affirmations. In fact, we don't actually get what we want at all. We get *what our most fragile self feels* about what we want!

According to the universal principle called the *law of attraction*, the energetic magnet that attracts what we desire is *how we feel* about what we desire. The desire is merely the context. It is the substance of the intention we set; the wish and hope we affirm. However, what draws that which we desire into our experience is the *tone* with which we deliver our intention. It depends on how accepting we are of our self and how deserving we feel about our desire. If we feel good about ourselves and feel worthy of our desires, there is no resistance, no block to our allowing our dreams to manifest. But when we don't feel good about the person we are our dreams get eclipsed by our unworthiness.

Our unworthiness is based on the fear we are not good enough to succeed. We may shoot out arrows of intent or desire, but they get shot down by the weight of our doubts, fears, and shame—all of which are related to negative beliefs we developed as a child. Those beliefs became the cornerstone of our self-esteem, and our self-esteem determines the feeling tone or vibrational energy, we send out to our world and to the Universe.

All things are energy—thoughts, and feelings as well. What we think and feel emits a vibrational frequency which then magnetically attracts its vibrational match. Every desire begins with a thought. We think it. We want it. We begin to dream about it. If the feelings associated with that desire are pure, without hindrance, we will allow the desire to manifest and appear in our physical world with acceptance and ease. If, however, the desire gets high-jacked by unconscious fears and doubts, the Universe will respond in kind by sending back the exact match for the desire, laced with this same fear and doubt.

Those feelings of unworthiness—the ones that follow us into adulthood from childhood—the ones that result in a form of vibrational resistance—thwart our mastery. This resistance fuels our Inner Child's need to sabotage. The impact of this sabotage is most evident in the on-going conversation we are having in our own mind. It is the emotion associated with this constant chatter that gets transmitted to the Universe and ultimately attracts into our experience things that match the vibrational frequency of that resistance. So, again, literally, what we feel we attract!

Now we were not born with these feelings of resistance. We extended into this life from the vibration of the pure, positive, energy of our non-physical self which vibrationally exists in an energy field of unconditional love. Some call this energy field, or this non-physical reality, God, the Divine Matrix, the Vortex, All-That-Is or Spirit. The essence of us that exists in this non-physical reality is referred to as our Inner Being, Divine Self, God-Self, Holy Christ Self, or Higher Self. However you refer to these energy fields, it is from that non-physical dimension that we extend when we take on the density of physical form. Our non-physical self vibrates at a higher vibrational frequency than our physical self.

This again is significant because according to the law of attraction, everything is vibrational—everything is energy. *But the "frequency of vibration" of all things varies.* The energy in the physical dimension *vibrates* at a significantly lower frequency than that of the non-physical one. In fact, the energy vibration slows down to such a degree that this very alignment with the physical realm results in a form of spiritual amnesia. So even though we are not separate from this all-loving, Inner or Higher Self, we ultimately lose conscious contact with it and experience it as such.

This Inner Self is the source of our authenticity. Connection to it is what allows us to feel whole, complete. Those of us who are on a spiritual path dedicate much of our life to attaining, and then sustaining, this connection. A disconnection from our source of authenticity results in our feeling anxious and alone. This loss is perhaps the source of all of the other losses we experience. This disconnection leads to our feeling despair, anger, shame, and grief as we progressively exchange the connection we feel to our authentic self for a connection sought from others in our physical world.

This exchange and ultimate loss of our connection to our Authentic Self slowly occur during the first six years of our life during which time our brains are operating at the theta level. The minute we are born, and perhaps even while in the womb, we begin to download, without discretion, every impression of our physical world. We begin to establish the very fabric of the person we are to become, based on the introjections of parents, teachers, the media, and society as a whole.

We are, in effect, progressively disconnecting from Source energy while simultaneously experiencing the process of socialization. Like a computer, our subconscious mind is being programmed. We are downloading the instruction manual on how to fit in and how to be like everyone else. These ingested beliefs are infused with feelings and expectations which ultimately become the operating system from which we *attract*. The degree of tension associated with each of these responses determines the density of the vibrational energy which, in turn, dictates the speed with which we are able to manifest our desires—the heavier our emotional state the slower our manifestation.

Over time this disconnection from our authenticity leads to the loss of our sense of self and our ability to accept ourselves as the person we are. This disconnection from our Higher Self, and the ultimate loss of our authentic self are the underlying core of every loss we need to grieve.

Our self-acceptance becomes anchored in how others treat us. We lose sight of the person we are. We become the person we are expected to be. Every experience magnetized after that serves to verify this inherited set of beliefs which, for better or worse, reflects the values of others but defies the essence of our true and authentic self. The very things we struggle to attract and invest in attracting, hold a value for us based on these beliefs and expectations embedded in our subconscious programming since childhood. They are based on the disconnection from our authentic self and motivated by the impending feeling that we are not acceptable, and therefore not worthy, just the way we are.

In desperation, we begin to believe that if we can just succeed in making our dreams come true their acquisition will prove our worthiness and our lives will be fulfilled. The caveat is that our dreams are launched from a sense of lack and the belief system that the acquisition of this desire will take care of that lack. But in truth, we cannot attract anything from the vibration of lack. Instead, we continue to attract situations which mirror our experience of lack because we can only attract our heart's desires when we are in vibrational alignment with those desires. And we are only in alignment with them when we are in alignment with our authentic self which is a direct extension of our Higher Self.

So we get caught in this vicious circle. We try to rectify our feelings of unworthiness with actions that will get us what we want based on the faulty assumption that the acquisition of our desire will result in our feeling good about ourselves. Unfortunately, this is not the case. It is just the other way around. We have to feel abundant and observe abundance in our world before we can attract the abundance we desire. We have to see love in the world before we can attract the love for which we long. We have to love what we do in order to attract a career in which we can do what we love.

And the trick to getting all of this into alignment is first to experience it as the adult and then, in turn, help the fractured, Inner Child feel worthy enough to have it. We have to first attain the level of self-esteem to be able to "see" ourselves as deserving of that which we want, and then help those fragile parts within us move beyond the fear and experience that deservedness as well. We have to discover the gifts and then share them. We can't do this as a child. As a child, we respond to life from a disempowered place. But by the time we become adults we have acquired certain skills and experiences that provide the point of reference needed to cope. Our ability to cope is what makes us believable to the Inner Child. It is why we can teach the fragile Inner Child how to feel safe enough to risk wanting without fear.

And how are those fears evident in your day-to-day life? They are obvious in the areas of your life where you feel the least satisfaction. Those areas of your life in which you struggle hold the invaluable information needed to begin your journey to getting what you want. Within them lays the vibration and expression of your lack of self–esteem to which the Universe is responding. Those areas are your mirrors—your reflection. They offer the content of your work. If you simply look at the contrast between what you want and what you have, the information is right before you. The losses you have incurred in response to your relationship to your body, to your family and friends, to your career, your finances, your passion and your self-esteem, hold the nuggets of the focus of your work—the focus of your grief—the focus of your healing—a healing that happens in layers.

To further enrich your understanding of this let's first take a look at this dynamic from another perspective.

WHERE DID IT ALL BEGIN—A Psychological And Vibrational Perspective

The actual focus of setting one's intention and attracting what is desired began decades ago. However, it actually became "popularized" early this century when an explosion occurred and the laws of the universe, and most specifically the law of attraction, suddenly caught the attention of the masses. An electrical current disseminated as a plethora of information became available to the mainstream in a new way. Workshops offered by Esther Hicks, who brings forth the group of Light Beings called "Abraham", and J.Z. Knight, who channels an entity referred to as "Ramtha.", drew fresh audiences. Movies such as The Secret and What the Bleep Do We Know? took the world by storm as they revealed the magic of these ancient laws.

A QUICK REVIEW OF LAW OF ATTRACTION

We already have covered the fact that universal law simply states that what we think and feel emits a *vibrational* frequency of energy which attracts a *vibrational* match—what we see and feel we create. With the onslaught of the movies mentioned above, this information was delivered cinematically for the first time, and therefore, began to reach those who had not previously found these truths through the written word. These concepts entered the mainstream. People got excited. Lives began to change. There was magic all around as many began to experience the law of attraction first-hand. They manifested those pre-paved parking places; their desired relationships; that divine-right job. Many felt empowered and exuberant.

But for most it was short-lived. The magic began to dampen. Some became frightened and disillusioned. Many assumed they were doing something wrong. They experienced fear—then shame—then anger—then despair. What few realized was that the very act of setting an intention pushed some part of them out of its comfort zone—coming face to face with its doubts and fears. They had not been prepared for the resistance, the backlash, the sabotage.

And for many, this is still true today. They discover these principles, begin practicing them, and then all of a sudden are met with resistance and failure. They begin to fear true mastery. Their wounded Inner Child takes center stage and begins the process of sabotage. It sabotages the efforts to succeed in an attempt to protect from failure. It sabotages efforts to succeed because, simply, it is terrified of success. And as you have seen, whatever that part of us fears, we attract into our experience.

What we conceive we achieve. This is a scientifically-proven fact. Our mind does not know the difference between what is real and what is imagined.

This truth was portrayed quite eloquently in the movie, What the Bleep Do We Know? The storyline wove together a woman's addictive battles with quirky animation to depict the impact our thoughts have in every cell of our body. Sprinkled between the real and imaginary scenes were interviews with some of the world's most renowned quantum physicists, spiritualists, and alternative healers who substantiated the movie's suggestions with compelling research and extraordinary possibilities.

One significant scene featured the work of Dr. Masaru Emoto who discovered that:

"...crystals formed in frozen water reveal changes when specific, concentrated thoughts are directed toward them. Emoto found, "that water from clear springs and water that has been exposed to loving words shows brilliant, complex, and colorful, snowflake patterns. In contrast, polluted water, or water exposed to negative thoughts, forms incomplete, asymmetrical patterns with dull colors..."

This substantiates what was talked about in the previously that when you focus positive, loving thoughts on your dreams your mind starts the process of creating them. If there is no resistance you begin to allow the manifestation. But when those thoughts get ambushed by your doubts and fears you disallow your dreams, and instead, create chaos and frustration.

It has become widely accepted and understood that if terror, betrayal, fear of abandonment or shame, are attached to the manifestation of our desires they will eventually be annihilated by that negativity. As many have seen, when hopes and dreams are externally based on the values of others, instead of on our internal values, we deny the essence of our true self. Manifestation is vibrationally contingent on our being connected to our true self. When we are not connected, we feel a loss—not only of our dreams—but also the loss of our true self!

And again, this loss of our true self evolves when we adapt to another's expectations and become who we think we need to be in hopes of feeling accepted and loved. This loss activates the process of grief. It is involuntary. It is a natural, predictable series of emotional responses encountered any time we experience a loss of any kind. These emotional responses affect the way we think and the manner in which we express our emotions.

What the Bleep Do We Know?, and subsequent scientific research supports the existence of a biochemical component linked to these emotional responses. What we think, feel, and say plays such a profound role that we literally can (and subconsciously do) use our thoughts, feelings, and statements to impact our cells.

Athletes know this. Cancer survivors know this. They have long known the power of positive, deliberate, intention and affirmation. They employ these techniques with great success.

What most of us do not keep in mind on a day-to-day basis, however, is the fact that when our thoughts, feelings, and statements are negative they produce negative results. Our cells flat-line and become lethargic. They are programmed to energetically attract exactly what we think and envision. If we tell ourselves we are fat—our cells create fat. If we tell ourselves we are a failure—we create situations in which we fail. If we fear getting hurt—we attract hurtful situations. This pattern of negative belief systems, self-negating feelings, and incriminating self-talk may begin in childhood in response to our non-filtered download, but they become magnified the first moment we confront not feeling safe and experience that "essential wound."

The Essential Wound

Each of us experiences a defining moment in our lives when we realize we are not safe. It is part of the human experience. Again, Hal Bennett, in his book, Follow Your Bliss, was the first to refer to this moment as the *essential wound*. Our psyche experiences a trauma which shatters our basic assumption about our world. It also corrupts the value system we downloaded. Things in our life begin to go awry. What we thought would lead to safety all of a sudden does not. This trauma can be a result of neglect, sexual or physical abuse, or mental cruelty through shame and belittlement. It can be experienced in this lifetime, or can even be carried over from a previous lifetime. The DNA blueprint of our first remembered Soul experience of feeling unsafe has been shown to be carried in the etheric body and can impact the force field of our current incarnation.

In response to this realization, irrespective of its origin, our psyche goes into shock. We either dissociate from the emotion of the event or bury recall of the event, thus banishing the memory deep into the unconscious mind. The stress of these traumas, however, gets recorded in the electrical systems of our bodies and ultimately emerges as symptoms of what is called Post Traumatic Stress Disorder. There are two kinds of PTSD: simple and complex. Complex PTSD usually results from multiple incidents of abuse and violence such as child abuse or domestic violence. Simple PTSD is related to an isolated incident which is beyond the scope of ordinary coping abilities.

POST TRAUMATIC STRESS DISORDER-PTSD

Until recently it was thought that PTSD impacted only combat veterans or victims of isolated, one-time events such as 911 or a natural disaster. The psychological community has come to understand that, in fact, there is another form of PTSD which is now referred to as complex PTSD. Not only are survivors of atrocities such as the Holocaust, torture, war, natural disasters, catastrophic illnesses, and horrific accidents susceptible to PTSD—anyone who is exposed to an on-going threat to his or her safety, (such as physical or sexual abuse, rape, domestic violence, family alcoholism, or any experience which threatens one's basic survival) can develop a form of PTSD.

Remarkably, this holds true even if a person *witnesses* a traumatic event. If, as a child, you observed the abuse of your mother or the abuse of a sibling, you can develop debilitating PTS symptoms from just having been a witness. Traumas of great magnitude shatter our basic assumption about the world and our experience of personal safety. The impact can leave us feeling alienated, distrustful or overly clinging. These responses are buried and emerge only when a trigger brings these feelings back to the surface.

Our affirmations serve as this trigger. Underneath the surface, the electrically-charged emotions related to these traumas are forever encoded in our bodies and are conditioning our cells to attract exactly that which we most fear. The process becomes circular—our fear perpetuates this Post Traumatic Stress response, and our PTS response perpetuates our fear. Fear creates anxiety. Anxiety is the first stage of grief. We are perpetually responding to the never-ending loss of our true self. Why? Because when we feel unsafe, we deny our true self and develop the adapted self as we evolve into the person we think we need to be if we are to experience love and protection.

THE BIOCHEMICAL PERSPECTIVE

Author, Candace Pert—a neuroscientist who is also featured in the film, *What the Bleep Do We Know?* provides a very compelling, biochemical, explanation for the circular impact of our perpetual grief. When asked why we keep getting into the same kinds of relationships, having the same kinds of arguments, repeating the same patterns, she replies:

> *...Every emotion circulates through our body as chemicals called neuropeptides—"short-chain" amino acids—that talk to every cell of our body deciding what is worth paying attention to. When these peptides repeatedly bombard the receptor sites, the sites become less sensitive and require more peptides to be stimulated. Receptors actually begin to crave the neuropeptides they are designed to receive. In this sense, our bodies become addicted to emotional states. When we have repeated experiences that generate the same emotional response, our bodies develop an appetite for these experiences. Like addicts, we will draw experiences toward us that give us that fix...*

If we are constantly being exposed to neglect and abuse we develop an almost hyper-vigilant anticipation of the abuse—and when we anticipate it, we attract and create it.

Lynn Grabhorn, in her best-selling book entitled, Excuse Me, Your Life Is Waiting, states:

> *...Modern-day physicists have finally come to agree that energy and matter are one and the same...everything vibrates because everything—what you can see and not see—is energy, pure, pulsing, ever-flowing energy. Just like the sound which pours out of a musical instrument, some energy vibrates fast from high frequencies, and some vibrate slowly at low frequencies...the energy that flows out from us comes from our highly-charged emotions which create highly charged electromagnetic wave patterns of energy, making us powerful—but volatile—walking magnets. "Like attracts like." When we're experiencing anything that isn't joy or love, such as fear, worry, guilt ... we are sending out low-frequency vibrations ...*

they're going to attract only cruddy stuff back to us ... It is always a vibrational match...

In my over three decades of experience helping individuals arrest their addictive behavior and heal their childhood and Soul wounds, I have observed this same dynamic from a slightly different angle. I have observed that most of us, when conditioned to anxiously anticipate a certain response, unsuccessfully attempt to manage that anxiety. Our psyches cannot sustain the on-going experience of the tension, and ultimately, symptoms of our PTS develop. In an attempt to manage our emotions we flip between the second, third, and fourth, stages of grief which are bargaining, rage, and despair. This attempt to manage our feeling unsafe becomes what I have coined, our "codependent bargain™."

OUR CO-DEPENDENT BARGAIN™

We cannot heal our core issues and truly manifest our heart's desires until we identify and work with that bargain we made in this lifetime with the parent we identify as the one who could have loved and protected us—but didn't. We assume they didn't because of our deficiency—which becomes the source of our shame. In response to this shame and our perceived "lack," we enter into this unconscious agreement to "earn" their love in hopes they will finally love us enough to keep us safe.

When our co-dependent bargain™ doesn't work we feel tension. This tension is uncomfortable and must be discharged. We discharge it by developing compulsive, perfectionistic, behaviors which later can easily set the stage for our addictions. In our adult life, whatever we do in excess—its intent is in response to this unconscious, and yet ineffective, unmet bargain. Because this bargain is unconscious we engage in this dynamic over and over. Our perpetual belief which permeates every interaction and relationship is that if we can just figure out what needs to be changed or fixed then things will be the way we need them to be and we will feel safe, loved, and protected. This act is a response to the "bargaining" stage of grief. It is an attempt to deal with the first stage of grief which is the anxiety and panic we feel in response to not feeling safe and fearing abandonment.

But it never works. No matter how much we try to be perfect—no matter how much we try to fix things so they will be better—we always fail because unfortunately, the source of the dysfunction is not us—it is the dysfunction in the parental system or our caretaker's addiction, negligence, or inabilities, to provide for us. As children, we did nothing to deserve being unloved. So we can never be "good enough" to impact or change what is wrong so things will get better. We get caught in the vicious cycle of attempting to be perfect—failing—then acting out compulsively or addictively to discharge the energy of that failure. This cycle keeps us active in our compulsions and addictions as well as disconnected from our authentic self and Source. This cycle is enacted by what I have come to call our *cherished saboteur*™.

THE CHERISHED SABOTEUR™

All of us have that one central character within us who sabotages our best efforts to succeed. When we come up against this relentless part of self—a self who feels bigger than even our most desired goals—we have come into relationship with what I call the *cherished saboteur*™. The foundation of this saboteur is embedded in the co-dependent bargain™. In every endeavor we pursue we encounter this resistance and a loyalty which springs from our original, co-dependent bargain™. This part of self knows nothing else.

This cherished saboteur™ is engrained in our beingness to such a degree that we often come to believe it is our true self. It is the essence of our DNA makeup, the root of our energy disturbances and energetic imbalances. It is this biochemical response which reinforces this pattern over and over and continually bombards the receptor sites with the peptides which disarm us. Its patterns give rise to our righteous indignation as we defend this saboteur's legitimacy. And it's tricky. It can shape-shift—change forms—jump from one area of our lives to another—always leaving us with that one thread in our perfect tapestry which needs to be rewoven—that one brick in our successful fortress which needs to be replaced—that core issue is embedded in a continual reenactment of our co-dependent bargain™.

Self-preservation—the dance between the Co-dependent bargain™, Rage, and Despair

When we muster up enough courage to begin the process of confronting our childhood pain, it soon becomes apparent that at a very young age—when faced with an experience which shattered our basic sense of safety—we either became active in early co-dependent behavior, lashed out in anger at others, or shut down, became sullen, depressed, and closed off to feeling anything.

I call this the *fight, flight, or make it right* response! All responses are attempts to cover up the underlying feeling of loss (or grief) related to believing we are not good enough to be loved and protected. Again, we begin to believe the problem is with us. Our parents are not protecting us or making us feel safe because there is something wrong with us. This is the source of our negative self-talk which sets off the cycle of what I call the "shame/blame" game.

The Cycle of Shame and Blame

Our shame is the source of self-incrimination. We assume we need to be perfect in order to be loved and when we fail, we feel shame, or we project the feelings out onto others and blame them for our deficiencies and disappointments. We super-impose the experiences of our past onto the situations of our present. The faces of strangers become the faces of those who betrayed and disappointed us. We forever get caught in the cycle of feeling shame for not being good enough or placing blame on those who disappointed and hurt us. The shame/blame game creates a cycle which is never-ending, and that cycle is the process of grief.

The process of grief has five stages. The first stage is panic and is experienced in the form of our PTSD. To manage this panic, we again fluctuate between the second, third and fourth stages of grief. We bargain, rage, or feel despair. If we get caught in the loop of the second stage, we bargain with the experience by attempting to make deals with the lost object in hopes of retrieving it. If the loss is our sense of safety, we attempt to retrieve that safety by fixing the situation which resulted in the loss in the first place. If a loss such as this occurs in childhood, we develop behaviors whose intent is to win back the favor of the disapproving or abusive parent.

Our bargain goes something like this…"*Mommy, if I am a good little girl and never make you angry—then will you love me enough to make me feel safe?*" Of course, we can never be perfect enough to be reinstated to this sense of safety. So we can perpetually get caught in the bargaining stage of grief enacted through our co-dependent behavior of "trying" … trying to fix a situation over which we actually have no control. We can spend lifetimes trying to be reinstated to this lost sense of safety.

When this does not work, you can shift between the third and fourth stages of grief—anger, and despair. If your anger is turned outward and projected onto others, you are operating in the third stage of grief. If the anger is turned inward in the form of depression or despair, you are operating in the fourth stage of grief. Until your grief is processed through expression and neutralized with a technique such as tapping, you will be forever caught in this vicious cycle.

Our PTSD activates our need to manage this discomfort. We react with either a fight (anger), flight (despair) or make it right (co-dependency) response. We may find moments of peace—but the cycle of our grief is raging just below the surface and emerges whenever we encounter a situation which resonates with our original, essential wound.

THE SHAME OF OUR IMPERFECTIONS

The motivating force behind the grief process—and its perpetual re-enactment—is our feeble attempt to ward off the insurmountable fear of abandonment and loss resulting from the shame of our imperfections. The panic which accompanies this ever-present fear is intolerable. It fuels the Inner Child's sabotage. It continually circulates through our body sending messages to our cells that not only are we not safe (which triggers panic), but our lack of safety is our fault (which triggers shame). We come to believe we are not worthy and lovable enough to be protected. We enter into that unconscious agreement of our *co-dependent bargain*™ as we hold onto the hope that if we can just be good enough—perfect enough—"they" will come through for us and be able and willing to love us and make us feel safe. This inner belief becomes the foundation of our need to be perfect. Our pursuit of perfection gives us a focus for the tension created by the fear we may fail.

But we do fail. We fail because there is no such thing as perfection. When we fail, we end up back in the middle of the tumultuous emotions of our essential wound—the fear—the panic—the disconnection from our true self. We end up back in the cycle of grief. This cycle is the essence of the twists and bends in our DNA make-up. It is the root of our cherished saboteur's™ energy disturbances and energetic imbalances. It is fueled by this biochemical response which reinforces this pattern and keeps continually bombarding the receptor sites with the peptides which disarm us.

How It Can Be Healed

To become fulfilled and healthy adults who can manifest our heart's desire we have to intervene in this cycle. We have to *revise our false belief* that we are not good enough and *challenge our pursuit of perfection*. We have to *grieve the original loss* of safety—*express and process the anger and despair of the Post Traumatic Stress* associated with our loss, and ultimately *reprogram the cellular encoding of our DNA.*

My *Seven-Layer Healing Process* teaches you to use your breathing, guided meditations, journal exercises, and Interactive tapping™ sequences (to which you were introduced in the last section) to address this.

REVISING YOUR FALSE BELIEF WITH INTERACTIVE TAPPING™

This revision begins by dealing with the mental body and the belief systems which developed in response to your Inner Child not feeling safe. The mental body or mind carries the need to understand. It is the part of you who reads with such diligence to try to make sense of what happened and understand what needs to happen, for things to change. Knowledge is power. When you come to know that the only true source of safety is the Divine, you step into the empowerment of your Adult Self who can orchestrate our own healing. As John Bradshaw stated in the mid-eighties, "There is no human security!"

The only way to challenge the belief system of your perfectionism—the source of your shame—the belief that you are not good enough—is to operate from the Illuminated Adult Self. It is he or she who is connected enough to the Higher Source to be able to respond to, and retrieve, the wounded Inner Child or Soul part who felt the loss in the first place. That wounded self will let go of the old belief system when he or she experiences a different reality in the interaction with this Illuminated Adult you. With the interactive tapping™ sequences you slowly neutralize and, in essence, erase the old belief by assuring the wounded one that the Adult is now present and able to create something new. You begin to create your own reality, and therefore, you are empowered to envision a new experience for this wounded self.

In the *Seven-Layer Healing Process*, you are again encouraged to use your breathing to inflate you with the essence of the Divine. You begin your life with your first breath, and you complete your life with your last breath. Each breath, from birth to death, gives you the opportunity to reconnect.

This is accomplished in Layer One of the healing process. You learn how to empower your Adult Self. Once connected, you proceed through the remaining six Layers of healing and use the interactive tapping™ sequences to retrieve the adapted self. You neutralize and heal his or her feelings and create whatever reality he or she needs to feel safe. Once empowered in that First Layer of healing you are equipped to move through the remaining Six Layers which begin with separating enough from the wounded one so you can help him or her grieve and feel safe.

GRIEVING THE ORIGINAL LOSS WITH INTERACTIVE TAPPING™

Targeting your Inner Child's grief with interactive tapping™ sequences and the exercises that follow offers a viable method for your Adult Self to neutralize the effects of this anxiety and grief. When this anxiety is neutralized, the Inner Child witnesses that he or she can survive. In fact, being rescued by the Adult Self is proof of this. You now have a part of you who can escort the wounded self through all of the feelings of grief and the interactive tapping™ sequences provide the vehicle to do so. You step into your Empowered Self with your breathing and then use energy tapping to support your vulnerable self through the stages of grief as you neutralize the franticness of trying to control the situations that are beyond your control.

By first neutralizing your panic, and then addressing your frantic need to bargain, you are able to move into the rage of the loss. The Adult Self helps the Inner Child get the anger out of his or her body. And when the Inner Child has expressed and neutralized the rage he or she can collapse into despair. True despair is standing in the center of the void of the loss. When the Adult Self is able to tolerate that emptiness the Inner Child has no need to distract with compulsions and addictions. He or she does not have to deny with disruptions. You stand side-by-side with your Inner Child, naked in the truth of the loss, able to embrace its rawness without fear. The tumultuous emotions of your childhood grief emerge to be neutralized, so the cycle of your PTS can subside. There are entire sections in this book dedicated to processing the grief, both as the Adult and as the Inner Child. But this release can only be experienced once the truth has been spoken and heard.

This is true whether you are dealing with the current experience of your Adult Self, the memory of an Inner Child, or the recall of an aspect of your Soul. When you have successfully reconnected with your Authentic Self and neutralized and released the unexpressed emotions, the circuitry of both the physical and etheric bodies is forever changed. You are then able to download a new program into the DNA make-up of each cell.

REPROGRAMMING YOUR DNA WITH SOURCE ENERGY AND INTERACTIVE TAPPING™ SEQUENCES

You will see how in the preview of the *Seven-Layer Healing Process,* you are lead through an exercise in which you do this reprogramming. However, for your conscious mind to support your efforts, it is useful to have a conceptual understanding of this exact process.

First of all, DNA is a large molecule, shaped like a double helix and found primarily in the chromosomes of the cell nucleus. The DNA contains the genetic information of the cell. The DNA forms a double helix, two elongated molecular chains (like staircases) that wrap around each other. DNA tells our cells what they have been; what they will continue to be; and what they will become. The DNA is the blueprint for our life processes. Each cell of our bodies contains the complete genetic code for the whole body.

According to Margaret Ruby, founder of *The Possibilities DNA Vibrational Healing School, (https://www.facebook.com/dnaofhealing)*

"…Our body's communication systems have been broken down due to feelings of limiting beliefs. There is a vibrational interference pattern attached to this limiting belief causing negative, low vibrational emotions, which affect and distort our DNA. When two energy waves (thoughts and feelings) pass the same point and are out of phase, they interact and create a low vibrational, low wave interference that can, in turn, create physical or emotional imbalance…DNA then replicates this interference pattern which has a twist and slight bend to it…"

These twists and bends have to be neutralized if we are to heal and manifest a productive, successful and satisfactory life.

Dr. Joe Dispenza (http://www.drjoedispenza.com/) —also featured in *What the Bleep Do We Know?* comments,"…*the remarkable component to this dynamic is the fact that as our cells split—and they do split and recreate—they carry the energy of the old cell. It does not split with a fresh start. A cell's off-spring carries the imprint of the parent cell at the time of the split. Negativity begets negativity, and positive reinforcement begets positive reinforcement!"*

There are trillions of cells in your body and within each and every cell is the nucleus, the mastermind for the blueprint of your life. The stories recorded in your DNA determine the course of your relationships, your wealth, your health and your career. What happens to you on your life journey is a result of what is written in the life code of your DNA. When this blueprint becomes faulty—the communication between each cell is faulty. This faulty communication is in response to the wounds experienced in childhood. It is established in response to the fears, disappointments, and hurts encountered when you were unable to fend for yourself.

Connecting with your Higher Self, accomplished through breathing and interactive tapping™ sequences, enables the Adult Self to repair this faulty communication. By activating your DNA and reprogramming and infusing it with the vibration of Source Energy, your most Illuminated Adult Self re-establishes a connection with its intuition and then helps the wounded Inner Child do the same. The twists and bends, which create the interference patterns of the DNA in every cell in your body, are neutralized, and the cells can once again be infused with this vibration of Source Energy.

But not only can the cells be reprogrammed, now, with the new brain science and epigenetics, it is understood that it is possible to even rewire the brain and construct new neural pathways which sustain a healing of this kind.

REWIRING YOUR BRAIN WITH INTERACTIVE TAPPING™

As you have hopefully gathered, the basic cornerstone of my model is that; "the healing agent for the old wound, which results in your sabotaging behavior, is the interaction between your wounded one and a part within you who can respond with compassion, love, and care." And furthermore, I hope by now I have effectively explained that in order to achieve this healing you must develop a soothing inner voice which can respond to the wound and need of a younger self. But as you have seen, this interaction is often eclipsed by the stress that followed you into adulthood and gets expressed in your day-to-day life. So, instead of being able to respond, you collapse into the wound and react to the current situation in the same way you did as the child.

My understanding of this principle was enhanced when I listened to a New Brain Series, hosted by Ruth Buczynski, Ph.D. of the National Institute for the Application of Behavioral Medicine. http://www.mentalhealthexcellence.org/new-brain-series/

In that series I was introduced to the work of Dr. Richard Hanson author of the Buddha's Brain, and Hardwiring Happiness. http://www.rickhanson.net/ His work inspired me to integrate some of the new brain concepts into my *Seven–Layer Healing Process.* Interactive tapping™ in itself rewires the brain in that it positions a negative experience with a positive one. But infusing this process and modality with this new science makes it even more effective.

In my *Seven-Layer Healing Process* the meditative interactions, supercharged with the new interactive tapping™ sequences, successfully replaces the old reactive experience with a calmer, more compassionate, response. Your brain is then equipped to send your body the new messages that are more life-giving.

The Adult Self can give a face to those saboteurs who run rampant with their negative statements and destructive behaviors. This Illuminated Self learns how to relate to those wounded ones with care and love and helps them grieve what was originally lost. The essential wound is repaired as the true essence of self is invited back into the vibration of your force field where it can be safe. The body learns how to relax. There is a part within who is willing to learn how to cope and is about to learn how to grieve. This is the promise when you learn how to administer the basic interactive tapping™ sequences that enable you to address your grief. And where we start is with our universal fear that we each experience—the underlying fear that we will not survive—that life will present us with an experience with which we will be unable to cope.

Our Underlying Fear—The Fear We Will Not Be Able To Cope

Our mastery is thwarted and the manifestations of our desires blocked because of an underlying fear we will not be able to survive if we lose something or someone we are unprepared to live without. The object of our feared loss is unique to each of us, but its undercurrent permeates every dream—every hope—every disappointment.

EXERCISE: TAKE A MOMENT

Take a moment to think of those times in your own life when you were most distraught. Then respond to these questions in your healing journal.

1. Tune into the anxiety of that stress.

2. What is its source? What is at stake?

3. What do fear you may lose?

4. What do you envision would happen if you were faced with such a loss?

5. What are those people, places, or things in your life about which you might hear yourself say, "If I ever lost _____, I would never survive."

In Layer One you work with this greatest fear and begin to address the stages of grief related to that fear. For most, it goes back to the exact moment we first experienced the world as unsafe, when we first lost trust in our environment when we first feared we would not be able to cope. But it didn't stop there. That underlying fear followed us into adulthood and it needs to be cleared before we can ever hope to help the Inner Child resolve the original pain.

My signature *Seven-Layer Healing Process* teaches you the layered process on how to access this information and gives you concrete ways to work with it. It shows you how to use the new energy therapy of tapping and how to apply the metaphysical concepts of the law of attraction to create the life you desire and deserve. *The Seven Layers of Healing,* to which you are about to be introduced, provides you with all you need to heal your Inner Child so you can share the gifts of the universe and invite them to share in the magic with you.

But first, you need to understand the components of the *Seven Layers of Healing* so you will be prepared to implement all that you learn.

SECTION TWO:
THE COMPONENTS OF HEALING ...

Components Of Healing

General Thoughts On The Process Of Grief

We all grieve. Much of the time we are not even aware we are grieving. We associate grief with a major loss such as that of a loved one or the loss of our security when we lose our house or a job. But as you will see in this material, it is my experience that we are in one of the five stages of grief all the time. Every major feeling we have fits into one of the stages of grief. Grief is a way we let go. Grief is a way we expand. Grief is a way we grow. We are constantly dealing with the evolution of change, and change requires that we let go of what was and embrace what is unfolding and emerging. It is the process of the ebb and flow of living life itself.

In this section, whether you are dealing with the loss of a loved one through death or divorce; the loss of a possession of comfort such as a house or even a car; the loss of a pet, or a hobby that has provided comfort, companionship, and support; the loss experienced physically with an injury, an accident, or the process of aging itself; or even the loss of a wallet, a cell phone, or an item of sentimental value; you will go through the five stages of grief. If those emotional reactions are not in some way resolved they will get stuck in your body and come back to haunt you physically, emotionally, or mentally. So, needless to say, it is in your best interest to fully understand the process of grief so you can embrace it, resolve it, and grow from it. My hope is that this following material will help you do just that!

But to do so it is essential that you get comfortable with grief. To do so, it is useful to have a fuller understanding of grief because most cultures do not embrace grief. They support a more stoic approach to loss and encourage the "buck up and bear it," philosophy. In the long run, that approach does not work. That approach did not work when we were children. It does not work when we confront loss as an adult, and when dealing with multidimensional grief from other times and places it doesn't work.

As children, we did not have the emotional maturity and capacity to process the intense emotions of grief. And if you choose to explore other realms and other lifetimes you will most often find that the fragment of your Soul did not have a choice either. But today, now, in this time and space, you do have a choice. And today, in this evolution of our growth you have ample support and technique to deal with grief. So my hope, in addressing grief more fully here, is that I will be offering you that choice and hopefully, you will be inspired to, and equipped to deal with your grief irrespective of its source.

So let's begin at the beginning.

Grief results from the stress response to fight, flee or freeze. When we experience trauma as a child our efforts to resolve these moments of stress get interrupted. Instead, we get locked into the stress response and spend much of our life bouncing amidst situations to which we react. As we have already discussed the psychological community is now referring to this response to our world as a complex form of "post-traumatic stress disorder", or simply PTSD. What is relevant for this grief overview is that when PTS, which originated in childhood, is coupled with a major loss in adulthood, the coping mechanisms of the past trauma will dictate the response to the current crisis at hand. In fact, even if we have not suffered from PTS, most experience at least some residual, childhood grief that has not been resolved.

Research now suggests that the essential wound we encounter the first time we experience the world as unsafe establishes the blueprint with which we will deal with loss throughout our lives. The context and intensity of our unresolved loss may differ. However, the commonality is that the lack of resolution is based on the conscious, or unconscious, fear that we will not be able to cope if we confront the depth of intense feeling associated with loss. What few realize, and what most cultures do not support, is the fact that *learning to embrace the process of grief is the antidote for our fear that we will be unable to cope.* Learning how to process grief is the most promising way to live a fulfilling life because it enables us to truly live life without fear.

Most of us are somewhat familiar with grief. We have experienced loss. We relate to grief as a process that must be endured, but only when there is a *major* loss, a measurable loss, one that has a beginning and an end.

However, as I suggested earlier, grief is a predictable process we experience on a regular basis in response to the many challenges we face each day. These commonly accepted stages of grief are experienced in response to even the little moments of loss—minute losses—like the momentary loss of self-esteem we feel when we do not live up to our own potential, or the loss of trust we might feel when a friend does not live up to our expectations. We can even experience grief when we fail to achieve a "personal best" in some desired endeavor. Without realizing it, we progress through the five predictable stages of grief even in response to these minor infractions.

Often, the process takes as little as ten minutes. But irrespective of how long it takes, we do progress through the same stages of feelings one experiences when confronted with a major loss. We feel anxious, (stage one—denial, panic, anxiety) which is mitigated by a desire to fix, control, or change the situation, (stage two—bargaining). When this fails, we feel anger and irritation, (stage three—anger). When we are exhausted by our anger, we begin to let go. We collapse into the truth of the loss and feel the deep despair, (stage four—despair). If we are lucky, with time, we do resign ourselves to the loss. We accept the loss. And, depending on the severity of the loss, we do reinvest and move on, (stage five—acceptance and resolution).

But many are not that lucky. An individual can get stuck in any one of these five stages of grief. If one's PTS is triggered, he or she can ruminate about the situation for days. If this occurs then, irrespective of the nature of the loss, the individual will continue to get retriggered at the stage of grief he or she was unable to resolve in the first place. This person simply goes from one triggering experience to the next, forever caught in a state or reactivity, experiencing few moments of peace and calm. Anxiety-ridden and overly active in co-dependent behavior, he or she can approach the world with rage and anger, or suffer from depression and despair.

Nonetheless, whether our childhood trauma was severe or not, most of us find we are living in a society in which unresolved grief has become an epidemic. The current economic situation, continued threats of terrorism, and relentless wars coupled with current stresses of daily life leave us afraid and confused—triggering childhood wounds and adult doubts about our ability to cope. We are thrown into the stages of grief as we express our unresolved anxiety, confusion, fear, anger, and sadness, which often are expressed through compulsive and addictive behaviors.

We may eat too much; drink, drug or smoke too much; love, shop, work, gamble, or worry too much. But we live out of fear rather than faith—compulsion rather than choice—isolation rather than unity, as we long to feel safe and secure. But there is little human security. Whatever excessive behavior we choose, it simply serves to numb the fear of the unknown, the pain of our grief.

Millions are pharmaceutically treated for depression, anxiety disorders, and post-traumatic stress. Each of these ailments has its roots in unresolved grief. When our grief is not processed, the lingering feelings of loss accumulate. They erode our hope and often lead to rage and despair. When faced with a major loss, these unresolved feelings roar deep within and exacerbate the current crisis. The depth of emotion can become a source of fear—fear that we will not cope.

And there is some truth to this possibility. The underlying effects of our grief get stored in our body, morph into physical ailments, and become a steady source of emotional, physical, mental, and spiritual, decline. The emotions may get numbed by our addictions, but our grief does not go away. It lays dormant, threatening to resurface with a vengeance, demanding the attention it deserves.

Yes, it is my experience that grief is deserving of our attention? It is deserving because these five stages of emotion are a natural response to living our life fully. It is deserving because dealing with the contrast and the resolution of that contrast is what invites our Soul to grow. It inspires us to work with our Inner Children so they can be safe. It relieves our body of storing the unexpressed emotions related to the perpetual loss we feel from just being human in this unpredictable world. And it allows us to live non-addictively, free to embrace, without fear, all that life has to offer.

Why?

Because if we have the tools to grieve we have the ability to cope. And, again, our biggest fear when confronting loss is that we will not cope. When we trust our ability to cope with whatever life brings us we have no need to fear what life brings us. And life certainly brings us experiences that will challenge, and inspire. But life also offers a myriad of opportunities to be triumphant.

So what's the first step to dealing with your grief? You first have to acknowledge it. You begin to identify the challenges of loss by recognizing those moments when, in response to challenging emotions, you restrict and contract. That very response shows you where you are out of alignment with your Higher Self or Inner Being with respect to something in your life. You are out of alignment with your most illuminated self. In response to some unexpected experience in your life, you have collapsed into an old fear and your job is to explore and resolve the exact source of that collapse. If you understand the five stages of grief we have a starting point for that exploration because every challenging emotion you encounter can be categorized as one of these five stages of grief. And every contrasting feeling, when resolved, holds the opportunity for expansion and growth.

When we experience loss, it is indicative of our attachment to someone or something. The attachment itself can be healthy and fluid—the resolution of its loss expanding and illuminating. When we lose someone we love or lose something of great value, our feelings of grief are a testament to how much that someone or something truly meant to us. It is a sign that we allowed ourselves to love, to be attached, to care. To grieve is to be alive. Grieving is a way we let go and allow a new form of the relationship or situation to emerge. That is the promise of the fifth stage of grief. We accept the loss of what was. We open up for a new form of connection to unfold and take its place. This is even true when we lose something of sentimental value, an object that we would prefer not to live without. Perhaps it is a piece of jewelry passed on as a family heirloom. It can even be that favorite pen or a book given to us by a special friend. What is the new form of a loss such as this? It is letting go with grace. It is finding a way to release and let go. That is indeed the final stage of grieving anything lost. Finding the grace to accept and let go so we can emotionally move on, and be filled with what life has to offer when we are not holding on to something that is gone.

As I look back on the experiences I have had with all of the moments of grief I have felt during this lifetime, I feel a sense of fulfillment. Being able to breathe through the grief and get to the place where I felt completion enabled me to stay connected to my Creator, to my Inner Being, my Higher Self. That connection enabled me to get out of my way and let the situation of loss morph into its next evolution. Trusting the process of grief empowered me to love without fear. That trust is what enabled me to stay connected to those I lost, during and after, their passing, in profound ways. My life is richer because I do not fear love. It is richer because I do not fear attachment. It is richer because I do not fear emotion.

When you can stay connected to your spiritual source, ask for, and receive, insight regarding the higher purpose of even your momentary losses, and fearlessly embrace the process of grief, you can rest assured you will be able to successfully live life unafraid to love. You will re-establish your trust in being able to cope. You will come to have faith in your ability to breathe through the anxiety, embrace the momentary anger, disillusionment, and despair, and with grace, return to a state of resolution and acceptance involved in everyday losses. When you can grieve, you can live life without hesitation. When you can grieve, you can nestle safely in the comfort of the arms of your Higher Power and feel bigger than your fears.

It is said there are two predominant states of emotion—love and fear. We are either feeling afraid or feeling love. Every other emotion falls somewhere in between. We cannot feel love and fear at the same time.

What can you do when you slip from the safety and comfort of trusting your Higher Power into the depths of fear that you will not survive? You guessed it! You can embrace the process of grief.

But to embrace grief, you have to understand grief in a more practical and non-intimidating way. To do so it is important to fully comprehend and accept that *you are already in a constant state of grief.* Let me give you a simple example. Although you might not realize it, as was suggested earlier, you can experience the five stages of grief every time you miss a phone call. Well, at least every time you miss a phone call you wanted to receive. Picture for a moment those times you've heard your cell phone ring but could not get to it in time. You hurriedly dropped what you were doing but to no avail. You got there too late. The caller had hung up.

What was your response?

Whether identified as such or not, it was most often the first stage of grief—denial. This was followed by the tension and anxiety related to what you perceive you have missed. You may find yourself pushing 'call back,' but with no luck. The caller is leaving you a message or has gone on to another call. What happens then? You feel frustrated. You try to manage the situation by calling again. And this cat-and-mouse game can go on for several minutes.

Have you ever talked to your phone as if you are talking to the person trying to reach you? "Pick up! Pick Up," you command. In today's world, you most likely send a text message commanding a response. That's when you slip into the second stage of grief. You find yourself bargaining with the dead phone as you hear yourself plea,"Just, pick up! I'm here—just callback!" But inevitably the other person has shut off the phone, or is engaged and cannot connect. What do you feel when "managing the situation" does not work? Most often you experience anger and disappointment, and sometimes sadness and despair.

The feelings may be mild. But they are the feelings of grief nonetheless. The sadness does give way to the knowledge that the person will indeed call back, or the call comes through and you breathe a sigh of relief for the need has been met. However, you come to terms with this incident; a resolution does ensue.

You first experienced disbelief that you had missed the call. This disbelief covered up the initial anxiety (stage one) which got denied as you tried to manage the situation (stage two). When this did not work, you most likely felt irritation or even anger (stage three), which then gave way to despair (stage four). And then, ultimately, you resigned yourself (stage five) to the fact that the person would indeed call back. In a period of several minutes, you experienced the five stages of grief. If you recognize these steps, you move through them and do not get stuck. The more you befriend this process, the more moments of contentment you will experience.

So I encourage you to have the courage to befriend this process. Learn as much from this material as you can, then seize the opportunity of your loss to learn more elsewhere. Relate to grief as a way to manage and resolve all of life's challenges and disappointments. Don't deny it. Treat grief as a friend. Learn how to breathe through your anxiety, let go, and give up your attempts to control the outcomes of situations over which you have no control. Give yourself permission to beat on a pillow, scream in the mirror, or throw a tantrum in the safety of your own home, as you rid yourself of the energy of your anger. Learn how to befriend the void and emptiness of your despair, so that place within you can be cleansed and prepared for you to bring in something new. Find that serene point of reference, then make that your goal to constantly process whatever keeps you from sustaining a sense of calm and peace.

Experience life. Stay present for life by identifying the stages of grief. Your comfort with grief is a sign that you are not afraid to live.

It is a sign you have the courage to love. If you are willing to actively engage in the process of grief, if you know how to graciously move through those stages, you will have a method by which you can deal with whatever life hands you. And life does hand you challenges. It hands us all challenges. Part of the human experience is to bump up against the glitches in our daily life.

No matter how good you are, you are going to have to deal with life's challenges. You are going to get stuck in traffic jams. Friends are going to disappoint you. Things are not going to turn out as you had hoped. You are going to collapse into old family roles or simply have "bad days."

But if you can become comfortable with the process of grief, you can live fearlessly with the assurance that you will indeed be able to cope. If you can cope, you can love and live from your heart. If you can cope, you can succeed!

INTERACTIVE TAPPING™—
The Marriage between Inner Child Work and EFT

One of the most expeditious ways to process through the five stages of grief is to do so with the energy therapy of EFT. And interfacing the grief stages with the interactive tapping™ sequences, as we do in this material, supercharges the effectiveness because you are working with the part of you that grieves and the part of you who can support the process of grief.

As you have seen throughout this material it is the interaction between the Adult Self and the Inner Child that is the healing agent of change. This interaction enables you to build a relationship with the parts of you who are afraid to succeed due to their sense of unworthiness. As you are well aware of by now those feelings are rooted in the antiquated beliefs formed in childhood. Combing the concepts of Inner Child work with energy tapping that is more relationship–focused serves to rid your consciousness of those unwanted and outdated beliefs. Once done, you can plant new thoughts and beliefs in a fresh, more fertile, environment. This new perspective supports your more fragile and frightened parts to allow, without risk, the manifestation of all that you want and deserve.

INNER CHILD WORK

Let's begin first with a more in-depth discussion of the Inner Child?

We all have one thing in common—we were all once children. Each of us progressed through predictable developmental stages of childhood. Inner Children are those aspects of us that carry not only our child-like sense of wonderment but also our childhood fears. The term Inner Child is simply a way to give a face to all of those feelings we brought into adulthood from when we were children.

If your life *is working* you have successfully brought positive experiences into your adulthood as a solid foundation for trust safety. Your Inner Child is, therefore, the source of your joy and excitement.

However, if your life *is not working* then it is most likely because you learned early in life it was not safe to feel or trust. That perspective is now the source of your sabotage to success. Those experiences influence your fears, your willingness to trust, your anticipation of abandonment and betrayal. And, as was discussed in the previous section—what we expect we attract. What we perceive and conceive we achieve.

The goal of Inner Child work is to explore the strengths and challenges that followed you into adulthood. Once identified, you can reinforce the attributes that contribute to the success and work on resolving the aspects of you who challenge and block that success. It is from these experiences that the reflection of the person you are takes form.

A positive reflection of self can get eclipsed by childhood betrayal, abandonment, and abuse. As you saw in the prior section, in an attempt to protect the psyche from being hurt again that child within us learned very early how to block anything that risked pain from occurring. A part of us got stuck in those old patterns and reacts in a knee-jerk manner anytime it feels threatened or at risk. The intent may be to protect, but the impact is sabotage. Your wounded Inner Child can sabotage fulfilling relationships because of the fear of abandonment, prosperity because of shame and guilt, or career success for fear of not being good enough.

What is the antidote for such sabotage? It is using the technique that combines these concepts with the energy therapy of EFT.

EMOTIONAL FREEDOM TECHNIQUES

https://www.emofree.com/ Commonly known as EFT

As you will witness the main ingredient in dealing with your past is having the capacity to cope with your feelings of grief. One of the most effective ways to do this is to neutralize them with the self-administered form of acupressure called EFT. I am a big fan of tapping. Tapping is what gave me a viable method to successfully move through many gut-wrenching emotions I have had to resolve in my own healing. It is the backbone of my *Seven-Layer Healing Process* and the cornerstone of every book I have written since 2007. So before we explore the stages of grief related to your present and your past, I want to introduce you to energy tapping. I will also provide you with a worksheet on how to design your own tapping sequences so you can begin to befriend this process yourself. However, never be afraid to seek professional guidance. Grief can be treacherous. You sometimes will need a guide. But it is standard procedure before you do engage in any self-administered form of EFT to understand that the use of energy treatment within the field of psychotherapy is a relatively new development. At this time there is only limited published research in established scientific journals investigating these methods.

While clinical reports of successful outcomes using these methods do exist in the published literature of the field known as energy psychology, and the methods are being developed and refined under the auspices of organizations such as the Association for Comprehensive Energy Psychology, it is important to understand before you continue, and certainly before you engage in any of the tapping sequences provided in this material, that these techniques are still considered experimental by the scientific and medical communities, as well as the *American Psychological Association*. The founder of EFT, Gary Craig is one of those contributing to this research. So please note that the following overview of traditional tapping is paraphrased from Gary's EFT Web Site which again is: www.emofree.com

> *Energy Tapping, commonly referred to as Emotional Freedom Techniques (EFT) by Gary Craig, is based on a discovery that has provided thousands with relief from pain, addictions, diseases, and emotional issues. Simply stated, it is an emotional version of acupuncture except needles aren't necessary. Instead, you stimulate well-established energy meridian points on your body by tapping on them with your fingertips. The process is easy to memorize and is portable so you can do it anywhere. The process launches off the EFT Discovery Statement which says...*

> ## "The cause of all negative emotions is a disruption in the body's energy system."

> *The commonsense approach of EFT draws its power from two sources. The time-honored Eastern discoveries that have been around for over 5,000 years and Albert Einstein, who told us back in the 1920's that everything, including our bodies, is composed of energy. These two sources and ideas have been largely ignored by Western Healing Practices, and that is why energy tapping often works where nothing else will. Emotions are energy and can, therefore be managed by working with the energy systems in one's body.*

What Exactly Does Energy Tapping Do?

Tapping on prescribed endpoints along the meridians of the body sends an electrical impulse to the electrical energy system of your body which is being affected by the unresolved feelings. When you simultaneously stimulate the meridian points while stating phrases which represent your current discomfort, you "neutralize" the energy associated with that emotion. Tapping addresses every feeling you experience when processing any form of pain. It essentially unties the knot of your tension and enables you to experience a state of calm and peace. Once the tension is released, the system affected can relax and energy can more effectively flow through your entire body.

The Procedure

The EFT process begins with three setup phrases. I use the setup phrases to identify the ambivalence and contrasting feelings of any issue. When using my signature brand of tapping I again call, interactive tapping™, and I speak of the contrast of feelings, I am referring to the conflicting feelings you experience with respect to the part of you who holds the pain (usually a younger part of self) and the part of you who is spiritually and psychologically advanced enough to be able to respond to the pain. This interaction between the wounded part of you and the Healer within you is the agent of the resolution of your wounding issue. In the focus questions provided before each stage of grief, you will be able to identify the belief systems and patterns which impact your ability to experience that respective stage of grief. Your Adult Self obviously grieves as well. But the resolution of your grief usually involves dealing with the impact of your childhood grief which has been triggered by the current loss.

Each setup phrase positions a challenging feeling with a more positive affirmation. Sometimes, as in traditional tapping, the dichotomous statements are symptom-related. In "interactive tapping™, " the contrasting feelings are relationship–related. They are those of the younger self who is more traumatized, and the healthier part of you who can cope, and can, therefore, comfort and support.

The tapping procedure itself is divided into three sections. You first *neutralize the negative* thoughts and feelings, then introduce the *possibility of change,* and finish with a strong *conviction to change.* Sometimes this is done in three segments. Sometimes the second and third segments are merged together to create more of a flow between the two.

Please Note: You begin the sequence with three setup statements which you state while tapping on the karate chop. Called a psychological reversal, the wording combines a statement about the problem with a statement of affirmation accepting the problem. This combination prepares your psyche and body to accept the energetic correction of this imbalance.

The Tapping Points

I have provided this graphic which illustrates the places upon which you will want to tap. It takes only a few rounds to get the hang of the sequences, but until you feel comfortable with the procedure, this graphic will be a nice reminder.

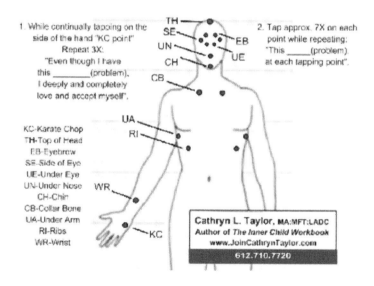

1. While continually tapping on the side of the hand "KC point" Repeat 3X: "Even though I have this _____ (problem), I deeply and completely love and accept myself".

2. Tap approx. 7X on each point while repeating: "This _____ (problem) at each tapping point".

KC-Karate Chop
TH-Top of Head
EB-Eyebrow
SE-Side of Eye
UE-Under Eye
UN-Under Nose
CH-Chin
CB-Collar Bone
UA-Under Arm
RI-Ribs
WR-Wrist

Cathryn L. Taylor, MA:MFT:LADC
Author of *The Inner Child Workbook*
www.JoinCathrynTaylor.com
612.710.7720

Again, just to reiterate, traditional energy tapping targets the symptoms of your grief. My signature method of interactive tapping™ addresses the symptoms from a relationship perspective. In other words, I focus on the interaction between the part of you who is experiencing the intense emotions, and the Healer within you who can respond. It is this interaction that facilitates such profound healing.

When I was experiencing the multidimensional events shared in Antoinette's Story I did not know about tapping. It would have been a great help had I known about it. But once I did learn about EFT I found it invaluable in dealing with and processing the residual grief of other times and other places. And by the time I experienced the losses addressed in my book, Beyond Compassion, I found that both the traditional approach and my advanced approach of tapping had merit. If my Adult Self was raw with emotion I used traditional tapping methods to address my immediate gut-wrenching reactions. If I had identified the emotions as being those of a younger part of me and needed to externalize the more emotionally distraught part of me then I used my style of "relationship" tapping or now commonly called interactive tapping™. I cleared my Adult Self so that part of me could ultimately deal with the more provocative feelings of the younger self who had collapsed into the unresolved grief of my past. I have found this to be true irrespective of the issue I am addressing.

In fact, before we begin this process I want to guide you through a simple procedure of clearing your Adult Self. That way, if, during any of the healing exercises, you do begin to feel a strong emotion, you will be equipped with a way to respond. Please refer to the graphic of the tapping points. The sequences for clearing your Adult Self follow.

Exercise: *Tapping Sequence to Clear the Adult Self (Click on the title to access the mp3 of this exercise)*

Begin by continuously tapping on the karate point while stating the following:

Even though there may be some things I am not totally in harmony with today, I choose, for this time, to suspend those feelings so I can now focus entirely on being present for this inner work.

So even though I may need to neutralize some general irritations, I am going to do that now because I am committed to clearing this up so I can be present for this work.

So even though I may not be in total harmony, I am willing to suspend any feelings that may distract me right now so I can be clear and open enough to be present for this work.

Next, you will do the general neutralizing. It involves stating reminder phrases while you tap on the designated endpoints.

Neutralizing the Negative

Eyebrow: Generally disturbed. A little bit antsy. Clear out any anger.

Side of the Eye: Clear out all distraction.

Under the Eye: Any frustration.

Upper Lip: A little bit fatigued.

Under the lip: But choose to feel empowered to do this work.

Collarbone: Am excited to show up for this work.

Under the Arm: Have committed to showing up to do this work.

Rib: I feel empowered to respond—I am ready to be present and to begin to do this work.

Wrist: I ask my Higher Guidance to assist…

Head: … so that I can move forward, clear this disturbance, and heal.

These statements are just an example of how you would neutralize anything that is currently in your day-to-day life. Continue to tap on each of the endpoints until you move through any resistance to being present to address the feelings which need to be embraced.

This tapping sequence provides the opportunity for you to step into the vibration of a healthy, Adult Self. The next step is to construct a strong connection between this Adult Self and your Higher Self. Obtaining and sustaining a spiritual connection while confronting these stages of grief is necessary. It gives your pain a purpose and helps you move from being a victim of your loss to being a student of your loss. It is this relationship that will enable you to embrace these exercises, and especially the subsequent stages of grief so prevalent in this process, with the courage and confidence needed to trust you can heal.

INTERACTIVE TAPPING™ FURTHER EXPLAINED

When tapping is combined with my interactive meditations these energetic blueprints impacting the Adult Self are directly addressed and neutralized. When we combine the tapping while interacting with the Inner Child, we can literally neutralize the blueprint which originated in childhood.

As you have witnessed repeatedly if these blueprints are not addressed they continue to trigger the same stress response as was experienced in childhood. Whenever a situation arises that vibrationally and energetically feels the same as it did when you were young your Adult Self can collapse and react in a child-like manner. Targeted, interactive tapping™ sequences respond to the Inner Child's pain and dissolve the antiquated, knee-jerk reaction to discomfort.

To emphasize this point a little further take a moment to think about a recent time you experienced a challenge and you found yourself feeling like you did as a child. You may have even heard yourself say, "Wow, I just felt about 3, (or 5, or even 10 or15) years old?" This is an example of a time when you collapsed into those antiquated feelings and experienced the knee-jerk reaction to the current situation whose response was embedded in your past. This occurrence is when your past and present collide and you "energetically" regress to the coping mechanisms of a younger time. So this combination, the context of the Inner Child with the methods of the energy tapping provides you with perhaps one of the most empowering avenues for working with those parts within you who sabotage your best efforts to succeed.

It is worthwhile to reiterate that it is not the intention of our wounded ones to hold us back. Their efforts are merely aimed at sustaining a sense of safety. They do not realize their actions sabotage the inner adult's success. They are frightened and are responding in the knee-jerk manner they developed in response to the original wound. It is the only way they knew then, and they know now, how to attempt to stay safe. When you empower your Adult Self and connect to your authenticity you provide these wounded ones with someone who can respond. You—in that state of empowerment—are the one for whom he or she has been waiting.

It's as simple as that. What heals your past is the ability to have some part within you be able to respond to the old wound in a way that makes that younger self feel safe.

That is what he or she was missing. But that was then and this is now. As an adult, you have acquired a great many experiences and can now be the champion for the little one within you. This is when the healing can truly begin.

Once the response has been made you will find you have a wealth of energy which can now be redirected. That redirection is what allows you to match the vibration of your non-physical self or your higher self, inner self or God-self—whatever you call it. Your authentic self is that physical part of you who can expand enough to begin to allow all of your dreams to come true with ease and eagerness instead of effort and worry.

This three-part progression of tapping presented in each of the seven Layers and the subsequent modules that feature the *Seven-Layers of Healing* offers you a method to step into this vibration of your healthy, authentic, Adult Self. This, in turn, allows you to come into alignment with your wounded Inner Child so you can heal, befriend, and ultimately merge with his or her divine joy.

Make no mistake. There is no magic greater than the vibration of a child.

But a wounded Inner Child holds on strong to that which kept it safe. It is prudent to re-emphasize that in order to regain his or her trust so you can heal you *must* have a part of you who can respond in a nurturing and healthy manner and who can orchestrate a sequential process of healing. It is necessary to come into this healing process with an empowered Adult Self who can respond in a compassionate, authentic manner.

If you begin digging into your past with no new way to respond to that pain, you simply pull the band-aid off of an old wound while offering no hope of healing it.

And, yes, I know you are getting tired of hearing this ... but ... again, the healing agent for an old wound is the interaction between the wounded one and an authentic, inner adult who can respond with compassion, love, and care. It is this interaction which changes the experience of the Inner Child and "creates the new reality." And since our mind does not know the difference between what is real and what is imagined, just as we program our future with intentions and "pretend" exercises, we can do the same thing by returning to the time of the wound and *changing the experience* of the part of us who holds onto the pain. When our Adult Self is believable enough to the wounded Inner Child to intervene we step into the original, wounding scene and, on behalf of the Inner Child, and protect, retrieve, and rescue him or her from the hurtful experience. Once healed, we are able to merge with our Inner Child enough to allow success.

Bring a child's imagination and wonderment into any intention and the vibrational frequency increases ten-fold.

This process systematically enables you, as the adult, to help your Inner Child heal so it can be taught to experience the magic of the law of attraction. Each Layer explained in detail in the next section uses Interactive tapping™ to accomplish the task stated. The first step in the tapping process is to do three setup phrases. These phrases state what you are feeling and what you want to feel. They establish the foundation for the interactive tapping™ because they identify the two parts which emerge within all of us when we are attempting to change.

And those two parts always exist when we approach change because as soon as we have a desire, we give birth to that part of us who is inspired to grow, expand, and pursue change. But the minute we give voice to that aspect of us who wants more it shines the light on the part of us who is afraid and does not want to move forward. Every subject has two sides. The very act of desire pushes some part of us—the part that is committed to the way things are—out of its comfort zone and the result is sabotage.

And actually, when you think about it, it stands to reason that as we set our intentions for our hearts' desire we flush out the old fears which sabotage our success. When we bring in more light we also illuminate our shadow selves, the wounded parts who inadvertently sabotage our efforts to grow and expand. But, if we give a face to those saboteurs who run wild with their negative statements and destructive behaviors; if we learn how to relate to those wounded ones with care and love, we *can* repair that wound and invite that essence back into the energetic force field of our authentic self where it can be safe. Not only does this halt the sabotage, it augments the magic with which we can manifest.

This is why there actually is truth in the statement that, "We really do not attract our heart's desires. We attract *how we feel about* our heart's desires." We attract the current, energetic vibration of what we fear. We attract what we expect, not what we want. And again, this is called your resistance, and it is the outgrowth of what I call your cherished saboteur™. This disparity is neutralized through the interactive tapping™ sequences and through what you will learn to be your *expand/release* breathing. The result is that your resistance will slowly fade. Your fears and doubts subside and you are able to move into a "state of allowing" because your fearful selves feel safe enough to get out of your way.

In the modules that are included in the last section of this book, you will be able to identify the sabotaging voice related to each of the featured areas of concern—intimate relationships, abundance, right livelihood, and reciprocal relationships. You can then determine the belief systems and patterns which sabotage your efforts to get what you want with respect to each area. This discovery readies you to apply the *Seven-Layer Healing Process* to these four areas that tend to be the most troublesome for most of us. You can pick and choose.

The tapping that is provided offers the setup phrases that position this sabotage against a positive affirmation. It puts words to that which you desire and that which prohibits you from attaining it— and thus the goal of the tapping is established and the sequences respond accordingly. You then will be guided to tap on the respective meridian points found on your face and body as depicted in the chart already included.

By following this chart, and the tapping scripts which I provide, you will, round by round, neutralize your fears and open the pathway for the positive feelings to take the lead. You will then tap until you reinforce the positive feelings enough to match the vibration of what you want.

As you will again see when we get to the tapping section I divide the neutralizing procedure into three targeted sequences. We will first *neutralize the negative* thoughts and feelings—then introduce the *possibility of change,* and finish with a strong infusion of your *conviction* to establishing a new way of accepting the part of you who is sabotaging your allowing success. This very acceptance diminishes the fear of not being safe and gives way to your ability to allow your heart's desire to manifest without disruption or fear.

Bringing It All Together

Combining the context of the Inner Child with the energetic interventions of EFT provides you with perhaps one of the most empowering avenues for working with those parts within you that sabotage your best efforts to succeed. Again, remember that it is not the intention of our wounded ones to hold us back. Their efforts are merely aimed at sustaining a sense of safety; they do not realize that their actions sabotage the inner adult's success. They are frightened and are responding in the knee-jerk manner they developed in response to the original wound. It is the only way they know how to attempt to stay safe. When you empower your Adult Self, you provide these wounded ones with someone who can respond. You will then discover you have a wealth of energy that you can redirect and thus give birth to your ever-evolving future self.

The following progression of the layered interactive tapping™ sequences offers you a method to step into the vibration of a healthy Adult Self. The sequences assist you in becoming empowered and coming into alignment with your wounded Inner Child that strongly holds on to that which keeps it safe. You then are able to heal and befriend this wounded one, so it can merge with you and experience joy. In order to regain his/her trust and thus heal, you must have a part of you that can respond in a nurturing and healthy manner and that can orchestrate a sequential progress. You must come into this interaction with an empowered adult who can respond in a compassionate manner. Why?

> *The healing agent for an old wound is the interaction between the wounded one and an inner adult that can respond with compassion, love, and care.*

THE FINAL COMPONENT—The Seven Layers of Healing

The following is a brief introduction to these respective Layers. This overview will give you a feel for the total modality. In the next section, each Layer is fully explained and combined with the tapping sequences that facilitate the healing for that Layer. The YouTube video links are taken from my YouTube channel and provide a more personal overview as well. They too give you a fuller experience of these Layers. Please ignore any references to my blog—any information you need is included in this e-book.

This process systematically enables you, as the adult, to help the Inner Child heal and ultimately learn how to experience the magic of the law of attraction. Each Layer uses my interactive tapping™ sequences to accomplish the task stated. Because this process takes you through a step-by-step process, each Layer respectively uses the pronouns appropriate to the task at hand. You 1) identify the contrasting feelings; 2) separate from and externalize that feeling so, as the adult, you can 3) respond to and, therefore, heal the contrasting emotion by relating to the feeling as an emotional expression of the child within that is afraid.

Also–Please, before you do any tapping
Read the following Disclaimer

Disclaimer: Although there have been remarkable results from EFT— it is still relatively new, should not be confused with or substituted for therapy and is done at your own risk. This information is provided for educational purposes only and IS NOT intended as a substitute for professional medical advice, diagnosis or treatment. Always seek professional medical advice from your physician or another qualified healthcare provider with any questions you may have regarding a medical condition.

1ST LAYER: EMPOWERING THE ADULT SELF

This sequence neutralizes all disturbances currently being experienced in our day-to-day life. The stress we felt yesterday with respect to this topic is where we start. We use the pronoun, "I" to own any disturbance that is housed in the force field of our Adult Self.

2ND LAYER: EXTERNALIZING THE PAIN

When we separate from the part within us that experiences the disturbance, we externalize the disturbance and set up a dyad between the part of us that carries the wound and the part of us that can respond to the wound. This is a crucial step because this separation allows us to interact; the interaction between the wounded one and the Healer within us creates the ultimate healing. We use the pronoun "he/she" to begin the separation process.

3ʳᴅ Layer: The Interactive Layer

We use the pronoun "you" to begin the interactive process. It is building a trusting relationship between our most illuminate/ nurturing self and the wounded Inner Child/Soul shadow. We are now doing a form of surrogate tapping (tapping on behalf of another). This creates the internal experience for the wounded aspect that finally someone is responding to his/her pain and is operating on his/her behalf. (This is true irrespective of the dimension of time or consciousness, be it an Inner Child or an aspect of your Soul. It is all a form of time travel anyway.)

The result, however, is that this interaction introduces the wounded one to the experience of deservedness and nourishes a sense of importance. Having the inner adult operate on its behalf invites this part to feel worthy of attention and care. This is an important step in the process of building trust because often the Inner Child has felt abandoned and left to fend for itself. This is true for aspects of your Soul as well. They sustain a state of suspension waiting to be discovered, rescued, and healed. When we travel back in time to respond to their situation and to heal their pain, they are finally free to return to the light.

4ᵀᴴ Layer: The Teaching Step: Healing your Inner Child and Soul

Now, we shift into a meditative state and begin to teach our wounded Inner Child the technique for this neutralization process. In our mind's eye, we imagine we return to the scene of the wound. We go through a meditation that invites our wounded one to show us his/her pain. Together, you and your wounded one determine what needs to be healed, and you then assist this little one in tapping through his/her pain. You use the pronoun "I", but it is now being said from the experience of your wounded one. You are merely asking him/her to repeat, follow along, and experience how this technique can heal the antiquated pain.

5TH LAYER: THE INTEGRATION AND MERGER STEP

This Layer is used predominantly for the Inner Child only. With aspects of your Soul, you want to simply escort them back into the light, so their energy can be freed. But with an aspect of your personality from this lifetime, you want to partner with him/her and build a bonding, cooperative relationship. Combining the neutralization process with the personal pronoun, "we" enables you to set up the merger and integration. Partnering with the Inner Child in this manner empowers him/her to return to your force field in a healed state. It enables you and your Inner Child to reclaim the magic that was lost while experiencing the wound. When you bring this magic back, the essence of the believability you have as a child returns as well. If you then infuse your manifestation with this vibration, you create magic tenfold!

6TH LAYER: REWIRING YOUR BRAIN; REPROGRAMMING YOUR DNA; RECONFIGURING THE ELECTROMAGNETIC FIELD

This next sequence neutralizes any disturbance that your body has held on your behalf. In all dimensions of time and consciousness, this sequence restores your DNA to the recalibrated vibration that can now hold your new alignment and intention. This process gives substance to who you want to become. You first clear the disturbance from your body by asking for its forgiveness, give it permission to release, and infuse it with the vibration of the new you. This reprograms the DNA in every cell to hold your new vibration. A meditation, specific to this purpose, guides you through this process.

7ᵀᴴ Layer: Giving Back to the World

Using EFT, this final sequence takes all you have neutralized and realigned; it then sends this energy into the Universe as an offering for planetary healing. It reinforces the fact that you are part of something bigger than yourself. You are a valuable agent of change for mankind.

In Section Three I provide an overview of each respective Layer and offer suggestions for of the Interactive tapping™ Sequences that will effectuate your Healing. You will also be provided with a formula for designing your own sequences. This will enable you to customize your tapping sequences to better fit your unique challenges and intentions.

Designing Your Own Unique Sequences—A Worksheet

This worksheet is provided so you can begin to design the sequences that will more effectively target your specific concerns. Play with it until you can make the process of tapping your own. Always begin by getting a sense of where you are at and where you want to go. What is your concern? How do you feel about that concern? And how do you want to feel about this concern? That way, you design statements that reflect the challenge, the goal and the conviction of a new response. Once you get comfortable with creating your own sequences this tool will become one of your most important remedies for distress.

Focus for the Tapping Setup: When you are designing the setup phrases for this tapping sequence you may want to revisit or redo to the weeding-out exercise you did in the previous section. This will give you an idea of what your goal is in this tapping. Then use the reminder phrases to address all of the aspects of your concern.

When you you're your issues determine what the intensity level of feeling is regarding this concern. Rate: 1 (being low) –10 (being high) intensity level: _____

What I want to feel:

Setup Statements–State each of these while tapping on the karate chop point:

Even though a part of me _____, I accept all aspects of me completely and fully or _____.

Even though that part of me _____, I accept all aspects of me completely and fully or _____.

Even though that part of me won't _____, I choose to try something new on its behalf or _____.

Now refer to your responses above and use the worksheet on the next page to design your own unique reminder phrases. Remember, you are moving first through your negative feelings, then to the possibility of change, then to a conviction for change. Come up with a reminder phrase for each endpoint. Then tap on this point 5–7 times while repeating your phrase.

Neutralizing the Negative

Eyebrow: _____

Side of the Eye: _____

Under the Eye: _____

Upper Lip: _____

Under the Lip: _____

Collarbone: _____

Under the Arm: _____

Chest Bone: _____

Wrist: _____

Head: _____

Repeat sequences, altering words accordingly, until, on a scale from 1–10, you feel at least a 2 or 3. Then proceed. When you are ready to move into the possibility that something different can occur, come up with a reminder phrase for each of the endpoints below, then tap on this point 5–7 times while repeating your phrase.

Possibility of Change

Eyebrow: _____

Side of the Eye: _____

Under the Eye: _____

Upper Lip: _____

Under the Lip: _____

Collarbone: _____

Under the Arm: _____

Chest Bone: _____

Wrist: _____

Head: _____

To complete this series, come up with phrases which capture your true conviction to feel or do something new. When you are ready to move into strengthening that conviction, tap on each of the endpoints on the EFT graph 5–7 times while repeating your phrase.

Conviction to Change

Eyebrow: _____

Side of the Eye: _____

Under the Eye: _____

Upper Lip: _____

Under the Lip: _____

Collarbone: _____

Under the Arm: _____

Chest Bone: _____

Wrist: _____

Head: _____

Other Techniques To Heal

Before we begin I want to introduce you to several profound techniques that are available to assist you in coping with and processing your pain. These are several other energy therapies of EMDR and the new innovative Trauma Release Exercises (TRE©). They are self-administering methods that are easy to learn and will definitely assist you in your release.

Eye Movement Desensitization and Reprocessing (EMDR)

EMDR stands for Eye Movement Desensitization and Reprocessing. It is a form of psychotherapy developed by Francine Shapiro which uses eye movements or other forms of bilateral stimulation to purportedly assist in processing distressing memories and beliefs. It is commonly used for the treatment of post-traumatic stress disorder. The theory behind the treatment assumes that when a traumatic or distressing experience occurs that overwhelms normal coping mechanisms, the memory, and associated stimuli are inadequately processed and stored in an isolated memory network. The therapy involves recalling distressing images while receiving one of several types of bilateral sensory input, such as side-to-side eye movements or hand tapping.

I was originally trained in EMDR in the mid-'90's, but when I was introduced to EFT a decade later I found that preferable because it was self-administered. I have recently been re-introduced to EMDR and was pleased to realize that now, in the era of YouTube; there are a plethora of self-administered videos available that can calm down a reaction to stress. For the purposes of this material, I developed and included the techniques of EFT. In fact, my YouTube channel has over 100 instructional EFT videos. However, I do encourage you to go to YouTube and search the EMDR self-administered videos as well. It is well worth your effort to explore this tool for yourself.

One particular video I recommend is called EMDR Celestial. If you are reading this material in its Kindle version, then click on that title. It should take you right to it. If not, simply search it on

YouTube and you should find it as well. If you find you are drawn to this modality I would suggest you do your research and find a practitioner to guide you through the deeper processes.

Trauma Release Exercises (TRE©)

Trauma Release Exercises or TRE® is another self-administered protocol that is proving to be invaluable in terms of dealing with the stress housed in the body in response to any form of trauma. The following is taken directly from their official website which is: https://traumaprevention.com/ (I encourage you to visit this site as it has a very informative video on the home page that will give you a clear idea of what this technique is really all about. But for a general introduction, read below.)

TRE® is an innovative series of exercises. Each exercise assists the body in releasing deep muscular patterns of stress, tension, and trauma. The exercises safely activate a natural reflex mechanism of shaking or vibrating that releases muscular tension, calming down the nervous system. When this muscular shaking/vibrating mechanism is activated in a safe and controlled environment, the body is encouraged to return back to a state of balance.

TRE® is based on the fundamental idea, backed by research, that stress, tension, and trauma are both psychological and physical. TRE®'s reflexive muscle vibrations generally feel pleasant and soothing. After doing TRE®, many people report feelings of peace and well-being. TRE® has helped many thousands of people globally.

TRE® is designed to be a self-help tool that, once learned, can be used independently as needed throughout one's life, thereby continuously supporting and promoting personal health and wellness.

I would suggest finding an introductory class in which you learn the basic exercises, but once learned, it is intended to be a self-induced form of release and relaxation. In the training I have received it has proven to be one of the gentlest approaches to inviting the body to rid itself of the stored tension from past and present-day situations.

Using EMDR, TRE©, as well as the many EFT tapping sequences provided in this material and on YouTube can be invaluable when you find yourself triggered by limited in-person resources.

For the purposes of this material, I will introduce you to the technique known as EFT, and most specifically to my brand of energy therapy, I call interactive tapping™.

SECTION THREE:
THE SEVEN—LAYER HEALING PROCESS

Introduction:
Layers One through Seven

When you have positive experiences but fail to sustain them—
When you find yourself forever caught in the recycling of insults and rejections—
When you long for love but repel finding it—
When you spiral into shame and guilt then get frozen there—
It is because your brain is hardwired to do so!
According to the new brain science, our brain over learns negative responses to life to ensure survival.

However, it is now understood that this self-preserving mechanism can be interrupted, rewired, and redirected and my newly, revised *Seven-Layer Healing* Process provides you with the very course that maps your way!

Layer by Layer I introduce you to my new, step-by-step, Interactive tapping™ Formula for Rewiring your Brain, Reconditioning your Heart; Reprogramming your Body and Reframing the Tasks of your Soul !—the New and Supercharged Seven-Layer Healing Process—a process that contains everything you need to know to take charge of your life.

Seven-Layer Healing Process—
Introduction

As is evident in all of my writing, the heart of my model is that the healing agent for the old wound, which results in your sabotaging behavior, is the interaction between your wounded one and a part within you who can respond with compassion, love, and care. However, in order to achieve this healing, you must develop a soothing inner voice which can respond to the wounds and needs of this younger self.

Unfortunately, this interaction is often eclipsed by the stress we feel in our day-to-day life. This dynamic was further substantiated when recently I was introduced to a series on the New Brain Science. As I referenced in the previous section when I listened to the New Brain Series, hosted by Ruth Buczynski, Ph.D. of the National Institute for the Application of Behavioral Medicine, I was inspired to expand my *Seven–Layer Healing Process.* I already knew in 2006, when I first developed this healing process, that tapping, in itself, rewired the brain in that it positions a negative experience with a positive one. But infusing it with the basic tenets of this new science makes it even more effective. By simply adding the very language the brain understands one can more effectively promote sustainability of growth by building new, positive, neuropathways in the brain.

This is essential in facilitating the movement of new paradigms from the short-term memory of your brain to its long-term storage. So before we can even begin to discuss the First Layer of healing, which is *Empowering your Adult Self,* it will be useful to explore the new brain science itself. Once you have some basic understanding of these new discoveries you will be more equipped to understand and implement the *Seven-Layer Healing Process.*

How The Brain Works

As Dr. Richard Hanson, (again the guest speaker on the New Brain Science webinar and author of the Buddha's Brain, and Hardwiring Happiness*)*, explains that,

> *When discussing how the brain works, it is important to note that our negative reactivity originates in the amygdala, or lower brain, which ignites our fight, flight, or freeze, response. In order for change to occur new experiences need to be lodged in the hippocampus where it can be stored in a long-term memory. The prefrontal cortex, or the Higher Brain, whose* basic activity is considered to be the orchestration of thoughts and actions in accordance with internal goals, can *then draw on this new experience from the hippocampus and use it to determine new behaviors. In short, stress responses can be changed and new behaviors sustained when new experiences are lodged in the hippocampus and are accessible to the prefrontal cortex.*

But in order to do this, **we** *have to learn how to retrain the brain to hold positive experiences.*

A major contribution of this recent discovery is the fact that this is not our natural state. In fact, it is quite the opposite. It is more common to default to the short-term memory of the amygdala which is hardwired to detect everything as a threat which keeps us in a perpetual state of stress.

This is a proven fact. Neuroscientists did indeed discover that our brain is not only hardwired to deal with stress—it is hardwired to look for negativity and focus on anything perceived to be a threat.

In fact, when our brain registers that one of our basic needs such as safety, satisfaction, and connection, is not met, it fires up the fight, flight, or freeze response as a way for us to survive.

This knee-jerk response is anchored in the First Layer of the brain, and it served our ancestors very well, for a very long time. It enabled them to determine if an object was a rock or a lion, and if it was a lion, they had the adrenalin to respond. The stress was short-term. If he or she survived then this outburst was followed by the return to a recovery state. This enabled the organism to refuel, renew, and repair—which in essence enabled mankind to survive.

Today, the threat of being eaten by a lion has been replaced with modern-day threats, such as the rejection experienced through the insult or abuse of a friend or lover; the fears of making ends meet; the inability to find a life-supporting job, or even the general unrest that is ever-present in the air! Our lower brain, the amygdala, is hardwired with all of these cues and our present-day psyche goes about finding experiences in life which confirm that this "need to be on alert" is indeed warranted if we are to survive. The result is chronic stress and the impact is failure and shame. So, in today's world, this survival mechanism creates a challenge and that challenge occurs in two ways.

The first way is the one which was just mentioned—those threats that are being perpetually triggered keep us in a sustained state of fight or flight, which results in anxiety and despair. We can also freeze and become immobile, which keeps us in a state of dissociation—disconnected from ourselves and others in our world.

But the second, more insidious, way this presents a challenge is that these threats trigger those deeper fears that have been pushed down in our unconscious from childhood and lurk, undetected, in our psyche. These fears run deep, often have no name or face, but interrupt our ability to live a peaceful and productive life. In other words, in an attempt to survive, our brain is actually hardwired to continually keep us on alert and reinforce these unconscious fears and suspicions for which we are forced to find a context. We fidget around trying to find a reason for this fear because we believe if we find "the" reason we will be able to resolve it and return to a state of peace and calm.

We are not aware of the fact that our brain is constantly searching for things for us to fear. Unaware we are hardwired to feel this way most of us assume it is our deficiency, our maladaptive way of relating to the circumstances of our life. We feel shame and inadequacy because we anxiously, and inappropriately, respond to life with the assumption that it is our inability to cope.

The Brain's Evolution

Over the past six-hundred million years our brain has evolved in three stages: the brain stem, the subcortical region that includes the hippocampus, and then the third, and most recent stage, the cortex, which sits on top.

On the webinar, Dr. Hanson stated, *http://www.rickhanson.net/*
Our three basic human needs, safety, satisfaction, and connection, are managed by overarching brain systems aimed to avoid harm, approach awards, and attach to others. The brain stem manages the ongoing survival/ maintenance of the body. The subcortical region includes the hypothalamus, the thalamus, the basal ganglia, the hippocampus, and the amygdala, and regulates the stress response. The human prefrontal cortex, which has roughly tripled in volume over the last three million years of evolution, is the seat of judgment and helps us regulate our attention, feelings, and desires.

So, long story short, any animal—whether it is a fruit fly or a human being–needs to be safe and avoid harm, needs to be satisfied and therefore approach rewards, and needs to, in one way or another, connect with others of its kind. When there is a basic sense of safety, satisfaction, and connection, the brain defaults to the responsive mode.

Dr. Hanson calls this the "green zone"." But when we default to what he refers to as the "red zone", the body burns resources faster than it takes them in. In terms of avoiding, approaching, and attaching, the mind is colored with a sense of fear, frustration, and heartache. In modern life, we are exposed to an on-going mild stress; Dr. Hanson refers to as the "pink zone." There is very little time to recover. Our nervous system never gets a chance to fully reset. We internalize this distress and assume it is the result of our own dysfunction. We assume we are doing something wrong—that it is our fault.

So the "red zone" tears us down, and the "green zone" builds us. But most of us exist in the "pink zone "where our brain is hardwired to be in a state of floating anxiety and fear. We are unaware of the source so we never know how to discharge the adrenalin of the stress. We get caught in a state of self-blame and self-recrimination. And the field of psychology supports this perception. With all of its diagnoses, disorders, and maladaptive behaviors that field has inadvertently supported this annihilation of the trust in self by labeling everything as maladaptive and neurotic.

Now I believe this is huge because what this has essentially done is support the idea that there is something wrong with us! It has fostered shame and guilt which separates us even more from our true self. We expect to be happy, and when we are not, we assume we are deficient, "screwed up," not normal. So now we add shame to the pot of our unworthiness!

Well, newsflash! It's not your fault.

In truth, it is your very nature to be suspicious and non-trusting. Your brain always defaults to negativity. It is hardwired to do so. So you have the capacity to respond positively, but this response has to be fostered, and it has to override the very nature of defensive reactivity.

Just take a moment to imagine what it would feel like if the next time you complained to someone about how awful you felt they turned to you and said, "Of course you feel lousy! It's not you! You are hardwired to feel lousy—you have to train your own heart, mind, body, and Soul to be positive, relaxed, and at ease."

My *Seven-Layer Healing Process* gives you the formula to do just that. It offers you the interactive tapping™ sequences (*supercharged* with the new brain science language) that target rewiring the brain activity with deliberate intent.

Layer One:
"Empowering The Adult Self"

In Layer One
We work with the first,
Essential level of healing—
Empowering your Adult Self.
This is crucial
if you are to ever step into
your Masterful Self
and succeed
in embodying
the Healer Within you.

LAYER ONE—Empowering the Adult Self

(Click on the heading to be taken to the YouTube overview of this Layer)

OVERVIEW—Empowering The Illuminated Adult Self

W hether you are wanting to: grieve the loss of a loved one (featured in Beyond Compassion), reestablish a healthy relationship with your body (the focus of SOUL STEPS), rewire your brain and teach your Inner Child the laws of the universe (as presented in Share the Gift), deal with addictions and compulsions (the content of The Four Stages of Recovery-Living Life Beyond Addictions and Fear), or heal a fragment of your Soul which is addressed in Which Lifetime Is This Anyway, you need to be in an empowered state to do so. If you begin digging into your past pain with no fresh method to respond to that pain, you simply pull off the band-aid of an old wound while offering no hope of healing it.

In order to regain trust, and thus heal, we must establish that part of us that can respond in a nurturing and healthy manner. That part of we can orchestrate a sequential progression of tapping and meditative exercises. The healing agent for our old wounds is this very interaction between the wounded parts of us and this empowered Adult Self that can respond with compassion, love, and care. So that is where we begin. We begin by empowering your Adult Self.

A key ingredient in this empowerment is our ability to bring attention to events during which we felt confident and competent— when we indeed felt empowered. Recall of these incidents gives us a point of reference for empowerment. And if we cannot recall such experiences we invent them. Because, remember, our mind does not know the difference between what is real and what is imagined. Just as we program our future with intentions and pretend exercises, we can do the same thing by returning to the time of the wound and changing the experience of the part of us that holds onto the pain.

Again, the only reason this is possible, and I know I keep hammering on this point, but it is because it is so essential, is that you have attained the level of spiritual evolvement that enables you to intervene. You are finally, after decades, (and sometimes lifetimes) equipped to step into the original scene of the wound; and on behalf of the wounded one—protect, retrieve, and rescue him or her from the hurtful experience.

I encourage you to again execute the following tapping sequence to clear your Adult Self for this journey. You were introduced to this sequence in the previous section but I strongly suggest you clear your Adult Self anytime you engage in your inner work. It enables you to get present, and when you are present your efforts are much more effective.

TAPPING SEQUENCE TO CLEAR THE ADULT SELF

(Click on the heading to be taken to the mp3 version of this exercise)

Begin by continuously tapping on the karate point while stating the following:

Even though there may be some things I am not totally in harmony with today, I choose, for this time, to suspend those feelings so I can now focus entirely on being present for this inner work.

So even though I may need to neutralize some general irritations, I am going to do that now because I am committed to clearing this up so I can be present for this work.

So even though I may not be in total harmony, I am willing to suspend any feelings that may distract me right now so I can be clear and open enough to be present for this work.

As before, you begin with the general neutralizing. It involves stating reminder phrases while you tap on the designated endpoints.

Neutralizing the Distraction—Reinforcing the Commitment to be Present

> *Eyebrow: Generally disturbed. A little bit antsy. Clear out any anger.*
>
> *Side of the Eye: Clear out all distraction.*
>
> *Under the Eye: Any frustration.*
>
> *Upper Lip: A little bit fatigued.*
>
> *Under the Lip: But choose to feel empowered to do this work.*
>
> *Collarbone: Am excited to show up for this work.*
>
> *Under the Arm: Have committed to showing up to do this work.*
>
> *Rib: I feel empowered to respond–I am ready to be present and to begin to do this work.*
>
> *Wrist: I ask my Higher Guidance to assist…*
>
> *Head: … so that I can move forward, clear this disturbance, and heal.*

Again, the wording here is just an example of how you would neutralize anything that is currently in your day-to-day life. Just always continue to tap on each of the endpoints until you move through any resistance to being present to address the feelings which need to be embraced.

Once you have stepped into the vibration of your healthy, Adult Self the next step is to construct a strong connection between this Adult Self and your Higher Self. Obtaining and sustaining a spiritual connection while confronting these layers of healing is necessary. It gives your pain a purpose and helps you move from being a victim of your loss to being a student of your loss. It is this relationship that will enable you to embrace these exercises—and especially the subsequent stages of grief so prevalent in this process—with the courage and confidence needed to trust you can heal.

BUILDING A BRIDGE BETWEEN YOUR HUMAN SELF AND SPIRITUAL SELF

As you have progressed in your adult life, you have had experiences that have strengthened your ability to deal with the world. But some losses are above and beyond those normal experiences. Loss often needs a spiritual context. That context takes place when you form a partnership between your Adult Self and your Higher Self. Some call this self their "Inner Being," the "Higher Self," the "Spiritual Self." It doesn't matter what you call that expanded part of you. What is relevant is that you find a way to develop this partnership.

Interactive tapping™ fosters this partnership. My interactive brand of tapping is built on the principle that, again, as an adult, you have acquired the skills to respond in a protective and nurturing manner. If this is not the case, then it would be useful to find role models that you can emulate. You can mimic them and "act as if" you have a similar nurturing voice until you develop the ability to find your own self-soothing language that can quiet your feelings of unrest. "Acting as if" (pretending you are someone else who is compassionate and accepting) is a way your Inner Adult learns how to respond in a way which invites trust. Partnering with the Higher Self teaches you how to raise your vibration to the point where you can experience compassion and acceptance for the more fragile parts that may not be quite as mature and able to cope.

Breathing is the primary method that enables you to merge with this more peaceful and compassionate Higher Self. Every time you breathe in you have the opportunity to fill yourself with the energy of the Universe. Every time you exhale, you are invited to release your earthly tension and fear. Inhaling expands your vibrational frequency so you can more easily merge with your Higher Self which ensures more ability to cope.

Exercise: Breath Exercise—Getting Present

Simply close your eyes and breathe in and breathe out. I suggest you place your left hand on your solar plexus and your right hand on your heart. Then breathe into your left hand and expand, and breathe out your right hand and release and let go. Do this repeatedly until you feel your energy shift and you feel relaxed and empowered. This audio version will give you more concrete instructions and assistance. Breathing into the Adult Empowered, Self (Click on the title to access the mp3 of this exercise)

The Chakra/Breath Exercise Explained (Click on the title to access the mp3 of this exercise)

In this next exercise, your breathing awakens the energy centers of your body called chakras. Each of us has seven primary energy centers which connect our spiritual body to our physical one. They operate on subtle levels and are invisible to the naked eye, yet affect every aspect of our life. In effect, these seven centers act as transformers—or sending and receiving stations—negotiating the flow of energy which comes from us and to us moment to moment. They are situated in the etheric fields along the spinal column at the base of the spine, the pelvic area, midway between the base and the navel, near the heart, throat, and brow or "third eye" area and at the top of the head.

These chakras are the central processing centers for every aspect of our being. The blockage we carry into adulthood from the losses we encountered in childhood will show up as energetic dysfunctions in the chakras. These, in turn, usually give rise to disorders in the body. These blockages disrupt how we think, feel, and connect with our Higher Guidance and Authentic Self. A defect in the energy flow through any given chakra will impair the entire energy field's ability to process energy—affecting all levels of the being. Our energy field is a holistic entity—every part of it affects every other part. Tapping and clearing our chakra system connects our physical self with our non-physical self. It constructs this necessary bridge.

In this exercise, you will be guided to gently tap on each of the correlating centers in your physical form. This diagram shows you where to tap. The tapping itself is done with your open hand. You just gently tap on each area of your body as if you were bouncing a small ball. This tapping sequence was inspired by EFT Practitioner, Carol Tuttle www.caroltuttle.com/. The complete instruction on energy tapping, and most specifically my signature form of tapping I call, Interactive tapping™, was explained in the last section. But for the purposes of this exercise, the open-handed tapping is sufficient to facilitate building the bridge between your Higher Self and Adult Self.

To begin, simply tap gently on the designated location of each energy center— again, as if you were bouncing a small ball—while simultaneously stating the words associated with clearing each chakra. This exercise will get your energy flowing in the right direction. Start with the root chakra (or first chakra) and move up.

The Chakra Breath Exercise (Click on the title to access the mp3 of this exercise)

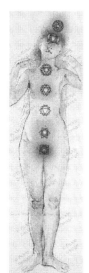

1st Chakra–red root chakra–the center of connection and safety and trust–State while you tap–*I am willing to feel safe enough to trust and connect.*

2nd Chakra–orange pleasure center–State while you tap–*I am willing to have faith in myself and my ability to discern–to set the limits and boundaries that allow me to connect with my authentic self.*

3rd Chakra–yellow power center–State while you tap–*I am willing to allow myself the feeling of empowerment–to release all attachment to feeling like a victim and instead allow myself to experience the feeling of expansion and empowerment.*

4th Chakra–green heart center–State while you tap–*I am now willing to open my heart to unconditional love so I can experience the true connection between my spiritual and physical selves.*

5th Chakra–blue truth center–State while you tap–*I am now willing to release and let go of all reluctance to speak what I know. I am willing to speak my truth with integrity, accountability, and trust. I am willing to receive all that I deserve.*

6th Chakra–violet higher vision center–State while you tap–*I am now willing to see through the eyes of my authentic self–to open the door to my intuition with the confidence and certainty that I am connected with my higher truth and am committed to attracting my highest desires.*

7th Chakra–white or golden God Center–State while you tap–*I am now willing to align myself with my authentic self, to connect with integrity, honesty, and trust.*

Now that you are present and connected you are ready to use the following exercise to attain a point of reference for your empowerment. Since the brain defaults to the negativity, it is necessary to retrain it to bring focus a positive experience which can then become the point of reference for empowerment. This enables you to begin to build the new neural pathways that reconstruct and rewire your brain.

RECALLING/INVENTING AN EMPOWERING MOMENT

(Click on the heading to be taken to the mp3 version of this exercise)

Think of a recent time when you felt empowered. If you cannot recall an event, invent one. Pretend you felt empowered in a situation even if you did not. Bring in as many details of this real or, imagined event, as you can. Record your responses in your journal.

1. *See, sense, or feel, the experience.*

2. *Let yourself envision the situation. Notice as many details in your environment as you can. How does it feel?*

3. *What are your thoughts?*

4. *Embody this experience as much as you can and then try to hold it in your mind's eye for at least a minute.*

Again, this exercise gives your brain a method by which it can construct new, neural pathways. The more you envision this empowering moment the more your brain will sustain it and build on it. Take a moment to record your experience. Then if you want more information regarding this concept I encourage you to check out this TED TALK video presentation of Dr. Hanson. It will also inspire you to access this more empowered self part of you. *https://www.youtube. com/watch?v=jpuDyGgIeh0*

THE ILLUMINATED SELF—A Clear Definition

As you touch into that moment when you were most empowered it becomes clear that this illuminated part of you actually *holds the balance* of both your *masculine and feminine traits.* The feminine characteristics are the more intuitive, compassionate and loving aspects of you. The masculine traits make up what I refer to as the Operation's Manager. This part of you takes care of business and makes sure you adhere to the protocols and disciplines which ensure illumination. You cannot experience that moment of empowerment without these parts of you being in sync.

> *Therefore, I define the Illuminated Self as the Partnership between your Masculine and Feminine selves!*

This makes it easier to internalize this concept and put it into practice.

Being able to vibrationally embody your Illuminated Adult Self is paramount to your being able to stay present. Being present means you are conscious. You have to be conscious if you are going to heal. Staying present is a result of shifting from defaulting into a reactive and negative mode to defaulting, instead, into a relaxed and calm mode. In order to *get relaxed* and to *stay calm,* you need the *nurturing,* compassionate self-talk of your *feminine self* and the *disciplined* and accountable follow through of the *masculine self.*

It is this *combination,* and the *harmony* between the two, that *inspires* that feeling and confidence of *empowerment.* By tuning into that frequency on a regular basis you will be able to more easily *access* that *Illuminated aspect* of you when your wounded ones are in need of a healthy, reliable and nurturing response.

It is for this reason it is essential that you practice expanding
Into that vibration as often as you can.

EXERCISE: REMEMBER AND EXPAND

This exercise will reinforce your remembering to expand and embody this Illuminated Self so that it becomes more and more the norm for how you live.

Simply close your eyes and recall a moment when you were embodying your most Illuminate, Adult Self—a moment when you were aware of the integration between the masculine and feminine selves—the partnership between this integrated self and your Higher Self. Remember—or invent— everything you can about the circumstances of this moment. Hold the memory of that moment—breathe into its essence—the sights, sounds, tastes, smells, sensations of that moment. Hold that essence for a solid 17 seconds as you breathe in and out.

Now, this time experiment with breathing into your heart and out your third eye by placing your left palm on your heart and the right palm on our forehead. On the inhale expand into the image and on the exhale let yourself release any resistance or fear. Spend several moments just breathing in and out. Allow yourself to really anchor in this expanded experience.

Then speak from that state of empowerment for 68 seconds. This gives the Universe the right amount of time to pick up this vibration and begin the process of gathering the necessary components to sustain this empowerment. Speak in current time. Speak about your achievements as if they have already been attained. Speak about how good it feels to hold this essence—to be aware of the integration between the masculine and feminine parts of you. Then take another moment to envision this integration as it is bridged with your Higher Self. Each of these expansions serves to fortify the Illuminated Adult Self who will orchestrate the healing of your most wounded parts within.

Suggestion: Use this meditation (or create your own) and record your 68 seconds on your cell phone and then play it over and over again as needed.

Your *Illuminated Adult Self* is the epitome of your most *Masterful Self.* This is the energetic form you want to *attain* and *sustain* as much as possible. He or she is the aspect of you that embrace that fragile self and teach him or her how to attract all that which you desire. This is the part of you that can flow in the river of success because he or she is a vibrational match to success. So it is in your best interest to practice accessing this vibration until it becomes *automatic to "live" in that vibration.*

What does it mean to "live" in that vibration?

It means that you spend more and more time in that *green zone of relaxation and health* and less and less time stressed.

It means that you *progressively manage your life* more and more from this Illuminated perspective.

It means that this becomes the *normal, expected, state of your consciousness,* and therefore, the *standard* for your response to your day-to-day world.

It means you develop a keen sense of awareness as to when you *slip from the green zone into the pink one,* and you *have the tools* to *neutralize* the feelings of the pink zone so you can return to a sense of peace and calm.

It means you have *developed the intuitive skills* to *recognize* when a part of you has been triggered and *collapse*d, and, through mastering the *Seven-Layer Healing Process,* you have acquired the tools to know how to *respond appropriately.*

That's what it means to live from your expanded, integrated state but what's happening when you are not harmonious and yet, you do not have a clue as to what's happening?

The Energetic, Addcitve Response

There are those times when our energy is off, but we cannot put a face to the emotion. It is general, non-specific, and unrelated to an incident or situation. I believe this is just floating anxiety related to all of those unconscious separations about which we have no recall. It's that existential loss that manifests as a feeling of unrest which keeps us out of harmony and disconnected from the calm and peaceful place held by our Illuminated Adult Self.

The distinction between these two energetic experiences is relevant because the way you resolve the tension from the addictive energy that is looking to be discharged and the energy evident in the collapse of a wounded Inner Child or Soul fragment that needs to be resolved is significantly different. Traditional tapping (or EFT) addresses the *energetic addictive response* and my interactive tapping™ addresses the collapse. You do not need to interact with the addictive response—you just need to clear the symptom and the energy. But if there has been a triggering event then you have collapsed into a younger set of coping mechanisms. You cannot climb out of that collapse if you do not have your Illuminated Adult Self to separate and respond to the collapsed self.

Again, this is why it is so important in this First Layer that you identify and really practice embodying your Illuminated Adult Self— the partnership between your masculine and feminine selves— because without this partnership you will be forever caught in the reaction with no promise of resolution. You will have no part of you who can identify when you are out of sync with your higher intention, let alone be able to orchestrate the separation that is necessary if you are to respond and heal the wounded one.

Your Illuminated Adult Self becomes the MENTOR for your wounded ones. But you have to be able to SEPARATE the two in order for this to work.

So let's backtrack again for a moment.

The reward, in establishing that healthy Illuminated Adult Self, is that you are then able to maintain that reverent and present, conscious response to life which ensures success. You are able to stay grounded and operate from a place of *being* instead of *doing*. I call this being Spirit-infused rather than ego-driven. Spiritual-infusion means you are centered enough to be in touch with your Higher Self, and conscious enough to see the world through its eyes. It takes work, and it is the partnership between your masculine and feminine selves that makes this possible.

EXERCISE: PARTNERING WITH THE MASCULINE AND FEMININE SELVES:

Take a task such as cleaning your house. Now focus your conscious mind on completing that task. If you are vacuuming be aware of that activity, the feel of the vacuum handle in your hand. Become aware of the suction cleaning your carpet or floor. Yes, get into the "Zen" of vacuuming. Engage in this task with a sense of reverence and presence. Experience the task getting completed in a relaxed and conscious manner.

This is a suggestion of the benefits of this partnership—the partnership between the masculine and feminine parts of self.

I am not suggesting you engage in the completion of every task in this manner. But experimenting with this exercise gives you a tangible point of reference for the merger. It gives these two parts of you a concrete mission to accomplish so that you can see how they flow and work together. Sustaining the empowerment of your Illuminated Adult Self cannot occur if this partnership is not intact. It's easier to feel stressed when you are not integrated. It is easier to slide into that pink zone and to act out addictively.

The energetic addictive response is a sign you are not in harmony.

That day-to-day stress gets expressed in that energetic, addictive response which ultimately silences the voice of your Inner Child, severs your connection to your Higher Self, and sabotages your ability to be in harmony with your Illuminated Adult Self.

Again that addictive response is an expression of your living in that pink zone of irritation, boredom, and restlessness. When you are in that addictive energy you are not illuminated. You are not taking care of the business of your life. You are simply reacting and discharging the disruptive energy without any resolution of its underlying cause.

You are stuck in a reactive mode and cannot be conscious or present enough to separate from your wounded ones—let alone be in a position to heal them.

So you can see how important this integration or harmony between these two parts of you actually is. It is essential that you begin to identify your addictive acting out because as long as you deal with stress in this way your life will not work. It is like trying to launch into action while standing in quicksand. You keep sinking and cannot propel forward.

The success of this is on-going, progressive, and in a constant need of assessment. The goal is to perpetually be in the process of aspiring for this harmony— to be able to assess when you are disharmonious—and to have the tools to reestablish that harmony. It requires an ever-present awareness and willingness to be accountable for your reactions and to have the skills and tools to self-correct when stress does occur.

But the Adult Self has to be ready and willing to acquire the methods to become empowered and learn ways to rewire the brain; recondition the heart; reprogram the body and reframe the tasks of your Soul. Your adult needs to stay open to learning, to be willing to be master and student, Healer and healed.

The *SEVEN-LAYER HEALING PROCESS* Supercharged With The New Brain Science.

To assist your Adult Self in this expansion and development we begin our journey by weaving the First Layer of the *Seven-Healing Process* in with Dr. Hanson's H.E.A.L. process. Dr. Hanson's acronym assists the Adult Self in the process of rewiring the brain's responses.

As you will see the brain is programmed to react. Those reactions are based on the perceptions you made as a child—the perceptions your Soul developed in response to traumas in your past. In this model, those perceptions have a purpose. That purpose is to provide the exact tension you need to inspire you to grow. But in order to grow, you have to have a part of you who can lead and identify the parts of you who need help. My *Seven-Layer Healing Process* does just that. And this process begins with empowering your Adult Self. It is the Adult Self who can accomplish the first three steps of Dr. Hanson's HEAL process.

THE BASIC TENETS OF DR. RICHARD HANSON'S H.E.A.L. PROCESS
http://www.rickhanson.net/

This acronym covers the *activation* and *installation* process necessary to successfully rewire the brain. The first three letters stand for Heal, Enrich, and Absorb. Each of these steps is an integral part of empowering your Adult Self. The final letter, "L," means "to link." Linking your positive experiences attained as an adult to the wounding experiences of your Inner Child and Soul enables you to build the new pathways necessary to rewire your brain and create new possibilities of responding to your world.

So let's break this down letter by letter—step by step.

Again, the *H* in HEAL stands for *Have*. You have to *have* the positive experience in the first place—either because you noticed an experience you are already having or because you actually create one.

Use this following exercise to refresh your memory on how to address this first step.

Refresher Exercise: Think again of that recent time when you felt empowered. Again, bring in as many details as you can—see, sense, or feel the experience. By doing so you are reactivating the memory and making it available to be anchored into long-term storage. You are moving it from short-term memory to a more lasting station in the brain—the hippocampus. By engaging, and re-engaging, you recapture the positive experience you will need to do this process.

Now let's move to the next step of the HEAL process. The "E" in the **H.E.A.L.** acronym stands for "enriching" which is the 2nd step of the activation experience.

Borrowing or turning to the famous saying in neuroscience that *"Neurons that fire together wire together"*, you want to get a lot of neurons firing together so that they start wiring together. In other words, just having the experience does not suffice. In order for the experience to have value, it has to be transferred from the short-term memory to the long-term storage. The challenge, as Dr. Hanson states, is that ... *most experiences are momentarily pleasant, but if they do not transfer from short-term memory buffers to long-term storage, there is no lasting value.* This is why all of the positive thinking in the world does not result in change because this transfer is not made.

So you can see why it is so important to really supercharge your positive experience. The following pointers may help because as Dr. Hanson discussed in the Series, there are several well-known factors in the neuropsychology of learning which promote installation and enrich this step of the activation process. You can do one of them or all of them, but each offers a way to augment the effectiveness of your experience.

The Main Factors in the Neuropsychology of Learning are as follows:

Duration—the longer you stay with the experience, the more it will sink in. *(Tapping reinforces the duration and provides your body, mind, heart, and Soul the time needed to truly anchor in the experience.)*

Intensity—the more intense you have the experience, maybe it is an emotion, maybe it is a body state, maybe it is an inclination of commitment, maybe it is an insight into your own psychology— but whatever it is, the more intense it is, the more there will be the formation of neural structure. *(The tapping sequences are designed to instruct your body to hold the vibration of the emotion so the neurons can begin to fire off and create new pathways.)*

Multimodality is the third factor—The more that you bring experiences down into your body and have them be emotionally rich, maybe even enact the experience, like sitting up a little straighter to support an experience of determination or inner strength —the more neural structure they will build. Again, borrowing or turning to the famous saying in neuroscience that, "Neurons that fire together wire together", you want to get a lot of neurons firing together so that they start wiring together." *(By using the focus of the tapping statements to instruct your body to anchor in the experience you support the revision of your energetic blueprint from being negative in reaction to positive in response.)*

Novelty is the fourth factor— the brain is a big novelty detector. Research shows that relating to things that are new augments our learning. *(In the second round of my formula you learn how to "introduce the possibility of change." This introduction informs your brain that something new is being introduced. It engages the brain in new possibilities and options.)*

Personal Relevance is the last factor—"Why does this matter to me? Why is it salient to me?" (In this *Seven-Layer Healing Process*, you are encouraged to access the information from your Soul to determine the purpose of your pain—the relevance of your experience. *(In your own work you design ways to communicate with your Soul and to build the partnership with your Spiritual Self so that this information is available to you in your day-to-day life.)*

Those are the factors that help you *enrich* your positive experience. But once you enrich the experience you have to *absorb* it.

To absorb the experience you have to prime the memory system by sensitizing it and owning the new thought processes. Owning them is evident when you can bump into resistance and not get derailed. Again, Interactive tapping™ provides you with three sets of rounds that address this possibility. You first *neutralize your negative feelings,* then you tap on *introducing the possibility of change* to your psyche, and you complete the sequence by anchoring in the new behavior with a tapping round that *reinforces your conviction to change.*

Have, Enrich, and *Absorb* are the three fundamental steps of taking in the good and installing a positive experience as a lasting neural trait. You, in essence, delete the old, energetic blueprint and upload a new one. Hanson suggests that even holding this new state for 12-15 seconds does the trick. By doing this repeatedly, "you will help your brain turn these activated, useful, mental states into something of lasting value woven into your brain and thus into your life."

For those of you who follow my work, I often refer to the Teachings of Abraham material in which it is suggested that in order to activate a new reality you need to hold the vibration of that new thought and feeling for just 17 seconds. To give the thought enough energy to be picked by the Universe so it can begin to gather the components necessary to manifest it you hold and nourish it for 68 seconds. You do this by talking about the thought in full description as if what you are trying to create is already created.

Either way, there are great benefits to repeatedly taking in the good and these benefits fall into three categories.

The first is that you are growing specific resources inside. The second benefit is that you are getting better control over your attention and begin to treat yourself like you matter. You are being active. You are being present in our own life. And thirdly, research is beginning to indicate that through repeatedly taking in the good, you can gradually sensitize the brain to become more and more efficient at converting positive mental states into lasting neural traits. This is the tipping point when you begin to really experience the benefits of all of your hard work.

But the essential ingredient in sustaining this activation so it can successfully be installed in what Hanson calls "linking."

Linking is simply holding the negative and positive thoughts at the same time. You simultaneously HOLD in YOUR awareness positive and negative experience. The setup phrase in traditional tapping is designed to do just this. Traditional tapping is based on two therapies—exposure therapy and cognitive therapy—exposing and accepting the wound and then reframing the wound in a compassionate and unconditional way.

And, as most of us know, this is where it gets challenging. It is often quite hard to simply sustain an enjoyable experience for a dozen seconds, let alone 17 or 68 seconds!

What happens, both clinically and in everyday life, when we start doing this practice is that we often bump into various blocks and saboteurs. It is startling to realize how unwilling the mind is to give the gift to oneself of a positive experience—let alone be empowered enough to share this gift with your Inner Child.

As you have seen over and over in this material some part of us does not feel we deserve to feel good or that we shouldn't try to feel good. Our job is to make others feel good—even though, as most of us know, the more we fill our own cup, the more we have to offer to others.

And this is where the installation process blends nicely with the Inner Child/ Soul work. It is the *interaction* between your wounded one and your Illuminated Adult Self, supercharged with the tapping as we do in my interactive tapping™ technique that enables you to secure the installation. It enables you to create a different pathway in the brain, and thus, the rewiring occurs.

Your Adult Self, through experience and maturity, is able to see your life's experiences beyond the wound. This enables you, in present time, to shift your point of reference and develop a new point of reference for the context of the wound.

Now here is a sideline that is worthy of mention! The brain is constantly allocating its resources—it is a very metabolically expensive organ, and even though it is just two to three percent of body weight, it uses twenty to twenty-five percent of the oxygen and glucose in our blood. As animals evolved, anything that was new signaled either a threat or an opportunity. If it was a threat, they really needed to pay attention to it. If it was an opportunity that was new, they needed to pursue it. If we bring our *beginner's mind,* and therefore a sense of novelty and freshness to the experience, it will build more neural structure, which in turn augments our ability to sustain the positive feelings which then envelopes or neutralizes the negative pulls and enables us to remain more connected.

In my original *Seven-Layer Healing Process* each essential human need is addressed and each step of Dr. Hanson's HEAL acronym is presented.

- Layers One and Two relate to *having* the experience and *enriching* it.

- Layers Three and Four relate to linking it.

- Layer Five supports the integration and merger, Layer Six gives it relevance.

- And the last Layer meets the need to feel connected to the world and to something bigger than self.

The following are links to broadcasts of my, EFT for Your Inner Child and Soul. During the year of 2015, I conducted a series of episodes that covered these Layers sequentially. When appropriate I will provide those links for those of you who are reading this in the Kindle format.

The first broadcast provides you with the Overview. Blog Talk Radio Broadcast of Overview In this second broadcast I offer sequences that begin to prepare your body, mind, heart, and Soul for the linking process of this formula. Click here to listen: Rewire Your Brain; Recondition Your Heart; Reprogram Your Body; Reframe the Purpose of Your Pain!

And in the third broadcast, you begin preparing the Adult Self so that he or she can be adequately charged to respond in such a way to the wounded one that a new pathway can be built. The cumulative effect of repeatedly engaging the brain in this new manner prepares you to shift from defaulting into the negative patterns of behavior to defaulting into positive ones which can support your ultimate goals!

Click here to listen: New Interactive Formula to Rewire Your Brain

Step-By-Step Instructions On Empowering The Illuminated Adult Self

The following worksheet gives you the step-by-step outline to empower your Adult Self.

GET PRESENT

(Do a short round of tapping that addresses your being present at the moment.) For example, you can use this as your setup. *"Even though I have a lot going on right now I choose to bring my full attention to this moment so I can be present for the work that I am committed to doing…"* You can also refer back to the *Clearing the Adult* sequence offered earlier. But once you have completed the setup then do several rounds neutralizing the challenge, presenting the possibility of putting all those distractions on the back burner for now, and then coming into the conviction to be present, alert, and ready to respond.

HAVE, CREATE, REFLECT ON THE POSITIVE EXPERIENCE.

(Establish a point of reference for your expanded experience. This is recognizing and giving essence to your "green zone" … the state of consciousness in which your mind is quiet; your heart is calm; your body is relaxed, and you are in contact with your expanded self.) This can be considered your "happy place." I actually call it, my *go-to-place."* It is that place you can go to in your mind when you need to come into total alignment and experience a state of peace. So, to get there … *think of a moment when you felt safe. Think of a moment when you felt satisfied. Think of a moment when you felt connected to your Higher Self, to others and to all there is.* Each of these basic needs, when addressed and satisfied, enables you to feel calm. Once you have that place in your mind's eye make, what I call, a "photo memory" of it. That way you can pull it up any time there is a need. When done, make a note of your experience in your journal for future reference.

ENRICH THIS EXPERIENCE

Again bring your focus to your "happy place." Fill it with color, with sound, with sensations. Can you feel the sun shining on your face or a breeze brushing your cheek? Can you smell the ocean, the flowers, or the trees? Record any additions in your journal. Really describe in present time—using as many adjectives as possible—this happy place, this happy moment. Then reinforce this enrichment by tapping on your endpoints while you use as many adjectives as possible to describe this experience. As you do so feel your energy increasing. You may feel a rush of energy going up or down your spine or you might experience your whole being lighting up like a lamp. This is where you ignite the experience and get the neurons engaged in the explosion of energy.

ABSORB THE ENERGY

While holding the "buzz" of this energetic infusion in your mind's eye and in your physical form bring one hand to your heart and the other hand to your third eye. Slowly begin to breathe into your heart and out your third eye. Take 17 breaths as you do this. Once done, take the fist of your right hand with your thumb pointing outwards and gently thump in the center of your chest while you hold your "go-to" place in your mind's eye. Continue to breathe normally, but verbally describe the experience with as many adjectives as possible. Do this for at least 68 seconds. This resets your central nervous system and allows your brain to fire off the neurons that connect with your Higher Self. It balances you and gets you grounded. Watch this demonstration video for further explanation and instruction. Thymus Thump.

You have now successfully established that empowered state of consciousness for your Illuminated Adult Self The more you do this the stronger your new, neural pathway will be built. Ultimately, you get to the point when anytime you feel stress you automatically tap on the center of your chest and reconnect to your "go-to" place with ease. The goal is to attain and sustain that sense of calm as much as possible. If you feel really triggered then I suggest you simply tap on the endpoints while you repeat, *"God's love (The Universe, whatever you choose) resolves this situation here and now."* Continue to repeat this until you move back into a state of peace. You do not have to understand its Source. You just have to change the energy.

The following offers additional exercises you can do to reinforce and build the new default response which your Adult Self can progressively sustain.

Daily Activities you can do to reinforce the empowerment of your Adult Self.

1. Get into the habit of making a gratitude list every day. List the moments you had during the previous 24 hours when you felt empowered, felt safe, felt connected, satisfied, and at peace. *This retrains your mind to look for the good instead of defaulting to being on guard for the negative. You can reinforce this by tapping on your endpoints while you state each item on your list. It does not matter if your list is repetitive.* Each time you write it strengthens the energy of the new neural pathway.

2. To further reinforce your brain's new habit do the Super Brain Yoga once a day for 14 breaths. Refer to this short video **Super Brain Yoga**

3. To reinforce the heart, tune into your vulnerable self and say hello to your Inner Child. Again, while tapping on the endpoints, repeat the following. *I am safe, you are safe, together we are safe in the arms of our Higher Self, (of God, of the Universe)*

4. To reinforce your body do a minimum of five minutes of stretching a day. Be present while doing so. Really breathe into your body the essence of your Higher Self.

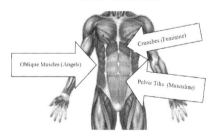

CORE MUSCLES

When you do your pelvic tilt exercise say hello to the masculine energy within you, while doing your crunches say hello to the feminine energy within you. While exercising your oblique muscles, welcome in the energy of the Angels.

5. A) To reinforce your connection to your Higher Self simply put your right hand on your third eye and your left hand on your heart. Breathe into your heart and expand. Breathe out your third eye and release. With each breath you take in you increase your energy, and therefore, the frequency with which

you vibrate. Again, breathe until you experience a "buzz" of energy, but not to the point where you get light-headed. B) While in that energy simultaneously say your spiritual prayers. You can even tap as you do so.

6. B0NUS—You can also say your prayers while you walk, run, bike, or while your body is in motion in any fashion. Refer to my book, Soul Steps for further instruction on what I call "conscious aerobic exercise."

7. Create a list of affirmations and say them in the mirror while you tap.

Part of empowering your Illuminated Adult Self is to acquire the skills to live your life with ease. In order to do this, and in order to be equipped to help your Inner Child be able to heal, you have to master the art of knowing how to grieve. In this next section, I give you the necessary methods to deal with any loss that may emerge in your day-to-day life. This is important because you can rest assured that any loss confronted as an adult will surely dislodge the residual grief from childhood. Therefore, if you are to heal you have to be able to deal with present losses and then be equipped to help the Inner Child grieve the losses from his or her past.

The Five Stages Of Grieving Current Losses

Stage One—Panic, Denial, Anxiety

Discussion: Our first response to the loss of any kind is panic. We go into the fight or flight response, or we freeze, shut down, deny, and go into a state of shock, (called psychic numbing). We want to deny the truth of the challenge. Embracing the loss would leave us too raw. The anxiety is the tension we feel in the pit of our stomach when we try to imagine life without this attachment. It is the response we feel when something has been ripped from our very core. We become panic-stricken. We can even experience a psychological split because we cannot endure the pain. Some even get aggressive and hostile, others become depressed.

And of course, there is always the option to compulsively or addictively act out. As was discussed in the previous section, addictively medicating our grief quiets the tumultuous feelings of grief sometimes for decades.

Ultimately, we even lose sight of the original loss. We simply experience a restlessness quieted by our addictive or destructive behavior. Eventually, we either die of the addiction or find ourselves in recovery. If we make it into recovery, the unresolved loss is waiting for us. We begin the journey through the stages of grief—the bargaining, anger, and despair. But now there is the grief of the time lost as we ran from our grief. Those feelings also need to be addressed and processed if we are to ever come to a resolution.

Focus Questions—Use these following thought-provoking questions to identify how you feel.

1. *How have you dealt with the anxiety regarding the given situation upon which you now want to focus?*

2. *Have you channeled your tension related to your loss into work?*

3. *Did you deflect your attention to another person, or activity— implode and become riddled with depression—or perhaps consumed with shame and guilt over your regrets?*

4. *Did you numb out with process addictions by excessively eating, smoking, exercising, compulsively spending, or gambling?*

5. *If any or all of the above are true, how long ago did the actual loss that you now need to address occur?*

6. *Take a moment to really ponder how you have dealt with your tension and anxiety. How you have avoided the feelings you felt you could not bear.*

7. *Bring your focus back to that moment when you first realized this challenge. Notice how you managed the anxiety that accompanied this experience.*

8. *Notice where in your body you held your anxiety?*

9. *Record your thoughts and feelings in your journal.*

Suggested Exercises: "Draw your Anxiety"

You might want to further your exploration by drawing a picture of your anxiety. This gives your psyche an alternative way to express this tension. You will then be better able to neutralize your challenging emotions with tapping as you introduce the possibility of feeling something new, which in turn, can morph into your conviction to embrace the feelings of this stage of grief.

EFT for Anxiety

While tapping on your karate point state the following:

Even though I felt anxious in this situation, and I can feel it in the pit of my stomach, the back of my neck, or in the stress, I hold in my shoulders, I love myself fully and completely.

Even though I feel great anxiety with respect to the perceived loss, I now choose to work with this fear, release it from my body, so I can begin to resolve this grief.

Even though I am experiencing great anxiety about this situation, I choose to believe I am in the arms of my Higher Power and, with that support, I choose to begin to let go.

Now tap on your endpoints. Refer to the graph if necessary.

Neutralizing the Negative

Eyebrow: Really feel anxious, feel it in my stomach, shoulders, or neck...

Side of the Eye: Cannot imagine surviving this loss ...

Under the Eye: Really frightened regarding this loss ...

Upper lip Am afraid I won't survive ...

Under the Lip: What if I don't survive ...

Collarbone: So frightened I won't survive ...

Under the Arm: Just want this fear to go away... want it out of my body and Soul ...

Rib: So afraid I won't survive ...

Rib: This anxiety has been with me for so long …

Wrist: Will it ever go away?

Head: Just want this fear gone … out of my body and Soul …

Moving from the Possibility of Change to Conviction …

Eyebrow: Maybe if I bury myself in the arms of my Higher Power …

Side of the Eye: Maybe I can let go and Let God …

Under the Eye: Please Higher Power fill this void …

Upper Lip: Help me move beyond this gut-wrenching loss and fear …

Under the Lip: Just want to feel safe and believe I can cope …

Collarbone: Maybe with help, I can survive …

Rib: Maybe I can find the support from above and within

Wrist: I can connect with my Inner Child and then give this anxiety to God

Under the Arm: I choose now to turn this over …

Rib: I choose to surrender to my Higher Power and God …

Head: I am strong enough … I can survive.

If you feel a shift in energy enough to move on, then do so. If not, continue to tap until you feel some relief. Feel free to adjust the words as you like.

As long as you are tapping, even if you say nothing, your body will begin to let go and relax. Your goal is to move out of your anxious place. It is also at this juncture that I might go to YouTube and play that EMDR Celestial video. When I do this I simply let my eyes move back and forth without saying a word. I have found this practice to also be effective in moving me out of the anxious state. If you have experienced the exercises of TRE® or any kind of breathing technique you might want to try these as well. Irrespective of which method you use, the goal with each of these stages of grief is to always move out of the reactivity back to a state of peace and calm.

STAGE TWO—BARGAINING

Discussion: When we can no longer tolerate the rawness of the loss we try to regain some sense of control by focusing on how we can change or fix the circumstances. Even though our attempts fail, the activity allows us to discharge some of the energy which gets stuck. These attempts are called the bargaining phase because we start making agreements with our self and with the object of our loss. We try to bargain with the circumstances of the loss. In a frantic manner, we try to manage the situation to ward off the inevitable pain.

Focus Questions—Respond to the following questions:

1. *How did you try to make this situation better?*

2. *What did you do behaviorally to try to change this situation or ignore this situation to pretend it did not exist?*

3. *This was your attempt to bargain with these circumstances. Did it work? If not, did you try something else or did you collapse into your anger or despair?*

4. *Is there anything about which you feel regret? If so, try to describe the circumstances and the accompanying feelings. This can be the source of much of your grief. It is important to flush those feelings out and address them.*

Suggested Exercises: "Attempts to Manage the Loss"

If it feels useful to do so, explore the deeper meaning of your attempts to manage the loss. Determine who inside feels such a need to change this situation. Who finds your present circumstances so intolerable? What motivates you to change, fix, or control, this situation in your adult world. You will find this motivation can be entirely different than what you experienced as a child. If you separate these two motivations and focus now on the adult's need to bargain, the process will be more effective. The Inner Child's feelings and need to bargain and control will be addressed in the next section. For now, use the tapping sequences to begin to manage your own need to manage.

EFT for the Bargaining Stage

Tap on your karate point while stating the phrases below. Customize these to fit your needs.

Even though I tried but failed to control, fix, or change, this situation (imagine it in your mind's eye), I love myself fully and completely.

Even though I have put great effort into changing this situation to no avail, and have exhausted myself in my attempts, I love myself fully and completely and am willing to tap this need to control away.

Even though I have tried so very hard, I now realize it is not my place to alter this situation, and I love myself enough to choose instead to detach and let the outcome go.

Use the following samples to begin your neutralization process. Add your own phrases accordingly but continue to tap around the endpoints saying your reminder phrase until you have neutralized the negative, introduced the possibility of change, and feel conviction with respect to your new stance.

Neutralizing the Negative

Eyebrow: Really tried so very hard …

Side of the Eye: Am exhausted with my attempts …

Under the Eye: Just wish I could let it go …

Upper Lip: But fight this need to control and fix …

Under the Lip: It is so in my nature to jump in …

Collarbone: Wish I could just let go and let God …

Under the Arm: But this need to do something takes over …

Rib: And I just don't seem to be able to let it go …

Rib: Feel too much anxiety to let go…

Wrist: Hard to give up the hope …

Head: Wish I could relax and let it go …

Moving from the Possibility of Change to Conviction ...

Eyebrow: Maybe I can begin to try something new ...

Side of the Eye: Maybe I can tap instead of reacting...

Under the Eye: Maybe what I can change is the way I respond ...

Upper Lip: Maybe I don't always have to be the one ...

Under the Lip: I am going to tap until I can let go ...

Collarbone: Tap myself through the need to respond ...

Under the Arm: I can deal with the panic, and let it go ...

Rib: I have a new way of coping ...

Wrist: I really want to respond in a new way ...

Head: I feel strong and secure in my ability to let go!

Again, use whatever method necessary to move from the tension of your need to control to a release and a letting go.

STAGE THREE—ANGER

Discussion: Anger seeps in once we realize our bargaining is not going to work or we simply feel angry and agitated at the loss of our cherished situation. This is often expressed as crankiness or being critical of everything around us. The irritation enables us to discharge some of the energy of the anger but keeps us from totally letting go of an attachment that can no longer exist.

But part of us does not want to let go. We feel angry that we even have to let go. We do not want to feel the loss. Often our anger is covert and even misdirected. It may be expressed at our self for blowing it. "*It's not nice to be angry.*" We can feel shame or guilt for feeling angry. On the other hand, we may project our anger onto another–blaming that person for everything under the sun. Either way, the anger is not resolved. This criticalness or complaining does reduce the tension, but it does so without ever actually severing the tie to that which we lost. The transition from our blame/shame frame of mind occurs when we can no longer suppress it, and our feelings seep out in rage.

This rage is often raw and unfiltered. It fuels our courage, whether willingly or unwillingly, to embrace the depth of grief which accompanies our loss. Sometimes it is done with great volume because we don't know how to speak it without volume. Use the following focus questions to help you find your truth and prepare yourself to speak it.

Focus Questions—Respond to the following questions in your journal:

1. *Take a moment to think about your loss. Determine when and how you experience or have experienced the irritation or anger at this stage of your grief.*

2. *Do, or did, you recall feeling irritated at anything/everything around you? If so, that is covert anger.*

3. *Do, or did, you feel righteous—vindictive—aggressive? This is an expression of overt anger—misdirected anger.*

4. *Do, or did, you have a shorter temper with others–with yourself—with the circumstances in your life? This is a suggestion of generalized anger.*

5. *Do, or did, you feel like you wanted revenge? This is a suggestion of revenge anger.*

All forms of anger are valid and need to be expressed. If it feels safe, use the following exercises to revisit that rage and anger now.

Suggested Exercises "Transmuting the Energy of Anger"

Pick and choose which of the following methods appeal to you. However, I do recommend that you always begin with the first one. Sealing your anger before you release it is just the responsible thing to do. Otherwise, the disruptive energy spews out into the universe and coagulates with another vibrational rage as well. This is why some are reluctant to express the anger–they don't want to put that energy out into the world. But if you take responsibility for working with it in a transformative way this does not happen. It is just energy that is recycled and transmuted for another higher use. So again, I recommend you always begin with creating protection around you and the release of your anger.

1. Creating Protection—first, so that you can always feel safe, close your eyes and imagine that you surround yourself with that bubble light. Sometimes I call in an Angel or a Master or Loved One to assist. Then, ask that your anger is being encased in this Light and that as you express it the anger be transmuted in Violet Light, then be sent directly to the great central sun to be transformed. This will seal your anger so that its energy does not bleed out into other areas. When you feel complete and secure proceed with any or all of the following exercises.

2. The Silent Scream—aka—Whisper Yelling—to do the silent scream you can take a pillow and simply scream into it. Scream by opening your mouth but blocking the volume from coming out. It releases the frustration without alarming anyone around you.

3. The Private Scream—If you really need to release the volume of your anger then this method is an option. Scream in a car or in the woods where you will not be heard.

4. Throwing a tantrum—this is a wonderful exercise or activity that enables you to jump up and down, flailing your arms around and making grunting noises, or yelling "No," to what you are releasing and then ultimately yelling "Yes," to that which you wish to attract. This resets the central nervous system immediately. Animals do this naturally when they have been stressed by a life-threatening experience. In fact, TRE© is founded on this principle so it definitely works!

5. Exercising—this releases the energy and makes it more manageable.

   (Note: aerobic exercise, such as jogging, etc., reduces current anger, anaerobic exercise, such as yoga, swimming, etc. reaches anger that is more deeply rooted in the muscular fibers.)

6. Meditation—using the breathing techniques you were introduced to in the last section, let yourself relax and go into a meditative state. When you tap you can hold this image in your mind's eye as well. That combination augments this method even more.

7. Journal Writing—I recommend when you record your responses in a journal that you use it for stream-of-consciousness writing, recording without censure whatever thoughts and feelings come to mind. By the time you have finished your inner work, you will have a rich collection of the feelings you identified, experienced, resolved, and healed. It will be similar to having a photo album that documents your inner journey.

8. Drawing—expressing your pain through drawing accesses your creativity and lets you give form to the feelings of anger. Describing the voice of the angry self with words can be limiting; drawing often gives you a richer symbolic means of expression.

9. *Mirror Work*—mirror work involves sitting in front of a mirror and having a dialogue with your angry self. It allows you to see for yourself how your shoulders slump or the mannerisms present when you express your anger. Tapping on your endpoints while you look at yourself in the mirror can accelerate this technique. You do not have to say anything, although you can, it is not necessary. Just observe and tap and see where it takes you. Looking at your own image in a mirror is also one of the most effective ways of finding that higher, more evolved part of yourself. By facing yourself eye to eye, you can look beyond your physical deficiencies and see the wise, Inner Being within you. The tapping below will also help you get started, but again, draw on any resource you may have acquired on your way to spiritual fitness and health.

EFT for Anger:

Tap on your karate point while stating the phrases below. Customize these to fit your needs.

Even though I felt/feel rage (anger, revenge, etc.) in this situation (imagine it in your mind's eye), I love myself fully and completely."

Continue with tapping around the points saying your reminder phrase until you feel flat.)

Even though I felt righteous and wanted revenge in this situation, I know it was my wounded one, and I want to be able to respond instead of collapsing into the pain."

Even though I felt anger inside but did not dare to express it for fear of retaliation, I want to neutralize that feeling, so I can speak my truth and let go.

Now tap on the endpoint to begin to resolve the energy of your anger and your rage. If it gets too intense always opt to seek support. Call a practitioner, schedule an appointment with someone you trust and give yourself the assistance you deserve.

Neutralizing the Negative

Eyebrow: All of this rage....

Side of the Eye: ... this anger and rage...

Under the Eye: ... really uncomfortable with the feelings of anger.

Upper Lip: But I feel so violated and betrayed.

Under the Lip: Isn't it wrong to feel this much rage?

Collarbone: It's not okay to feel such anger ...

Under the Arm: ... better stuff it again...

Rib: So uncomfortable with this rage ...

Wrist: ...and yet it won't go away...

Head: All of this anger... can't silence that voice... it's too late.

Moving from the Possibility of Change to Conviction ...

Eyebrow: But maybe I can tap it away

Side of the Eye: I can give myself permission to speak my truth...

Under the Eye: I choose to speak my truth while I tap it away...

Upper Lip: It sure has not worked to push it down...

Under the Lip: I need to figure out a new way ...

Collarbone: Perhaps if I tap while I vent to my Inner Being

Under the Arm: I will finally be able to speak my truth and invite my Inner Child to do the same.

Rib: Somewhere in time, this truth needs to be stated and heard.

Wrist: If not now, when?

Head: If I want to be real I have to be able to speak what I feel.

Truly embrace the energy of your anger. Remember, this is the force that will let you move on and allow the new form of the relationship to that which you lost to unfold. When you speak your truth, you free yourself from the denial. You free yourself to be real.

When we can truly, and honestly, embrace our anger, the volume diminishes. We speak our truth authentically which opens the door to great sadness. We admit how angry we are with our loss. The anger ultimately severs the hope that we can alter the reality of the loss. This surrender brings relief. We are finally free to stand in the void of the emptiness left by our loss as we collapse into the next stage of grief–the sadness, and the despair.

STAGE FOUR—DESPAIR

Discussion: After allowing the severing of your hope there is usually an exhaustion–an emotional and physical exhaustion. It takes energy to hold on to those feelings of loss. Despair over this situation can feel like complete hopelessness—sadness—numbness. Despair is that experience of apathy and of giving up which leads to a sense of surrender. But most often the surrender begins with that apathy of complete hopelessness.

You will feel tired and worn out. You will need to sleep a great deal and let the reality of this loss settle into your psyche. You are readjusting to life without this challenge. Many mistake despair for depression. In reality, it is the exact opposite. Although the two feeling states feel the same their function is quite different.

Depression is a result of stuffing down feelings we feel unable to cope. It is the equivalent to stuffing socks into a bag until it is bulging. The emotions are suppressed, cramped together, and ultimately become toxic to the body and Soul, Despair, on the other hand, is experienced when we have the courage to feel the sadness appropriate to the loss of something that we valued. It is the emptiness, the void—a void that cannot be filled until it is felt.

Feeling your despair is embracing it. It is standing in the center of the space once filled with the object of your loss and allowing yourself to confront the bareness of its absence. It is the last stage of letting go of the physical way you have related to what you are now losing. Once you can endure that emptiness, and let go of the attachment to relating to your loss, the void can be filled with a new vibration.

How do you do this? You simply breathe through it. Allow the void to be embraced. From this allowance comes the resurgence of something new. For this re-emergence to occur, you have to put a form to and embrace your despair. Use the focus questions below to assist you.

Focus Questions—Respond to the following questions:

1. What is one of your favorite, most loving, moments or experiences related to the object of your loss?

2. Describe this memory in as much detail as possible? Focusing on this memory recreates the vibration of attachment from which you will draw when you begin to allow the new form of relationship to emerge. *For instance, when I had to grieve no longer being able to run for exercise because my knee gave out I had to let myself really acknowledge the joy I felt when running. I revisited every race I had run and every trail I had experienced.*

3. What is it you will truly miss about this object of your loss?

4. How will your daily life be affected?

5. Imagine you are standing in an empty room. Allow yourself to really feel the absence of everything related to the object of your loss. Imagine no stimulation-no distraction-no mementos that hold the memory of this loss. It is gone. Truly see how it feels to be without that which you lost. Facing the relevance running held for me—really admitting that running had enabled me to cope and had kept me balanced and in connection with my Higher Self was riveting. It made me realize the true depth of the loss. And when I faced that truth-that running was indeed the primary avenue of release and connection I had to grieve before I could replace it with something new. In fact, I even had to admit I was grieving! For a while, I just felt the apathy and despair but had not identified it as being connected to not being able to run anymore. Only when I identified that I was grieving was I able to embrace those feelings and move on. Completing the suggested exercise below was one of the methods I used to accomplish the task.

6. When you have answered the above questions then go on to the suggested exercise and let yourself admit and speak your truth.

Suggested Exercises "Letter to Your Loss"

Write a letter to the object of your loss. Tell him, her, or it, all that you are going to miss about no longer having this object be part of your life. If you were involved with this object of your loss on a daily basis then speak about the void that you must now face. Say what you were perhaps unable to admit or even realize as long as there was not this void. If it is a pet or a person you have lost through death or divorce, say what you may not even have known you felt when your loved one was around. Put it all down on paper.

When we write our feelings out like this, we get the energy of the feelings out of our body. We externalize the feelings thus bringing them from the unconscious to the conscious mind. The feelings are then more stimulated and present in the energetic meridian system, and therefore, more susceptible to being neutralized and released with our tapping.

Each of the focus questions and journal exercises above will assist you in embracing your despair more fully. The more you allow that emptiness to be there the more room you will have to allow the relationship to morph into a new form and the more benefit you will get from your tapping sequences.

EFT for Despair

Tap on your karate point while stating the phrases below. Customize these to fit your needs.

"Even though I felt/feel sad, despair, or hopeless in this situation (imagine it in your mind's eye) I love myself fully and completely."

"Even though this sadness is more than I can bear, it feels good to finally acknowledge the truth, to be honest with myself so I can begin to heal.

"So even though this truth has been buried for a very long time, it feels so relieving to lance his wound, so my Inner Child and I can begin to heal."

Continue with tapping around the points saying your reminder phrase until you feel flat or have very little emotional charge. Then proceed to the reminder phrases.

Neutralizing the Negative

Eyebrow: So much sadness…

Side of the Eye: Have run from it for many years…

Under the Eye: Not sure how to feel …

Upper Lip: I have cut off from this truth for so long…

Under the Lip: The sadness, the despair, the emptiness is so big…

Collarbone: Will I ever be able to move beyond it and really heal?

Under the Arm: I feel so alone, what if I do not survive?

Rib: No wonder I did not feel safe.

Wrist: This loneliness is almost more than I can bear.

Head: What if I don't survive?

Moving from the Possibility of Change to Conviction …

Eyebrow: But I am not alone, not like before.

Side of the Eye: I do have a support system …

Under the Eye: My Inner Child and I can survive.

Upper Lip: I want to draw on all of the resources I have gathered along the way.

Under the Lip: I have done a lot of work on myself.

Collarbone: I have a lot to offer my wounded one from my past.

Under the Arm: Together we will neutralize the pain, return to safety, and heal.

Rib: I have come a very long way on this journey… I am not alone…

Wrist: I have my Higher Self-inner child and I can release and let go.

Head: It truly is time to let go to let God handle this, so we can heal.

Again, draw from whatever methods you have at hand to assist you in embracing the depth of this void and despair. When you feel ready to move on then go to that stage where you feel some relief.

STAGE FIVE—ACCEPTANCE AND RESOLUTION

Discussion: This stage is when you resolve the grief related to your current loss. You are ready to allow a new form of attachment to unfold. You have embraced each stage of your loss, and have dealt with the void. You are now ready to replenish with something new–to replace the old form of attachment with a new form, a form as of yet, unknown.

This final stage is when your Adult Self gets to make peace with the loss because you have dealt with the feelings of the immediate loss. The loss is replaced with a feeling of wholeness, of being complete. You are finally safe to bring in something new. Trust in self, and your Higher Power can be restored. The healing of the residual losses endured by your Inner Child will soon begin.

But first, you want to complete this process with your Adult Self. This completion comes when you sense you are ready to address the higher purpose of your loss. You are ready to go into meditation with your Healing Team and inquire about the purpose of your loss. You are receptive to asking how the resolution of your loss can benefit you spiritually and contribute to the expansion of your Soul,

When we address our healing in such a way, we move from being a victim of our loss to being a student of it. We recognize the spiritual significance of this loss. We begin to understand that having embraced the stages of grief so courageously, and having accepted our loss so authentically, opened our hearts. It expands our consciousness and enables us to see our life without this object of our loss differently.

In dealing with the loss of a loved one you may come to understand more and more that there truly is no loss. You may have experienced signs or visitations–those extraordinary experiences that give you the inclination that your loved one has not gone far. You can begin to comprehend that there is merely a change in the form of the relationship.

But this all begins when we are ready for the higher purpose of our pain to be revealed. The following exercise will help move you in this direction. However, this pursuit is one that will continue indefinitely. It has been over thirty years since my father passed away, and I continue to learn from the relationship we have today. The evolution is truly endless.

Focus Questions—Respond to the following questions.

1. *Take a moment to picture the source of your loss in your mind's eye. What's it like to tune into the vibration of your heart?*

2. *How was your heart attached to that which you lost?*

3. *How did you respond to the loss at the time of its occurrence?*

4. *Ask who inside felt such grief and what does he or she need from you now? How do you want to respond to this pain and loss? Comfort your little one and assure him or her that you are going to assist in resolving the hurt, the sadness, the anger, and despair. But now is not the time. Now you need to step away from the depth of the loss and look at the loss through the eyes of your elevated self.*

You may want to return to the breathing exercises in which you bridged from your Adult Self to your higher self. It is from this expanded state of consciousness that you can begin to address questions of this higher, spiritual nature. When, as adults, we have an understanding of the higher purpose of our pain we are in a much better position to later assist our more fragile Inner Child in dealing with his or her original experience of the loss of safety and love.

Suggested Exercises *"I am willing to see the bigger picture of my Loss."*

1. *Now imagine you are standing before your Guardians and your Higher Self.*

2. *Ask about the higher purpose of this loss.*

3. *What was it your Soul may have wanted you to experience in dealing with this loss?*

4. *What was its purpose? What were its promise and reward?*

5. *Record your responses to this interaction with your Healing Team. Include your thoughts about this higher, more spiritual perspective on your recent loss? How are you now different than you were before enduring and resolving this loss? How have you grown?*

Meditation Tapping for Acceptance and Resolution—Rewire the Brain

Meditation tapping is very powerful in that it augments the vibrational intensity of anything you are affirming or intending. The text for this meditation is based on the principles of the "law of attraction." Keep this in mind as you begin to redirect your attention to a new form of connection with the object of your loss. When you do this you will be creating a new vibrational resonance. This vibration or buzz is what will attract the new object or experience into your life. The buzz is usually felt as a tingling all over your body, or a surge of energy up your spine.

According to quantum physicists, this surge, buzz, vibration, signals that the neurons in your brain are firing the neurotransmitters that support the emotional response or vibrational response to the affirmations included in this meditation. According to the Teachings of Abraham, if you hold this "buzz" for 17 seconds it energetically takes the vibrational form needed to be launched as a desire. If you hold it for 68 seconds, your DNA begins to replicate the picture and attract its vibrational match.

Tap on the endpoints while you recite this following meditation as an affirmation and an intention setting tool.

> *I am now ready to fully let go and allow this new evolution to occur. I have honored my attachment to that which I have lost. I really am ready to expand my consciousness–to vibrationally merge with my Higher Self–for it is from that vibrational point I can create an attachment after that which I lost. There does not have to be a void–a loss. The vibrational connection has merely changed. I can expand enough to connect and recreate in a new way. I now have the courage to do just that.*

You may want to add variations to this meditative tapping sequence, but those words should give you the idea of what you are trying to accomplish. When you feel that connection is secure, proceed to your last tapping sequence for processing the grief of your Adult Self which will prepare you to address the unresolved grief of your Inner Child. There may be other momentary flashes of anxiety, anger, or despair. But you have given yourself a model for breathing through those responses to your grief to the point where you will never be a victim of your multidimensional loss again.

You have freed up the energy you had tied up in your multidimensional grief. You can now work with the residue of your past; learn about your Inner Child's pain, bring him or her home. You can now assure those parts of you that they can be free to feel their feelings. You will not abandon them in their pain. You will get the help you need, pray for the guidance required, so you can assist them in letting go and feeling safe. Your current loss inspired this healing so you can finally learn how to live your life without fear.

Layer Two: "Externalizing The Pain"

Separating from the Wounded One

In Layer Two we work with the Separation Layer
of healing.
When we externalize the disturbance we set up a
dyad between
the part of us that carries the wound and
the part of us who can respond to the wound.
This is a crucial step in that it is this very separation
which allows us to interact—and the interaction
between the wounded one
and the Healer within us is what creates the healing.
When we interact with our wounded one
we not only establish the target for the healing,
we also identify the exact need.
This builds the foundation to be able to
respond instead of react.
We use the "he" or "she" to
begin the separation process

LAYER TWO—Externalizing the Pain

(Click on the heading to be taken to the YouTube Overview)

OVERVIEW—Separate And Externalize The Pain

Layer Two has to do with addressing the dual aspect of our psyche. It is recognizing that you have a part of you who feels wounded and afraid and a part of you who has evolved enough to be able to respond to that wound. It involves realizing you are bigger than your wounds. In Layer Two you begin to acknowledge the skills you have acquired as an adult. These are the skills that enable you to separate from the pain of your past and become the Healer within who can respond. It is externalizing the pain by using the pronouns "he" and "she" to first establish a separation between, and then to acknowledge the relationship between the parts of you who carries your wounds and the part of you who can orchestrate the healing of those wounds. However, you cannot separate from the pain until you have acknowledged that adult part of you who is bigger than your pain.

We accomplished that step in Layer One. By adulthood, because of the very nature of your life's experiences, you have acquired a different point of reference than you had as a child. Furthermore, the Human Self, in this incarnation, has evolved and has most likely developed more spiritual awareness than the embodiments you had in previous lifetimes. You hopefully have attained more consciousness and therefore operate at a higher level of frequency. This empowers you to facilitate a healing, not only of your Inner Child but also for the fragmented aspects of your Soul which remain suspended in other dimensions of time and consciousness waiting to be healed and escorted into the Light.

Your evolution has, in itself, provided you with the specific techniques needed to separate from your wounds, even if you have not recognized this to be the case. It is this acknowledgment you build on as you embody your most Illuminated Adult Self who has attained a higher level of mastery and empowerment.

You begin this Separation Layer the moment you gain enough awareness to understand that in response to your life's challenges there were debilitating patterns of behavior you developed. These old patterns leave you vulnerable to repeatedly collapsing into your old wounds. In fact, sometimes you most likely feel as though you will never be able to let go of the past. Only when you are not in a collapsed state can you recognize the contrast of when you are in a collapsed state and when you are not. That recognition is born out of spiritual evolvement and self-reflection. But recognition is not enough on its own.

Once you have identified the faulty belief systems you have to be able to rework them. No matter how much work you do on yourself if you are not rewiring your brain; reconditioning your heart; reprogramming your body, and reframing the purpose of your pain, you are going to continue to default into that coping mechanism that your brain is hardwired to implement. You are going to continue to scan the horizon to constantly assess for possible risk because that is the only way you know how to survive.

So how does this happen? How did it occur that we became so identified with our pain that we came to believe that is all there is? What happens when we keep recycling those same old patterns? How do we ever get over those old wounds?

Layer Two deals with this dilemma. It is a dilemma that many of us find ourselves confronting.

Where The Separation Begins

Separation begins when we first lose the connection to our Source. We come into our physical body connected to Spirit. Our higher brain or pre-frontal cortex is hardwired to experience Divine joy and peace. However, in response to our environment and the experiences of being unsafe, we slowly *prune* out the neurons that promote joy and continually reinforce those that keep us safe. As you read in the Introduction, your lower brain actually becomes hardwired to look for the negative and to be very hyper-vigilant in keeping you safe.

So to begin the Separation Layer we have to go back to the very beginning of our lifetime when we were still in spirit form. Again, we were connected, not separate. But as we took on physical form we naturally became more and more disconnected from our Source energy. Separation, by its very nature, means that we experience loss. And that first loss we experience is what I call the *Soul's essential wound*. It is that existential angst we all experience throughout our embodiment. It is the hole in our bellies that each of us tries to fill with our addictions and excessive behaviors, our pharmaceuticals and drugs.

It occurs when we break away from our Spiritual Source and we come into physical form. Suddenly our consciousness has to deal with the density and the weight of our earthly body, our human self. This densification results in tension—tension related to being separated from the all loving essence of our spiritual self. But we cannot identify it as such because we do not have the cognitive abilities in infancy to determine this is the case.

We just experience a discomfort.

Add to this the emotional climate of our mother. If our mother experienced stress during her pregnancy her tension got transmitted to us as well. This stress is compounded by the natural interaction with our environment. Through the very progression of the stages of our emotional development, the process of separation from our caretaker begins. Slowly we experience the fact that we and our mother are not one. This results in another layer of loss and anxiety. Both mother and child have mixed reactions to this ensuing individuation. The way each of us deals with this transition from symbiosis to independence and separateness determines whether the process progresses gracefully or traumatically.

If we are gracefully escorted into that stage of autonomy (which occurs between the ages of eighteen and thirty-six months) if our caretaker is healthy enough to assist us in this transition, then we do so with ease. But very few mothers or caretakers can assist their child that gracefully.

Mothers are human. They have needs and agendas of their own. Many mothers lean towards wanting to hold onto that connection and that symbiosis with their child. When this is the case the very individuation of the child triggers loss in the mother. Often she holds on to the child, even more, to ward off her own grief and anxiety. Because the child and the mother are still merged, her anxiety gets transmitted to her child.

On the other hand, if the mother is uncomfortable with that dependency and that symbiosis then she often pushes the toddler out of the safety net too soon. The child, unprepared for that abrupt abandonment, develops the pattern of being overly-dependent and wanting to merge with any potential source of safety.

Each of us falls somewhere on this continuum of attachment versus detachment. Add to this any degree of dysfunction in the family system itself and you can imagine the degree of tension our little body had to process as we tried to navigate the trials and tribulations of early childhood.

The third separation process that we have to deal with is that of separating from our True Self. As we adapt to our environment we become more and disconnected and separated from our real essence. We begin to adapt our behavior to please those we determine can meet our needs. We first try to please our parents; then the other adults in our life; and ultimately our peers, employers, and our partners. This list can go on and on!

So, even though we come in connected to Spirit, in response to our environment and the experiences of being unsafe we slowly become more and more disconnected. And our brains follow our lead. Our brains prune out the neurons that promote joy and continually reinforce those that keep us on alert. Slowly we become more and more separate—from our creator, from others, and even from ourselves.

Separation means loss, and loss means anxiety.

To summarize, the first separation is from our Spiritual Essence, the second is our separation as the child from our parent or caretaker, and finally, the third separation occurs when we disconnect from our Authentic Self. We adjust to the cues from our environment as we adapt to the circumstances of our life. And our brain follows. It follows through that process called synaptic pruning, a process that leaves us in a perpetual state of anxiety and grief.

SYNAPTIC PRUNING

Synaptic pruning is the process by which neurons that are used frequently develop stronger connections, and those that are rarely or never used, eventually die. By developing new connections and pruning away weak ones, the brain is able to adapt to the changing environment. But in so doing, the brain becomes hardwired to expect stress and pain. And the more stressful our environment is the more hardwired our brain becomes to prepare us to expect stress.

This gets compounded the first time we experience our essential wound—that first experience of our world being unsafe. Our energetic blueprint gets established and embedded in who we are to become. In response, we begin the process of Soul loss as we move from connection to separation, from safety to risk and fear.

Each experience of separation results in a loss of a part of our Soul. And when there is loss there is a need to grieve.

A RETURN TO GRIEF

When we experience grief we get stuck in the anxiety, panic, fear, anger, rage, shame, guilt, regret, depression or despair. We remain either engaged in these knee-jerk reactions to life, or we go into denial and these feelings get buried. As we explored in working with the grief of current losses the residual losses of childhood stay buried until an incident pulls the band-aid off. Once this happens we are left exposed, vulnerable, and afraid. These feelings get bundled up and become what we most often experience as "floating anxiety." There is an unrest that begins to bubble just below the consciousness. We cannot name it or get a sense of its origin. But nonetheless, it is there and morphs into what we ultimately refer to as our "saboteur."

Then, as you have read, the brain follows our lead. Even though this unrest is taking place below the surface of our consciousness our brain is deciphering which neurons to support and which ones to discard. Our brain gets very astute at keeping us safe and begins to focus on situations which alert us we are at risk. Once assessed, our brain cues our body to go into the fight, flight, or freeze response all of which is fueled by fear— the fear we will not be able to cope.

This is why I say our biggest fear is we will not cope.
Our anxiety has a purpose.
And there is a reason we cannot trust.

Our anxiety shows us that something is wrong. We cannot trust because we perceive we have no choice. If we trust we are at risk. If we trust we will not be safe. This can lead to our being biochemically imbalanced. Our brain fires off the neurons that cue us to go into stress mode. Our body produces the cortisol and adrenaline to react and we collapse into the emotional angst of our Inner Child or Soul. So our biggest fear is that we will not cope. We use our anxiety to ward off that fear——to protect ourselves with our unworthiness and shame so we can avoid the risk of getting hurt.

The good news is that this vibrational glitch that carries your pain is repairable. The energetic blueprint which keeps this process in motion can be interrupted and changed.

And it is changed when you develop the ability to separate from your pain, to externalize your pain, so you can build the bridge needed to **respond** to your wounded ones with the compassion and love that can heal.

THE INTERVENTION—How This Can Be Repaired

How does repair occur? What is intervention?

When, as an Adult, we have acquired the skills to respond, we are able to go see the pain of our past through a different lens. We are able to recognize that we are now more than our wound. The wound is carried by a more compromised, fragile self.

This separation from the wounded one and the externalization of our pain that takes place in Layer Two is the cornerstone for rewiring the brain, reconditioning the heart, reprogramming the body, and reframing the purpose of your Soul's pain. Layer Two begins the journey of our partnering with our wounded ones and helping them grieve their loss of safety. This prepares us to return to the time of their wound in Layers Three and Four when we prune the old experiences and exchange them with new ones. We systematically change these experiences and build new pathways in the brain.

Gradually your brain begins to default to these positive experiences instead of the negative ones. You can begin to live life non-addictively without fear. You can move into a state of mastery which allows you to the heal anything that keeps you disconnected from your true source. It is this ability that defines your level of self-mastery. Not that you will sustain this mastery. It is a fluid state from which you move in and out.

But what you do master is that ability to move in and out of that contrast of feelings so you can gracefully separate from the stress and respond and heal the fragments within your Soul and personality. What you master is the ability to sustain a willingness to deal with any aspect of your personality or Soul whose unresolved pain pulls you from your Source. What you master is your ability to give up judgment and fear. You learn to embrace those wounds—see their relevance and skillfully resolve what needs to be healed so you can return to that state of peace and calm—that green zone in which your body, mind, heart, and Soul can heal.

As you will see in Layers Three and Four, the Adult Self summons your healing team and together they return to the scenes of your childhood, and ultimately to the situations in which the fragments of your Soul are suspended. Once there, the healing team steps in on behalf of the wounded ones. Wrongs are righted. The wounded ones receive the help they need. The loss is resolved and healed.

It is this very activity that meets the installation stage of rewiring the brain. This meditative interaction, supercharged with the interactive tapping™ sequences, successfully replaces the old, reactive experience with a calmer, more compassionate, response, thus enabling the brain to send the body a new message. The new message is that there is no risk. There is no tiger. And the body can remain calm and relaxed.

But in order to be able to accomplish this task, you have to be able to separate from the pain so you can respond. Only then can you determine what needs to be addressed. Only then can you determine what belief system needs to be rewired—assess how your heart needs to be reconditioned—what it needs to be retrained to expect connection, safety, and the satisfaction of your needs. With this information, you can then reprogram your body to expect joy and peace. The stress response cycle has been interrupted. You are able to spend more time in the "green zone" where you can heal and feel safe.

To summarize, building new pathways in your brain enables you to interrupt the default coping mechanism which has been conditioned to default to negativity in response to your need to survive. This perception of risk was perceived through the eyes of your Inner Child. Your Illuminated Adult Self has acquired the skills to view the world differently. The negative response can be replaced with the positive reaction which allows the stress response to default to the positive memory or vibration of your "happy place" created or experienced by your Illuminated Adult Self.

This supports a state of relaxation instead of fear, response instead of reactivity. Your Adult Self, along with the support of your Healing Team, can begin to begin to recondition the heart of your Inner Child by responding to his or her need.

When this need is fulfilled your emotional self can relax.

If there is no emotional cue to fight or flee the body does not have to freeze. You are not disconnected from your body. Your body can be reprogrammed to stay calm because there is no perceived danger.

When your body is calm you can look at your day-to-day events through the eyes of your Soul. This new perspective gives your pain relevance. It enables you to pull the threads back to the origin of the pain. Once there, you can assess the context of the painful situation. You can ask your Soul what it wanted you to learn. You can determine the purpose of the original experience and gather the information needed to heal the aspect of your Soul who is suspended in time.

If your pain is relevant, it is useful.

If it is useful you are not deficient.

If you are not deficient, there is no need to feel shame.

If you don't collapse into shame you can exchange fear for faith; self-loathing for self-love; and judgment for compassion and trust.

But all of this is possible only when we are separate enough from the parts of us who hold the pain so we can respond to them and help them heal. This is the purpose of Layer Two—to establish this duality—to respond instead of collapse. But how is that purpose realized? What are the steps we take to separate from our past? How do we pull the threads that link our anxiety to our fear?

IMPLEMENTING LAYER TWO—Separating From The Triggered Self In Order To Respond And Heal

The gift of the separation process is that we begin to identify the trigger point of where we stepped out of our green zone. We begin to put a time and place to the eruption of our discomfort. Unlike the floating anxiety which results from the general, the specific anxiety we experience in response to the three, original, separation experiences previously discussed, holds the unique vibration of the original trauma. It is not "floating." It is not generic. It is very specific and carries a personal, energetic blueprint. This blueprint is formed by the unique, very personal, incident which occurred that pushed our younger self out of his or her safety zone. This incident carried a perceived threat, which got coupled with it a specific belief system, fueled by an emotion which resulted in a reactive behavior, aimed to return to a state of safety. This reaction carried with it a certain vibration which followed us into adulthood. And now, anytime we encounter a similar experience which resonates with that original vibration, we collapse into the coping mechanisms we experienced at the time of this original, essential wound.

The second task of Layer Two deals with these incidents. When this takes place we plummet into what Hanson calls the red zone and experience a full-blown collapse. Irrespective of our chronological age, we see the current situation through the eyes of the younger self who has determined he or she is at risk.

If there is a collapse there is a trigger.

If there is a trigger there is an old wound.

If there is an old wound the experience carries the face of an Inner Child or the energetic blueprint of a suspended, fragment of your Soul.

Both of these blueprints are expressions of events that were left unresolved and are therefore suspended in time waiting to be healed.

This first task of Layer Two is to separate from the pain. The second task is to acknowledge that because of that separation the Adult Self can now see that "this is now not then." Layer Two does not involve your "relating" to this wounded self, as we do in Layer Three. It is merely acknowledging that a wounded self has gotten triggered.

But the trigger is outdated. In reality, we are not at risk in the way this wounded self has perceived.

The antidote for a collapse such as this is
tapping while you state over and over again,
"Even though he or she got triggered by this situation,
this is now not then!"

Exercise: Think of a recent situation when you felt you had regressed. Really look at that situation. Get very clear about what it was about that interaction that resulted in the collapse. Begin to externalize these feelings by referring to them as his or her feelings. Addressing the emotional collapse in this manner begins the separation process. This sets up the dyad needed to respond and heal.

Using the terms he or she externalizes the emotion and enables your Illuminated Adult Self to separate enough to respond.

The operative questions to ask are:

1. Who was involved in this situation?

2. How did my Inner Child or Soul fragment feel?

3. When did this part of me first feel this way?

4. What were the beliefs this part of me held at the time of the original wound?

Key Question To Ask

What do I now know that my Inner Child did not know at the time of the wound? Your Adult Self has encountered experiences that enabled you to survive and move forward. You are no longer in that powerless position you once were as a child.

The collapsed part needs to be walked into the present and the words, "This is now not then, help you do this!"

So how do you put This Layer into action? You weave the inter-active language with the tapping. You use the tapping sequences to establish the necessary dyad so you can separate enough to be prepared to relate to him or her in Layer Three. Externalizing the discomfort in the third person, by referring to it as the "feelings of a younger self," sets up the dyad between the wounded ones within and your Illuminated Adult Self who can respond. In this next section, you will be introduced to the interactive tapping™ sequences which facilitate this separation between your Illuminated Adult Self and your wounded one. This separation, which is based on using the pronouns "he" and "she", prepares you to begin, in Layer Three, to relate to this wounded one so he/she can begin to feel some relief.

Step-By-Step Instructions For Separation Layer

IDENTIFY ZONE OF EXPERIENCE

"If you are in it—you cannot heal it!" Your first task in Layer Two is to "notice" you are not in your green zone. This requires that you recognize when you have veered from that relaxed state into the pink zone of "floating anxiety" or boredom and complacency and are acting out your energetic addictive response. Or perhaps you have slid into a full-blown collapse—into the red zone—and into the wounds of an Inner Child or unresolved trauma of a fragment of your Soul, Your goal is to stay in the green zone of relaxation with which we have the ability to heal. The reality is that most of us live in the pink zone made up of the stress of our unidentified, floating anxiety or the stress of our boredom and complacency. The result is that we are sitting ducks to collapse into that red zone of reactivity.

WHAT TOOK YOU OUT OF RELATIONSHIP TO YOURSELF?

To determine this you must first notice you have slipped into vulnerability. If the goal is to stay in that relaxed green zone, then you will progressively get more attuned to those times when you slip out of that state of consciousness. But it is important you assess if you are in the pink zone or the red zone because, again, the responses that lead to resolution are different.

Exercise: "Assessing Source of the Zone" Use the following questions to assist you in assessing the source of your reaction so you can determine the most effective next step that will take you back into the green zone of relaxation, peace, and calm.

When you notice you are out of relationship with yourself, pause. Take a moment to get "conscious." Use the following to trace your experience back to when you slipped out of that green zone.

1. Make a list of the behaviors, thought patterns and/or feelings that took you out of your green zone of relaxation and empowerment.

2. Can you identify a time and place, a situation that triggered this collapse? Or are you experiencing that sense of floating anxiety and are in need of coming back into a state of balance?

3. What is your point of intervention? To whom or to what do you need to respond?

4. Are you in the pink zone, feeling anxious, irritated or afraid? Or are you in the red zone and in the middle of a full-blown collapse?

Once you have identified what the state of consciousness is that you are in you can determine which set of tapping sequences would most effectively resolve the energy.

ASSESS *"POINT OF INTERVENTION"*

Discussion: There are three points of intervention. They are: 1) the pure *energetic addictive response* to the floating anxiety we feel in response to the disconnection from source energy; 2) the *collapse of an Inner Child who feels at risk* in response to our day-to-day inter-actions with those in our adult life, and 3) a *multidimensional bleed through from a fragment of our Soul* from other times and other places.

HOW DO YOU DEAL WITH AN *ENERGETIC ADDICTIVE RESPONSE*?

As we discussed in Part A the goal, when you recognize you are in this state, is to get out of that energy as quickly as possible. This is a reactive energy that has been stimulated either by a biochemical imbalance or a general, energetic collapse resulting from being compromised because of an imbalance between your masculine and feminine selves. The goal is to neutralize the energy so you can return to that partnership required to step back into your most illuminated Adult Self.

We will be using traditional tapping sequence to help you get started. This tapping process begins with three setup phrases. The setup phrases position the symptoms of your energetic addictive response against a positive affirmation. The reminder sequence is divided into three sections. You first neutralize the negative reaction, then introduce the possibility of change, and finish with a strong infusion of your conviction to release the stress and return to that green zone of relaxation and a state of peace and calm. Continue with the first round of sequences until you feel ready to move to the next one. You will intuitively feel an energetic shift when you are done with the negative and your psyche is ready to consider something new. The second set of sequences usually does not take as long. It just softens the psyche so it is ready to claim the right to feel convicted about the return to the relaxed state. The last set should leave you feeling strong and energized in your new conviction. It should escort you back to the green zone where you can feel relaxed and calm.

EXERCISE: "USING TRADITIONAL TAPPING TO ALLEVIATE THE TENSION OF ENERGETIC ADDICTIVE RESPONSE."

Here is an example of an interactive tapping™ sequence that will begin this process. Again, this is just traditional tapping. You focus on the symptom, the discomfort, and disturbance and neutralize the negativity, move into the possibility of change and then reinforce your conviction to make good choices instead of stay stuck in your addictive acting out.

Even though I am feeling restless and stressed for reasons known and unknown, I choose now to neutralize this energy so I can return to that green zone, to that state of peace and calm.

Even though my brain is firing off the neurons that keep me irritated and afraid, there is no threat. I am safe. And I deserve to return to a state of peace and calm.

Even though I am addictively acting out right now, and feel this floating anxiety from tension I cannot even name, I choose to discharge this energy through tapping instead of acting out. I want to tap this out so I can return to that state of peace and calm.

That completes the setup phrases and sets the stage for you to continue with the reminder phrases. Here are some sample rounds. But continue your tapping until the energy has relaxed and you once again feel calm and relaxed.

Neutralizing the Negativity

Eyebrow: All of this tension.

Side of the Eye: Feel restless, anxious and scared.

Under the Eye: This desire to act out …

Upper Lip: …for reasons unclear.

Under the Lip: So much tension,

Collarbone: discomfort, restlessness, and fear.

Under the Arm: Just want to act out.

Rib: So much tension and fear.

Head: Will I ever be able to just release this tension and fear?

Introducing the Possibility of Change

Eyebrow: Maybe I can relax and let go.

Side of the Eye: Maybe I can let God's love resolve this tension and fear.

Under the Eye: Maybe I can let go and let the Universe take over.

Upper Lip: Maybe I can calm myself down and direct my brain to reduce the cortisol …

Under the Lip: … to cue more serotonin so I can just let go.

Collarbone: Maybe I can really rewire my brain.

Under the Arm: Maybe I can teach it to be calm, show it there is no threat.

Rib: I don't want to run this addictive energy that keeps me so stuck.

Head: I really want to just let it go.

Affirming the Conviction

Eyebrow: I'm so ready to release and let go.

Side of the Eye: I am so glad to release this addictive urge … to calm down my brain …

Under the Eye: … to restore my sense of balance … and to once again feel calm.

Upper Lip: I AM capable of neutralizing this energy and getting calm.

Under the Lip: I really can calm myself down.

Collarbone: Every cell in my body DOES feel relaxed.

Under the Arm: There is no threat. I am not at risk.

Rib: I am safe. My brain has relaxed.

Head: And I am willing to now be calm.

Continue to work with these sequences until you feel you have neutralized that energetic addictive response and you no longer feel the need to act it out. Only then can you be present enough to even assess if you have collapsed into a younger self and are resonating from his or her energetic blueprint of tension and pain.

You can also throw in a round of this phrase, *"God's love resolves this pain here and now."*

Eyebrow: God's love resolves this pain here and now.

Side of the Eye: God's love resolves this pain here and now.

Under the Eye: God's love resolves this pain here and now.

Upper Lip: God's love resolves this pain here and now.

Under the Lip: God's love resolves this pain here and now.

Under the Arm: God's love resolves this pain here and now.

Rib: God's love resolves this pain here and now.

Head: God's love resolves this pain here and now.

Identifying A Full—Blown Collapse

If your feelings are in response to a situation or an interaction with another, then you have collapsed into the experience of an Inner Child, and you are seeing the situation through his or her eyes. This collapse may be fueled by the vibrational resonance from a fragment of your Soul, but for this Layer, you are just concerned with setting up a dyad from which you can establish a separation from the wounded one. You know you have collapsed because the distress is aimed at a person or a situation.

You know it is a full-blown collapse because the internal dialogue is specific and aimed at another or at berating yourself because of an unacceptable response to a situation. The reactions are in response to a tangible event.

In Layer Three you will do more work with putting a face to the wounds. But in Layer Two you just want to establish the separation and give form to the energy as you assess if it is merely an energetic addictive response or the feelings of a regressed state. You do not have to be concerned with which Inner Child this is, or whether this collapse is taking you back to a multidimensional self from another time and place. You are not putting a face to this energy. You are not yet "interacting" with this energy. You are just separating from it so you can begin to respond and experience the duality of the part of you who is triggered and the part of you who can respond.

You accomplish this with interactive tapping™ sequences in which you use the pronouns "he" or "she", or his and hers to externalize the pain. This creates the dyad needed to respond and heal.

However, as with every Layer, before you begin your work and *start dealing with a collapsed state, it is important to first clear* the Adult Self so you can step back into that illuminated balance. Just by going back to that moment you are stepping into a balanced state between your masculine and feminine selves. You would not have experienced that moment if this balance had not been in place. This balanced state IS AN EXPRESSION OF the Illuminated Adult Self, and it is this aspect of you that will most effectively establish this separation.

It is therefore essential that you get clear of any current, distracting emotions or thoughts so you can be present for the separation.

EXERCISE: *"GETTING PRESENT"* A RETURN TO THE 1ST LAYER—EMPOWERING THE ILLUMINATED ADULT SELF

Take a moment to go to your special place—that special moment when you were embodying your most illuminated, masterful self.

1. *Have the experience, enrich the experience with feelings and using each of your five senses, then absorb the experience by holding it for first the 17 seconds.*

2. While in this energy *reaffirm your intention to heal and talk about how great this feels to be present for 68 seconds.*

3. *Anchor it in by doing your Super Brain Yoga breaths 14 times.*

Once you have embodied that Illuminated Adult Self you want to bring that experience into the present moment by clearing any distractions from your present-day life. Once done you are ready to separate from the stress of the younger part of you that has gotten triggered. I use the setup phrases to establish the intention of separating from the distress so you can establish the dyad between the part of you who has gotten triggered and the part of you who wants to remain separate so you can respond. The "reminder phrases" identify the distraction and then set the stage for you to choose to "be here now." Since the statement, "This is now, not then," is so crucial to this separation, you need to get present in the "here and now" before you can begin to address the collapse.

EXERCISE: TAPPING INTO *"BEING HERE NOW"*

Begin by tapping on the karate point while stating the following:

Even though there may be some things I am not totally in harmony with today ... I choose, for this time, to suspend those feelings so I can be present enough to separate enough to focus entirely on the sequences for this work.

So even though I may need to neutralize some general irritations … I am going to do that before I engage in this work because I love myself and my triggered self enough to externalize his or her pain and help him or her heal.

So even though I may not be in total harmony right now I am willing to suspend any distractions I have at this time because I want to be clear and open enough to do this work.

Next, you will do the general neutralizing so you can "be here now." State the reminder phrases while you tap on the designated endpoints.

Neutralizing the Negative

Eyebrow: Generally disturbed … A little bit antsy … Want to clear out any anger, frustration, or fear.

Side of the Eye: Clear out all distraction.

Under the Eye: All frustration.

Upper Lip: Any fatigue, restlessness, boredom, panic, or fear.

Under the Lip: But choose to feel empowered to do this work.

Collarbone: Am excited to be present enough to do this layer of work.

Under the Arm: Have committed to showing up to do this work.

Rib: Excited to be present enough to externalize this pain.

Head: I ask my Higher Guidance to be of assistance so that I can move forward and separate from this stress and prepare the road to healing.

That completes the examples of sequences. This is just a suggestion of how you *would neutralize anything that is currently in your day-to-day life.* Continue to tap on each of the endpoints until you move through any resistance to being present and responsive to your efforts to separate from this pain and establish the dyad between that part of you that feels stressed and the part of you who can be separate enough to respond.

Now that you are present you are ready to move to the next exercise in which you begin to actually separate from him or her and "externalize" the feelings of tension and fear. When you externalize the disturbance you set up a dyad between the part of you who carries the wound that has been triggered and the part of us who can respond to that trigger.

Again, you will be using the pronouns "he" or "she" to begin the separation process. This is a crucial step in that it is this very separation that prepares the way for you to interact in Layer Three, and the interaction between the wounded one and the Healer within you is what creates the healing. Keep in mind you do not have to be concerned with "who inside" is feeling this. You are not putting a face to this part of you yet. You are simply acknowledging the dyad of the parts within you so you can facilitate the separation needed to interact and respond in Layer Three.

Exercise: Giving Form to Feelings of Triggered Self"

If you are certain your Adult Self is clear take a moment to get in touch with one of the uncomfortable feelings about the recent situation which resulted in this collapse. Know that this is the emergence of a wounded one who perceived danger in this recent situation and is holding onto tension and fear.

Once you tap through the separation in the first set of sequences you will be introducing the "possibility" that you can separate from this collapse enough to be able, in Layer Three, to respond instead of react. You want to realize that "this is now not then" and that you are not stuck back in time when you were at risk. You have acquired the skills to deal with the current situation in an adult manner, and you are able, ultimately, to help this wounded one feel safe.

State the setup phrase while tapping on the karate point.

*Even though I collapsed into a part of me that got triggered in response to this situation, I know this is only a part of me, that this is **now not then**. I am capable of handling this situation. It is safe to return to a state of calm.*

Even though a part of me really got triggered, and I collapsed into his or her pain, I now choose to separate from this reaction, to embody the essence of my Illuminated Adult Self and respond to this situation with calm.

*So even though a part of me really collapsed into his or her old fear, I am ready to respond to his or her needs because **this is now not then** and I know I have the adult skills to respond and be safe.*

That completes the setup phrases. Again, notice all we are doing in Layer Two is acknowledging that we collapsed and we are now choosing to separate enough to respond as the adult instead of reacting from the feelings of this wounded child within. If you feel ready then proceed with the reminder phrases. Continue to repeat the three sets of reminder phrases until you move through any resistance to your being willing to respond to this part of you, and you feel fully anchored in the illuminated part of you who is skilled and confident enough to respond. Remember you do not have to worry about "who got triggered." You do not have to put a face to the pain or "follow the threads to another life." You just want to get into the "here and now" and acknowledge the duality so you can set up the platform to respond and heal.

Neutralizing the Negative

Eyebrow: Really collapsed into his or her pain.

Side of the Eye: Fell right back into that old fear and rage.

Under the Eye: Felt so triggered, triggered and afraid.

Upper Lip: I really collapsed and fell right back into the fear of being unsafe.

Under the Lip: Feel like such a victim when I collapse.

Collarbone: Fill up with such anger, fear, and rage.

Under the Arm: He or she cannot imagine being protected, loved or safe.

Rib: So much fear when I collapse into his or her pain.

Head: Wonder if I will ever be able to get separate enough to trust I can respond instead of collapse.

Introducing the Possibility of Change

Eyebrow: But this really is "now not then."

Side of the Eye: Maybe I can help him or her to feel safe and secure.

Under the Eye: Maybe I can get separate enough and help restore his or her faith.

Upper Lip: Maybe I can help him or her feel safe enough to let go.

Under the Lip: Really want to help him or her let it go.

Collarbone: Maybe he or she can trust enough to let go.

Under the Arm: Maybe I can respond and make him or her feel safe.

Rib: I don't want this part of me to feel so much fear.

Head: I really want to help him or her. I want to separate enough so he or she can just let it go.

Affirming the Conviction

Eyebrow: I'm going to help, help him or her let go.

Side of the Eye: I am trustworthy. I can separate enough to respond.

Under the Eye: I do have the skills to help this part of me feel safe.

Upper Lip: I can feel compassion enough to help him or her let go.

Under the Lip: I really do have the skills to adequately deal with this situation so he or she does not have to feel fear.

Collarbone: Every cell in my body feels the compassion I need to stay separate enough to respond.

Under the Arm: This IS now not then.

Rib: Every cell, every fiber vibrates with the confidence I need. Every cell now invites him or her to trust.

Head: I can help him or her replace this fear with trust.

Continue to work with these sequences. Modify them according to what you need until you feel complete with this initial clearing and are prepared to proceed.

MULTIDIMENSIONAL BLEED-THROUGH

As I have mentioned, in the Separation Layer it is not important to even assess if this collapse is from another time or place. You are not yet ready to relate, interact, or heal this energetic collapse. Layer Two is just about identifying the difference between the undifferentiated, energetic addictive response and the collapse when you are clearly looking through the eyes of a younger self. It is about acknowledging your duality. It is about accepting that it is possible to feel two ways simultaneously and that you can have a part of how is scared and a part of you who has the skills to respond. LAYER TWO is about acknowledging the dual nature of our existence and establishing enough separation between these two parts of self so that you can externalize the pain in Layer Two and be prepared for Layer Three when you begin to interact. That's all it is.

Layer Three:
The Interactive Layer—
"Building A Relationship With
The Wounded One"

In LAYER THREE we use the pronoun "you" to begin the interactive process. Referring to our wounded one in the second person begins to build that trusting relationship between our most illuminate and nurturing self and the wounded Inner Child or Fragment of our Soul.

You are introduced to a form of "surrogate tapping." (Tapping on behalf of another) This creates an internal experience for the wounded aspect of you that finally someone is responding to his or her pain and operating on its behalf. This is true irrespective of the dimension of time or consciousness, be it Inner Child or an aspect of your Soul (It is all a form of time travel anyway.)

The result, however, is that this invites the experience of deservedness and nourishes a sense of importance—having the Inner Adult operate on its behalf makes this part feel worthy of attention and care. This is an important step in the process of building trust because often your younger selves have felt abandoned and left to fend for themselves. This is true for aspects of your Soul as well. They sustain a state of suspension, waiting to be discovered, rescued and healed.

LAYER THREE—The Interactive Layer

(Click here to be taken to the YouTube Overview)

OVERVIEW-Building The Relationship With Your Wounded One

In Layer One you identified your Illuminated Adult Self. You gave concrete form to him or her so you could continue its evolution. This is essential because the Illuminated Adult Self is the part within you who orchestrates your self-healing. It is this more illuminated part of you who can respond instead of collapse.

In Layer Two you saw the power of externalizing your pain. When you collapse into the pain you are fully submerged in that experience. If I say, "I am so angry," the "I" that is being referenced is the "I" that is in vibration of the anger. When you are in that vibration it is very difficult to move out of it. Traditional tapping can neutralize the reaction. The very fact that you are tapping and working with a discomfort, putting that discomfort in alignment with an affirmation you are already beginning to work with rewiring the brain and changing the paradigm by which you live. But it does not dissolve the trigger. Nor does it rewire the brain.

With Layer Three—*The Interactive Layer*—we take this a step further. Dr. Richard Hanson's formula for rewiring the brain stresses how important it is to anchor a new response into the long-term memory. This only occurs when we link the Inner Child's response to the challenging experience to the positive response of the illuminated, nurturing Adult.

But, as we explored in Layer Two, this cannot happen unless we have the skills to separate from the pain. We do this by referring to the wounded one in the third person and by referencing our pain as his or her pain. This enables us to externalize our pain. It helps us recognize that we are bigger than our pain.

In Layer Three, we build on that separation we created in the Layer Two. We begin to nurture a relationship with our wounded one. We do this by referring to this part of us in the second person.

Using the pronoun, "you," establishes that relationship. It sets up the dyad between the Illuminated Adult Self and the Inner Child so a dialogue can begin to take place. The focus of Layer Three is to learn how to create the nurturing dialogue that your Inner Child needs in order to begin to build trust. You learn how to extend your hand to your Inner Child and say, *Look, I am your Illuminated Adult Self, and I am here for you. I am the one you have been waiting for. I am going to keep you safe. It's ok. It's ok to have these feelings. It is ok to move beyond them. I love and accept you just the way you are.* This is now the role your Illuminated Adult Self plays in terms of your internal work.

One component of showing up for your Inner Child is learning how to tap on your Inner Child's behalf. This is called surrogate tapping. It builds trust between the two of you. Surrogate tapping is a gesture of goodwill. It establishes your intent to respond and heal.

In traditional EFT surrogate tapping is used as a way to tap on others that are not present or, for some reason, are not able to tap on themselves. There is a sender and a recipient. What interactive tapping™ invites you to do is to use surrogate tapping to address, respond, and give to that younger part of you.

I want to reiterate that Inner Child work is simply giving a face to the variety of feelings which originated in childhood. It is not separating out different personality states. It does not lead to a multiple personality disorder. You are not schizophrenic. It is simply *acknowledging* different feeling states. You may perceive your Inner Child as the same figure, or you may see different Inner Children at different ages. It is unique for each person, and there is no right or wrong way to envision him or her. It is simply giving a face to the aspects of you, those younger parts of you, who carry your shame, guilt, anger, and despair.

For example, you may recall situations when you were interacting with someone like a boss, or a loved one, and he or she said something that you experienced as shaming. When we experience shame we regress. We collapse. We feel deficient. We feel about three inches tall. That's the moment when you have collapsed into that younger state of self. In Layer Two you learned how to recognize you were there by remembering to "be here now." You learned the power of the setup phrase:

Even though he or she got triggered in response to this situation, this is now, not then. As the adult, I can choose to respond differently. I am not at risk. This is now, not then. I have acquired the skills to respond and to stay safe.

In Layer Three you begin to relate to that younger part of you who got triggered. You learn to ask the most essential question of Inner Child work is— *Who inside is feeling this ... who inside just collapsed and what do you need from me to feel safe?* Layer Three of this *Seven-Layer Healing Process* teaches you that even if you are vibrating at the frequency level of your regressed self, that just by forming those words ... *who inside is feeling this way, and what is it that you need from me ...* you establish the separation and create the necessary dyad that enables you to interact.

So how can you facilitate this interaction on behalf of your Inner Child? What are the most effective methods for developing this relationship which is such an integral part of your healing?

Methods To Interact

Journaling

The most common way to interact with your Inner Child is to do so through journal writing. You simply write down the question ... *Who inside is feeling this way, and what do you need from me?* Once you have written these words it is useful to switch to your least dominant hand to respond. Why? Because when you do so your rational mind has to focus on the mechanics of writing the letters. This allows the feelings of your younger self, which are often buried in the subconscious, to emerge without being censored by fear. When doing this try to write down as much as you can about the voice inside that is feeling this pain. The very fact that you are willing to do this gets the pain out your body. You are externalizing the discomfort. You are creating that dyad and once that dyad is established you can facilitate the internal interaction which allows you to respond and ultimately heal.

JOURNAL TAPPING

Reading the conversation you have just written while you tap on the endpoints supercharges the effectiveness of this exercise. You simply read it and systematically tap on each endpoint about five to seven times. You do not have to create a setup phrase. You just simply tap as you read what you have written.

MIRROR WORK

Another method to try is to simply stand in front of a mirror and experience the dialogue between these two parts of you. Now the trick to mirror work is that you want to just look eye-to-eye. When I first incorporated this method into my inner work I found I could only use a little hand mirror. I held it up close to my face, just so I could see my eyes. If it reflected my full face and/or body my critical eye would begin its assessment. It was too tempting to be self-critical. Therefore I recommend you ease into mirror work by simply looking eye-to-eye while you state—*Who inside feels this, and what to you need from me?*

If you continue to repeat these words while you look eye-to-eye then ultimately your more illuminated part of you will begin to respond. Even if you begin the exercise in the regressed state the repetition pulls out a response that comes from your more illuminated self—and sometimes even from the Soul self. These parts of self are differentiated simply by the vibrational frequency that you experience. Tapping while you are conversing in front of the mirror increases the effectiveness of this sequence ten-fold.

Our goal in this healing process is to progressively live from a higher and higher vibrational frequency. *Share the Gift,* and its *Seven-Layer of Healing Process,* offers you the methods to accomplish this task. You learn to establish fluid contact with that Spiritual Self—to see your life through the eyes of your Soul and feel more and more connected to All That Is.

It is important to remember that the Inner Child from whom you are separating operates at a denser frequency. The more challenging the emotion—the more intense the feeling—the denser the energy is. Likewise, the more positive you feel—the more expanded you feel—the more conscious you are. Being conscious of your surroundings, of your connection to all that is, enables you as the Adult to live at a higher frequency. Our opportunity, as well as obligation, is to take that higher frequency of vibration attained as our Illuminated Adult Self, and begin to respond to the denser parts of us, the more wounded parts of us, so we can relate to them and reinstate a sense of safety and peace.

Several years ago I created an audio recording during which I tap down a series of feelings that the Teachings of Abraham www.abraham-hicks.com refers to as the

ABRAHAM'S EMOTIONAL GUIDANCE SCALE

(http://www.abraham-hicks.com/lawofattractionsource/askitisgiven.php)

This recording brings you into relationship with your more vulnerable "feeling states." You begin by stepping into the vibration of what you have come to know as your most Illuminated Adult Self. Once there, I escort you down the scale by having you progressively acknowledge the denser emotional states while tapping and addressing each of these emotional states with the pronoun "you."

Ultimately you get down to the real gut-wrenching emotions of shame, grief, and deceit. At each emotional juncture, you relate to that feeling state by giving it a face and responding to his or her fear so together you can heal. This is a wonderful way to begin to acknowledge your multiplicity. I have included the audio link here for your convenience. You can also find it on my YouTube channel.

Tapping Down Abraham's Emotional Guidance Scale

As you progressively give a face or a form to those aspects of you through the interactive tapping™ sequences you are basically experiencing Layer Three in action. You are acknowledging the feelings of your wounded ones. You are giving them the form needed to establish the relationship that will enable you to do the actual healing in Layer Four. As you introduce yourself to each of the children within you are creating enough separation to be able to say—*I am the one you have been waiting for. I am acknowledging you. I am identifying you, and I am going to tap on your behalf so that you and I can begin to heal.*

To begin to surrogate tap for your Inner Child you need to first get a vision in your mind's eye of a present-day challenge during which you collapsed. Try it right now. Respond to the following questions and record them in your journal.

Exercise: Present-day Challenge

Take a deep breath and bring your focus back to that situation. Again, it may have been an interaction with a boss or a loved one. But retrieve a recent time when you really felt emotionally challenged.

1. Find, where in your body, you hold the tension. You may see, sense, or feel the energy of our younger self. Once you've established that dyad you begin your dialogue.

2. Bring your focus to that part of your body and pose your question: *Who inside feels scared, compromised, unprotected, and at risk? Who inside feels this? And what do you need from me?*

3. Take a deep breath again. Keep in mind that simply by posing those questions you are creating that separation you need to relate to the more wounded part of you.

4. Once you have established this relationship you tap on your endpoints and begin to dialogue with this younger part of you. The purpose of the dialogue is to build that connection and rapport so the Inner Child can begin to trust you. The

first task of this conversation is to introduce yourself to this younger part of you—i.e. *I am your Illuminated Adult Self.* (Notice that I continue to use the pronoun "you.") *I am the one you have been waiting for. I am here to help you heal. I am here to respond to your needs.*

"I AM THE ONE YOU HAVE BEEN WAITING FOR..."

It is essential to understand that this one statement, this exact response, is the key component to rewiring your brain and changing the experience of your wounded one. You create a new reality. That's what rewiring your brain means. You erase an old experience and create a new one. You, in essence, use your imagination to upload a new experience. Remember, your mind does not know the difference between what's real and what's imagined. So editing out old experiences and replacing them with new ones is definitely doable. You just have to trust that this can occur.

This exercise implements the last letter of Dr. Hanson's H.E.A.L. acronym because, in essence, with that response, you are "linking" your positive experience with a challenging collapse. You are giving your Inner Child a different point of reference. That is why the statement—*I am the one you have been waiting for*—is so powerful. You are saying to that Inner Child that you have acquired the skills his or her parents, or caretaker, did not have when he or she was at such a young age.

This is true even when you are dealing with the timeline of an aspect of your Soul. It doesn't matter which dimension of time you are working with because both, the Inner Child in this physical dimension (which is part of your personalities time continuum), or an aspect of your Soul (existing on the timeline of your Soul continuum) are suspended in time. In that suspended state he or she holds the energetic blueprint experienced in response to the original trauma. It became problematic because the response to the traumatizing event was never expressed and resolved. Your system went into shock and he or she never got to process the emotions and reset the central nervous system.

This is why I believe the Trauma Release Exercises are so beneficial. I first heard about the TRE modality that I covered in the Introduction during a conversation I had with Dr. Erik Robins. One interesting reference he made was about the response a gazelle has to a life and death threat in the jungle. If a gazelle survives the attack, unlike a human being, it does not suffer from post-traumatic stress. Instead, the gazelle instinctively goes into this spontaneous shaking. The animal literally resets its own central nervous system by discharging the energy of the trauma.

What happens in our childhood, or even what occurred with a fragmented aspect of our Soul, is that when we experienced a real or perceived threat we were unable to discharge the stress chemicals that were transmitted from the brain in an attempt to respond to the threat. We were unable to reset our central nervous system. Instead, our system went into shock. In order to live with that shock, in order to survive, we developed beliefs, accompanied by a feeling response, which ultimately became a pattern of behavior anchored in our muscular and cellular structure.

We got forever locked into that trauma and developed the energetic blueprint that supported the experience. This included developing certain beliefs about our safety. These beliefs were then laced with a set of emotions which ultimately dictates our behavioral responses to any situation which resonated with this original threat. This behavioral response becomes our way of coping with similar situations.

From then on, any situation in which we are involved that resonates with that original trauma cues that same response. And this is where our energetic blueprints emerge.

Again, this was substantiated by Candace Pert, www.candacepert.com/ the American neuroscientist and pharmacologist who discovered the opiate receptor sites in the brain. She spoke about our actually becoming addicted to certain emotional experiences. As was mentioned earlier, we develop these receptor sites that then become addicted to craving depression, rejection, betrayal—to the point where we actually begin to expect those emotional responses. We biochemically get addicted to craving the rush of depression, anger, anxiety, and even despair. Our body becomes familiar with that biochemical response. "Running that stress" becomes so familiar to us that we literally crave that biochemical stress-response and actually experience withdrawal when we are out of that experience. In Dr. Hanson's HEAL process we literally crave operating in the pink and even sometimes in the red zone. That becomes the new normal. We begin to crave the stress when we are calm and operating in the green zone. That is one of the reasons why we continue to repeat patterns.

As was mentioned before the most recent research has shown that if a young child, who has experienced the trauma of molestation— especially a one-time incident— is given the opportunity to speak about the abuse without shame or guilt, post-traumatic stress does not develop. When survivors were given the opportunity to talk about the event, they did not develop post-traumatic stress. If they were supported, believed, and assisted in discharging the emotional stress response then, in effect, their central nervous system was reset. There was no reason to hold on to experience or the response to the experience. No energetic blueprint was created.

In Layer Three we begin to complete this PTS process. We begin to rewire the brain and learn how to target the Inner Child who experienced the original trauma and developed the default coping mechanisms as a way to survive. In Layer Three we pull the thread from our adult patterns back to the activation point in childhood and then ultimately back to the wound of the Soul. It is at that suspended place in our Soul's history where the energetic blueprint first origi-nated. It is for this reason your Soul charted experiences that would resonate with that Soul wound. You come to accept that this is the purpose of your pain. That thread is what inspires you to evolve and grow … because, at some point, it becomes too painful not to evolve and heal.

Now how do you get back to the Soul pattern of this energetic blueprint once you have identified the Inner Child? You start by looking at what is not working in your current life. Because whatever is not working in your day-to-day life indicates where you are disconnected from your Illuminated Adult Self.

Again, there are three primary sources of challenge which explain this disconnection. Either: a) your childhood wounds haunt you, b) the adult blueprints remain ineffective, or c) your spiritual evolvement has not been adequately anchored into your day-to-day life and into your physical form.

If there are still wounds from your childhood which need to be addressed, they will haunt you until you address them. If however, you have done a significant amount of work on your Inner Child issues and still find your life is not working, then perhaps you have healed the childhood pain but have failed to redesign the belief systems dictating the patterns for failure and success in adulthood.

Your unique blueprint is based on the experiences you endured in childhood and the belief systems and accompanying behaviors which originated from these experiences. To redesign them you will need to identify the wound and determine the belief systems, as well as the connective, dysfunctional behaviors, which prohibit you from achieving the mastery you desire. It is also common, however, that the process of anchoring spiritual evolvement into daily pursuits, and into your physical form, has not occurred, and therefore, true mastery in adulthood cannot be attained.

The dysfunctional patterns we develop in childhood not only manifest as maladaptive blueprints in adulthood—they also hold the keys to the unlearned lessons our Soul has charted to complete in this lifetime. In other words, *the progressive developmental stages of childhood evolve into the progressive steps of adult mastery which open the door to the progressive lessons confronted in one's pursuit of spiritual empowerment.* A predictable, identifiable, and similar process is evident in the progression of each of these areas of development.

The process is circular. By pulling a thread from one area of development one can begin the process of healing the other two areas because the lessons of the Soul are revealed through the wounds incurred in childhood which manifest as ineffective blueprints in adulthood which impact mastery in our day-to-day pursuits which, when confronted, give us clues about the lessons of the Soul, It is circular. It is multi-faceted—and any block prohibiting this circular flow requires a healing which can be facilitated with interactive tapping™.

But before we move into the tapping sequences it is imperative to understand a bigger piece of this puzzle and that is that we all have one thing in common—we were all once children. And again, as children, we progressed through predictable stages of developmental tasks which required resolution. These tasks hold the keys to our Soul lessons and the themes of resolution which we unconsciously or consciously pursue.

The following is an overview of each of those developmental stages. They are followed by a look at how these childhood tasks, if not mastered in each developmental stage, may have not only manifested in your adult life as dysfunctional blueprints but may also provide valuable clues into the origin of the tasks of your Soul. If this is part of your belief system then it is relevant to understand that the emotional vibrational response to current life events resonates with the same vibration of situations which occurred in another lifetime and in another dimension of time.

An aspect of this metaphysical belief system suggests that prior to each incarnation our Soul meets with a team of advisors and determines what experiences are to be offered to the personality who will house the spirit of our Soul. Because of free will, it is unknown as to whether the personality will achieve or even aspire to master the lessons' the Soul has charted. The "flight plan" is nonetheless designed and the opportunities for growth mapped out. Soul agreements are made and the seeds for life events are planted. These seeds usually sprout in the first three stages of development; are revisited in the three stages of adolescence; come into full bloom in adulthood, and are evident in the behaviors and patterns we exhibit in our day-to-day life. Again, what the personality chooses is determined by free will. We can repeat the pattern of victimization, or rise to the occasion, see the situation through the eyes of the Soul, and respond accordingly.

The following overview will offer you a broad glimpse of the circularity of issues we have been discussing. You will be able to see how the issues of childhood are reflected in the patterns exhibited in adulthood and how these patterns may reveal the vibrational context of the lessons of the Soul. This metaphysical extension does not necessarily interest everyone who is reading this book. If you are not interested then use your discretion to ignore the Soul references. You have the absolute right to pick and choose what fits and to discard what does not.

From The Seven Developmental Stages To The Seven Adult Patterns To The Seven Lessons Of The Soul

Please Note: Where appropriate I have included YouTube or mp3 links that will enrich your understanding of the material being presented. Most of my recordings were taped as part of other on-going programs and include a tapping sequence to assist in working with the concept being discussed. I suggest you gauge your own interest with respect to these files. They may carry more significance the second or third time you work these exercises.

From Abandonment to Union

Developmental Tasks in Infancy (Birth to Eighteen Months)

The first developmental stage in childhood is infancy. This stage begins at birth and lasts until approximately eighteen months of age. The task in infancy is to develop a sense of trust and safety in relation to our environment. This is accomplished through the relationship we have with our mother, our primary caretaker. From her, we learn, body to body, what it means to be safe. If she transmits acceptance, calmness, and security, we internalize that experience to the depth of our physical being and trust that it is safe to exist and take form. When we experience this sense of safety and trust we are free to experience mastery in every area of our life. However, if she is tentative about her mothering skills, ambivalent about motherhood, distracted from her tasks because of an external life crisis which demands her attention, we internalize unrest, feel unsafe and relate to our environment in a tentative and ambivalent manner.

As infants, we cannot assess when our mother's reactions are in response to us and when they are in response to external circumstances. We self-reference every event and organically assume responsibility for all reactions to us. These reactions become the blueprint which ultimately dictates the degree of safety we feel in trusting and in attaching. As infants, if we do not trust, we cannot bond. If we cannot bond, we cannot successfully attach. This inability results in a longing. We long for that attachment.

A sense of safety is built on healthy ego development which involves being able to adequately attach. Once we attach we then have something from which to detach. It is this attachment/detachment process that the personality uses to establish an identifiable form. The mirrored reactions and interactions we experience with our primary caretaker in these early months enable us to begin to develop our unique identity. This exchange enables us to claim our right to exist and thus take form. We first experience mastering this task in relation to our family, but it is once again revisited between the ages of seventeen and twenty-one when we confront this task with respect to fitting into the world.

How Patterns May Have Been Carried Into Adulthood

If, as a child, we had difficulty taking form, we will not have the internal point of reference needed in adulthood to give form to anything in our day-to-day lives. The adult challenge which relates to this developmental stage is to give form to ideas, goals, to a self-image, body image, financial plan, and exercise plan or to anything in our lives we want to create.

Every endeavor we pursue requires a beginning, a seed, a birth. Every inspiration which leads to action begins with the birth of an idea which is then nurtured and given substance and form. If the original blueprint for conception and formation is faulty, the process of giving birth to that which we want to manifest will be faulty. Just as an infant has to endure and survive the birthing process before it can obtain the feedback which allows it to take form, the universal challenge of the first step to adult mastery is to have our ideas and goals survive their own birth so they can develop and thus take a tangible form.

Once the idea has taken form or the goal has been established, the second component of this first step to mastery is to successfully bond with the external object of choice. This requires developing trust and faith in the idea or goal sufficiently enough to "bond" with it. This bonding may occur with a parental projection, such as a corporation, a church or spiritual source, a significant other or any external structure. We may simply "bond" with the creation of a new idea or to the commitment to a new pursuit such as financial security or physical exercise. It is this experience which gives us the foundation to conceive of a new idea or to give birth to a new goal and then to nurture this idea or goal until it develops a substantial and tangible identity of its own.

Potential Lesson of the Soul (YouTube Overview/Tapping Sequence)

A potential Soul lesson which can extend from this developmental stage and this step of mastery is the theme of needing to attain and maintain trust in a spiritual source, a power greater than that which your personality knows. The challenge may be to mentally attain and hold a belief system which incorporates unity with a divine power and to then be able to anchor that spiritual energy into your day-to-day activities and endeavor.

Difficulties in any of the above areas may indicate you would benefit from exploring the origin of such difficulties. Perhaps in a past life, you were abandoned by your spiritual group and therefore came to believe that God had deserted you. Now in your present day life, it is difficult to trust and put your faith in any power greater than self. It is hard to believe and have faith.

How do you relate to what you have just read? Review the times in your adult life when you have been confronted with starting something new. How did you commit? Do you have a difficult time bonding with a new idea or pursuit?

If you believe your Soul charted the course of your life, if you believe your Soul chose the parents you needed to have in order to learn this Soul lesson, begin to reflect on what your Soul could possibly learn from the experiences you encounter when beginning something new or being in a position to have to commit to a new endeavor. How might this experience reflect the unresolved issues of your Soul which originated when you first separated from the Universal Source? Record any findings in your journal.

From Betrayal to Trust

Developmental Tasks in Toddler Stage (Eighteen Months–Three Years)

This stage of development is when you first began to experiment with being separate from your caretaker and experienced a taste of the independence which resulted from that separation. Remember you cannot separate if you never attached. This step of mastery builds on the first step. Your separation and independence enable you to step back and discern what works and what does not work. As a toddler, you begin to trust yourself enough to make adjustments in your behavior and to experiment with who you are. For the toddler, mastering the art of discernment is based upon feeling secure enough to experiment with what does and does not feel good and then developing the ability to distinguish between the two—to instinctively notice the contrast of feelings between the two.

The toddler years were the first time in your development you were mobile enough to walk away from your caretaker and verbal enough to refuse and protest. This was when you began the transition from dependency to autonomy. It is a process which continues throughout your life, but learning how to establish and maintain personal boundaries is essential if you are to successfully establish a sense of self. Boundaries are emotional and physical separations from your caretaker. Boundaries are the manner in which you establish your independence. They enable you to experience control over yourself and your environment.

Learning to say "no" gave you this sense of control. Hearing "No" was also important. Having a caretaker who gave you clear boundaries helped you feel safe. It gave you clear limits and an idea of what was expected of you. It also gave you a way to experience your separateness. It gave you the opportunity to begin to experience the tension of your separateness.

You were, for the first time, exposed to the life-long conflict of choosing between self versus others. "Do I respond to the needs of others or meet the needs of self?" You vacillated between compliance and defiance as you refined the definition of self. Working with this struggle set the stage for you to learn how to distinguish between what you felt and what others felt… how to distinguish between what felt good to you and what did not feel good to you. It taught you how to discern contrast. What we do not master in this stage of development is carried into the adolescent stage of the fifteen-to-seventeen-year-old when we are learning how to define ourselves with respect to our peers and to the world.

How Patterns May Have Been Carried Into Adulthood

To successfully mature into emotionally healthy adults we needed to have experienced in childhood that it was acceptable to say "no" without being punished and encouraged to hear "no" when it was for our safety and protection. Few of us received this encouragement because it required our caretaker to allow us the luxury of experimenting with testing their limits and setting our boundaries. The healthiest way a caretaker can do this is by providing a set of choices which empowers the toddler to choose between two acceptable options. This empowers the toddler and yet allows the parent to still be in charge of the parameters of choice. Most often our caretakers were ambivalent about letting go and therefore gave us mixed messages about our acting independently.

They may have responded with a rigid structure or with no structure at all. If they responded rigidly we would have never been able to develop the internal structure needed to establish our own separateness. Instead, they would have overpowered us, forcing us into submission through ridicule and/or abuse. If they provided no structure then we would have experienced difficulty in discerning where they ended and we began because we would have no clear point of reference for the division between us. If as toddlers we were given too much control over our lives we would have begun to melt into boundaryless oblivion. We would have experienced tension in response to feeling unprotected and unsafe. Either approach from our caretakers would have left its mark.

In adulthood, this impairs our ability to experiment with and to explore limitations between ourselves and external structures. It makes it difficult to assess where we end and the outside world begins… to determine where we end and our loved ones begin. It makes it challenging to have a clear idea of the expectations of our responsibilities at work. We may be ill-equipped to say No in our day-to-day world, to set limits for ourselves with our bosses, loved ones, and friends. Likewise, we may find ourselves confused about how to deal with others saying "No"…with how to deal with limitations being set for us due to circumstances or situations.

In order to be prepared for the third stage of development which teaches us how to make adjustments and modify and revise any life goals we have established, we will need to learn how to assess what is working and what is not. We do this by experiencing the "contrast" between how we feel when the energy in our lives flows and how we feel when it seems blocked. Carrying this ability to experience contrast into adulthood enables us to begin to consciously assess what we want and do not want. It puts us in a position to consciously set intentions regarding what we want. Through prayers and affirmations, we begin to focus on creating and attracting that which we have discerned we want.

This practice is called "deliberate creation." It involves identifying what we want; envisioning those wants and, through prayers and affirmations, mastering the ability to command universal law of attraction to manifest and attract what we want. The vibration you attain through mastery of this ability is the vibration of joy—because the frequency of energy required to intend in this manner is a joy! Joy is an expression of trusting ourselves enough to be able to set boundaries and limitations.

Potential Lesson of the Soul (YouTube Overview/Tapping Sequence)

A potential lesson which extends from this developmental stage and this step of mastery is the need to experiment with and explore limitations experienced between your earthly and spiritual bodies or your personality and your Soul, You might find yourself pondering the limits your physical form has created for your spiritual being-ness. You may begin to have past life memories of being wounded when you set limits or times when you suffered, were killed, maimed or harmed for speaking your truth. It will also become apparent as to how well you deal with the ambivalence of being in the density of your physical form versus the freedom felt in the spiritual world.

The unresolved issues of your Soul and the themes your Soul charted to focus on during this lifetime may have originated from a time when you first separated from the Universal Source and had to deal with the limitations of body and the temptations of the earthly plane. Most often the experience of boundaries and limitations which emerge in adulthood carry the same vibration of how we responded to boundaries we experienced in other times and other places. These Soul experiences may even carry life and death themes. There may be times in the history of your Soul when you were abandoned or killed for saying "No" or for claiming an independent position in response to a structure or person of authority. If this pattern resonates with you it would be worth exploring through the Ten-Step Formula provided for you at the end of this section.

FROM SHAME AND GUILT TO UNCONDITIONAL REGARD

Developmental Tasks from Ages Three-to-Six

This next developmental stage involves assessing the positive and negative aspects of your pursuits and beginning to make the appropriate adjustments. You have gathered information regarding the behaviors sabotaging your efforts. In the toddler stage, these behaviors were the result of the encroachment or abandonment experienced in response to your new found independence. The behaviors exhibited are the result of those within you who have translated their fears experienced as a toddler into the character traits exhibited as a three to six-year-old.

By the age of three, we begin to assume any problems in our family are with us and we begin to experience shame and guilt. We are introduced to feeling self-conscious in our body and uncomfortable with our natural sense of curiosity. These issues relate back to this stage of development which because it is this time in your life when you first encounter the tasks of dealing with these aspects of your character. How you feel about yourself and your body and how you deal with and respect the positive and negative qualities in yourself and others are related to how you experienced these issues when you were between the ages of three and six.

In this stage of development, you begin to work with the positive and negatives of who you are. When you were good (acting like the adults in your life expected and wanted you to act) you were rewarded. When you were bad (acting in ways that were unacceptable to these adults) you were punished. The rewards may have been in the form of praise or you may have been given special food, toys or outings. Punishment may have been emotional: you may have been humiliated or teased, or your parents may have ignored you. Perhaps you were punished physically–spanked or slapped or sent to your room. Fearing punishments and desiring rewards you quickly learned what was acceptable and what was not.

Your developmental task during this stage is to learn how to negotiate between the good and bad, right and wrong and positive and negative aspects of self. You have developed enough cognitive ability to determine what is acceptable and what is not acceptable and can, therefore, calculate which behaviors bring rewards and which behaviors result in punishment. You begin to make choices accordingly. You also begin to compromise who you are as a way to avoid risking rejection or judgment. This stage of development is the origin of shame and guilt.

By the age of three, you are figuring out how to relate to other people. You know what to do to get what you need. Unfortunately, if you were raised in a dysfunctional home your needs were probably ignored or even ridiculed. You may have been the object of anger because you even *had* needs. The words you heard others use to describe you become the words you use to describe yourself. If you were told you were bad you would begin to believe you are bad. If you were told you were stupid, you would begin to believe you are stupid. If you were teased or told to shut up anytime you were curious and asked a question you would learn it was not safe or wise to inquire about anything. If you were shamed, humiliated or teased about your body, if you were violated or the physical boundaries were not honored you would grow up to believe you had little right to physical or emotional privacy and that your body was bad or perhaps even evil. These beliefs would have become the foundation for who you became as an adult. They are again revisited during the adolescent stage of your twelve-to-fifteen-year-old when you begin to wrestle with self-consciousness versus self-confidence and struggle with getting comfortable with discomfort.

How Patterns May Have Been Carried Into Adulthood

This stage of development sets the arena in adulthood for our ability to negotiate with the positive and negatives of any life situation and to know how to make the necessary adjustments. In adulthood, in order to successfully discern strengths and challenges, we have to have developed a healthy relationship with our humanness. This means developing the ability to relate to ourselves with compassion. We have to be able to assess our positive and negative qualities and blend the good with the challenging to create our unique self. This sense of self empowers us to negotiate our differences with others and to reach an acceptable compromise without feeling overpowering or disempowered.

To be successful in our adult activities we need to have developed the ability to assess our internal value system as it compares to an external one. For example, in your career or job, you may have bonded significantly enough with a position or the ideas of a company to where you can determine what aspects of the company resonate with who you are and where you need to make adjustments to fit in. You can determine if these adjustments can be made without losing your integrity.

The same can be said in our relationships with others. This blending, which requires compromise, is built on a clear under-standing and acceptance of the person we are—identifying where we can bend and where we need to stay true to ourselves so we do not violate our own value system. This negotiation and adjustment phase involves sorting out what is going to work for us and what is going to have to be challenged. We begin to speak our truth and attempt to work things out in a negotiating manner. It is in this adjustment phase when we juggle our values with the other person's values or the organization or the corporate value system and try to mediate agreement or at least peaceful coexistence. This is the "process" stage. The first and second stages involved bonding and connecting, then butting up against limits and boundaries. This step involves the process of working with those limitations and finding acceptable resolutions.

This developmental stage represents all of the basic tasks we need to master so we can be balanced on the physical plane. It allows us the opportunity to experiment with staying anchored in our body as we encounter such issues as judgment and projection; shame, blame and guilt and comfort or discomfort with our bodies. This is the key developmental stage when we anchor into our bodies and consciously experience all of the density of the physical plane. Because of this, special topics need to be covered and addressed with respect to this stage of development because the impact these issues have on our adult life is paramount to our developing the ability to succeed in our pursuit of mastery.

Our Initial Dilemma—The Socialization Process

When we take a physical form we are subjected to a socialization process which serves to shift us from trusting our God-Self to trusting those in charge of us on the physical…i.e., parents. We are taught to externally reference, that it is not safe to trust ourselves or our God-self.

We learn very quickly who we are and what we do is not always acceptable. So we lose trust in ourselves to discern right from wrong. Instead of being given the guidance to experience life and learn its lessons based on our inner truths we are taught to discount our inner knowingness and to trust, instead, the adults who can use guilt and shame, withdrawal and fear to socialize us so we can fit into a world of others who do the same. It results in a community full of people who are attempting to get their needs meet in a horizontal manner by looking to each other—instead of looking up to their God-Self and the Divine for their vertical connection which can then illuminate their connections to others.

Parents believe they have to imprint their child with a sense of right and wrong. I believe the God-self already carries that programming for each of us and that as parents we can ally with that God-self and help the child learn to believe in and trust his or her basic goodness. Between the ages of 3-6, a child begins to separate from his or her God-self and develop the ego-self—but if as children we are given the message that we are basically good and we can trust ourselves the ego is illuminated with the essence of our God-self instead of severed from it. In the process of our healing our childhood, we have the opportunity to give this to our children within.

Our Body and Our Need to Respect It as Sacred

One of the issues most of us need to heal is our relationship with our bodies. We have spent many years, and perhaps lifetimes, de-valuing our bodies and its needs believing the physical form is too dense and of such a low vibration that we need to tend to our spiritual path instead of our bodily needs. I have found that since I am in body and must do my spiritual work from this plane that it is absolutely essential for me to hold sacred this physical form which enables me to do this work.

In exploring this for myself I realized that the "I" who I identify as my human and physical self had a right to be in an equal relationship with my connection to the God-Source or my higher or God-Self. This thought inspired me to begin to explore how I became disconnected from respecting my body in the first place. I realized that as children we are taught to be shy about our bodies, that our curiosity about our bodies is not acceptable and that, at best, the body is an object to be taken care of but not to be taken too seriously. However, since every mineral and cell found in our bodies is also found in the makeup of Mother Earth, wouldn't it be wonderful if, as children, we were taught to respect our bodies as a gift from Mother Earth. To learn that she has given of herself to give us a physical form that can house the gift of spirit we have received from God.

If in childhood we could learn to respect the land and the trees as our relatives—the rocks and the rivers as the libraries of the earth; if we could be taught to listen to the land; to say hello to Grandfather Sun and to bid Grandmother Moon good-night; if as a child we were taught that it is from Mother Earth and her animal and mineral creatures from which our food comes. If we were taught that we, too, come of the earth and if we can just wake up in the mornings saying hello to ourselves when we brush their teeth and thanking our feet when we put on our shoes; paying proper respect to our bellies when it digests our food, we would be so much more connected to ourselves, to the earth and to the God-source around us. Being taught to relate to one's body in this way would allow us as children to stay connected to our physical form, to accept our curious nature, to respect and to expect to be respected for our physical boundaries and needs. Relating to our children within in this manner can at least begin to facilitate your own connection to your physical form and could undo some of this disconnection which took place in our own life. It can restore our trust in our body to tell us what it needs so we can make the appropriate choices.

One of the ways I have tried to re-instate my connection to Mother Earth and my physical form is that at meal time I not only thank God for the meal but also thank the food, the farmers, the grocery store clerks, every person or element that has been involved in getting this food from its source to our table. It re-educates my Inner Child in the sequence of this nourishment and sets the stage for her to not be so disconnected from her origin. This serves as a metaphor for my Inner Child and facilitates a reconnection to appreciate the gifts of Mother Earth as well as from the God-Source.

Judgments and Projections

Children observe—they do not judge. They are taught to judge by the adults around them when good and bad is applied to their responses to their world. Children, at a very early age, speak the truth and often their parents become mortified... parents get embarrassed because they look at their child as an extension of themselves and fear being judged. Children do not know how to use tact—but they do speak the truth without judgment—I believe it is a parent's reaction which then becomes internalized and places a value of right and wrong on any person, place or thing.

For instance, when a child sees a person in a wheelchair— the child comments or stares and can speak the truth of how this is different. The parent often silences the child... the child gets the impression that there is something wrong with being in a wheelchair and a prejudice is set up. A separation between another human being and the child is implanted and the foundation for the superior/inferior value system is imprinted. There are many examples, but the fact remains that whatever we did experience in childhood gets internalized as our values and is carried into our adult lives where they are projected onto others in a manner in which we feel entitled to judge another as good or bad, right or wrong.

I believe there is a difference between having an observation about someone and having an observation laced with an emotional charge, which is really a judgment. This judgment then gets projected onto others. Rather than focusing on changing someone else, we can, when emotionally charged, look at what that projection carries for us and use that information to further illuminate our own path.

Dealing with Shame

Shame is when we feel we are not good enough. The first time in our lives we have the cognitive ability to associate the feeling of not being good enough with the way we behave and the manner in which the adults in our lives react to that behavior is between the ages of three to six. When the adults in our lives do not like what we do, they attempt to control our behavior by humiliating us, neglecting us, abandoning us or sometimes even abusing us. Shame can also result from being sexually abused. Our perpetrators can hold us responsible for the sexually inappropriate behavior; we, therefore, begin to feel as though the abuse was our fault. We did something to deserve it.

Shame can even occur if our parents or caretaker make us "too" important in their lives. If we were overindulged we can sense our parent(s) are living vicariously through us and it results in a tension that we may let them down. If we sense the parental expectation that we should always be the best at everything we do we can become burdened and fearful with that responsibility. We can develop the fear that we will be left, humiliated or even violated if we fail to live up to that parental expectation.

Either source results in our coming to believe that the problem is with us. We develop this belief because it would be too painful, in fact almost impossible, at such a young age, to admit the adults in our lives are incompetent. We cannot afford to feel that powerless and unprotected. So, instead, we take it on as our deficiency. *If only we were better, we say to ourselves, we would be loved and protected.* Or we tell ourselves, *I'd better be perfect so I don't let "them" down.*

This inner belief becomes the foundation of our need to be perfect. Our pursuit of perfection gives us a focus for the tension created by the fear we may fail. It gives us the illusion we have some control over a situation which is beyond our control. This creates a dynamic which I call "functional shame" because it allows us to survive in childhood but ultimately prevents us from becoming self-fulfilled adults.

In order to become fulfilled and healthy adults, we have to give up the *false belief* we are not good enough and challenge our *pursuit of perfection.* This requires we give up the antiquated hope our parents will become who we need them to be. As a child, and as an adult, giving up this hope is more than we can bear. So we remain loyal. We unconsciously hold onto the hope that if we can just be good enough—perfect enough— "they" will come through for us and be able and willing to love us and make us feel safe.

In adulthood, the THEY expands beyond our parents and gets projected into our intimate relationships, our relationships with co-workers and onto any person who is a candidate to protect, love or value us. We overdo in hopes of winning their love. Over and over we become involved in relationships in which we feel we must overdo to warrant being loved. Each of these dysfunctional relationships ultimately gives us the opportunity to heal our shame.

To look at this dynamic through the eyes of the Soul we would be taken into times in our Soul's history when we felt too unworthy or imperfect to hold the Light of our Source. Spiritual shame resulted when, in response to our "free choice," we were unable to hold the light, and instead, made choices that resulted in our turning away from Source.

In order to change this pattern in all dimensions of time and consciousness, we must heal our shame on all levels. We begin by going back to a recent/current experience when we felt shame. We trace this thread back to the first remembered time we felt that same sensation in our childhood. We re-parent our Inner Child and help her accept that it was not her fault. We help her begin to believe she is enough just way she is. We then follow that thread back to the origin of our shame in a past life because we are in a position to heal the shame of our Soul,

Our Co-dependent Bargain™

We cannot heal our shame until we identify and work with the bargain we made in response to our shame. I called this bargain the co-dependent bargain™— it is made in this lifetime with the parent we identify as the one who could love and protect us—but didn't. Again, we assume they didn't because of our deficiency—so we enter into an unconscious agreement to "earn" their love in hopes that we will finally be made to feel safe.

When our co-dependent bargain™ doesn't work we feel tension. This tension is uncomfortable and must be discharged. We discharge it by engaging in compulsive and addictive behaviors. Whatever we do in excess—its intent is most likely in response to this unconscious, and yet ineffective, unmet bargain.

Because this bargain is unconscious, we engage in this dynamic over and over. Our perpetual belief that if we can just figure out what needs to be changed or fixed then things will be the way we need them to be and we will feel safe, loved and protected.

It never works. No matter how much we try to be perfect—no matter how much we try to fix things so they will be better—we always fail because unfortunately, the source of the dysfunction is the system, not us. So we can never be "good enough" to impact or change what is wrong so things can get better. We get caught in the vicious cycle of attempting to be perfect—failing—then acting out compulsively or addictively to discharge the energy of that failure. This cycle keeps us active in our compulsions and addictions as well as disconnected from our authentic self and Source. This cycle is the source of our saboteurs—of those behaviors that derail us and keep us from coming fully into the commitments and intentions of our pursuit of mastery.

OUR GOAL IS TO REALIZE IT ISN'T OUR FAULT AND OUR SAFETY MUST BE FOUND VERTICALLY NOT HORIZONTALLY!

However, in order to look vertically instead of horizontally, we need to first identify our own addictive and compulsive behaviors and this includes confronting our own co-dependency. It means exploring our own unique co-dependent bargain™ and the degree to which we focus on others instead of ourselves. It means we need to determine the degree of tension which surrounds our co-dependent behavior and honestly address the degree to which we use our compulsions and addictions to mitigate that tension.

Potential Lesson of the Soul
(YouTube Overview/Tapping Sequence)

A potential lesson which extends from this developmental stage and this step of mastery is learning to express compassion for self and others, learning to be non-judgmental of self and others, confronting and dissolving multidimensional shame and guilt and finding the threads of shame in your Soul 's history when you may have turned away from your Source.

It is this source of Soul issues which can escort us to the trials and tribulations of being a physical being in a spiritual world. I have never worked with an individual who did not have at least one central life theme which originated at this stage of development and which was in need of resolution.

FROM REJECTION TO ACCEPTANCE
Developmental Tasks from Ages Six-to-Twelve

As you enter into the realm of issues from your grade school self you will be invited to explore how these concerns and strengths interface with your peers, co-workers, friends, acquaintances, and family. You will be visiting potential issues involving feeling left out – your discomfort and pride regarding your inclusion or exclusion in the "in-crowd." Competition with others will also emerge for examination. You may find you compare yourself ruthlessly to others and feeling either superior or inferior. Although either experience can breed stress, bringing awareness to these feelings will give you the opportunity to confront how you deal with feeling "better than" or "lesser than" someone else. This whole teeter-totter of comparison with others can become a source of tension no matter which side you slide into. Much to your surprise, you may find that feeling superior to others brings about just as much fear as feeling inferior.

How well you fit into your social groups, the degree of comfort you feel with your co-workers and close friends, the degree of success you experience when you have to perform or compete and the success you experience in a career or when you start and complete projects are all related to how well you mastered these tasks when you were between the ages of six and twelve. These years are called the middle years because they span the time between the rapid physical growth of your first six years and the marked changes that arise with puberty. your attention was more on mastering tasks of a social rather than psychological nature. Your focus moved from being internally referenced to being externally referenced.

Exclusion versus Inclusion

This was perhaps the first time you moved from the safety (or lack thereof) experienced in your family and entered the outside world. You began to focus on issues involving your relationship with peers. *Do I fit in? Am I the same as others or different? Am I accepted by my peers?* Whatever experience you had at this time your life has followed you into adulthood and is reflected in how well you feel you belong or how much you fear being excluded.

Mastery or Fear of Public Speaking

Another area of exploration which emerges is the degree of comfort you experience when you speak in public. Since this was the time in your life when you were first expected to get up in front of your class and give reports and presentations your comfort or discomfort will be related back to these childhood experiences. If you are able to do this with ease then you developed the confidence necessary to feel comfortable with such self-disclosure. This confidence is also evident whenever you are expected to give presentations in your work and other environments. Since, other than death, public speaking is the number one fear, few moved through this task with ease.

Task Completion (Beginning and Completing Projects)

Completing tasks and learning the discipline needed to begin and finish projects is also related to what you experienced during this time in your life. Starting and completing tasks is a skill which needs to be learned—it is not innate and you are not "lazy" if you did not master it. Many factors influence your success at mastering this ability. It depends upon how much assistance you received from your caretakers in following through with your homework. It can be influenced by how secure you felt in your peer groups. It can also be affected by how much emotional energy you had to devote to this lesson. If you were distracted from this focus by family dysfunction– if your energy was directed towards worrying about what was going on at home–whether your mother was drinking or your father had found a job—then you would not have had the emotional energy to focus on such task developments and your mastery would have been stifled.

You may have grown up having great challenges in completing projects and now interpret this trait as evidence of your being lazy or unmotivated. In truth, many adults are unable to begin and complete projects because they simply were never taught how to put one foot ahead of the other as a way to take the steps necessary to succeed. Those who are able to complete tasks with ease were often forced to focus on this area of their life as a way to survive. They had been the parentified child who was selected as the member of the family who had to hold the order.

Even though this accomplishment can be a strength in adulthood, it can carry underpinnings of grief and sadness because of its origin.

Loyalty to Your Dysfunctional Family System

Perhaps, however, the most profound pattern which originates from this developmental stage is the pattern of sabotage related to being loyal to your dysfunctional parenting unit. Seldom have I worked with an adult on their Inner Child issues without us having to confront this grade school self who has developed a loyalty to one or both parents. This dynamic emerges as sabotaging any efforts which would result in that person's surpassing their parents and succeeding in areas where their parents were unable to succeed. The purpose for this is embedded in the fact that, as children, we need to think of our parents as "all-knowing." It is the only way we can survive. We hold onto the unconscious belief exhibited in the plea of our co-dependent bargain™ that if only we can "do what is needed" then our parents will be able to become the parents we need them to be in order to survive. As we grow into adulthood we take this unconscious belief into our day-to-day lives.

We remain loyal to the contract and sabotage any efforts which would result in our succeeding in areas our parents have been unable to experience success. Why? Because it is too frightening for this part of self to excel and surpass his or her parents—this brings on too much grief and fear of being alone. We would then be expected to be the experts of our own lives and that fear alone can catapult us into despair, a sense of isolation and fear of failure. So we focus on our weight or our finances or our dysfunctional relationships—any dysfunction which allows us to feel less than our parents.

How Patterns May Have Been Carried Into Adulthood

So how does all of this material filter into your adult life? The pattern exhibited in adulthood which relates to this stage of development is found in your need to be recognized by your peers and acknowledged for your accomplishments. Your agenda is to find outside activities and interests. You begin to search for a support system which matches your inner value system. You begin to gravitate towards a group which mirrors your specific styles and with whom you feel you "fit." You may also find you begin to develop hobbies or a line of work which gives you the feeling of being good at something. Your psyche can and is drawn to success in at least some areas of your life—as long as that one sacred area remains untouched you can succeed without risk of being disloyal to the parent with whom you still long for connection.

This stage of development and adult pattern reflect the transition made from being a novice to being seasoned. You will see this represented in your present level of achievement in your career or in the manner in which you relate to loved ones and family members. You may see evidence of these threads emerging in the way you attract prosperity; create your life's passion; relate to your sexuality, your body in general and your sense of self and adult belief systems about success. This transition prepares you for entry into your refinement phase of adolescence when true mastery can occur.

Potential Lesson of the Soul
(YouTube Overview/Tapping Sequence)

This time in your life and the issues which emerge in this stage of the pursuit of your mastery give you the opportunity to look at the moments in your Soul 's history when you perhaps joined a group which led you away from your Source or perhaps a time when you put your loyalty into a false source.

You may be inspired to examine your success at establishing a co-creatorship between our Higher Self and our Human Self from a more reciprocal perspective as you recognize and show appreciation for all you have had to endure in human form. This time in your life and in your journey towards mastery offers you the opportunity to come to terms with the tasks your Soul may have charted for you in this human form and the degree to which you have actualized them.

FROM SELF-CONSCIOUSNESS TO SELF-CONFIDENCE
Developmental Tasks from Ages Twelve-to-Fifteen

Stepping into puberty, and into the twelve-to-fifteen-year-old stage of development, marks the beginning of your transition into adulthood. Most of us made this shift physically much more quickly than we did mentally or socially. We spent most of our adolescent years trying to settle into who we were becoming. All of the tasks mastered up to that point in our development paved the way for this transition. The bonding and trust we learned as infants provided the security we needed as we risked relating to the opposite sex. The ability to set limits and to say No provided us with the foundation needed to establish and discern boundaries. The confrontation of good and bad within prepared us for the comparisons which so ruthlessly emerged in the early teen years. The social and education skills mastered in grade school set the tone for the academic and social adventures which greeted us as budding young adults.

Each of these agendas has been mirrored in the successes and challenges you have encountered in showing up for your exploration. You have laid the foundation for your plan, worked with the dichotomous feelings and confronted the co-dependent bargain™. You have looked at the sources of shame and guilt, your false loyalties, your need to please and your fear of being left. All of the above has paved the way for you to now step into the emerging you with a sense of ownership which is often associated with a fear of exposure. Why? Because whatever you were able or unable to master before you turned twelve became major building or stumbling blocks. Even under the best of circumstances, the move into adolescence is awkward. Discomfort with the sexual attraction you felt towards others and your struggles with social awkwardness and isolation became key issues. The need for peer approval became even greater because your entire self-image rested in the judgments of those around you.

Dependency on Peers for Approval

In our adult lives, it is important to feel we can ask someone what they think—we all need feedback. Dependency on another's opinion, however, is another thing. This form of dependency results when we completely lose sight of what we feel or think because we are so heavily influenced by the opinions of others.

Indicators of a dependency such as this are evident when you have to poll your friends before you feel confident about making a decision. This is further indicated if you continue to do this— over and over again. Asking for feedback and asking someone else to tell you what to do are two distinctly, different agendas. Asking for feedback invites those close to you to shed light on the areas of your life to which you may be blind—but the inability to take that feedback and co-mingle it with your own intuition as to what direction would be most beneficial to go is a result of not trusting yourself and your connection to your Source.

As a teenager, this was a way we felt connected to our peers and became a part of the "in-crowd." As an adult, this dependency can become a problem. In your pursuit of mastery, it can hinder you from moving into feeling comfortable with what you are achieving thus far in your goals. Your successes will only be valid when compared to the successes of others.

Between twelve and fifteen years, teens are primarily involved in same-sex activities. When sexual interest did begin to spark, however, few knew what to do with it. This new interest was also accompanied by rapid physical changes. The teen years were a time of baby fat, acne, and voices that cracked. The emotional and physical bodies were at odds. It was a time when we were perhaps the most self-conscious physically and yet the most compelled to take emotional risks. This tension between the emotional and physical is what made us feel so hopelessly awkward.

Social Awkwardness

A carry-over from this stage of our lives is revealed in our level of comfort or discomfort in social situations. If we were unable to learn how to cope with our sense of self-consciousness then we would have never developed that internal sense of self-confidence. This would be most apparent when we find ourselves in social situations in which we fear judgment. Those experiences when you feel exposed—when it is as if you are walking across a lunchroom and all eyes are on you—are threads from this stage of development. If these situations in your adult life are still gut-wrenching then this is a stage which will need some work. If you never learned how to cope with this discomfort and how to contain that anxiety without acting it out, then as you progress in your maturity you will have to face those issues and learn what was never learned.

Using Compulsions and Addictions as A Way to Cope

So what did most of us do to quiet these anxieties? We withdrew and began a long history of resolving this angst through compulsive and addictive behaviors. If your coping mechanism involved using chemicals then you learned how to cope with discomfort by drinking, smoking dope or doing mind-altering drugs—or perhaps by smoking cigarettes or overeating. If you were physiologically predisposed then you may have even activated an addictive disease. Your co-dependency may have taken root. Your "pusher-driver" and will to survive may have emerged and you assuaged your discomfort not by learning how to process your feelings and coping with them but rather by rising above them and channeling that discomfort into competitive sports or academic ventures.

Irrespective of how you directed this surge of hormonal energy—it was directed in some manner and that manner, destructive or constructive, would have followed you into your adult life. It would have set the stage for your challenge between self-confidence and self–consciousness with respect to entering new situations, new groups and new ventures.

The last focus which needs to be addressed with this age is sexual promiscuity. Sexual promiscuity is a learned behavior. It was either learned from watching your parents misuse their sexual energy or developed in response to having been sexually abused and incorporating this experience into your blueprint for being loved. The result is that you learn to use your body to get your needs met—to "attract" love because that is what you learned as a child.

What results is a shame-based approach to one's sexuality. If you were molested as a child on some level you sensed this was wrong and you internalized this "wrongness" as being related to something you did. You could have also been told you were being molested because you were the "chosen one." You were special… so the way in which you would attempt to get your needs for feeling loved and accepted could be through sexual activity. How? By your using your newly budding sexuality to manipulate your world in hopes of getting your needs met. The context of this sexual acting out is embedded in the fact that as a child your body was exploited and you developed the belief system that the manner in which you could get your needs met was by physicalizing your need for love.

For some, the sexual molestation began at this age. Because a young teenage body is developing, it can suddenly be exploited by others. Perhaps a step-father began to turn to you to meet his sexual needs and by not protecting you, your mother unconsciously allowed and even sanctioned it. Incest cannot happen unless there is a breakdown in the communication between the daughter and the mother. If a strong bond exists then the daughter would feel free to tell her mother what was happening and the abuse would stop.

For many, their attempts to get help were met with accusations, ridicule, and disbelief which only compounded the guilt, fear, and tendency to take responsibility for the abuse and make it your fault. If you had never developed clear boundaries and had witnessed one or both of your parents being promiscuous you may have been more inclined to become promiscuous yourself. If you were experimenting with drugs and alcohol this would have contributed to the loosening of your inhibitions.

How Patterns May Have Been Carried Into Adulthood

As we move into mastery and autonomy we go through a stage where we experience discomfort with our new self-image. We may feel as though we don't quite fit into this new self. It mimics the issues we experienced between the ages of 12 and 15 when we were moving into a new frame of reference with respect to our body, our families, and our peers. Our hormones were running rampant and this created great anxiety and discomfort. Our self-confidence was compromised by our self-consciousness. This experience is often recreated in any new endeavor which we pursue.

We go through that period when we have moved into a new area of expertise, yet, we do not feel quite comfortable with our new role. Our self-concept of success is tried on, but it needs adjustments. These alterations are made in the next stage of development which is adolescence. It is then when we become comfortable enough with the new role to pepper it with our own unique ingredients. We first go through that time when we transition from being a novice to being seasoned. You will see this represented in the degree of comfort versus discomfort you experience with respect to the attainment of your goals. How comfortable do you feel in telling others about your achievements? Do you feel conceited? Embarrassed? Shy?

This stage of development and adult patterns reflect the transition made from being a novice to being seasoned. You will see this represented in your present level of achievement. This transition prepares you for entry into your refinement phase of adolescence when true mastery can begin to occur.

Potential Lesson of the Soul
(YouTube Overview/Tapping Sequence)

So what may the potential lesson of your Soul look like? The answer to this would be found in exploring when, in the history of the Soul, you experienced discomfort in holding the frequency of Light or lacked the self-confidence to appropriately express your creative and sexual passion. There may have been a time in your Soul's past when you began to attain spiritual mastery but felt insecure with your new powers and, therefore, acted without integrity.

You may discover a lifetime or Soul situation when you moved into a position of authority before you felt confident enough to hold that energy and you were left with an uneasiness of having possibly bitten off more than you could chew. The lessons related to this stage of development which would be reflected in this stage of your journey have to do with a discomfort with the newness. You may have completed one goal and now, all of a sudden, fear that new expectations will be put upon you from some unknown source. This could relate to a time in your Soul's past when a similar experience occurred. As you work with these issues keep your mind open to their original source.

From Rebellion to Reverence
Developmental Tasks from Ages Fifteen to Seventeen

As we reached mid-adolescence, rebellion became essential if we were to move into the final stage of development – preparing for our place in the adult world. We did begin to settle down in terms of sexual feelings. We started "going steady." Couples were still paired within groups, as the group provided the base for identification, but we were beginning to learn skills necessary for a long-term relationship—although, for an adolescent, long-term usually meant from six-weeks to six-months.

Peer acceptance became more important than parental acceptance. Even though we wanted to sprout our wings, we still needed to feel the safety of home. Of course, we never would have said that. We behaved more rebellious than we were. It was a time when we began to define a self outside of the family. To be different than our parents meant to be separate from them. We defined that self by separating from our parents and family, and by struggling, self-consciously, to be different. That was what growing up involved.

This stage of development was similar to the toddler stage because we again learn to say no. Whatever our Adult Self has difficulty saying no to, our fifteen-to-seventeen-year-old will rebel against through behavior. When the Adult Self is able to set limits and say no, this adolescent within rebels less, but until then, this part of self will continue to rebel. We are rebelling against things which feel unsafe or unfair— things which threaten to compromise our individual nature.

Developing a self was the primary task in this developmental stage. Rebellion was and still is a response to anything which threatens this definition. This inner teenager will act up to be separate and different. If you are around someone who tries to control you and "make you over in their image," this part of you will rebel. This is the part of you who holds your individuality as the prime importance and anything which threatens it will butt up against its wrath. Again, this was evident in the angry adolescent voice I had to work with before I could clear the path for me to go to Washington DC and continue with my work. Underneath her wrath, however, was the wound of the younger, more vulnerable self who was being protected by the armored adolescent. This part of us is the gatekeeper to our pain and unless we can gain enough courage to confront it, we will never earn the trust needed for these parts to reveal themselves with the confidence that they can now be healed.

Standing Up For Yourself

The barometer for how much we stand up for ourselves is evident in those moments when we feel betrayed. Most often, when we examine these feelings more closely, we can detect the exact moment when we sold ourselves out. Long before another betrays us we have, most often, betrayed ourselves. They have given us signs of their untrustworthiness, but we chose to ignore them.

Standing up for yourself simply means that you are astute enough to identify your truth and then have enough courage to speak it. Working with this stage will give you an opportunity to examine the points where you sell yourself out and project your self-betrayal onto the person you empowered to betray you.

Being Caught Up In an Active State of Rebellion or Passivity

Rebelling when you were an adolescent was essential if you were to move into the final stage of development—preparing for your place in the adult world. There may have been many reasons this rebellion did not occur. In order to rebel there had to be someone you cared enough about to rebel against, and there had to be a structure against which you could safely rebel. The degree to which you were allowed to rebel will determine the degree to which you were able to define yourself as separate from your caretakers. If you were restricted from this feat you may have become passive and instead projected your rebellious nature onto others. You may have externalized this feeling by attracting those who would act out your rebellion for you.

Needing To Be Right

Another expression of this stage of development in your adult life is when you find yourself becoming righteously indignant about some cause or issue. Your ego may be invested in being seen as the expert—your self-esteem may be intertwined with assuming, if you are a grown-up, then you know what is best. You may find yourself fighting battles you don't even care about just so you can prove the other person wrong. If this rings true, it is time for you to ask your inner adolescent who he or she is really angry at and what truth has not been spoken which now needs to be expressed?

Defining and Owning Your Uniqueness

This stage invites you to clearly define for yourself the difference between being selfish and being self-caring; between having a healthy self-esteem and a nauseating sense of self-importance; between being conceited and holding an "earned appreciation" for your uniqueness.

Now, I understand in some circles, to even claim you are unique is a step towards relapse, but having a solid connection with your true source, while at the same time having an appreciation for your unique expression of that source, can be a sign of maturity. As you learn to appreciate your unique characteristics without being attached to them you can further appreciate and revere the uniqueness of others.

How Patterns May Have Been Carried Into Adulthood

So how does all of this material filter into your adult life? The pattern exhibited in adulthood which relates to this stage of development is found in your need to hold onto an identity or at least to establish one. This is the part of you who does not want to be the same as everyone else—who will rebel against the mundane—who, through our very beingness, will challenge others to stretch beyond their comfort zone. This is the part of you who will harshly set limits or let others know what you like and dislike.

If you feel angry or betrayed, it is your adolescent who is responding to a perceived betrayal. If you feel repressed, there is most likely an inner adolescent who fears butting up against someone he or she perceives to be in authority and this part of you does not like it! In order to operate in sync with this part of self, the adult part within you needs to meet the challenges of holding your authenticity. Anything which emerges that is less than this pursuit will be met with the rage of your inner adolescent.

This rage or depression can emerge at any point in your journey. You may find yourself rebelling against those in your life who held the notion you would not succeed. You may find yourself feeling righteously indignant about injustices which relate to some unspoken aspect of your inner self. This is when you will begin to shed the old ways and defiantly carve out a new you—to break away from any external structure which has been used as a false source of identity. You may find yourself breaking away from your role of wife/husband, or a negative self-image such as being "no good", or "too fat" or "too thin", or not smart enough, educated enough or any and all of the above. As an adult, you may feel rebellious against any external structure which has served as a point of reference for the old you as you then replace it with a more current and refined point of reference for the new you.

This is the step where your true signature is put on any endeavor or relationship—where the idea or the job becomes "yours"! This is when you become settled in your role with others. You have more comfort at being who you are and in allowing the rest of the world to accept or reject you. Your reference point for self-worth is no longer externally projected; it is now internalized and based on the process of self-referencing.

Potential Lesson of the Soul
(YouTube Overview/Tapping Sequence)

So what may the potential lesson of your Soul look like? The answer to this would be found in exploring when in the history of the Soul you experienced a rebellion or betrayal with respect to your Higher Source. When did you turn away from God and betray your inner knowingness, only to then blame the Higher Source for abandoning you? When did you fail to set the appropriate limits for yourself spiritually and then blame it on the organization to which you belonged? There may have been a time in your Soul 's past when you attained spiritual mastery but felt uneasy with your authority and either misused it or let it go dormant. You may discover a lifetime or Soul situation when you moved into a position of authority before you felt confident enough to hold that energy, leaving you with an uneasiness of having bitten off more than you could chew.

The lessons related to this stage of development, and which would be reflected in your pursuit of mastery have to do with any area of your life where you do not stand in your truth. You may have achieved some mastery or completed a goal and now, all of a sudden, fear that new expectations will be put upon you from some unknown source. This could relate to a time in your Soul 's past when a similar experience occurred. As you work with these issues keep your mind open to their original source. Also, invite your Higher Guidance to reveal to you times in your Soul 's history when you have mastered this task and can now draw on that Higher Self as a mentor for who you are in your current incarnation.

FROM MEDIOCRITY TO MASTERY

Developmental Tasks for Ages Seventeen-to-Twenty-one

How effectively you run your life—how responsible you are with respect to the daily habits which enable you to manage your life in a productive manner; your relationship to the masculine and feminine traits within you and your relationship to your internalized value system are all related to what you learned or did not learn during the last years of your official childhood. These years are the years when you are supposed to have the opportunity to practice being an adult while still living within the safety of your family.

Between the ages of seventeen and twenty-one, you began to be treated as an adult. Learning how to be responsible and manage your life were important issues. You began to relate to others more maturely. You learned how to provide and fend for yourself as you prepared for college, got married, or found a job and moved into an independent living situation. Goals became more concrete as you began to discover what you wanted from life and made plans to achieve those goals.

At least, that is how it was supposed to be! Some of you moved away from home but remained dependent emotionally, perhaps even financially on your parents. Others moved right from the home of your parents to the home of your wife or husband and never had an opportunity to experience autonomy in the adult world. Yet others moved out even before this time—unprepared for the adult world—but thrown into the mix with what you had on your back and in your "tool chest." You had to fend for yourself and act as if you were competent long before your time. Irrespective of what your transition was into adulthood, the patterns learned, and habits developed from this time will set the stage for how you master carrying your achievements into your day-to-day life in a meaningful and productive manner.

You will begin to explore how you want to use all you have learned from this structure to enhance your life. What habits have you developed over the course of your life which you can now incorporate on an on-going basis? What have you integrated? What is still left to be resolved? Each time you apply this structure to an endeavor, you will learn more about yourself and flush out the blocks which prohibit you from not only experiencing your joy but also, from sustaining it.

You will be invited to examine the origin and effectiveness of those values. The buzz word for this stage of development is an *evaluation*. The more comfortable you are with reviewing and examining your life and then making the appropriate adjustments, the more successful you will be with your continued evolution and growth. You will look at your personality through the lens of the masculine and feminine within you, and explore how these principles have or have not been integrated into your day-to-day life. You will be invited to evaluate your satisfaction with respect to your career, your relationships, your passions and your productivity.

You will have an opportunity to recall past dreams; to evaluate the realization of those dreams and to revise and recommit to new dreams. You will also be given the support to look at your life from a holistic angle—how integrated are your spiritual values into your day-to-day activities? How congruent are your thoughts on your feelings and your actions? What have you learned about your body and your relationship to your body over the last nine months that is useful? How have you internalized what you have learned? How can you now set new goals and commit to new aspirations?

Examining Your Values

Values are what give your life meaning. You develop your value system based on what you observe from those around you. Family, friends, and society at large play a huge role in your value development. You learn about the roles of men and women from what you observe. You learn the value of money, of integrity, of honesty from what you observe. You develop a work ethic and a blueprint for your relationships all by what you observe and then weave into your own unique formula for living. You are invited to ponder all of these values for yourself and determine which ones now support the new you, and which values need to be revised?

Focus first on your relationships. Look at the relationships you have in your life. How many people in your life are acquaintances? How many would you call good friends? How do you define a meaningful friendship? What do you value in your friendships? Look at your intimate relationships—and ponder what is valuable about them. What aspects of each relationship support your authentic self and which relationships require you to be a version of who you really are? What do you want to do with this new awareness? Take the time to ponder your relationships—notice how much courage it takes, to be honest, and to hold the truth of the quality of the relationships you have attracted into your life. What do your relationships say about you—how do they mirror your own strengths and challenges?

How you respond to these questions will be most influenced by the relationship you had with your same-sexed parent, because it is from this parent you learned what it meant to be an adult as a man or a woman. To have made this transition successfully would have required that you had a meaningful relationship with your same-sexed parent. It would have been necessary to have seen traits in your same-sexed parent which you wanted to emulate. The development of your masculine and feminine sides would have been most influenced by what you observed of the men and women involved in your life at that time. Teachers, clergy, bosses, mentors all would have played a positive or challenging role in who you became.

Your ability to weave the creative aspects with the side of you who can take that creativity and mold it into action originated with the models you had. How did the males in your life take action? How did the females express their creative talents? Were there mentors in your life who successfully tapped into their creativity and were able to express this creativity in the world in a meaningful way? Most of us are strong in one area but have challenges in the other. It will be useful to explore more fully the masculine and feminine within you and the degree to which they dance with ease.

Career Satisfaction

You will also want to turn your eye to how you make your living. In some ways, it does not matter what you do, but rather, how you do it. How do you feel about the ways you work in the world which enable you to provide for yourself? Do you provide for yourself? Have you always had to provide for yourself or have you been taken care of by others? What are your independent abilities? In what areas of your life are you interdependent? How do you feel about this? If you had to define a work ethic—what would yours be? How do you find value in what you do?

What you discover is going to relate directly back again to what you observed, and the models, positive and negative, you had for this integration. The value of examining these traits is that you then have a starting point from which you can begin your work. You cannot determine who you want to be until you are clear about whom you do not want to be. Part of becoming a functional and productive adult—one who has mastered integrating a higher value into the day-to-day activities is one who can muster up the courage for such self-reflection. If you can engage in this kind of perpetual self-inventory without shame or guilt then you are constantly in a position to modify and re-commit to a never-ending evolution of your highest form. You become a student of life's circumstances, not of a victim of them.

The Maturation of Your Spiritual Intent

The most promising component of this journey is the invitation to consciously integrate your spiritual aspirations into your day-to-day activities. The entire thrust of this material has been to provide you with a structure which can assist you in developing the habit of integrating your spiritual practice into your daily life. Taking all you learned now involves successfully weaving your spiritual values into the way you live your life on a day-to-day basis. Examining the following will assist you in this endeavor. How do you integrate your spiritual principles into the manner in which you treat your physical form? How do you weave it into your daily thoughts? What belief-systems have been altered? Use these questions to assist you in your self-examination.

There is more and more support for living a spiritual life in a physical body. More and more individuals are finding a way to integrate their belief in a higher source into the actions they take on a daily basis. It is helpful to examine your day-to-day life through this lens. What do you value spiritually? How do you integrate these values into how you treat others, how you treat yourself, how you treat your body, how you live your life? How do your friends and co-workers support or challenge your spiritual aspirations and what do you want to do about this?

Evaluating Your Achievements and Setting New Goals

In this final aspect of your exploration, you begin to look back and ahead. You are encouraged to look through the eyes of the newly, empowered self, feeling pride in what you have accomplished and intrigue and excitement about what you can now set your sights on. How can you set new goals? How can you establish a new vision for who you want to become next? Have you become the person you wanted to become? How does this new you compare to who you hoped you would be by this time in your journey? How do you feel about this? What are your disappointments and what aspects of your journey thus far make you feel proud?

Completing a leg of any journey always invites evaluation and recommitment. Acknowledging what you have accomplished while at the same time being able to set new goals is what keeps this whole process of living an adventure. When we stop setting new goals—we cease to make use of the time we have on this planet and in this body. Your progress can be defined only by you and your higher source— but when we feel we have no more to learn—we don't. We send a signal to our body that the time has come for us to begin the journey back home.

It is my belief that when we cease learning we begin dying. Some make their transition immediately—others take years to pull their energy from these forms and to transition back to the spiritual realm. Where are you on this journey? What are your new sights; new goals; new aspirations? How can you take the structure you have been invested in and give birth to a new way of living your life with feeling; non-addictively?

How Patterns May Have Been Carried Into Adulthood

So what is the purpose of all of these questions? How does all of this material fit into what you learned as a young adult? The same questions you have been invited to explore above are the same issues you had when you were in the developmental stage of seventeen to twenty-one. How prepared you are and how willing you are to be involved in a constant evaluation of your life originates from what you experienced at that time in your life; for this stage of development marked the first time you made a major transition—the transition into the adult world.

This stage of development and adult patterns developed, reflect the manner in which you shift from being a novice to being seasoned. You will see this represented in your present level of achievement with respect to your achievements—but the integration of this will be revealed in the ease with which you participate in this on-going evaluation. This transition prepares you for entry into any refinement phase where true mastery can be maintained.

Potential Lesson of the Soul
(YouTube Overview/Tapping Sequence)

So how does this material interface with what your Soul may be here to learn? Know that this is not the first time you have had to practice this transition into mastery. Just like serenity mastery is not a fixed state—it is a stance in life and in life's situations which you achieve, lose, revise and once again attain.

It is living, moment to moment, in the process of grief as you feel the anxiety of impending change; attempt to hold onto the old; use your anger and dissatisfaction to break free; allow yourself the luxury of standing naked in the void and then integrating the new vibration with ease. Each experience in life invites you to integrate more fully the vibration of joy. The manner in which you chose to do so will vary according to the Layer you are focusing on at that time. Nothing is constant–everything is ever-changing and each new day offers a new opportunity to be who you want, and know, you can be.

With this overview of the developmental stages, adult patterns, and lessons of the Soul you will hopefully be able to pinpoint some of the areas in your own life which could benefit from this kind of work.

Taking An Inventory To Assess The Issues Of Your Personality And Soul

In the following exercises, you will be given methods to identify the area of concern in which your ineffective blueprint manifests. The first task in redesigning your blueprint is to identify your potential Soul themes in which the difficulty is made evident. Responding to the following statements will assist you in this process. The statements provide the foundation for the exercises contained in the remainder of the Ten-Step Formula. These worksheets will help you take the information you received in the last section about the developmental stages being carried into adulthood and holding insight about the tasks of your Soul into specific areas of concern.

Take a moment to respond to the following statements of the respective worksheets. These statements reflect how these issues may be emerging in your day-to-day adult life. They are categorized into the specific seven developmental stages. Again, this inventory will help you explore the ways your issues from childhood are impacting your adult patterns and Soul tasks. By identifying the stage of development to which you most relate, you will begin to create a profile of your wounded one's themes.

I suggest you respond to all seven worksheets and then look them over and begin to decipher where patterns and repetitions appear.

INVENTORY FOR SELF-IMAGE

Read the following statements and check those with which you resonate.

Infant Stage (Birth to 18 Months)

_____1. I struggle with knowing who I am.

_____2. I have difficulty in clarifying own ideas.

_____3. I sometimes do not even feel I have a right to be alive.

_____4. I often feel I do not belong—like I cannot find my place in the world.

Toddler Stage (18 months to 3 Years)

_____1. If I say No, I fear abandonment.

_____2. I find it difficult to say No to those with whom I am involved.

_____3. I fear if I say yes, I will be expected to say yes all of the time.

_____4. I fight the limitations (rules) I experience in my external world.

Young Inner Child (3—6)

_____1. I am judgmental and critical of myself.

_____2. I am judgmental and critical of others.

_____3. I don't have a very good understanding of my strengths and challenges.

_____4. I do not respond well to constructive criticism.

Grade School Self (6—12)

_____1. I do not really feel seen for who I am by those in my life who I value.

_____2. I do not really have many outside interests that I pursue with regularity.

_____3. I often wish I could find a good support system of like-minded people.

_____4. In order to fit in, I will adjust my values to those of my peers.

Young Teen Within (12—15)

_____1. I feel self-conscious about my talents.

_____2. I dislike exposure and prefer to stay hidden.

_____3. I feel the right to claim my true self, but feel awkward in doing so.

_____4. I don't like being too vulnerable.

Adolescent (15—17)

_____1. I don't really know what I like or dislike.

_____2. I like to shock others with my ideas of what is important.

_____3. I am very determined about what I want to accomplish in my life.

_____4. I find other people's opinions about me irrelevant.

Young Inner Adult (17—21)

_____1. I like to hang around others who think and act as I act.

_____2. I wish I could feel authentic—but most of the time I don't.

_____3. I find it difficult to be honest about what I really feel or think.

_____4. I don't feel comfortable exposing who I am and how I feel.

INVENTORY FOR BELIEF-SYSTEMS

Read the following statements and check those with which you resonate.

Infant Stage (Birth to 18 Months)

_____1. I wouldn't say I really think for myself.

_____2. I find it hard for me to clarify my thoughts about matters of the world.

_____3. If someone asks me my opinion, I pretend I do not have one.

_____4. If someone asks me to come up with a plan, I panic!

Toddler Stage (18 months to 3 Years)

_____1. My ideas are usually different than the mainstream.

_____2. I base my ideas on the ideas of others.

_____3. I seldom have an idea of my own usually I am influenced by others.

_____4. I assume most people think as I think.

Young Inner Child (3—6)

_____1. I feel embarrassed when I learn something that makes me wrong.

_____2. I have strong opinions and even with new information, I do not adjust.

_____3. I don't like people that think differently than I do,

_____4. I keep my thoughts to myself for fear of being judged.

Grade School Self (6—12)

_____1. It is important to me that others agree with what I think.

_____2. I have creative ideas and want to be acknowledged for them.

_____3. It is essential that the organizations to which I belong believe as I do.

_____4. I study what others think so I can think that way as well.

Young Teen Within (12—15)

_____1. I express my thoughts but only if I know they are going to be accepted.

_____2. I cautiously test other's opinions to see if they think as I do.

_____3. If I state a truth that is different than others, I feel ill at ease.

_____4. It makes me feel nervous when I say what I think and feel judged.

Adolescent (15—17)

_____1. I speak what I think no matter what anyone else says.

_____2. I like to say things that shock others.

_____3. My thoughts may be inconsistent, but they are mine.

_____4. If someone disagrees with me, I will defend my view to the end!

Young Inner Adult (17—21)

_____1. My thoughts are not very formed and are ever-evolving.

_____2. I get nervous when I cannot determine what I want to be when I grow up.

_____3. My behavior seldom matches how I think.

_____4. I get uncomfortable expressing my thoughts.

INVENTORY FOR FAMILY, FRIENDS, AND ROMANCE

Read the following statements and check those with which you resonate.

Infant Stage (Birth to 18 Months)

_____1. I have difficulty being aware that I am interested in someone new.

_____2. My relationships with family members feel stagnant and confined.

_____3. Many of my relationships lack depth and trust.

_____4. I have difficulty initiating contact in new relationships.

Toddler Stage (18 months to 3 Years)

_____1. I dislike having to say No to a friend or loved one.

_____2. I would rather not ask than to risk being told No.

_____3. I fear if I say yes once, I will be obligated to say yes the next time.

_____4. If I do not know what I feel or want to do I remain quiet and simply go along.

Young Inner Child (3—6)

_____1. It is difficult for me to articulate what I feel about something.

_____2. If I state an opinion which is challenged, I wish I had remained silent.

_____3. If another's opinion differs from mine, I assume theirs is wrong.

_____4. If I give in and agree with someone else, I feel I give them my power.

Grade School Self (6—12)

_____1. I want more acknowledgment from those I love.

_____2. I feel invisible and unseen by most or some of my family members.

_____3. If I disagree with my partner, I stay silent rather than risk disapproval.

_____4. Even if I have strong feelings, I will still agree with others.

Young Teen Within (12—15)

_____1. I proceed with great caution when I exhibit a new behavior with others.

_____2. I get nervous when I attempt to break away from family ideas.

_____3. I figure nothing is going to change anyway, so why even try to be different.

_____4. I would rather avoid contact with some people rather than deal with the discomfort I feel at being different than them.

Adolescent (15—17)

_____1. Even though my family does not agree with my beliefs, I speak them.

_____2. Even if I agree, I like to disagree with someone just for the fun of it.

_____3. I find myself in situations where my values are unique and stand out.

_____4. I would rather be dishonest about how I feel than risk losing a close friend.

Young Inner Adult (17—21)

_____1. My relationships are not really based on mutual trust and appreciation.

_____2. I do not do very well with differences in the relationships I have with others.

_____3. If someone challenges my belief system, I have a hard time defending my position.

_____4. I am uncomfortable with others who "agree to disagree."

INVENTORY FOR SEXUALITY AND CREATIVITY

Read the following statements and check those with which you resonate.

Infant Stage (Birth to 18 Months)

_____1. I find it hard to express my creative ideas.

_____2. I feel like a creative person but don't do much with that feeling.

_____3. My sexual expression is more physical in nature than emotional.

_____4. I have difficulty initiating sexual contact.

Toddler Stage (18 months to 3 Years)

_____1. I have a hard time saying No to sexual advances.

_____2. I have a lot of creative ideas but not much discipline to manifest them.

_____3. I am afraid if I give in once, I will feel obligated to respond every time.

_____4. I have no idea what my sexual preferences are so I remain quiet.

Young Inner Child (3—6)

_____1. I have a hard time setting realistic goals for my creative efforts.

_____2. I feel passionate about my ideas but fear being judged if I express them.

_____3. I don't like to be around someone who is experimental with their sexuality.

_____4. I feel ashamed and shy about my sexual feelings.

Grade School Self (6—12)

_____1. My sexual preferences pretty much fit the societal norm.

_____2. My creative thoughts, which I share with few, are somewhat avant-garde.

_____3. I create a great deal but feel I get little recognition for my efforts.

_____4. I have strong sexual preferences but keep quiet to avoid criticism.

Young Teen Within (12—15)

_____1. I feel awkward about my sexuality.

_____2. My passion for life and for love frightens me.

_____3. I would rather eat, smoke, drink, or addict than let my passion emerge.

_____4. I avoid people who obviously have different sexual preferences than I do.

Adolescent (15—17)

_____1. I like to experiment with sexual preferences even if they are different.

_____2. I have creative talents but do not express them.

_____3. I find my sexual values are unique and stand out.

_____4. I am a person with great passion and will compromise it for nothing.

Young Inner Adult (17—21)

_____1. I wish I could see my sexuality as an extension of the Universal Source.

_____2. Sexuality is sacred,but I don't find manypartners who feel the same way.

_____3. If my creative projects are challenged, I feel they have little worth.

_____4. I know I am passionate about life but am afraid to express it.

Inventory for Job or Career

Read the following statements and check those with which you resonate.

Infant Stage (Birth to 18 Months)

_____1. I have difficulty trusting the value of my ideas.

_____2. If offered a position in a new job, I can't decide what to do.

_____3. The thought of being in business for myself terrifies me.

_____4. I experience great anxiety when beginning a new position.

Toddler Stage (18 months to 3 Years)

_____1. I find it hard to say No to my employer.

_____2. I would rather not ask for special treatment than to risk being told No.

_____3. If my boss is angry or in a bad mood, I assume I made a mistake.

_____4. If a co-worker asks me to do something, I do it even if I don't want to.

Young Inner Child (3—6)

_____1. I worry a great deal about what my co-workers and boss think of me.

_____2. I don't think many of my co-workers are as competent as I.

_____3. If I agree to do something, I stick with it until it's done.

_____4. I feel irritated when others do not have the same value for integrity as I.

Grade School Self (6—12)

_____1. I want more acknowledgment from those with whom I work.

_____2. I feel overlooked by my superiors.

_____3. I think about going into business for myself, but fear I wouldn't succeed.

_____4. I dread giving presentations and avoid promotions because of this.

Young Teen Within (12—15)

_____1. I feel very cautious when I try a new behavior at work.

_____2. I get nervous if I do something at work which calls attention to me.

_____3. If I don't like something, I keep quiet; why try to buck the system?

_____4. I have some ideas which excite me but I don't share them with anyone.

Adolescent (15—17)

_____1. I am determined to speak my mind, even if it gets me into trouble.

_____2. Even if I agree, I like to disagree with my co-workers, just for the fun of it.

_____3. I enjoy testing the company's rules.

_____4. I have strange ideas and I enjoy shocking others with them.

Young Inner Adult (17—21)

_____1. I wish I enjoyed what I do for a living.

_____2. I don't know what I want to do when I grow up.

_____3. If an evaluation challenges my self-image I feel deflated.

_____4. If only I could have had more training before I could go into business for myself.

INVENTORY FOR PROSPERITY AND ABUNDANCE

Read the following statements and check those with which you resonate.

Infant Stage (Birth to 18 Months)

_____1. I have difficulty conceiving of myself as a wealthy person.

_____2. Abundance seems really out of my immediate reach.

_____3. I am so used to struggling I don't know how it would feel to have money.

_____4. I have great wealth I just don't know what to spend it on.

Toddler Stage (18 months to 3 Years)

_____1. I devise a budget plan but then do not stick to it.

_____2. I wish I could spend money wisely, but don't.

_____3. I don't make a lot of money because I am afraid it would change me.

_____4. If I do get money, I feel a need to spend it right away.

Young Inner Child (3—6)

_____1. I want just enough money to meet my needs.

_____2. I feel everyone else has more than I.

_____3. I don't like to be around people who have a lot of money.

_____4. When abundant, I feel uncomfortable if I see someone who is not.

Grade School Self (6—12)

_____1. It is important to me to "keep up with the Jones'."

_____2. My job pays well and I like others to know this.

_____3. I feel less prosperous than most around me.

_____4. I feel abundant but keep it quiet rather than risk rejection or criticism.

Young Teen Within (12—15)

_____1. I feel inadequate when it comes to managing my money.

_____2. I don't have much passion for life or love.

_____3. I believe if I do what I love, the money will follow.

_____4. I avoid people who obviously have significantly more or less money than I.

Adolescent (15—17)

_____1. I spend money on items that most others would not.

_____2. I don't like spending time on anything that doesn't fit with who I am.

_____3. I refuse to spend money on items which are harmful to the planet.

_____4. I purchase only those things which reflect my individual spirit.

Young Inner Adult (17—21)

_____1. I wish my abundance was a direct extension of the Universal energy.

_____2. I feel abundant in my life but know there is room for improvement.

_____3. I do what I love; I just wish the money would follow.

_____4. When I look around the world, I wish I saw more abundance and prosperity.

Inventory for Body Image and Physical Health

Read the following statements and check those with which you resonate.

Infant Stage (Birth to 18 Months)

_____1. I would like to exercise but have difficulty getting started.

_____2. I find it impossible to decide what kind of exercise plan I want to follow.

_____3. I have a hard time staying present in my body and often dissociate.

_____4. I addict to food or drugs to stay disconnected from my body.

Toddler Stage (18 months to 3 Years)

_____1. I start an exercise plan but have trouble sticking with it.

_____2. I can adhere to a food plan very strictly, and then I splurge.

_____3. I have a hard time setting realistic physical health goals.

_____4. I am not good at assessing the best food plan for my system.

Young Inner Child (3—6)

_____1. Even if my exercise plan becomes too restrictive, I stick to it.

_____2. I am judgmental of my body type and wish it were different.

_____3. I wish I were more in shape, but don't have the time to exercise.

_____4. I am uncomfortable with people who "let themselves go."

Grade School Self (6—12)

_____1. I want my peers to acknowledge how good I stay in shape.

_____2. I am very conscientious about my eating habits and like acknowledgment.

_____3. I feel unaware of my body.

_____4. It is important my body is acceptably met by society's standards.

Young Teen Within (12—15)

_____1. I am self-conscious about my body.

_____2. If someone criticizes the way I look, I believe what they say.

_____3. I wish I could accept my body, but somehow am unable to do so.

_____4. I do not like to eat in front of others.

Adolescent (15—17)

_____1. I know exercising is good for me, but it is such a fad, I refuse to do it.

_____2. Even though certain foods do not agree with me, I eat them anyway

_____3. I eat, drink or addict when I am angry.

_____4. I don't like to relax, it makes me too nervous.

Young Inner Adult (17—21)

_____1. I wish I accepted my body just the way it is, but I don't.

_____2. I try to eat in a healthy and responsible way but am not really good at it.

_____3. I like would like to exercise at least 3-5 times a week but.....

_____4. I want to feel more comfortable in my body than I do now.

Review your responses to each area. Are there certain stages of development which emerge? Did specific themes become apparent? Record what you have learned about yourself in this experience. Make a note of the stage or stages of development you resonated with most predominantly.

INTERACTIVE TAPPING™ SEQUENCES FOR LAYER THREE

Again, in Layer Three we use the pronoun "you" to begin the interactive process. Referring to our wounded one in the second person begins to build that trusting relationship between your most illuminate and nurturing self and the wounded Inner Child or fragment of your Soul. You are introduced to the surrogate tapping which creates that internal experience for the wounded aspect of you that finally someone is responding to his or her pain and operating on its behalf.

The result is that this method of tapping invites in the experience of deservedness and nourishes a sense of importance. Having the Inner Adult operate on behalf of the Inner Child makes him or her feel worthy of attention and care. This is an important step in the process of building trust because often your younger selves have felt abandoned and left to fend for themselves. This is true for aspects of your Soul as well. They sustain a state of suspension, waiting to be discovered, rescued, and healed. When we travel back in time to respond to their situation and heal their pain, they are finally free to return to the Light.

STEP-BY-STEP FORMULA FOR LAYER THREE— *"Interacting With The Wounded Inner Child"*

As we discussed in the overview, your goal in Layer Three is to establish the relationship with your wounded Inner Children and ultimately gain the trust needed so that in Layer Four you can actually take him or her back in time and orchestrate the healing. This Inner Child holds the vibrational resonance with the aspect of your Soul whose traumatic experience continues to be transmitted through time and space and cues your fight, flight, or freeze response anytime you encounter a situation that holds a similar vibration of threat.

Keep in mind you do not need to *build a relationship* with the Soul aspect. In Layer Four you will simply take your healing team back in time and heal that energetic disturbance left from the unresolved trauma. But in order to do that, you have to pull the thread from this lifetime to that past one. So, in Layer Three, your focus is on building the relationship with the Inner Child who became wounded in response to the childhood situation that may have activated your Soul's energetic blueprint. It was he or she that endured the tension of the situation your Soul charted in hopes that you, in this body, would be inspired to pull the thread back to its origin so the wound could be healed.

But the Inner Child's issue is revealed to you through your current responses to your day-to-day life in adulthood. And the link between your triggers of today and the triggers from childhood is the stress that got stored in your body. As you read, your body is your most loyal servant. It will store your pain for you as long as it can or until you come back and resolve the issue first-hand. Therefore, your first task when working with This Layer is to identify the tension your body holds, and then to follow that tension to the voice of your wounded Inner Child.

To experiment with this task, think of a recent experience when you felt you collapsed into the fears of your younger self. Then follow the steps below to begin to separate, interact, and relate.

EXERCISE: PULLING THE THREAD OF CURRENT TRIGGER BACK TO ORIGIN OF INNER CHILD'S COLLAPSE

1. Once again you begin by taking a deep breath and bringing your focus back to a current situation. It may the same inter-action with a boss or a loved one you worked with before. Or your psyche may select a new point of reference. But retrieve a recent time when you really felt emotionally challenged.

2. Next, find where in your body you hold the tension. If this situation resulted in a collapse … it began with your feeling stress. That stress is registered as tension in your body and gets stored somewhere in your body until it is resolved or erupts as a physical ailment. Again, your body is your most loyal servant. It **WILL** store your pain for you as long as it can or until you come back and resolve the issue first hand.

3. So, bring your focus to that part of your body. It is this tension that becomes the thread you pull to take you into a relationship with the child within you who has gotten triggered. It is his or her tension. The way you invite this part of you to come forward is by asking the simple

question—*Who Inside feels scared, angry, or alone, and what do you need from me?*

4. The next task is to introduce yourself to this younger part of you. *I am your Illuminated Adult Self.* (Notice again that I continue to use the pronoun "you.") *I am the one you have been waiting for. I am here to help you heal. I am here to respond to your needs.*

5. Take a deep breath. Again, keep in mind that simply by posing those questions you are creating that separation you need to relate to the more wounded part of you.

6. Once you have established this relationship you tap on your endpoints as you begin to dialogue with this younger part of you.

Please Note: The purpose of the dialogue is to build that connection and rapport so the Inner Child can begin to trust you. The reason why you tap as you do is because the tapping itself will begin to dislodge the hidden feelings from your subconscious. You will be taking the edge off of these feelings as you are simultaneously developing this relationship with this wounded one. If you take the edge off of the initial reaction you will more effectively get down to the core of your Inner Child's issue that is the focus of Layer Four.

It is essential that you understand that this one statement—this exact response —is the key component to rewiring your brain, reconditioning your heart; reprogramming your body and reframing the purpose of your pain.

Next, you want to you get more specificity so you can determine which Inner Child needs your attention. This is important because the age of the inner one triggered determines the parenting techniques you will want to use. Remember, you are beginning to "repair" an old wound by parenting this little one in a new, and more compassionate manner. That is why I coined the phrase, "repairenting." It captures the essence of this process.

The previous overview prepared you to think in terms of different developmental stages, tasks, and issues. With time you develop more of an intuitive sense as to which Inner Child has emerged.. In fact, initially, you often work primarily with the most wounded Inner Child or the part of you who grabs your attention first. But what I have found is that, with time, other patterns of behavior emerge that originated at different times in your life. Therefore, the intervention you design is constructed accordingly. For now, begin to work with the recent issue in the following way.

EXERCISE: COMBINING YOUR FINDINGS FROM THE INVENTORIES

Draw from what you discovered by combining your findings from the inventories with the above exercise then use the questions below to get more specific.

1. Use your feelings to determine the issues that got triggered by this recent situation. *Did the incident trigger a fear of abandonment or fear of trust? Did it involve your need to set limits or your feeling betrayed and walked on? Was your shame or guilt triggered—or was it your need to be respected and valued for who you are?*

2. Make a list in your journal of at least five or more feelings which became apparent in the above exercise.

3. Refer back to the inventories to which you previously responded.

4. How does this information fit into the profile of your wounded self? What common themes held the most charge for you? Which stage of development continually showed up?

5. Take each item and ponder its origin. Reflect on other recent times when you felt this way? What was the situation? Who was involved? How old did you feel, and, again, what

emotional themes did you notice? Record your findings in your journal.

By now certain memories should be emerging. Work with whatever is presented to you. When you can describe or feel a certain scene, apply the following formula to clear it in present time.

Exercise: Identifying Your Belief System and Subsequent Behavior

Now that you have selected the scene with which you will be working begin to respond to the following questions and gather as much information as possible for your work.

1. What belief system formed in response to this experience?

2. What feelings accompanied this belief?

3. What behavior developed in response to this experience?

4. *Record your beliefs and behaviors in your journal.*

This combination of beliefs formed, feelings experienced and behaviors designed to keep safe, make up your unique energetic blueprint.

With this in mind, take a moment to ponder these additional questions so you can begin to determine not only how this blueprint is currently impacting your ability to manifest all that you desire and deserve, but what you can do to resolve it.

Exercise:"Redesigning Your Energetic Blueprint

Keep in my mind that your blueprint is embedded in every inter-action you encounter which resonates with your core theme. It is this blueprint which results in your knee-jerk reactions to situations which get triggered. It is this blueprint that erupts in your current reactivity. So take some time to ponder how this blueprint truly impacts your day-to-day life and governs your responses to your world. Once you identify this blueprint it will more easily be updated and altered through the tapping sequences that follow. By updating the belief system and bringing this experience into the "now," you can begin to alter the behavior associated with it, This empowers you to be able to avoid the collapse into the abandonment of your Inner Child who has been waiting for someone to respond and keep him or her safe.

Use the following questions to assist you in working with and redesigning the blueprint associated with this core scene.

1. Is this belief still functional in your life today? Are the feelings that get triggered still appropriate for your current situation? Is that behavior still effective for you today?

2. How would you like to redesign the blueprint of these beliefs, feelings, and behaviors?

3. Take a moment to imagine what your life would be like if you implemented this new blueprint. Who would you be, how would you behave differently? How would your life look different?

4. Write one paragraph that encapsulates this intention. This is your ultimate truth statement. It will be your litmus test with respect to believability and trust.

5. Now read the UTS and see what feelings come up that challenge your being able to hold the essence of the UTS.

6. Record your findings in your journal.

Now that you have all of this information you want to begin your surrogate tapping so you can build on your relationship with this wounded one. We do this first by helping him or her take the edge off of the beliefs, feelings, the body's sensations, and the perspective of the pain. The interactive tapping™ sequences will dislodge any energetic disturbance that needs to be neutralized in your mind, body, heart, and Soul and opens the door for the theme of this issue to be revealed. Once revealed, we can bundle the baggage of this issue, and ultimately peel back the onion so that in Layer Four the Illuminated Adult Self will know exactly which scene is relevant to heal.

Tapping Sequences for the Mind, Heart, Body, and Soul

As you know my brand of tapping is called interactive tapping™ and you will now see its relevance. We are tapping on behalf of your Inner Child. We are doing surrogate tapping to help that little one within you to revise the belief systems, neutralize feelings, to let go of the body sensations, and to begin to understand how important his or her pain was with respect to the evolution of the Soul.

Begin by envisioning your little one standing or sitting in front of you. Explain that you are now going to tap on his or her behalf. Let this little one know that even though this technique may look a little ridiculous, it is going to help him or her feel safe. Explain that he or she can either watch or even participate—whatever makes him or her feel the most comfortable.

Grab your water so you can keep yourself hydrated then come to the karate point and begin to take the edge off of the limiting beliefs.

Even though, my little one, you have held the belief that it was your fault—the belief that you were not good enough—the belief that resulted in your feeling so unsafe; I am the one that you have been waiting for, and I am here to tap on your behalf so that together we can begin to heal.

So even though my precious one you have held these debilitating beliefs for so many years, I have come back in time to relate to you, to connect to you, to help you feel safe, so that together you and I can heal.

So even though, my wounded one, you have been so courageous in carrying this pain, I am now here to help you feel safe. I am here, so together you and I can heal.

Proceed with the reminder phrases.

Neutralizing the Negative

Eyebrow: These limiting beliefs …

Side of the Eye: They served a purpose for you.

Under the Eye: They established a blueprint which gave you the illusion of safety.

Upper Lip: But they are faulty beliefs. They are no longer necessary.

Under the Lip: And I am here to help you heal so you can let go.

Collar Bone: It is time to let go of all of those beliefs that the world is not safe…

Rib: …the beliefs that you are at risk…

Wrists: …the beliefs that you did something wrong…

Head: …the belief that you were deficient in some way…

Possibility of Something New

Eyebrow: …that it was your fault…

Side of the Eye: and it was your responsibility to make it right.

Under the Eye: Those were beliefs that enabled you to survive.

Upper Lip: But I have come back in time to help you heal.

Under the Lip: You are ok.

Collar Bone: It wasn't your fault.

Under the Arm: And I am going to keep you safe.

Rib: It's ok to delete those old belief systems.

Wrist: Through this process, you and I can upload a new paradigm,

Head: a paradigm that enables the front part of your brain to hold a new experience.

Conviction to Change

> *Eyebrow: Because you know that I will keep you safe.*
> *Side of the Eye: You are safe.*
> *Under the Eye: You are wonderful just the way you are.*
> *Upper Lip: It wasn't your fault.*
> *Under the Lip: You were way too little to have to endure that.*
> *Collar Bone: And I am so sorry it has taken me so long …*
> *Under the Arm: …to return…*
> *Rib: …to retrieve.*
> *Wrist: …to help you feel safe.*
> *Head: But I am here now and together you and I will heal.*

That begins your work with the belief systems. Next, we will begin to neutralize the feelings that accompanied those beliefs and led to the behaviors that have been keeping this little one safe. Once you delete the old belief and neutralize the behavior associated with that belief you will be ready for Layer Four in which you help this little one return to the original scene, right that wrong, and help him grieve and let go.

The most common feelings associated with not feeling safe; with feeling like it was your fault, that you were unworthy are shame, regret, panic, fear, denial, anger that you can't change it, and a sense of unworthiness for just not feeling good enough. It is now time to clean that up on behalf of your Inner Child.

Come to the Karate:

Even though my little one, you have spent so much time being in fear, feeling panic, experiencing the shame, the rage, powerlessness, and regret, I have come back in time to help you neutralize those devastating feelings. Together you and I can come back into a state of peace, harmony, and grace.

So even though, my little one, you have spent many years being in a state of fear, I have come back in time to assist you now. Together we will take the charge off of these feelings. It's time for you to relax. Your heart can be reconditioned, and you can finally come home.

Even though my precious one it is so difficult to trust and feel safe I am the one you have been waiting for—and together we will heal.

Shake your hands out. Take a drink of water so you keep yourself hydrated, and then begin to neutralize these feelings on behalf of your Inner Child so you can assist him or her in coming back into a state of calm. Again, we are using the pronoun "you" because we are tapping on behalf of that Inner Child. Remember that just by referencing the Inner Child in this manner you bond with that younger part of you. The Inner Child can finally feel important enough for someone to show up and return him or her to a state of peace and calm.

Begin with the first point:

Neutralizing the Negative
Eyebrow: Feeling of shame...
Side of the Eye: Your feelings of fear...
Under the Eye: Panic, regret, rage...
Upper Lip: Your fear about what you did wrong...
Under the Lip: Your focus on you could fix this...
Collar Bone: Thinking the problem was with you ...
Rib: Not understanding why you could not safe.
Wrist: That absolute panic that you wouldn't survive...
Head: ...it runs through your physical form...

Possibility of Something New
Eyebrow: ...and keeps you agitated,
Side of the Eye: hyper-vigilant,
Under the Eye: and afraid.
Upper Lip: But now we want to come into a relationship to each other.
Under the Lip: I am the one that you have waiting for.
Collar Bone: And I have come back in time so you can heal.
Rib: You can replace your shame for unconditional regard;
Wrist: Your sense of betrayal for trust;
Head: Your fear of abandonment for connection and safety;

Conviction to Change

Eyebrow: I am the one you have been waiting for…

Side of the Eye: …and I have come back in time to help you heal.

Under the Eye: Release all emotions.

Upper Lip: Let go of all fear.

Under the Lip: Take a deep breath my little one.

Collar Bone: For I have come back in time to bring you home.

Rib: You are finally safe.

Wrist: I am here.

Head: And together we will return to a state of safety and calm.

Breathe. Rub your hands together to change the energy. If you want to take another drink of water do so now. Next, you are going to work with the body of the Inner Child and help him or her begin to let go.

In your mind's eye see the body of that Inner Child. You are going to begin to address the sensations that have been held in your physical form. These sensations have served as a transmitter of the post-traumatic stress from another time. Your physical body is connected to the etheric body where the chakras transit energy from your environment, and also from you multi-dimensional selves, so you now need to help the body let go.

Again, imagine this little Inner Child standing or sitting in front of you. Keep in mind you are going to be talking directly to the body of your Inner Child. When you feel ready start by tapping on that karate point:

Even though your little body has been a conduit for this pain, I am her to help you let go of that vibration so that you can re-program your body's reaction, revise the faulty DNA, so your body can return to a state of relaxation, of peace, and calm.

So even though you have been cued to biochemically react, and the neurons in your brain have fired off that reactive fight or flight stress response, I have come back in time to help your body heal, to revise that sequence so that you begin to default to a more positive response that will enable you to trust you will cope, and survive. I am here to help your body release and let go so you can finally trust me enough to feel safe.

Take a deep breath. Take another deep breath, and then to begin neutralize the body's reactions start with the first point:

Neutralizing the Negative

Eyebrow: All of this stress in my physical form…

Side of the Eye: originating in your experience…

Under the Eye: from so long ago.

Upper Lip: And now, I am here to help the body heal.

Under the Lip: I give you permission my dear physical form…

Collar Bone: …to let go…

Under the Arm: …of all of the fear,

Rib: All of the reactivity,

Wrist: the panic, the grief, the remorse, the rage,

Head: …the powerlessness that is stuck in the fibers of our physical form.

Conviction to Change

Eyebrow: …from both then, as well as now.

Side of the Eye: I now give you my dear body.

Under the Eye: On behalf of my Illuminated Adult Self, the child with me, and the aspect of my Soul,

Upper Lip: I now give you

Under the Lip: Permission to release,

Collar Bone: To relax,

Under the Arm: To let go.

Rib: I am a child of God.

Wrist: You are a child of God.

Head: We are safe in the arms of God.

Another Round

> *Eyebrow: We are safe in the arms of our Higher Self.*
> *Side of the Eye: We are safe in each other's arms.*
> *Under the Eye: It's safe for our bodies to let go.*
> *Upper Lip: I now envision your little physical form*
> *Under the Lip: Being filled with the Divine light.*
> *Collar Bone: Every fiber of your being resonates with the frequency of peace.*
> *Under the Arm: So that together you and I can heal.*
> *Rib: It's safe.*
> *Wrist: It's safe to let go.*
> *Head: It's safe to release.*

Conviction to Change

> *Eyebrow: It's safe to plant a new expectation in the prefrontal cortex.*
> *Side of the Eye: So that our brain defaults to safety instead of fear;*
> *Under the Eye: Union instead of abandonment;*
> *Upper Lip: Trust instead of betrayal;*
> *Under the Lip: And unconditional love instead of shame and guilt.*
> *Collar Bone: It's ok.*
> *Rib: It is ok body, you can release.*
> *Wrist: It's safe.*
> *Head: I am now ready to do for this Inner Child what you have done for so many years.*
> *STAY ON HEAD: I am ready to keep him or her safe. Thank you, thank you thank you.*

We have neutralized the belief systems. We have worked with the emotions. We have started clearing out from the body. And now we are going to reaffirm the relevance of this Inner Child's pain. You will let him or her know that what was endured had meaning. It had a purpose. And you are so grateful that he or she was willing to endure.

So now come to the karate:

Even though my little one you are much too young to understand, there was a Spiritual significance to what you have endured, and I am so grateful you had the courage to oblige.

So even though you have held great pain and stress in your little physical form, and all these years you thought it was you. I, on behalf of our Soul, want to express my gratitude to you for all that you have endured.

Now shake your hands out and come to the first point:

Conviction to Change

Eyebrow: You are so brave my little one.

Side of the Eye: I am so thankful.

Under the Eye: Our Soul is thankful.

Upper Lip: You have done such a good job.

Under the Lip: And your pain has had a purpose in our growth.

Collar Bone: We thank you so much for all you have endured.

Rib: And we want you to know …

Wrist: … that it is finally safe.

Head: It is finally safe to let go and feel trust.

Now, take a deep breath. Put one hand on your heart and one hand on your third eye. Breathe into your heart and out your third eye. This is the final sequence. You are stepping into heart and mind coherence so that you can anchor this release in your mind, heart, body, and Soul.

So breathe into the heart.

Breathe out your third eye.

Breathe in and expand.

Breathe out, and release and let go.

Breathe in.

Breathe out.

Breathe in.

Breathe out.

You are safe to release and let go.

Clearing the mind, body, heart, and Soul prepares you to bundle the baggage of this Inner Child's pain. He or she will then feel connected enough to you to move into that Fourth Layer of Healing during which you actually help him or her to go back into the painful situation so it can be neutralized and healed.

Now, we will bundle the baggage of this issue so the true essence that needs to be revisited and resolved in Layer Four can be made known.

A note about "bundling the baggage"—This exercise was developed by EFT Master Lindsay Kenny. You simply draw a garbage bag and write down everything you want to neutralize regarding the incident during which you recently collapsed. You just want to capture the essence of the issue so write phrases or words that hold the energetic blueprint of this pattern. Use descriptive words that capture the feeling you want to release. Once done, you place the bag in front of you so that when you tap on the "bag" your psyche envelopes everything you have written.

What this accomplishes is that it "takes the edge off" of the issue. This exposes the core of the pattern so that in Layer Four you can help your wounded one return to the original incident to rework, and thus heal, the pattern of this experience that activated the energetic blueprint from the history of your Soul, Once your Inner Child's activation point is healed you have the thread that takes you back to the energetic blueprint of the Soul wound from which that post-traumatic stress signal is being sent.

From there, your healing can be completed. The purpose of your pain has been realized. The energetic blueprint is dissolved. The post-traumatic stress signal is interrupted, and the rewiring of your brain, the reconditioning of your heart, the reprogramming of the DNA of your body can take place. But first you have to get down to the core of the issue, and you do so by bundling the baggage of the triggered event so you are prepared to take your Inner Child back to the origin of his or her wound.

EXERCISE: BUNDLING THE BAGGAGE OF THE INNER CHILD'S WOUND

Preparation: Before you start your tapping bring your focus to your body. Just come into this moment. You are going to bundle the baggage of all that this Inner Child has held. Take a piece of paper upon which you have drawn a symbolic garbage bag. Reflect back on all that you recorded in your journal. Write down words and phrases that capture everything your Inner Child, the aspect of your Soul (if anything has emerged), or even your body, needs to release and let go. Get it all written out because just by writing it down in your garbage bag you are externalizing it. You have already, in the previous tapping sequences, taken the edge off of the belief systems, the fears, the feelings, the body sensations, the stress responses that were charted by your Soul to create that reactivity. But now you want to capture anything that is left. You may even uncover anger at your own Soul for agreeing to have this experience. Whatever is left over from the clearing we did earlier, whatever your Inner Child needs still to release; or the aspect of your Soul needs to bundle, write it down on the garbage bag now. We are going to bundle the baggage of this pain, the bag of this wound, and get rid of it.

Since we are *interacting* with the Inner Child you will continue to use the pronoun "You." You are *bundling the baggage* of this wound so you can get to its core. This prepares you for Layer Four in which you will actually help your Inner Child return to the original scene and heal the wound in his or her time. Once this is done you will be in a position to pull that thread and explore and respond to the etheric energetic blueprint of your Soul. But first, you need to tend to the Inner Child, for he or she is the one who accepted the reactivity of this lesson. It is this little one that has endured the pain necessary for you to notice, and to respond. Only then can you be prepared to follow this thread back to the original blueprint in the history of your Soul and clean it up in all dimensions of time and consciousness.

Tapping Sequence

So, shake your hands out. Take a drink of water. Place your garbage bag in front of you and get prepared to tap. Come to your Karate point:

Even though my little one, you have carried this bag of betrayal, abandonment, shame, and grief for so many years, I have now come back in time to help you release, let go, and feel safe.

So even though, my little one, you have carried this heavy, heavy bag for so many years, I am the one that you have been waiting for. I am the one that can keep you safe. I am the one that will bring you home.

So even though you have held this bag of stress and disappointment for so many years, it is now time to trust me enough to help you let it go.

Now shake your hands out, rub them together, take another drink of water, and let's do the first round of just neutralizing the bag.

Neutralizing the Negative

Eyebrow: This bag of abandonment…
Side of the Eye: This bag of betrayal …
Under the Eye: This heaviness of all that you have carried …
Upper Lip: It's time to neutralize it. It's time for you to let it go.
Below the Lip: Let go of all of the fear…
Collar Bond: …all of the broken promises…
Rib: …all of the abuses, the moments of neglect and shame.
Wrist: It's now safe little one to let it go.
Head: It's now safe to release and come home.

Next Round—Giving the Inner Child Permission to Let go

Eyebrow: Release the fear.
Side of the Eye: Release the shame.
Under the Eye: Release the regrets, the belief that it was your fault.
Upper Lip: Release and let go. There is no reason to hold on.

Under the Lip: You're safe. I am here to bring you home.

Collar Bone: Let it go.

Rib: Take that bag that you have been carrying.

Wrist: Give it to me.

Head: Hand it to me so that I can give it to the Angles above and ultimately exchange it for a basket of our gifts and talents.

Expressing Gratitude

Eyebrow: You have done such a wonderful job carrying this bag;

Side of the Eye: Being loyal;

Under the Eye: And suffering with this on your back.

Upper Lip: I am so sorry it has taken me so long to get back to you.

Under the Lip: But I am here now.

Collar Bone: I am the one you have been waiting for.

Rib: And I have truly come back in time to help you feel safe.

Wrist: Its time, it's time to let go.

Giving Permission to Let Go

Head: Its time, it's time to release.

Eyebrow: Its time, it's time to come home.

Side of the Eye: Because I am the one you have been waiting for.

Under the Eye: And I am the one that can keep you safe.

Upper Lip: Let it go my dear one.

Under the Lip: Let it go.

Collar Bone: Let the bag go.

Rib: So you and I can determine what's left to be healed.

Wrist: Let it go.

Head: Give it up.

Next Round

Eyebrow: It's safe.

Side of the Eye: You can trust me ... it really is safe.

Under the Eye: It's safe for me to take this bag.

Upper Lip: The Angles will discard it, neutralize it.

Under the Lip: So they can return it as a basket with your gifts and your talents.

Collar Bone: It's safe.

Rib: Let it go.

Wrist: It's safe.

Head: Let it go.

Another Round

Eyebrow: You are absolutely wonderful just the way you are.

Side of the Eye: It's safe.

Under the Eye: You can let it go.

Upper Lip: I am the one you have been waiting for.

Under the Lip: And together you and I are going to heal.

Collar Bone: I will not leave you this time.

Rib: And I may not always be perfect.

Wrist: But if I collapse and forget, the minute I remember…

Head: … I will come into relationship with you

Final Round

Eyebrow: I will apologize to you.

Side of the Eye: I can't promise I will be perfect.

Upper Lip: But I really am the one you have been waiting for.

Under the Lip: Together we can truly heal.

Under the Eye: But I will hold myself accountable.

Collar Bone: Because I am the one you that have been waiting for …

Rib: And I have returned to help you heal.
Wrist: I have returned to help you heal.
Head: Together, you and I will heal.

Now shake your hands out and take a moment to see that little one in front of you. *Check in with him or her to see how this younger part of you is doing. Does he or she need anything from you? Ask if he or she feels safe.* Record his or her response in your journal.

When you pull this thread and begin working with the aspect of your Soul it is a bit more elaborate. But that comes in Layer Four and only after you have gone back and cleared up the energetic blueprint established when this theme got activated in this physical form during a wounding experience now held by your Inner Child.

You are in now relationship with that little one so you will want to nourish that relationship by staying in touch and periodically asking what is needed for this part of you to remain safe. It is important to respond to his or needs. But in order to do so, you have to be conscious. You have to be attentive. You have to be in communication as you just have experienced. And that is what this Third Layer of healing is all about—is strengthening that relationship.

EXERCISE: CONTINUING TO STRENGTHEN YOUR RELATIONSHIP WITH YOUR INNER CHILD

Once you have moved through the tapping your next step is to create different activities which you and your Inner Child can share. Why? Because spending time with this little one builds a relationship. It gives this part of you the childhood he or she deserved. Your Inner Child has been so busy holding on to the pain that he or she did not get to have the experiences he or she should have had in a healthy childhood. So now you need to create that childhood before that child will trust you enough to go into Layer Four. You need to create that relationship; give space to that relationship, and develop that relationship.

EXERCISE: GETTING TO KNOW YOUR INNER CHILD

You do this by going into your mind's eye and imagining different activities that are shared between you and this little one. Remember your mind does not know the difference between what is real and imagined. So just by spending time with your Inner Child; by checking in with him or her on a daily basis; by asking what this little one needs from you; and by actually envisioning different activities, you create a new reality and establish a new point of reference for this little. And that, in essence, IS rewiring your brain, reconditioning your heart, and reprogramming your body.

So if your Inner Child never got to go to the park imagine taking your Inner Child to the park. If it was never safe for your Inner Child to bring friends home imagine that. Again, your mind does not know the difference between what is real and what is imagined. So now you get to create, with your Inner Child, not by yourself, but together with your Inner Child—you get to create the childhood this that little one within you deserves.

And that is the beginning of the inner healing that solidifies this relationship so that when you have to go back in time to really break down the wound, give that Inner Child a chance to state his or her truth, and step into empowerment, that little one is going to have the trust in you to walk through this process together.

It is really important that you spend time with your Inner Child; that you foster this relationship; that you envision yourself hanging out with the Inner Child and going for walks, and bicycle rides, and whatever the Inner Child needs to do.

However, I must say that it is important to distinguish between what happens in your mind's eye versus what happens in your day-to-day life. For instance, if you are on some food protocol which necessitates you do not eat sugar, and yet your Inner Child wants an ice cream cone you simply envision taking your Inner Child to your favorite ice cream shop and getting him or her an ice cream cone in the mind's eye. You do not have to put your body at risk. You do not have to eat that ice cream cone in current time. Remember, your mind does not know what is real or imagined. If you imagine your

Inner Child is getting that treat the experience of eating the ice cream cone will be transmitted.

And that's what is so beautiful about being able to work in that other dimension. You do not have to retrigger your body because, remember, your body was cued to hold a certain energetic response to the stress of a perceived threat. Your Inner Child experienced the wound; developed a belief system that was flavored with a set of feelings; which ultimately became the operating system for the Inner Child. But you have just corrected that response, and now you want to reinforce it.

You can then be relaxed enough for the new belief system to get embedded in the brain as a new response, which then allows your body to stay calm, and your feelings to stay relaxed and at peace.

Layer Four:
The Teaching Layer—Healing The Inner Child And Soul
Layer Five:
The Integration And Merger Layer

Layers Four and Five flow into one another because this is when you bring it all together. You step into your Illuminated Adult Self and use the following step-by-step process outlined below to go back in time and begin to help your Inner Child heal the pain of his or her past. This process is facilitated by using the pronoun "I." Once the Inner Child has been healed you are in a position to pull that energetic thread back to the history of your Soul when this pattern of behavior began.

A Soul healing is orchestrated in the same manner as with your Inner Child.

The difference comes in Layer Five with the integration and merger. With the use of the pronoun, "we" you merge the Inner Child back into the force field of your Illuminated Adult Self.

A fragment of your Soul, however, is sent back to the light. This is accomplished on behalf of this part of your Soul by referring to its essence as "you."

LAYER FOUR—The Teaching Layer—Healing The Inner Child And Soul

(Click on the heading to be taken to the YouTube Overviews of each of these Layers)

OVERVIEW OF LAYER FOUR —The Teaching Layer—Healing The Inner Child And Soul

Layers Four and Five flow into one another because this is when you bring it all together. You step into your Illuminated Adult Self and use the following step-by-step process outlined below to go back in time and begin to help your Inner Child heal the pain of his or her past. Once the Inner Child has been healed you are in a position to pull that energetic thread back to the history of your Soul when this pattern of behavior began. A Soul healing is orchestrated in the same manner as one is with your Inner Child. The difference comes in Layer Five with the integration and merger. When you have completed the healing for your Inner Child you integrate its essence back into the force field of your physical self and merge with the Inner Child as a way to sustain the connection. Some establish a sacred place where their Inner Child can reside. Others integrate the healed essence of their Inner Child into a sacred chamber within their own heart. I prefer the first option simply because it is easier to sustain the separation if the Inner Children are envisioned in their own safe place. But by the time you reach Layer Five, it really boils down to personal preference.

What's important is that once your healing is complete that natural spontaneity, the innocence, and presence you possessed as a child that got eclipsed when you experienced trauma, can be reclaimed. When you orchestrate a healing such as the one you will be conducting with your Inner Child you regain access to that innocence and spontaneity. When that wounded one is brought back into that protective force field acquired by your Illuminated Adult Self and is made to feel safe, faith, hope, and trust can return. You integrate the Inner Child back into your force field because he or she is a vital aspect of you that has been banished or denied.

On the contrary, when you resolve the tension of the energetic blueprint held in the etheric field of your Soul you return that essence back to the Source or the Light. This effectively unties the knot of tension that has been creating static in your force field and has been blocking manifestation and success. When you heal that suspended traumatized part of your Soul you assist its essence in being escorted back to the Light and Soul integration occurs.

The *Seven-Layered Healing Process* accomplishes this with sequential, interactive tapping™ sequences. In addition, the structure offered in the original Inner Child *Workbook* can be useful for Layer Four as well. It is perhaps one of the most comprehensive resources for orchestrating the healing for the Inner Children within you. In my 20-year Anniversary update, to enhance the work with each of the seven developmental stages, I went back and recorded the meditations and added the tapping sequences for this *Seven-Layer Healing Process.* The formula for multidimensional healing included in this chapter was originally developed for my book, *Which Lifetime Is This Anyway?* That material is an ideal step-by-step process which teaches you how to pull the thread of your current stress all the way back to its origin so it can heal in all dimensions of time and consciousness.

With the resources provided for you in each of these Layers, you should begin to feel more comfortable with the flow of the healing of your wounded ones. What follows is the step-by-step process you use to orchestrate your own healing. As you empower your Illuminated Adult Self he or she will, in turn, begin to mentor the children within you. This structure provides you with the formula to do just that.

EXERCISE: STEP-BY-STEP PROCESS TO HELP YOUR WOUNDED INNER CHILD HEAL

1. *Close your eyes and ask your Healing Team to step forward. (Your Healing Team consists of those in the unseen, characters that are real or imagined, alive, or on the other side, who can help and assist you in returning to the time of your Inner Child, and even the wounded aspect of your Soul, so the healing can take place.)*

2. *Imagine that you and your Healing Team are standing at the top of a stairway.*

3. *Before you begin to descend, reflect on the trigger you felt in the last Layer.*

4. *Where in your body do you now feel that tension?*

5. *Bring your focus to that tension. What intensity level would you give this tension? (#1 is very low and #10 is high and almost unmanageable.)*

6. *Either place your hand on this part of your body that holds this tension or simply bring your focus to it. This gesture enables you to communicate with this part of your body. You inform it that you are aware of the tension, and you are in the process of resolving it.*

7. *As you and your Healing Team proceed down each step imagine this tension intensifies.*

8. *Move to each step sequentially, and as you do so, the intensity level of this tension increases but not to the point where you need to abort this mission. It progresses but is still manageable. You do not want to re-traumatize your Adult Self. You are accessing the tension but not collapsing into it.*

9. *Once you reach the bottom of the stairway you pause for a moment. In front of you is a doorway. It is the threshold between the present and the past. Once you decide to cross over this threshold you are choosing to time-travel back to the time and place of the original event. Determine if you and your Healing Team are prepared to cross over this threshold because once you do so you will find yourself and your Healing Team back in the time and place where the wound in this body occurred.*

10. *Take time to notice the circumstances. Really explore the scene. When you locate your Inner Child, notice what he or she is doing. What is the situation here that ended up being so wounding?*

11. *Once you have a feel for the scene imagine you freeze the scene so an intervention can be designed and implemented.*

12. *The only character in this past scene that is not frozen is your Inner Child. Make contact with him or her.*

13. *Introduce yourself as his or her "Future Self, Higher Self, or the Adult Self. Explain that you have come back in time to help him or her heal.*

14. *Notice how this little one responds to you. Talk to this little one.*

15. *Ask him or her what is needed to feel safe. (This is crucial, because often, as we try to rescue our Inner Child, we go in and dictate what should or should not be done. We end up overriding what the Inner Child really needs based on what we believe he or she needs. The Inner Child can end up feeling overpowered and not heard. You want to partner with this little one so he or she feels supported but not controlled. Remember this is the Teaching Step. You are teaching this part of you how to cope with this situation—unless this little one is too young to stand up for itself. Then you need to step in and model for this little one that, you are the one he or she has been waiting for. You need to reassure this little one that you are now willing to step in and create the safety he or she deserves. In this case, you are teaching your Inner Child that 'it is safe to feel safe'. You are not teaching him or her how to create safety. This Inner Child may be too young for that.*

16. *When you have determined the intervention play this out in your mind's eye. Sometimes it is helpful to write the story of this healing. Imagine the situation in the way that would have kept the Inner Child safe. If there was a violation see the perpetrator being confronted and stopped. If there was a need that was not met, see that need being met now, preferably by you. Create the new story of this Inner Child then envision it taking place in your mind's eye. Right this wrong. Protect this Inner Child and help him or her heal. Meet the need of this little one so that he or she finally feels safe. Once you have completed this healing (by envisioning it in your mind's eye through meditation) you are ready to assist your Inner Child in reinforcing this healing by teaching him or her how to tap.*

You can also vicariously observe this process on my Blog Talk Radio broadcast which demonstrates an actual session during which these Layers of healing were conducted.

LIVE Demonstration Consult for the Seven-Layer Healing Process

As you will see, once you have created the new story, you will use the three-step interactive tapping™ process to first, neutralize the challenging feelings, second, introduce the possibility to the Inner Child that things can be different, and last, but not least, use the conviction sequences provided throughout this material to anchor the new paradigm into your prefrontal cortex.

This in itself begins the process of rewiring your brain enough to be able to pull this thread back to the origin of this wound in the history of your Soul. Then, in the Fifth Layer, you merge with your Inner Child, and/or assist the fragmented part of your Soul to return to the Light. Ultimately, in the Sixth Layer, you use your interactive tapping™ sequences to anchor this new paradigm into your cells, to recalibrate the electromagnetic field around you, and to build the new neural pathways which enable you to move this new experience from your short-term memory to long-term storage.

Let's now put this together with your interactive tapping™.

EXERCISE: PREPARATION FOR THE INTERACTIVE TAPPING™

Once you have completed the steps above and you are ready to teach your Inner Child how to tap you simply invite him or her to sit beside you or even to jump on your lap. Once you have his or her attention, again, explain how you want to teach him or her how to do this process so he or she can feel safe enough to release and let go. It is this relationship you must heal before this part of you will allow you to attract all that you so desire.

Return to your mind's eye. Ask your wounded one to take you back to the time and place when he or she first developed fears and doubts and began to feel unsafe. You will most likely be taken back to the moment of your essential wound.

Even though there may be experiences which built on this, if you can get back to the core it is easier to pull the cord and orchestrate a complete healing of your past. Be prepared that this little one might even begin by taking you back to an experience in which you, as the Adult, were the cause of its fear. If that occurs—neutralize this first exchange and complete the sequence with an apology. Every time you collapse into the fear and act from this part of you, your Inner Child experiences it as abandonment. As you progress in your work you will be able to recognize this more easily and respond more quickly.

If you are reading this in the Kindle format this meditation will help you get connected to your Inner Child and prepare him or her for the tapping that will take place. Use it if you feel you initially need more hands-on healing.

Meditation that Gets You and Inner Child Ready for this Teaching

If you need more prompting, inquire about past situations where he or she felt abandoned or experienced a lack of trust and faith. Who was involved? What did he or she hear or witness that resulted in so much fear, sadness, and pain? Spend time really exploring this past situation so you will be able to more effectively respond. You may want to record your responses in a journal so you have a record of them. Also seeing your response on paper can bring you even more clarity. It will help you design your own statements to customize your sequences in a way that will target your exact issue.

The Inner Child cannot heal until he or she has a chance to speak the truth. However, it is essential to be tapping while this is taking place. This will neutralize any residue or debris that would prohibit the Inner Child from releasing and letting go. The following guides you through the process of letting your Inner Child speak his or her truth. Once there, you will be given extensive instructions on how to help your Inner Child grieve and let go. However, I strongly recommend, that any time you are working with your Inner Child that you do so while tapping on your endpoints like you learned how to do in Layer Three. This will ensure more success and fullness in your healing.

EXERCISE: TAPPING SEQUENCE: THE INNER CHILD SPEAKS

You can use this example of tapping to give you a better idea of how this sequence flows. When you feel you have enough information and are ready to return to the scene where the wounding took place close your eyes.

Observe this scene for a moment. Then freeze the scene and pull your wounded one to the side. Invite him or her to either sit on your lap or sit cross-legged in front of you. In this first round, all you want is for your Inner Child to repeat what you say and to tap where you tap. Explain this so your little one understands you are stating these sequences as if you are him or her (using the word "I"), and you are asking that he or she repeats the phrases after you speak them while tapping where you tap.

When you feel this connection, begin to tap. In the first round imagine that both you and your Inner Child are tapping on the karate point while you speak and tap on his or her behalf. These are just suggested sequences. Determine if these statements need to be tweaked and feel free to customize them to your specific needs. Remember, by using the pronoun "I," you are giving your Inner Child a voice to speak his or her truth.

Even though I am really afraid to once again trust, and I have been so badly hurt in the past, I know you love me and I love myself enough to trust you to help me heal.

Even though this is really scary for me, and I am afraid to open up to experience this hurt, I feel safe enough with you that I trust it will be okay.

So even though moving ahead causes great fear, I am willing to experiment with this because I trust you enough to keep me safe.

Again, customize the setup phrases to your Inner Child's needs. When you feel ready to move into the neutralization sequences use the suggestions provided below. But you are going to want to experiment with this because this is really the Healing Layer of this entire process. It is here that you actively teach your Inner Child how to feel safe. This is where you truly "share the gift" with your wounded ones so together you can all heal.

As you will see, the sequencing gradually helps you identify the origin of the disturbance and then assists you in moving into the possibility of letting that go—the possibility that something really can be different—that this wound really can be healed. The sequences then end with the conviction that it is safe to let it go and once again feel faith and trust. Only then will your Inner Child be ready to trust you enough to help him or heal grieve what happened and let go. Follow this to get a feel for This Layer but, always feel free to experiment with your own words as well.

Neutralizing the Negative

Eyebrow: So much pain in this scene ... just remember feeling so unsafe ... so wounded and unable to trust.

Side of the Eye: Seldom felt safe.

Under the Eye: Always feared being left ... afraid I would not be safe.

Upper Lip: I remember the pain ... I am so afraid to once again open up and trust.

Under the Lip: Seldom felt safe ... so afraid to let go and feel trust.

Collarbone: I was so abandoned ... left alone to fend for myself.

Under the Arm: Wish they could just love me as I am.

Rib: So much fear ... will I ever be able to trust?

Wrist: Wish I wasn't so afraid ...

Head: Just don't know if it is safe to trust.

Another round...

Eyebrow: All that I hear is that I have too many needs.

Side of the Eye: Never felt safe ... always feared being left.

Under the Eye: So afraid of being left and will not survive.

Upper Lip: What if I am not good enough to be loved?

Under the Lip: That's how I feel ... when I look back.

Collarbone: Just wish I felt safe.

Under the Arm: I get so afraid of being left.

Rib: So afraid to trust.

Wrist: Don't want to be hurt or left.

Head: Just so afraid if I trust I will again be left.

Introducing the Possibility of Change

Eyebrow: Maybe this can change...

Side of the Eye: Maybe I can finally feel safe.

Under the Eye: I have always felt fear of being left.

Upper Lip: But maybe it is safe to trust.

Under the Lip: Maybe I can let this tension go.

Collarbone: Maybe my Adult Self is really here to help me heal this pain.

Under the Arm: Maybe I can let go of my need for Mom and Dad's love.

Rib: Maybe I don't have to carry this tension that I did not deserve.

Wrist: Maybe I can let go.

Head: Maybe it is safe to trust.

Conviction to Change

Eyebrow: I am going to let go and let my Adult Self in...

Side of the Eye: I am going to let go ... let go of the past.

Under the Eye: I am willing to let this go and trust my Adult Self.

Upper Lip: I am willing to let go and let God.

Under the Lip: I know I have carried this for so long.

Collarbone: But I am willing to let it go.

Under the Arm: I am willing to trust my Adult Self might be different than my parents.

Rib: I am willing to give it a try.

Wrist: I feel really good about joining forces with the Adult Self
Head: I am ready to let it go.

Again, this gives you suggestions on how to move through it. I encourage you to continue to work with these tapping sequences and these exercises. Keep going through these Layers. Incorporate this process so it becomes an effective way for you to continue to heal and evolve. Keep in mind there is no right or wrong with how you implement this teaching. Continue to work with this Inner Child until he or she is ready to let go and can begin to experience trust for you.

As with any issue, you will sense this part moving through the stages of grief, tension, and fear, acknowledging how badly he or she wanted to feel safe and to trust. You will notice the anger that emerges when this did not take place and how this anger caved into the total collapse of despair and fear. Ultimately your Inner Child will be ready to accompany you through the five stages of grief so that together you can both begin to heal.

As I stated in the general overview of grief, all feelings encountered as a human being can be linked in some way to the five stages of grief. When we help our Inner Child process the unresolved emotions of childhood—whether they are labeled as loss or not—we begin to build a relationship with him or her that restores the trust. This restoration is necessary for dealing with the present-day loss because the intensity of your loss as an adult is fueled by the unresolved emotions you experienced as a child. In the previous section, you dealt with the immediate feelings of loss—those related directly to recent losses experienced in your life as an adult. In this next section, you begin to dig deeper into those unresolved issues from your past—those issues which fuel your current response to life in ways you can only now begin to recognize and resolve.

Keep in mind what the Inner Child is grieving is the original loss of safety. If there were an actual loss, such as the death of a parent, or the trauma of a divorce, these situations would need to be targeted more specifically. But for now, you are just working with the residue of the loss of safety that is most likely getting triggered any time there is an experience in your current life that feels unsafe. For a deeper healing that is more age-specific, I recommend you obtain a copy of *The Inner Child Workbook*. Each developmental stage includes a section with instructions on how to help that particular Inner Child grieve. It can most easily be purchased through amazon.com.

Helping The Inner Child Grieve—With Interactive Tapping™ Sequences

Inevitably, when we suffer a loss as an adult, the residue of the past comes to haunt us. I remember what occurred when, as an adult, I lost my first pet. A plethora of unresolved grief erupted. It felt as though I were crying every tear I had ever repressed. The floodgates opened. The depth of feeling overwhelmed and frightened me. Luckily I had a talented counselor who helped me navigate through the rocky terrain of my unresolved childhood losses that had been triggered.

In my case, not only did my childhood grief emerge—the multidimensional grief of the history of my Soul seemed to collide with events in my present life as well. I found myself engulfed in a grief for which I had no context. With time the story revealed itself to me as the story of Antoinette which is shared in my book, *Which Lifetime Is This Anyway?* The same tools and methods I shared in that book that were used to heal that multidimensional bleed-through are offered below and can be applied to processing grief from any dimension and time.

How Our Past and Present Collide

Again, your essential wound occurred at the precise moment you realized you were not safe. You went into a panic and experienced terror you would not survive. This moment is the origin of your Post Traumatic Stress Disorder. It is this underlying trauma that gets reactivated whenever we experience any loss for which we must grieve. Symptoms of our PTS get activated anytime we experience a situation in our day-to-day life that resonates at all with the original neglect, judgment, shame, or abuse. The unresolved feelings related to this first experience of loss determine how we navigate through the feelings of the current losses irrespective of their intensity. They are the source of our loss of trust. They are the origin of our fear that we will be unable to cope.

As I stated in the general overview of grief, all feelings encountered as a human being can be linked in some way to the five stages of grief. When we help our Inner Child process the unresolved emotions of childhood—whether they are labeled as loss or not—we begin to build a relationship with him or her that restores the trust. This restoration is necessary for dealing with the present-day loss because the intensity of your loss as an adult is fueled by the unresolved emotions you experienced as a child.

In the previous section, you dealt with the immediate feelings of loss—those related directly to recent losses experienced in your life as an adult. In this next section, you begin to dig deeper into those unresolved issues from your past—those issues which fuel your current response to life in ways you can only now begin to recognize and resolve.

Keep in mind what the Inner Child is grieving is the original loss of safety. If there were an actual loss, such as the death of a parent, or the trauma of a divorce, these situations would need to be targeted more specifically. But for now, you are just working with the residue of the loss of safety that is most likely getting triggered any time there is an experience in your current life that feels unsafe. For a deeper healing that is more age-specific, I recommend you obtain a copy of *The Inner Child Workbook*. Each developmental stage includes a section with instructions on how to help that particular Inner Child grieve. It can most easily be purchased through Amazon.com.

STAGE ONE—DENIAL, PANIC AND ANXIETY "THE INITIAL AND CURRENT RESPONSE TO THE LOSS"

To reiterate, because we were too young to endure the panic and survive, we went into shock and experienced a numbing denial of the truth. Our body stored this pain in our electrical circuitry, and we developed what is called *Chronic Post Traumatic Stress Disorder.* Some of us dissociated and went into that dark hole previously referenced. Our emotional system simply shut down.

If, as an adult, you experience a lack of "affect", or it seems as though emotional expressiveness is missing, it is a sign that your Inner Child split off because he or she could not endure the pain. Sandra Ingerman's book, Soul *Retrieval,* refers to this as "Soul Loss." Her book covers this subject in much more detail than I am prepared to address in this material, but Soul *Retrieval* is certainly a worthwhile read and can also be purchased through amazon.com.

These next two exercises will assist you in identifying the possible Soul loss your Inner Child experienced that is now resurfacing in response to your current loss.

Exercise: Ponder your current loss. When you bring focus to the feelings, you are now revisiting try to recall the first remembered experience when you felt a similar set of emotions. Follow the thread of your emotions. Let that tension escort you back to that first remembered experience. Don't force it, just trust whatever thoughts or images emerge. This will give you an idea of the essential wound that may have been triggered. Then record your thoughts in your journal.

Exercise: Now take this experience one step further. When you experienced or re-experienced, this loss, and you did, or perhaps do not, have the mechanisms to cope, the energy is diverted. Think for a moment how you may have diverted your attention from this set of feelings related to your current loss.

Usually, we react with some excessive behavior. In fact, it is most likely in this arena your addictive behaviors emerged. So, think for a moment, how you cut off from the feelings with which you could not cope. Did you ignore them? Did you compulsively or addictively act out? Take a moment to make a list of the ways you acted out (and perhaps still do) to keep yourself from feeling the panic or discomfort of your loss. In other words, write down ways you have kept or keep yourself in denial! Record any thoughts you might have on this list in your journal.

Exercise: Take a plain piece of paper. Draw a great big garbage bag in the center of the page. It can be something as simple as what's featured here. Now write in the center of that garbage bag all the thoughts, feelings, and events, associated with your anxiety, denial, and panic. Include everything from your perspective, as well as from your Inner Child's perspective, that you want to tap on and ultimately release. Once done, have this garbage bag sitting in front of you. As you tap, know that your psyche is neutralizing everything you have put in that bag. The procedure is called, "bundling the baggage." It was developed by EFT Master Lindsay Kinney and is very effective in the processing of feelings associated with one subject. Everything that is written down and symbolically placed in the bag is neutralized by your psyche as you tap on the respective points of release.

A Note on Tapping for the Inner Child—The tapping process I will be facilitating for each stage of your Inner Child's grief uses the same three setup phrases to identify the unresolved feelings that would inhibit your Inner Child's ability to grieve. Creating an affirmation for the acceptance of the way in which your Inner Child coped is one of the first steps in winning the trust of your Inner Child. It is acknowledging the Inner Child's response to his or her situation while neutralizing any judgment you, as the adult, might have about the manner in which you, as a child, coped. This acceptance establishes the platform to begin to heal. For example, an Inner Child setup would look like this: "Even though as a child I was unable to cope and withdrew, I love myself and this little one fully and completely. I know this was the best she could do." The setup phrase states the obvious but does so in a way that accepts the Inner Child did the best job she or he could.

The sequences are then again divided into two, progressive sections. You first neutralize the negative thoughts and feelings your Inner Child had at the time of the loss. Sometimes you are speaking to the Inner Child, in which case you will be using the pronoun, "you." And sometimes, when using the pronoun, "I", you are giving your Inner Child a voice. I suggest you stay with each series of the sequences until you feel an energetic shift that signifies your Inner

Child is ready to move to the next round. However, be patient. Often this is the first time your Inner Child has been able to speak his or her true feelings about the trauma and fear experienced in childhood.

Also, though it is important to give your little one the room to vent, it is equally important to do so while you are tapping. Remember, tapping sends the electrical impulse through your body to untie the knot of tension experienced when you target these unresolved feelings. It is the tapping itself that ensures the feelings are being neutralized. To vent with no recourse for dissolution can lead to your ruminating and feeling retriggered all over again with no reprieve or resolve.

The second set of sequences introduces the possibility of change. This shift in the focus of the tapping softens the psyche and invites your Inner Child to consider the possibility that it is safe to trust the Inner Adult. This is a new concept for your Inner Child. He or she is not used to feeling accepted and allowed to speak. The last statements of tapping should leave you feeling strong and energized. They should reflect the shift in your Inner Child from fear to trust. Use the statements I have provided as an example but definitely customize your own sequences as well. Only you know exactly what needs to be targeted with respect to your childhood experience. Once this shift is accomplished, the two of you will be ready to progressively proceed through each of the respective stages of grief.

Tapping for your Inner Child's Anxiety

Now allow the feelings and thoughts you dislodged in the first part of this discussion to be infused with the words I have provided as you continuously tap on your karate endpoint stating each of the following setup statements at least three times:

Even though I felt anxious in this situation–and as a child I know I have felt this anxiety before–I can feel it in the pit of my stomach, the back of my neck, or in the stress, I hold in my shoulders, I love myself fully and completely.

Even though this has triggered many memories of previous losses, I now choose to work with this fear, release it from my body, so I can begin to resolve this residual grief of my Inner Child.

Even though I am experiencing great anxiety about this situation, I choose to believe I am in the arms of my Higher Power and, with that support, I choose, as the Adult Self, to begin to help my Inner Child express and release his or her fear.

Neutralizing the Negative for your Inner Child …

(Start out speaking as the adult…)

row: Really feel anxious … feel it in my stomach, shoulders, or neck.

Side of the Eye: He/she believes the loss cannot be survived…

Under the Eye: Really frightened regarding this loss …

Upper Lip: Afraid he or she won't survive …

(Now switch to the voice of the Inner Child …)

Under the Lip: What if "I" don't survive …

Collarbone: So frightened I won't survive …

Under the Arm: Just want this fear to go away …

Rib: So afraid I won't survive … I'm too young to feel this afraid.

Wrist: Will it ever go away?

Head: This anxiety has been with me for so long…

Moving from the Possibility of Change to Conviction …

Eyebrow: Maybe if I bury myself in the arms of my Adult Self …

Side of the Eye: Maybe I can let go and feel safe …

Under the Eye: Please help me fill this emptiness …

Upper lip: Help me move beyond this gut-wrenching loss and fear …

Under the Lip: Just want to feel safe …

Collarbone: Maybe with help, I can survive …

Wrist: I want to connect with my Adult Self and then let this fear go.

Rib: I want to trust my Adult Self …

Head: I am hoping he or she is trustworthy enough to help me survive.

Keep tapping until you really feel the energetic shift of releasing and letting go. Customize your own reminder phrases so you can address the unique way your Inner Child may be experiencing this stage of grief.

STAGE TWO—THE INNER CHILD'S BARGAIN "MAKING DEALS TO MANAGE THE LOSS WHICH WAS MITIGATED BY YOUR CO-DEPENDENT BARGAIN™

Again, the co-dependent bargain™ is the contract we made as a child with a parental figure, or with God, in which we agreed to do something in hopes of being lovable enough to warrant their willingness to keep us safe. The problem is that the other party was either unaware of this agreement or unable or unwilling to live up to this agreement. Consequently, we ended up feeling betrayed and full of rage when confronted with the fact that our bargain was not kept.

As adults, we integrate the shame of this failure into our self–talk, and it becomes the basis of our internal critic and our projected, judgmental self. The culprit who perpetuates this self-talk and protects us with mal-adaptive coping mechanisms is what I referred to previously as our *cherished saboteur*™.

Exercise: Lets now work with the Co-dependent bargain™.

This bargain was directed to the parent you were hoping would protect–the parent with whom, as a child, you were compromising and bargaining with in hopes of winning the approval needed to feel safe. Fill in the blanks according to what feels right.

Example: Mommy, I will be a good little girl, and do everything you ask, if only you will love me enough to stop hitting me so I can feel safe. Customize it to your Inner Child's experience and reality.

Your co-dependent bargain™, (*the parent with whom you are making the bargain*) I will _____ (*the agreement you tried to make–i.e.e, "I will be perfect; I will be good"*) if only you will (*what we hoped to get in return*) "keep me safe, you will love and protect me."* _____.

Write your co-dependent bargain ™ out:

_____

_____

Now bundle the baggage of all of your attempts to manage the situation over which you had no control... write in the center of that garbage bag all the thoughts, feelings, and events, associated with your attempts to bargain with your loss of safety as a child, the ways in which you compromised yourself in hopes of returning  *to a state of safety and peace. Include everything you can recall from your Inner Child's perspective, that you want to tap on and ultimately release.*

Tapping for the Bargaining Stage

Tap on your karate point while stating the phrases below. Customize these to fit your needs.

Even though I tried but failed to control, fix, or change, this situation (imagine it in your mind's eye), I love myself fully and completely.

Even though I tried very hard to change this situation I was just a little kid. But it is so nice to feel that my Adult Self loves me anyway. There really wasn't anything I could do.

So even though I did try so very, very hard, I now realize it was not my place to alter this situation. I was too young. It is so comforting to now know that my Adult Self loves me enough to detach and accept the outcome of what it was.

(Please Note: If, as the adult, this does not resonate, return to the tapping sequences to clear yourself of the distraction and unwillingness to be present for the healing of your Inner Child. If you are still carrying judgment about how you, as a child, handled this situation then this needs to be neutralized with your tapping before you can be an effective agent of change for this fragile one within you.)

Next, use the following examples to begin your neutralization process. Add your own phrases accordingly, but continue to tap around the endpoints saying your reminder phrase until you have neutralized the negative, introduced the possibility of change, and feel conviction with respect to your new stance.

Neutralizing the Negative for your Inner Child

Eyebrow: Really tried so very hard …

Side of the Eye: Am exhausted with my attempts …

Under the Eye: Just want to let it go …

Upper Lip: But fight this need to control and fix …

Under the Lip: It is so in my nature to jump in …

Collarbone: Wish I could just let go …

Under the Arm: But this need to do something took over …

Rib: And I just didn't seem to be able to let it go …

Wrist: Hard to give up the hope …

Head: Wish I could have relaxed and let it go …

Moving from the Possibility of Change to the Inner Child's Conviction …

Eyebrow: Maybe I can now begin to try something new …

Side of the Eye: Maybe I can turn to my Adult Self instead of feeling so scared.

Under the Eye: Maybe what I can change is the way I respond …

Upper Lip: Maybe I don't always have to be the one …

Under the Lip: Maybe my Adult Self can be in charge …

Collarbone: Maybe my Adult Self can help me move through the need to respond …

Under the Arm: I can give up control …

Rib: I can tolerate this panic and let it go …

Wrist: I really want to respond in a new way …

Head: I feel strong and secure in my ability to trust and to let go!

Keep tapping until you really feel the energetic shift of releasing and letting go. Customize your own reminder phrases so you can address the unique way you may experience this stage of grief.

Exercise: Designing a Nurturing Statement—To heal this bargain your Adult Self needs to design a nurturing statement that counters the compromise–a loving statement his compromising, wounded one needs to hear in order to give up the bargain. Design that statement now.

An example of Adult Self speaking to an Inner Child – "*Honey, you do not have to do anything other than be yourself. I love you and promise not to ever hurt you. You are safe with me, and deserve all the love and protection I can, and am willing to give.*"

Now come up with your own statement that fits your unique co-dependent bargain™. Record it in your journal.

Once you have your statement, tap on the endpoints as you imagine saying this statement to your Inner Child. Keep saying it over and over until you feel a connection has been made. Let the healing of these words really sink into the Inner Child's awareness. State it slowly and with heart. You are anchoring this new belief system into the Inner Child's experience. The tapping neutralizes your Inner Child's doubt and fear while progressively reinforcing his or her willingness to believe and trust.

Exercise—Revising the Belief System

This exercise overrides the old belief system housed in the codependent bargain and replaces it with a new way of thinking based on the trust that has been restored to you and your Inner Child. In essence, this proclamation is what the Adult Self can now say to the Inner Child that is believable once this bargain has been dissolved and trust has been restored.

Read each proclamation separately while repeatedly tapping on the endpoints. Read it first from the Adult Self to your Inner Child, and then, as your Inner Child, to your Adult Self. Customize the words if it feels right to do so.

Proclamation for the Adult Self: I, _____, (state your name) AM WORTHY OF YOUR TRUST. YOU ARE A CHILD OF THE UNIVERSE AND DESERVE TO BE PROTECTED AT ALL TIMES. IT IS MY JOB AND MY HONOR TO LOVE YOU AND TO KEEP YOU SAFE. AND I PROMISE THAT IF I AM NOT PERFECT, AND IF THERE ARE MOMENTS WHEN I FLOUNDER AND DO NOT FOLLOW THROUGH, I WILL HOLD MYSELF ACCOUNTABLE. I WILL ASSURE YOU IT WAS NOT YOUR FAULT, AND TOGETHER, WE WILL COME BACK INTO THE LIGHT WHERE WE CAN HEAL.

Proclamation for the Inner Child: I, _____, (state your name) AM WORTHY OF YOUR LOVE. I AM A TRUE CHILD OF THE UNIVERSE. I CAN TRUST YOU, MY ADULT SELF. I NOW BELIEVE I DESERVE TO BE PROTECTED AT ALL TIMES, AND I TRUST THAT YOU WILL KEEP ME SAFE. I UNDERSTAND THERE MAY BE TIMES WHEN THIS IS NOT THE CASE, BUT I BELIEVE YOU WHEN YOU SAY THAT YOU WILL NOT ABANDON ME. YOU WILL NOT BLAME ME. INSTEAD, YOU WILL ACKNOWLEDGE YOUR MISTAKE AND TELL ME YOU ARE SORRY SO THAT TOGETHER WE CAN HEAL AND TRUST.

It is this kind of dialogue you and your Inner Child need to have to enable the two of you to deal with the more intimidating feelings of anger and rage.

STAGE THREE—ANGER "THE UNSPOKEN TRUTH"

Anger seeped into our Inner Child's experience when the denial and bargaining no longer worked. It was anger at the loss, agitation at the loss. But for most that anger could not be expressed. It had to be camouflaged or repressed and ultimately became the source of our negative self-image. As you read in the overview of the development of the Inner Child's pain, it is easier to collapse into shame and believes there is something wrong with us then to hold the anger at our parents for not being strong enough to love us in the way we deserved. Making it our fault gives us the false impression that there is something we can do to impact a situation about which we feel totally helpless.

If we were not muted and silenced then the anger was most likely discharged through more overt behaviors such as hyperactivity, or the development of Attention Deficient Disorders. Those behaviors let off steam, but the underlying feelings are never addressed. Few children are ever truly able to embrace the full essence of their anger. Even as adults many of us continue to be afraid of our own anger and mute its expression.

Instead, we continue with our truth remaining unspoken. But the truth was that we did suffer a loss. And if we are ever to feel safe again that little part of us needs to acknowledge the truth of that loss, the gut-wrenching truth that he or she did not feel safe or protected.

Much of the anger you experience in your inner work is anger fueled by memories of loss experienced before you had the knowledge and tools to cope with it. The emotion was an instinctive response to feeling unsafe. What went unexpressed got lodged in the tissues of your body. And it remains there as an energy block (or, as Gary Craig, founder of EFT calls it, an energetic disturbance) until it can be physically released.

The thought of releasing anger is frightening for most people. The fear is that the anger will be endless. The fear is that if we take the cap off of our latent anger, we will not cope. But anger can be released, and it can be released in a constructive and beneficial way. To ensure this occurs I always recommend you begin your anger work with the same simple exercise you did when working with the anger of your present-day self.

Exercise: Creating Protection—To create the safety you and your Inner Child deserve, begin by closing your eyes and imagining that you are surrounded by a bubble of Light. Set the intention with the universe that your anger be encased in this Light. Ask that your anger is transmuted with a violet flame. And finally, request that the energy of your anger be sent directly into the Great Central Sun to be transformed. This practice will seal your anger so that its energy does not bleed out into other areas.

When we truly trace the threads of our anger we most often discover that the anger comes back to our being angry at ourselves for not saying no. We may even feel anger related to regrets about which we now feel shame. This anger is toxic–to us, and to all those around us.

However, when we responsibly express our anger we soon come to understand that the unresolved anger emerging is the residue from the grief of the past. The child within us did not have the option to deal with the emotions in any other way. We begin to realize that it is this level of unrest from the unexpressed anger of our Inner Child that keeps us from resolving our grief and moving into another form of a relationship with our current losses. But now that the anger has been identified it can be released and resolved.

The first step to flushing out the anger is to weed out all of the negating statements that block this anger from being realized. The following exercise will help you do this.

Exercise: Anger Exercise—Using your dominant hand, write in the first column, "I am angry." In column two, using your least dominant hand, write your immediate response. *See the example below.* The experience of going back and forth with these statements dislodges the self-talk that originated from your Inner Child's old belief systems. It also flushes out the responses that perhaps you as an adult have adopted as a way to continue the denial of these feelings.

The purpose of this exercise is to continue writing in the columns until you can righteously own the anger of your Inner Child. Your Inner Child most likely had a right to be angry. If you own it, when you do your tapping, the energy of that anger will be sufficiently stimulated in the electrical circuitry of your body so it can be neutralized. Try to continue until you can write, I am Angry," in both columns with no resistance.

Example:

1. I am angry.   1. But they did the best they could.

2. I am angry.   2. But it's not her fault she died.

3.

4.

5.

6.

7.

8.

9.

10. "I AM ANGRY!   10. "I AM ANGRY!"

Once done, bundle the baggage of your anger. I usually just draw the bag over the columns as a way of throwing them in one big bag. Then have your list in front of you when you do this round of tapping. Your psyche will automatically neutralize the anger on all levels available. You will also be able to use what you have written as your reminder phrases. You can do the few rounds I have provided, but then please tap using your own words. It will make your experience much richer.

Tapping for your Inner Child's Anger

Begin by tapping on the karate point for the setup statements. Then continue by tapping on each of the endpoints.

Even though I feel rage (anger, revenge, etc.) that I was left alone and felt so afraid, I want to finally feel safe and protected by my Adult Self; I want to trust that I can express these feelings and still be loved.

Even though I later felt righteous as an adolescent and my anger did enable me to survive, I know that anger was an expression of my hurt. I know it was triggered by this current loss, but it reminded me so much of when I had no power and felt so alone. But I'm not alone now. I want to trust enough to say what I felt–safe enough to speak my truth.

So even though I felt anger inside, I did not dare to express it. I feared retaliation. I was powerless and at risk. But that was then–not now. Now, I want to neutralize those feelings. I want to trust my Adult Self to keep me safe while I finally speak my truth. I want to let go of this pain and be able to trust enough to feel joy. I feared retaliation, but that was then and this is now.

Neutralizing the Negative

Eyebrow: All of this rage …

Side of the Eye: … this anger and rage …

Under the Eye: … really uncomfortable with these feelings of anger.

Upper Lip: But felt so abandoned and alone, so violated and betrayed.

Under the Lip: It felt unsafe and wrong to feel this much rage.

Collarbone: It was not okay to feel such anger.

Under the Arm: So I stuffed my feelings and pushed them back down… …

Rib: Even though it is so uncomfortable …

Wrist: … it won't go away …

Head: All of this anger… can't silence that voice… it's too late … no matter how afraid I feel.

Moving from the Possibility of Change to Conviction …

Eyebrow: So maybe I can give myself permission to speak my truth.

Side of the Eye: I want to find my courage …

Under the Eye: … to speak my truth while I tap with my adult …

Upper Lip: It sure has not worked to push it down …

Under the Lip: I need to figure out a new way …

Collarbone: Perhaps if I tap while I vent …

Under the Arm: I will finally be able to speak my truth … with the protection of my Adult Self…

Rib: Somewhere in time, this truth needs to be stated and heard.

Wrist: If not now, when?

Head: If not with my Adult Self, then who else can I trust, where else can I turn?

The Inner Child finally speaks his or her truth!

Eyebrow: I am angry!!!!

Side of the Eye: I didn't deserve what I got.

Under the Eye: I deserved to feel loved.

Under the Lip: I deserved to feel safe.

Collarbone: It was them not me!

Under the Arm: I am no longer willing to take the blame …

Rib: …to feel shame about the person I am!

Wrist: I am lovable! I did not deserve what I got…

Head: I can finally say that out loud and feel confident my words will be heard. I can trust and will still be loved!

Again, customize these statements and keep tapping on the endpoints until the anger is released and the Inner Child finally feels he or she has been heard and is still loved. Only then can the two of you, Inner Child and Adult Self, be free to move into the emptiness of the loss and, once and for all, acknowledge the void so it can be filled with love and light.

However, if there is still an edge to your anger, the following exercises will serve to rid your body of the energy. Some of these exercises are aimed at dislodging the Inner Child's anger. Some are simply to move the energy out of your body so you can let it go.

Additional Methods to Release Anger

I am again including these following methods to deal with the anger of your Inner Child. Remember to always begin with the first one. Sealing your anger before you release it is just the responsible thing to do. Otherwise, the disruptive energy spews out into the universe and coagulates with another vibrational rage as well. This is why some are reluctant to express the anger–they don't want to put that energy out into the world. But if you take responsibility for working with it in a transformative way this does not happen. It is just energy that is recycled and transmuted for another higher use. So again, I recommend you always begin with creating protection around you and the release of your anger.

1. Creating Protection—first so that you and your Inner Child can always feel safe close, your eyes and imagine that you surround yourself with that bubble light. Sometimes I call in an Angel or a Master or Loved One to assist. Then, ask that your anger is being encased in this Light and that as you express it the anger be transmuted in violet flame then be sent directly to the great central sun to be transformed. This will seal your anger so that its energy does not bleed out into other areas. When you feel complete and secure proceed with any or all of the following exercises.

2. The Silent Scream—aka—Whisper Yelling—to do this you can take a pillow and simply scream into it. Scream by opening your mouth but blocking the volume from coming out. It releases the frustration without alarming anyone around you.

3. The Private Scream—if you really need to release the volume of your anger then this method is an option. Scream in a car or in the woods where you will not be heard.

4. Throwing a tantrum—This is a wonderful exercise or activity that enables you to jump up and down, flailing your arms around and making grunting noises, or yelling "No," to what you are releasing and then ultimately yelling "Yes," to what you are want to attract. This resets the central nervous system immediately. Animals do this naturally when they have been stressed by a life-threatening experience. In fact, TRE© is founded on this principle so it definitely works.

5. Exercising—this releases the energy and makes it more manageable.

(Note: aerobic exercise, such as jogging, etc., reduces current anger, anaerobic exercise, such as yoga, swimming, etc. reaches anger that is more deeply rooted in the muscular fibers.)

6. Meditation—using the breathing techniques you were introduced to in the last section, relax and go into a meditative state. Then invite your Inner Child into your mind's eye and listen to your Inner Child's anger. Allow it; you do not have to change it or fix it. You just have to help him or her discharge it responsibly so it does not bleed into inappropriate acting out in your day-to-day life. This is useful if the tapping did not quite address the depth of your Inner Child's rage. You can tap as you hold this image in your mind's eye as well. That combination augments this method even more.

7. Journal Writing—I recommend when you record your responses in a journal that you use it for stream-of-consciousness writing, recording without censure whatever thoughts and feelings come to mind. By the time you have finished your inner work, you will have a rich collection of the feelings you identified, experienced, resolved, and healed. It will be similar to having a photo album that documents your inner journey.

8. Verbal and Written Dialogues—Dialoguing is a tool that involves talking to the different parts within you; orchestrating an interaction so that a healing can occur. It can be done verbally, when you are actually stating the feelings of the different parts involved in the exercise, or it can be done by writing the responses of each character. When you are dialoguing between the Adult Self and a younger Inner Child, again, I suggest you use your least-dominant hand to write your Inner Child's responses. It was difficult, as a child, to master the skill of writing. Sentences were shorter, words more direct. By using your least-dominant hand, you will find that this experience is recreated. The more mature response of the Adult Self is experienced by using the hand you are most

accustomed to using. This is true when you are dialoguing with the Inner Child about his or her anger. Ask questions.

9. Drawing—Drawing your pain unleashing your Inner Child's your creativity and lets you give form to the feelings and the different internal characters without using words. Describing the voice of the critical self with words can be limiting; drawing often gives you a richer symbolic means of expression.

10. Mirror Work—Mirror work involves sitting in front of a mirror and having a dialogue with your younger selves in order to observe the body and facial movements that accompany these parts within. It allows you to see for yourself how your shoulders slump when you speak from your child self, or how you wince when you express your Inner Child's fear. It also helps you see more clearly your physical demeanor from your adult point of view. Looking at yourself in a mirror is also one of the most effective ways of finding that higher, more evolved part of you. By facing yourself eye to eye, you can look beyond your physical deficiencies and see the wise, Inner Being within you.

Once you feel the energetic shift of this younger one within you, and you can sense he or she has let go, you are ready to move on to the next stage.

Stage Four—The Inner Child's Despair "Standing in the Void"

When our Inner Child has finally been allowed to speak the truth, he or she collapses into the arms of the Adult Self in complete exhaustion. The truth has been acknowledged and contained. The despair in childhood was masked by shyness, lethargy, fear to engage, often mistaken for "quietness." But usually, that quietness was a loss of trust and a fear of retaliation if the true self was revealed. To truly embrace the source of our loss at such a young age would have put us at too much risk—the risk of not surviving the fear— the risk of being exposed and punished—the risk of being shamed, blamed or humiliated.

So the despair for the Inner Child is more of an expression of the loneliness and the abandonment he or she felt at having to be so cut off from what was really felt. It was in response to the loss of the real self. As you saw in the overview of childhood grief, this stage of grief touches the loss of the real self, the angst felt in having to compromise the person we were in order to strive for the safety we needed to survive. The antidote for this despair is for you as the Adult Self to assure the Inner Child that you have indeed evolved to a place where this is no longer true. It is welcoming the Inner Child back to his or her true essence, accepting him or her for the unique individual he or she truly is. It is done by validating the Inner Child's truth as was done in stage three and now allowing the Inner Child to tolerate the loss of your support.

Exercise: Experiencing and Releasing Despair

1. Write a letter to the younger parts of you who have had to let go. Welcome them into your force field, into a relationship with your Higher Guidance and the part of you who can tolerate this loss. This letter serves as a way to gather those parts of you that had to be sacrificed and banished in order for the Inner Child to survive. Acknowledging them by assuring their feelings will be heard, their needs met, makes this release more complete.

2. Take another piece of paper, write a second letter and let the Inner Child speak. Use your least-dominant hand so the true feelings of the younger self can bypass the conscious mind and be spoken with honesty and truth.

Now write down all of your words, phrases, and pictures that capture the despair of your Inner Child. Let him or her draw the sadness, the emptiness, then throw all that you want to neutralize into your bag and bundle the despair so you can help your Inner Child heal.

Tapping for your Inner Child's Despair

Begin by tapping on the karate point for the setup statements. Then continue by tapping on each of the endpoints.

Even though I felt so much sadness, despair, and hopelessness back then I know it is now safe to let it go.

Even though this sadness has felt as though it were more than I can bear, it feels so good to finally acknowledge the truth, to be honest with my Adult Self, so together we can begin to heal.

So even though this truth has been buried for a very long time, it feels so relieving to lance this wound, to trust my Adult Self enough to open that door so ultimately we can begin to heal.

Continue with tapping around on the endpoints saying your reminder phrases until your feelings are neutralized and you can experience the courage to let go.

Neutralizing the Negative

Eyebrow: So much sadness …

Side of the Eye: Have tried to run from it but failed …

Under the Eye: Not sure how to feel …

Upper Lip: I have been cut off from this truth for so long …

Under the Lip: The sadness, the despair, the emptiness, is so big …

Collarbone: Never thought I would be able to move beyond it and really heal?

Under the Arm: Thought I was so alone like I would not survive?

Rib: It was so hard to tolerate that much emptiness … No wonder I did not feel safe.

Wrist: That loneliness is almost more than I can bear.

Head: Can hardly believe I survived.

Moving from the Possibility of Change to Conviction …

Eyebrow: But I am not alone, not like before.

Side of the Eye: I do have a support system …

Under the Eye: I am getting stronger. I do trust my Adult Self and know he or she can help me let go.

Upper Lip: I want to trust all of the resources he or she has gathered along the way.

Under the Lip: My Adult Self has done a lot of work since then …

Collarbone: … there's a lot to offer that can help me heal.

Under the Arm: Together we can neutralize the pain. I can feel safe enough to stand in the pain … I will not be standing alone.

Rib: We have come a very long way on this journey…

Wrist: I am not alone … This is now, not then. I can release and let go.

Head: It truly is time to let go, to let God handle this so that we can heal.

EXERCISE: THE INNER CHILD'S TRUTH ABOUT THE DESPAIR!

1. Go into a meditation and invite your Inner Child to write his or her pain of the void. Do so with your least-dominant hand so the true essence of that younger self can emerge.

2. Then picture yourself as the adult holding the Inner Child in your arms or having your Inner Child sit near you enough to feel safe. Quiet yourself and be present enough to support this vulnerable one's admission of how alone he or she really felt.

3. Tap on your endpoints while you are listening. If that is too cumbersome invite your Inner Child to write down the truth of the despair then imagine he or she reads it as you tap and neutralize the deeper levels of the pain.

Keep tapping until you really feel the energetic shift of releasing and letting go. Customize your own reminder phrases so you can address the unique way you may experience this stage of grief.

STAGE FIVE—ACCEPTANCE AND RESOLUTION "LETTING GO AND MOVING ON"

Acceptance and resolution of our loss mean we have processed the first four stages of grief. We have addressed the residue of our essential wound–this loss triggered in our Inner Child–loss felt when, as a child, we felt powerless and feared we would not survive. All of that grief has now been addressed and resolved.

The following tapping sequence will anchor this new reality into your force field and that force field of your Inner Child as well. This tapping meditation that follows is a wonderful way to wrap up the final stage of grief. With your Inner Child in your arms, you can now proceed on the journey of exploring the different realms of consciousness that enable you to pierce the veil between your physical world and the world of the unseen. But perhaps more importantly, you are now equipped to live your life with feelings, non-addictively, with the confidence that there is nothing with which you cannot cope. Your trust in self is an asset, that not only benefits you, but benefits all those in the world, and actually humanity itself.

Tapping for Acceptance and Resolution

Begin by tapping on the karate point for the setup statements. Then continue by tapping on each of the endpoints. This will anchor in this positive affirmation. Again, keep doing tapping rounds until you feel the "buzz." Hold the energy of this affirmation for 17 seconds as it takes form; then for another 68 seconds so the DNA can begin to replicate this new picture and attract its vibrational match.

Even though my Inner Child's grief got triggered in response to my recent loss, and he or she held this memory of not being safe, we have been reunited in trust and love. It IS safe to release all cellular memory of our grief, both present and past alike. We CAN now rewrite that cellular memory. With confidence, we know that we are loved by our Higher Source (God, Higher Power, etc.) enough to feel safe and to recommit.

So even though it has taken us a while to make peace, I am so grateful we navigated through this grief. I have finally found my way home, have reunited with my Inner Child, and am now ready to live a life beyond fear knowing I will be able to cope.

So even though this has been a long time coming, we have finally healed enough to allow ourselves to expand and attract.

Continue with tapping around the endpoints saying your reminder phrases until you feel flat or neutral.

Neutralizing the Residue of the Negative

Eyebrow: This has taken a very long time.

Side of the Eye: Sometimes it felt as though I would never find the strength!

Under the Eye: So many months for me …

Upper Lip: And years of my Inner Child!

Under the Lip: Wish I could have healed before… and not wasted so much time.

Collarbone: I wish we could have embarked on this journey before.

Under the Arm: Really wish I could have found peace at an earlier time.

Rib: … But I can now envision another level of this situation…

Wrist: And the truth is I needed the current loss to flush out the old wounds…

Head: … and that wounded one that really needed to be healed.

Moving from the Possibility of Change to Conviction ...

Eyebrow: I really could not know what I did not know ...

Side of the Eye: Each stage of grief was valid in its own way ...

Under the Eye: I would not have had the compassion any earlier ...

Upper Lip: and without compassion, I could not have healed my Inner Child.

Under the Lip: I want to focus on the fact that the time has finally come ...

Collarbone: I could not know what I did not know ...

Under the Arm: I did the best I could with the resources I had at the time.

Rib: I am just glad the time has finally arrived ...

Rib: We are now united, and the healing is done.

Wrist: My Inner Child and I are finally ready to move on.

Head: We are united, have let go, and I can now expand.

The last task of grieving involves forgiveness. What are you forgiving? Everything! You are ceremonialzing your forgiveness of your loved one for leaving you. Your Inner Child forgives you for taking so long to rescue him or her. Perhaps your Inner Child even forgives those who wronged him or her. And you forgive your higher guidance, understanding you were not a victim of this loss. And last but not least, you are asking your body to forgive you for its having to bear the brunt of your unresolved feelings and stress until you were truly ready to do for yourself what your body had been doing for you all these years.

The Hawaiian Forgiveness Ritual was given to me by a Hawaiian Elder named Josie. It is but one way to orchestrate a formal forgiveness. The shorter version is more popular and is included below. But I like to use this longer version when I am sealing a piece of work around grief. I use the shorter version for dissolving stress at the moment. Please feel free to use or create your own as well.

Exercise: Hawaiian Forgiveness Ritual—Ho'oponopono

Simply put, Ho'oponopono is based on the knowledge that anything that happens to you or that you perceive—the entire world where you live—is your own creation and thus, it is entirely your responsibility–a hundred percent, no exceptions. Your boss is a tyrant—it's your responsibility. Your children are not good students—it's your responsibility.

There are wars and you are feeling bad because you are a good person, a pacifist? The war is your responsibility. You see that children around the world are hungry and malnourished, if not starving? Their want is your responsibility. There are no exceptions. The world is your world. It is your creation. As Dr. Hew Len points out- "Didn't you notice that whenever you experience a problem, you are there?"

"It's your responsibility" doesn't mean "it's your fault." it means that you are responsible for healing yourself to heal whatever or whoever it is that appears to you as a problem.

It might sound crazy or just plain metaphorical, that the world is your creation. But if you look carefully, you will realize that whatever you call the world and perceive as the world is your world, it is the projection of your own mind. If you go to a party you can see how in the same place, with the same light, the same people, the same food, drink, music, and atmosphere, some will enjoy themselves while others will be bored. Some will be over-enthusiastic and some depressed, some will be talkative, and others will be silent. The "out there" for every one of them seems the same, but if one was to connect their brains to machines immediately, it would show how different areas of the brain would come alive, how different the perceptions there are from one person to the next. So even if they apparently share it, the "out there" is not the same for them, let alone their inner world, their emotions.

How do you heal yourself with Ho'oponopono? Three steps: by recognizing that whatever comes to you is your creation, the outcome of bad memories buried in your mind; by regretting whatever errors of the body, speech, and mind, caused those bad memories; and by requesting Divine Intelligence within yourself to release those memories, to set you free. Then, of course, you say Thank You. So what does that all really mean? It means that what you heal is your response to any of the issues in your world about which you have strong feelings. Dr. Hew Len healed a whole psych ward just by simply holding the files of the patients in his hands and saying the prayer on *his reactions* to their histories. His disgust or fear regarding their circumstances is what he asked to be released. And it worked. It took him four years but he healed every patient and the entire ward was closed! So I invite you to work with it in the same way. Heal your reactions to the world and you heal the world! Heal your reactions to loved ones and you heal your loved ones.

You do so by reciting the prayer. Below is the long version … I recite this while tapping on the endpoints. It augments the clearing and neutralizes anything I might be holding on to in the unconscious.

FORGIVE ME _____

    If I have hurt you

     In any way, shape or form,

    In thought, word or deed,

At any time, any place,

    Past, present or future

FORGIVE ME.

AND I, _____ FORGIVE YOU

    For hurting me

In any way, shape or form,

In thought, word or deed,

At any time, any place,

    Past, present or future

I FORGIVE YOU!

AND MAY THE CREATOR OF ALL THINGS FORGIVE US BOTH: ALL HO'OPONOPONO

IT IS DONE... SO BE IT!

This prayer can be said between you and another, between you and your body, between you and your Inner Child, between your Spirit and your Personality. It can be said to the one you have lost as a way to resolving their passing and a way to release the attachment so you both can move on.

The shorter, more popular version is simply:
I'm Sorry…Please Forgive Me
I love you…Thank You.

I repeat this over and over while tapping on my endpoints. Another one-liner I use to reduce the stress and anxiety before it even gets to stages two, three and four, is, **"'God' love resolves this situation, (these feelings of loss) here and now."** Again, I say that repeatedly as I tap on the endpoints until the gut-wrenching feelings of loss subside.

The losses of your life have been acknowledged, processed, and released. The residual grief triggered in your childhood has been addressed. You have learned how to relate to your fragile one in a new and more profound way. Being able to embrace those parts within you that feel more vulnerable ensures that you will be able to respond to your fears instead of collapsing into, and reacting to, them.

LAYER FIVE:
The Integration and Merger
(Click on the heading to be taken to the YouTube Overviews of each of these Layers)

OVERVIEW OF LAYER FIVE—Integration Of And Merger With The Inner Child And Soul

This Layer is perhaps one of the most empowering Layers. As mentioned before, the following process is used only for the integration of an Inner Child. For an aspect of your Soul, you will be given the exercises to just send it back into the Light in order to free that suspended energy. But with an aspect of your personality, from this lifetime (the Inner Child), you want to partner with him/her and build a bonding, cooperative, relationship.

With this set of interactive tapping™ sequences, you really begin to feel the rewards of your hard work. You have the opportunity to see exactly what has been severed within you as you and your Inner Child begin to merge and become one. As mentioned above, the following process is used only for the integration of an Inner Child. Obviously, I cannot say this enough. But rest assured, if you have uncovered a pattern which involves a Soul task, you will be instructed on how to send that essence back into the Light so that energy can be freed as well.

For this Layer, you will be using the pronoun "we" because you are stating the sequences as if the Inner Child and the Adult Self are saying them in unison. Combining the neutralization process with the pronoun, "we," enables you to begin to set up the merger and integration. Partnering with the Inner Child in this manner empowers him or her to return to your force field in a healed state. It empowers you and your Inner Child to reclaim the magic that was lost in the wounding experience. When you bring this magic back, the essence of the believability and trust we all have as children returns as well. If you then infuse your desires to allow and attract with this vibration, you experience magic ten-fold! The result will mirror this very relationship you have taken the time to heal.

Again, you can listen to this suggested tapping sequence to give you a better idea of how this flows.

EXERCISE: TAPPING SEQUENCE: THE MERGER BETWEEN ADULT AND THE INNER CHILD

When ready to move forward tap on the karate point while stating the setup phrase.

Even though we have both experienced many betrayals and have many reasons to not feel trust—and we have both experienced a lot of tension about not feeling safe, being left feeling unsure we would survive—we are

281

so excited we have found each other again … we love ourselves and each other enough to trust we can manifest all that we want and deserve.

Even though we both have experienced so many disappointments, betrayals, and reasons to not trust, we are so excited we have come together and are now able to feel safe enough with each other so we can heal.

So even though we have so many experiences with abandonment, so many reasons to not trust, we are so excited we have found each other, we have come home to each other and are ready to heal.

These are merely suggestions for the setup phrases. Please feel free to customize them and make them fit your particular situation. The following is further tapping suggestions you could use to augment this goal. It is really not as much of a process of neutralization as an infusion of what you have affirmed. But just to be on the safe side, I have provided one round to help you clear any resistance to come together in this fashion. Add more if you feel it would be useful.

Again, prepare to tap by beginning with the corner of your eyebrow.

Eyebrow: We are so excited to come together and heal.

Side of the Eye: We are just buzzing with enthusiasm and trust for each other.

Under the Eye: So excited we are going to finally manifest our heart's desire.

Upper Lip: Through the love of each other and the love of God, we know we deserve all we desire.

Under the Lip: We are so excited to come together to heal.

Collarbone: So excited we are together to heal … to attract the relationship we deserve.

Under the Arm: We are so full of energy, love, and light … we send this out to the entire world.

Rib: We are so excited we have done such good work.

Head: We are so proud of each other and love each other so much.

Now just keep going with that until you are really, really buzzing with the absolute glee of being reunited. Once your Inner Child feels safe and has been retrieved you can proceed to rescue and heal the aspect of your Soul that has been suspended in time and has been waiting for you to return and escort him or her home.

WORKING WITH A FRAGMENT OF YOUR SOUL

Next, to extend this exploration to the issues of your Soul, I recommend you begin to ponder what the purpose would be for your Soul to chart such pattern. What could it possibly learn from the experience you just resolved with your Inner Child? The thread of experience from childhood which becomes anchored in your behavior in adulthood can chart the map you may need in order to return to the original source of tension.

As was explained in the *Which Lifetime Is This Anyway?* our Soul charts experiences in childhood which vibrate to the same frequency of discomfort as situations from our past lives when we were wounded, violated, or abandoned. When we determine the specific themes we can then begin to ask what the higher purpose of that theme is. We can begin to ask why our Soul would chart such an experience. What was it trying to get you to experience?

The following review of Soul lessons will refresh your memory and assist you further in your exploration.

Soul Issues from Infant Stage—If you responded to the infant issues, then you will most likely be dealing with a lack of attachment or an issue of trust. This particular lesson is embedded in your experience as an infant and your behavior exhibited as an adult. A possible lesson which extends from this developmental stage and this step of mastery is the need to attain and maintain trust in a spiritual source, a power greater than that which your personality knows. The challenge may be to mentally attain and hold a belief system that incorporates unity with a divine power and to then be able to anchor that spiritual energy into your day-to-day activities and endeavors.

Soul Issues from Toddler Stage—A potential lesson which extends from this developmental stage and this step of mastery is the need to experiment with, and to explore, limitations between your earthly and spiritual self. What limits does your physical form have to put on your spiritual being-ness? When have you been wounded with respect to setting limits? When have you suffered, been killed, maimed or harmed for speaking your truth? How well do you deal with the ambivalence of being in the density of your physical form versus the freedom felt in your spiritual existence?

Soul Issues from 3–6 Year Old Stage— A potential lesson which extends from this developmental stage and this step of mastery is learning to express compassion for self and others, learning to be non-judgmental of self and others, confronting and dissolving multi-dimensional shame and guilt, and finding the threads of shame in your Soul's history when you may have turned away from your Source.

Soul Issues from 6–12 Year Old Stage—This time in your life and the issues which emerge in this stage of your pursuit of your mastery give you the opportunity to look at the moments in your Soul's history when you perhaps joined a group that led you away from your Source or perhaps a time when you put your loyalty into a false source. You may be inspired to examine your success at establishing a co-creatorship between our Higher Self and our Human Self from a more reciprocal perspective as you recognize and show appreciation for all you have had to endure in human form. This time in your life and in your program offers you the supreme chance to come to terms with what your soul's intentions were and how, in this human form, you have actualized them.

*Soul Issues from 12– 15-Year-Old Stage—*So what may the potential lesson of your Soul look like? The answer to this would be found in exploring when in the history of the Soul you experienced discomfort in holding the frequency of Light or lacked the self-confidence to appropriately express your creative and sexual passion. There may have been a time in your Soul's past when you began to attain spiritual mastery but felt insecure with your new powers and, therefore, acted without integrity. You may discover a lifetime or Soul situation when you moved into a position of authority before you felt confident enough to hold that energy, leaving you with an uneasiness of having bitten off more than you could chew. The lessons related to this stage of development and which would be reflected in this stage of your program have to do with a discomfort with the newness. You may have completed your event and now, all of a sudden, fear that new expectations will be put upon you from some unknown source. This could relate to a time in your Soul's past when a similar experience occurred. As you work with these issues, keep your mind open to their original source.

Soul Issues from 15– 17-Year-Old Stage—The lessons related to this stage of development, and would be reflected in your pursuit of mastery, have to do with any area of your life where you do not stand in your truth. You may have completed your event and now, all of a sudden, fear that new expectations will be put upon you from some unknown source. This could relate to a time in your Soul's past when a similar experience occurred. As you work with these issues keep your mind open to their original source. Also, invite your Higher Guidance to reveal to you the times in your Soul's history when you have mastered this task and can now draw on that Soul self as a mentor for who you are in your current incarnation.

Soul Issues from 17– 21-Year-Old Stage—So how does this material interface with what your Soul may be here to learn? Know that this is not the first time you have had to practice this transition into mastery. Just like serenity – mastery is not a fixed state – it is a stance in life and in life's situations which you achieve, lose, revise and once again attain. It is living, moment to moment, in the process of grief as you feel the anxiety of impending change; attempt to hold onto the old; use your anger and dissatisfaction to break free; allow yourself the luxury of standing naked in the void and then integrating the new vibration with ease. Each experience in life invites you to integrate more fully the vibration of Joy; the manner in which you chose to do so will vary according to the Layer you are focusing on at that time. Nothing is constant—everything is ever-changing and each new day offers a new opportunity to be who you want and know you can be.

EXERCISE: IDENTIFYING THE LESSON OF YOUR SOUL –

1. If you believe that your Soul charted the course of your life if you believe your Soul chose the experiences you needed to have in order to learn this Soul lesson, then begin to reflect on what your Soul can learn from the experience you had in this situation. How do the issues you discovered in the previous exercise mirror what your Soul may have wanted you to learn? How do you feel about that discovery?

2. Record your thoughts in your journal.

EXERCISE: THREADS TO THE LESSONS OF YOUR SOUL

1. Surround yourself with Light. Next, go into a meditation and notify your guidance that you would like to be shown the threads which lead you back to the original experience which distracts you from attaining mastery in all areas of your life. This sets the intention for your work.

2. Next, begin by reflecting on a recent time in your adult life when these same patterns were evident? When you can recall an incident such as this, record it in your journal.

   Please Note: It is often most helpful to begin by focusing on a current situation, then take the feelings from that situation and follow them back to when you felt this same way in childhood. This provides your Guidance with the vibrational feeling needed to connect you to the images of previous lifetimes when this issue originated. Your emotional responses to situations are the tools needed to connect you from one dimension of time to another. The characters faces may change and the surroundings may be different – but what remains constant and gets passed on from lifetime to lifetime is the emotional experience and the subsequent choices of behavior which then became attached to that experience.

3. Next, as you hold the image of this activity in your mind's eye, imagine that your Guidance escorts you back into your

childhood experience and you metaphorically witness the original situation.

4. Record these findings in your journal.

5. Now, in your mind's eye, return to that image and request that your Guidance uses the threads from this childhood scene to take you back to your Soul memory of this same issue. You may see an actual scene from a past life. You may experience a sensation of your theme. Just trust what your guidance reveals to you and when it feels comfortable, open your eyes and record the sensations, images or feelings that you had.

6. Ponder what this tells you about the lesson your Soul has to learn from the task and challenge of your current life? How does this lesson manifest in your ability to achieve mastery?

7. Having obtained that information, now ask for guidance from the Highest voice within you to assist you in designing a new blueprint which will enable you to achieve mastery in your day-to-day life. Redesign the belief system and the behavior which accompanies that belief system.

8. When you have the new blueprint intact, ask to be returned to the original scene, rescue the wounded Soul self and reassure that aspect of your Soul that you are now able to do what he or she was unable to do. Reassure that part of your Soul that it is now safe to rewrite this blueprint for you have acquired the skills needed to ensure success.

EXERCISE: COMPLETION OF YOUR HEALING

By going through this process you will be reclaiming the aspects of your Soul who split off because they were unable to cope with the circumstances of your life at that time. By taking the clues from your current life and resolving the conflicts which manifest in your specific areas of concern you are acquiring the skills needed to succeed in the very situations you were previously unable to succeed.

Once you have completed this process you will be able to see how the failures and successes in your current life relate back to the wounds you endured in childhood and how the purpose of these wounds originated with a wound in your Soul's past which now needed to be healed. By redesigning your blueprint and acquiring the skills needed to succeed, you are arming yourself with the coping mechanisms and skills needed to assure your Soul part that it is safe to come home and back into the Light.

EXERCISE: RETURNING OF THE SOUL FRAGMENT TO THE LIGHT

1. Go back into meditation. Imagine you are standing in the beam of a magnificent, brilliant Light. Call forth the wounded parts of your personality and your Soul. Welcome them and then ask if they are ready to be returned to the Light. When they agree, imagine that this beam of Light begins to escort your wounded selves back to their original Source. Watch until these wounded selves are out of your vision.

2. In Layer Six we will begin to reprogram your DNA to match the new vibrational frequency which you are now capable of sustaining. Every cell in your body will be recalibrated to hold this new energy. Once done, you will be instructed to fill yourself with the Light and affirm that your faulty blueprint has been eternally changed in all dimensions of time and consciousness and that your etheric blueprint mirrors the same.

Layer Six:
Rewiring The Brain;
Reprogramming The Dna Of The Body And Reconfiguring The Electromagnetic Field
Layer Seven:
Giving Back To The World

Layers Six and Seven—

You and Inner Child have done your work.
You have returned the fragments of your Soul back
to the Light.
You are now ready to complete your healing by:
1. building new neural pathways from your lower
brain to your higher brain;
2. infusing every cell with the higher vibration of
your most Illuminated, Adult Self,
And reconfiguring the electromagnetic field around
you.

Once completed, you are ready to give back to the
world and contribute to the Mandala of Healing
energy that has, and is, surrounding this planet
called Mother Earth.

LAYER SIX: Rewiring the Brain; Reprogramming DNA; Reconfiguring the Electromagnetic Field

(Click on the heading to be taken to the YouTube overview of this Layer)

OVERVIEW OF LAYER SIX—Rewire The Brain; Reprogram The DNA, And Reconfigure The Electromagnetic Field

*N*o healing is complete until you clear the energy and patterns from your body. Before we move forward I want to preface this next set of tapping sequences with an interesting quote I found on the website of Carol Look (EFT Master) about your body. It substantiates this point. "Whenever we have been traumatized, hurt, betrayed or scared, our body records the feelings on an energetic and cellular level.

As the well-known trauma specialist, Bessel van der Kolk says, 'Your body keeps the score. When we have a car accident, the bruises or broken bones are evident, physical, visible to the eye, and painful when touched. When we cut ourselves with a knife or burn ourselves in the kitchen, the scars can last indefinitely—proof that yes, we endured, yet, made it through a hardship of some kind. But when we've been screamed at, abandoned, or threatened, we have no visible "scars" to see or show others. Our bodies do indeed make and keep excellent records of these incidents in our electricity and our energy fields." (carollookeft.com)

The pain does not go away—the patterns do not change if you do not have the methods to clear the energy from your body. How do you begin? You first use your tapping sequences to clear the energetic disturbance. Then you ask for your body's forgiveness. And finally, you give your body permission to release and let go. The tension and stress can be replaced with a sense of relaxation and calm. You move from what Dr. Hanson referred to as the "red or pink zone" to the "green zone." The DNA in every cell is reprogrammed so that each cell can then hold an infusion of the new energetic vibration.

This implementation of this Layer was inspired by the New Brain Science, most specifically the work of Dr. Richard Hanson, and Margaret Ruby's work with reprogramming the DNA. You first clear the disturbance from your body, ask for its forgiveness then give it permission to release. This process reprograms the DNA in every cell of your physical form so it can hold your new vibration. I encourage you to experiment with the wording as much as your imagination will allow. Just keep tapping and saying affirming statements.

I have included an example but please experiment and try it on every feeling you think you have stored in your body in response to attracting the relationship you so desire. Make sure, however, you use this only after you and your Inner Child have moved to a low intensity on the scale from 1—to 10—because it will only be as effective as your energy system will allow.

Before you begin, do one round to clear any current triggers in your Adult Self and to neutralize any current disturbances that may be getting in the way of your giving your body permission to release.

I encourage you to experiment with the wording of these meditations and the interactive tapping™ sequences as much as your imagination will allow. The reprogramming is only as effective as your energy system will allow. I recommend that you use these reprogramming exercises each time you and your Inner Child have experienced a healing, or have done a piece of work. It is then that our body is the most receptive to this infusion.

When disparity does emerge (and it will because you are ever-evolving) then tap it away before you continue. I have included an example of an audio and text infusion, but please experiment. Try it on every feeling you think you have stored in your body that now eclipses your ability to attract your heart's desire.

I also encourage you to explore the benefits of EMDR and TRE which I mentioned earlier. I have found both of these practices useful in ridding the body of the tension left from unresolved traumas. Each of them, in their own unique way, assists the body in completing stress responses that got frozen in an event that could not be properly resolved.

REWIRING YOUR BRAIN

Your first task is to rewire your brain so that new neuro-pathways can be constructed and your cells can be reprogrammed. Use this following meditation to begin that process. As you read it I recommend you gently tap on your endpoints.

I now command you my dear brain to produce the right amount of serotonin and dopamine to create new neuro-pathways from the amygdala to the prefrontal cortex. I ask that the new paradigms and belief-systems be moved to long-term storage in the hippocampus so that my prefrontal cortex has access to these new ways of thinking and being. I progressively get better and better at being able to produce the right amount of neurotransmitters that support this new way of being.

I now command you my subconscious mind to relax and receive all that is for your Highest and best that is being transmitted to you. It is safe. You have discernment. You will only take in that which serves you for your Highest and best.

My brain is now able to transmit to every cell in my body the vibration of this new thought process. It is safe for my body to release. It is safe for my body to let go of all of the tension it has carried for me for so many years.

GIVING YOUR BODY PERMISSION TO RELEASE

You have now constructed new pathways in your brain and your cells are now ready to release and let go so they can be prepared to be reprogrammed. Before you begin, check in with yourself and see if there are any current triggers that need to be neutralized before you proceed. If so, do a round of tapping to get present. When ready state the setup phrase while tapping on the karate point. Imagine you are speaking directly to your body.

Setup for the Clearing

Even though I have needed you, my dear body, to store my pain, I am now strong enough to process this residue myself. I am now able, with full confidence, to finally instruct you on ways to release the tension and the stress. With great gratitude, I invite you to finally let it go.

So even though, my dear body, you diligently held the many feelings of tension related to my fears and my not feeling safe, I am now able to do for myself what you, for so many years, have done on my behalf. I can now, with full confidence, give you complete permission to let it all go.

And even though I know I had little choice back then … I really did not know what else to do … and for this, I now choose to forgive myself … but in turn, I ask you to forgive me as well. I do humbly apologize for needing you to hold this disturbance for me for so long … but I now give you total permission to release it and let it go. I firmly commit to you that I will now neutralize and dissolve all disturbances related to my lack of trust and my inability to feel safe. I am so appreciative of all you did on my behalf.

Repeat these setup phrases until you feel you have moved through all the resistance your body is storing for you. Really sincerely give your body permission to release what it has held. Reassure it that you are now completely willing to use the tools you have acquired to deal with whatever comes your way.

Eyebrow: My body has held onto all of this fear and mistrust.

Side of the Eye: This fear of abandonment … betrayal, and mistrust that my body has stored because I didn't know how to process the emotions and feel safe.

Under the Eye: My body has held onto this fear and mistrust … this lack of safety and fear to love.

Upper Lip: But I now give my body permission to let go.

Under the Lip: I release all of this mistrust, fear of abandonment, and inability to feel safe.

Collarbone: My body is now reprogrammed with faith and trust.

Rib: Every cell now holds this new DNA vibration of compassion and love.

Wrist: My body forgives me …

Under the Arm: … and vibrates with unconditional love.

Head: *I am so glad my body can finally let go and vibrate with safety and trust.*

As with all of these processes, the release is progressive. Each time you engage in this healing another frozen block in your body will thaw. Once you have cleared what can be cleared in this round you are ready to tap in a new program. When replenishing your body with a new vibration you are, in essence, reprogramming the DNA of every cell by infusing it with your new intention.

REPROGRAMMING THE CELLS OF YOUR BODY

Exercise: *Reprogramming the DNA of the Body*
(Click here to use this recording to guide you in this infusion but I have included the text below as well.)

Now let's begin by taking a deep breath and bringing your focus to the center of your belly. Feel that spark of light which rests in the very center of your being—envision that light expanding ever so gently so that every cell within your physical form can now be infused with this light and illuminated with its energy. In your mind's eye, see your entire physical form being illuminated by and infused with this light…and as you do so, envision this light expanding about 6 to 9 inches outside of your physical form—thus creating a column of protective light all around you. This builds a spiritual boundary around you which protects you as you open up your consciousness to higher frequencies…inviting a higher vibrational energy to infiltrate every cell within your body.

Now, bring your focus to the highest place in the Universe you can attain. It is here where you connect with your higher teachers and connect with the grid of unconditionality. It is here where you can extract the healing vibration of the Universe. It is here where you touch the wings of your Angels and where they make contact with you so they can be of service. Make your contact now. Invite your Highest Teachers to be present; your guardians, Ascended Masters, Spirit Guides, and Power Animals…ask for their assistance and blessing in this endeavor.

Now bring that new vibration of compassion and love right down to the center of your head into the pineal gland—and into the Master Cell. Infuse the DNA in the Master Cell with this new intent—awakening the chromosomes and the codons—the little computer chips which exist in the nucleus of each and every cell. Know that you are about to download a new program into your cellular makeup as you realign with the natural vibration with which the cells of your physical form long to resonate.

Once your Master Cell has been activated, bring that energy down the back of your head all the way along your spinal column, right to the base of your spine. It is here where you can infuse your Creator Cell with the same intent. Feel the energy of this vibration floating freely between your Master Cell and your Creator Cell—awakening and notifying every muscle, tendon, and ligament of your intention to infuse it with the vibration of the purest form of Light. I now invite you to bring your attention to your heart. Breathe into your heart now—peer into its center. There you will discover a secret chamber called the sacred heart. Within this sacred chamber exists a particle called the adamantine particle. This adamantine particle is the purest form of love which is known to mankind. Feel the vibration of this particle now and envision extending this vibration from the sacred chamber in your heart to every fiber of your being.

Repeat this sequence until you feel you have moved through all the resistance your body is holding for you. Give your body permission to release what it has held. Reassure it that you are now completely willing to deal with what comes your way with the tools you have acquired. When replenishing your body with a new vibration, you are acknowledging that the DNA has been reprogrammed. You infuse every cell with the new vibration of your intention.

THE AFFIRMATION FOR THE INFUSION

(Click here for the audio version of this meditation)

To replenish your cells after their reprogramming I suggest you gently tap on what is called your "sore spots" while you affirm the infusion of a new paradigm. The sore spots are located on your chest, several inches from your collarbone, and can be found by slowly tapping and putting pressure on this area of your body. Refer to the diagram below but you will know when you have hit the right spots for they will be a little tender.

Infusing a new affirmation is a way you can begin to tell the new story of a new intention. It marks a new beginning. Simply tap on the two sore spots as you tell your new story. Continue to tap for at least those 68 seconds while you tell your new story and until you feel the "buzz" (emotional charge) of your infusion. As I suggested earlier, it is this emotional "buzz" that energetically reprograms each cell. And again, according to the Teachings of Abraham, holding that "buzz" for these 68 seconds gives the Universe enough time to start to gather the necessary components to solidify what you intend and the process of manifestation can begin. The following is an example of how your affirmation might flow.

I now envision compassion and safety radiating from every cell of my body to every area of my life. All my needs and wants are fully realized in the presence of the Light. I am so fortunate to experience such acceptance and unconditional love. I feel so safe and am willing to respond with respect and love. Every area of my life is enriched with this sense of acceptance. Every cell is vibrating with the pure essence of joy.

This new vibration radiates out to all I attract. I absolutely love the rewards my actions bring back. I radiate unconditional love, and this vibration attracts the perfect people into my life; the perfect job, ample abundance, and harmony in all my endeavors. I am safe to be present in my body. I trust I can cope so my body does not have to take on my pain.

I am rich with experiences of love and Light. I see the magic of the Universe everywhere I look. I am truly a worthwhile being, and I exude that worthiness in every act! I am perfect in mind, body, heart, and Soul!

I deserve to be loved. I trust enough to allow all that I want to be created in my life.

Once you have reprogrammed your cells you are ready to extend this healing to the electromagnetic field all around you.

RECONFIGURING YOUR ELECTROMAGNETIC FIELD AROUND YOU

The electromagnetic field around you is your force field. It is that energy field that vibrationally extends beyond your physical form. It is embedded in the vibration of your Higher Self, as or as Abraham calls it, your Inner Being, The force field is where your chakras are located. It is the center of where your etheric body connects with your physical form. I picture it as being surrounded by Healing Light—like being encapsulated in healing energy.

"Meditation on Reconfiguring your Electromagnetic Field around You"
(Click here for the audio version of this meditation)

In your mind's eye see, sense, or feel this vibration you have just tapped in ... imagine the healing Light all around you. Make the command that the electromagnetic field around you is now recalibrated to hold this new intention and vibration. The recalibration enables you to better connect with your Divine Self, Inner Being, Higher Self. Breathe this experience in. Feel every cell in your body in its aliveness. Know that the neuropathways in your brain have been reconstructed to hold this new paradigm. For now, your healing is done!

LAYER SEVEN: Giving back to the World
(Click on the heading to be taken to the YouTube overview of this Layer.)

OVERVIEW OF LAYER SEVEN—Giving Back To The World

The final Layer of the *Seven-Layer Healing Process* invites you to share your healing with the world. Mother Earth also needs an infusion of compassionate, unconditional regard. Use the recording and the text below to take all you have neutralized and realigned and send this energy into the Universe as an offering for planetary healing. When you do this it dissolves isolation and contributes not only to increase of the Light on the planet but also to its healing. This gesture reinforces the fact that you are part of something bigger than yourself. You are a valuable agent of change for mankind. You have shared the gift with your Inner Child and the fragments of your Soul, You now have an opportunity to share it with the world.

Again, I encourage you to experiment with the wording as much as your imagination will allow. Just keep tapping and saying affirming statements. I have included a written example, as well as the audio version above, but please experiment, and try it on everything. I recommend, however, you use this only after you have experienced the reunion between your Adult Self and Inner Child, and the release of tension in your body because you want the energy you send out into the world to be as pure as possible.

MEDITATIVE TAPPING: GIVING BACK A PERCENTAGE OF THE HEALING TO THE UNIVERSE
(Click here for the audio version)

Enter into a meditative state. When you feel ready, begin again to tap on your sore spots while you say something like:

I feel so fortunate to have done this work. I now envision the cylinder of Light running from the center of Mother Earth to the grid of unconditional love about 60 feet above my head. This cylinder is filled with Healing Light.

I am so full of this Light and illuminated energy. From this highest place within myself, I now offer 10% or more of this healing back to heal the planet. I gift it to Mother Earth to use in her healing the energy wherever it is needed on the planet. I then contribute 10% of this healing to the Mandala of transformation that cloaks the planet, making it available to all who choose to tap into this healing energy and use it for their own expansion and growth.

I feel so fortunate I have been able to complete this work and am so grateful I am now in a position to share this gift. I love feeling safe. I love contributing this sense of safety to the world. Thank you, God, Goddess, Higher Power, Angels, Masters, and All Above, for your support and direction. Thank you for your support in my feeling safe. Thank you, fragments of my Soul for having the courage and fortitude to call me back to you in all dimensions of time and consciousness. And thank you my dear little ones for having the patience to await my return.

I love that we are healed and have methods to continue the ever-evolving healing within and without. I can now hold the Light which allows all within me to attract all that we choose. I so appreciate that we can now contribute to the expansion of this world in a supportive and safe way. Thank you, Thank you. Thank you.

This is, again, but an example. As you work in this fashion, the inspiration will come to you ... the words will come to you. But always keep in mind, as you go forward, that when you, as the Adult Self, are secure in knowing that no matter what happens you will not abandon this Inner Child, he or she will trust you ... will not feel at risk ... and will not need to sabotage your efforts to attract all that you desire and deserve. The sequence you just stated simply augments your willingness to allow yourself to receive because you are able to accept who you are and have learned how to share this gift with the children within you.

Whether it is harmony and peace, resolution of your grief, a renewed relationship with your body, the attraction of that intimate relationship, abundance, or right livelihood, when you are no longer being sabotaged by your Inner Child's fears, or high-jacked by the unresolved bleed-throughs from your Soul's past, you are free to *observe* the abundance, love, grace, and beauty of the world. Then, based on the simple law of attraction, what you observe, you attract—what you conceive, you achieve. You naturally begin to manifest grace, beauty, success, and abundance in ALL areas of your life.

But this can only happen when the fragments of your Soul have been healed and returned to the Light and when you and your Inner Child are one. My *Seven-Layer Healing Process* provides a map for you to confidently chart the course for your continuing journey of expansion, evolution, and growth.

DESIGNING YOUR OWN UNIQUE SEQUENCES:

This worksheet is provided so you can begin to design the sequences that will more effectively target your specific concerns. Play with it until you can make the process of tapping your own. Always begin by getting a sense of where you are at and where you want to go. What is your concern? How do you feel about that concern? And how do you want to feel about this concern? That way, you design statements that reflect the challenge, the goal and the conviction of a new response. Once you get comfortable with creating your own sequences this tool will become one of your most important remedies for distress.

Focus for the Tapping Setup: When you are designing the setup phrases for this tapping sequence you may want to revisit or redo to the weeding-out exercise you did in the previous section. This will give you an idea of what your goal is in this tapping. Then use the reminder phrases to address all of the aspects of your concern.

When you you're your issues determine what the intensity level of feeling is regarding this concern. Rate: 1 (being low) –10 (being high) intensity level: _____

What I want to feel:

Setup Statements–State each of these while tapping on the karate chop point:

Even though a part of me _____, I accept all aspects of me completely and fully or _____.

Even though that part of me _____, I accept all aspects of me completely and fully or _____.

Even though that part of me won't _____, I choose to try something new on its behalf or _____.

Now refer to your responses above and use the worksheet on the next page to design your own unique reminder phrases. Remember, you are moving first through your negative feelings, then to the possibility of change, then to a conviction for change. Come up with a reminder phrase for each endpoint. Then tap on this point 5–7 times while repeating your phrase.

Neutralizing the Negative

Eyebrow: _____

Side of the Eye: _____

Under the Eye: _____

Upper Lip: _____

Under the Lip: _____

Collarbone: _____

Under the Arm: _____

Chest Bone: _____

Wrist: _____

Head: _____

Repeat sequences, altering words accordingly, until, on a scale from 1–10, you feel at least a 2 or 3. Then proceed. When you are ready to move into the possibility that something different can occur, come up with a reminder phrase for each of the endpoints below, then tap on this point 5–7 times while repeating your phrase.

Possibility of Change

Eyebrow: _____

Side of the Eye: _____

Under the Eye: _____

Upper Lip: _____

Under the Lip: _____

Collarbone: _____

Under the Arm: _____

Chest Bone: _____

Wrist: _____

Head: _____

Share the Gift

To complete this series, come up with phrases which capture your true conviction to feel or do something new. When you are ready to move into strengthening that conviction, tap on each of the endpoints on the EFT graph 5–7 times while repeating your phrase.

Conviction of Change

Eyebrow: _____

Side of the Eye: _____

Under the Eye: _____

Upper Lip: _____

Under the Lip: _____

Collarbone: _____

Under the Arm: _____

Chest Bone: _____

Wrist: _____

Head: _____

Use this formula in whatever way is useful to you. Be creative. Be adventurous. Remember, you can do no wrong when it comes to tapping.

SECTION FOUR:
APPLICATION OF SEVEN-LAYER
HEALING PROCESS
TO FOUR MODULES:

Intimate Relationships:
Abundance:
Right Livelihood:
Reciprocal Partnerships.

OVERVIEW: The Ingredients used in each of the Modules––the Application of the *Seven-Layer Healing Process*

I n each of the Modules presented I add spice to the respective Inner Child issues with excerpts from the *Teachings of Abraham* to obtain the focus of the work and then offer the seven layers of interactive tapping™ sequences to produce the change. Through meditations and exercises you fortify the Illuminated, Adult Self; identify the state of negativity related to attracting your heart's desire; separate from that emotion; and respond to the Inner Child's wounded feelings. His or her painful experience can then be replaced with a more positive one. This new experience commingles with the adult's intention which now carries a higher vibrational frequency that can be sent out to the Universe to find its elevated, vibrational match. This is "sharing the gift" in action. It is teaching the Inner Child the law of attraction and inviting that Inner Child to sit at the manifestation table. The need for sabotage is neutralized and the intention being offered to the Universe can be delivered without resistance.

THE FIRST INGREDIENT—The Teachings Of Abraham

Each Module begins with an excerpt from the many teachings of Abraham. Jerry and Esther Hicks produce and present the leading-edge teachings of this non-physical entity. They have been traveling around the country since 1968 presenting workshops in which the participants are invited to discuss the topics of their choice and ask any question they desire. The answers are provided through Esther Hicks' channeling Abraham.

The *Teachings of Abraham* educate their followers about the law of attraction and the laws of the Universe. They emphasize the fact that everything is a vibration—and that we live in a vibrational environment. The manner in which we experience the circumstances of our life is dependent upon the vibrational frequency we energetically transmit to the Universe. I flavor your Inner Child's issues with this spiritual perspective to give your Inner Child's pain a spiritual relevance. The flavor of this ingredient with respect to each area of concern will be evident in the excerpts I have selected. They offer just a hint of the contribution the *Teachings of Abraham* can have on all of our journeys, but I greatly encourage you to visit their website and then consider attending one of their gatherings they conduct around the world. You will not be disappointed. You can go to their website for more information. www.abraham-hicks.com

The publisher for Esther and Jerry, Hay House, has produced numerous books, DVDs, and CDs; each offering hands-on information on spiritual practicality. The following excerpt is transcribed directly from what was originally offered as a DVD entitled, "The Secret behind the Secret", but is now offered as a streaming video. These words are boldly displayed in the first frame of the film in spellbinding fashion. They eloquently capture the essence of the message of this Divine Intelligence.

We Are Abraham.

We are Source.

You are Source Energy.

We are here because you asked.

We are here to answer your questions.

We are here to remind you of that which you are and have forgotten.

We are here to remind you of that which you now wish to remember.

And So Enters The Second Ingredient—Inner Child Work

What is it that we have forgotten? What is it we now wish to remember? As we talked about at the very beginning of this book, we make Soul agreements before we come into this physical world, but then the veil is pulled and we forget our true origin and intent.

The more socialized we become the more we forget who we truly are. Our amnesia is the result of the fears of your Inner Child. They hold us apart from that which we want to attract. In response to our childhood experiences, our wounded Inner Child developed belief systems and knee-jerk reactions to expansion. Expansion (getting bigger, being seen and comfortable with attracting attention) became equated with pain and risk.

As we discussed in Section Two: Layer Three, each reaction has a face and each face has a voice which holds clues as to what we have forgotten and what we now need to remember. In this material, those faces are represented by the seven developmental stages of childhood. Each holds a task and an opportunity for growth. These unmet needs of these developmental stages appear as the emotional responses we have to the respective areas of concern. The exploration of these responses assists us in determining what part of us is sabotaging our efforts to succeed, and what exactly he or she needs to feel safe enough so we can remember who we truly are, and therefore, feel deserving of that which we desire.

The remembrance is progressive. The more inner work you do the more access you have to your true self. One of the most effective methods to accomplish this task is the combination of traditional EFT with interactive meditations, thus enters the third ingredient to this process, the interactive tapping™ sequences which provide the vehicle for this *Seven-Layer Healing Process.*

THE THIRD INGREDIENT—EFT (Gary Craig's Emotional Freedom Techniques)

The Inner Child's insecurity gives rise to loads of fear. We neutralize this insecurity with the interactive tapping™ sequences— simply the combination of traditional EFT with interactive meditation. Again, EFT is an emotional version of acupuncture except needles aren't necessary. Instead, you stimulate well-established energy meridian points on your body by tapping on them with your fingertips. Combining the context of the Inner Child with the energetic interventions of EFT provides a very effective and efficient avenue for working with those parts within us that sabotage our best efforts to succeed. Again, always keep in mind that it is not the intention of our wounded ones to hold us back. Their efforts are merely aimed at sustaining a sense of safety; they do not realize their actions sabotage our success. They are frightened and are responding in the knee-jerk manner they developed in response to the original wound. It is the only way they knew how to stay safe.

As you have seen over and over in this material, the healing agent for an old wound is the interaction between the wounded one and an inner adult that can respond with compassion, love, and care. This interaction changes the experience of the Inner Child and creates a new reality. Since our mind does not know the difference between what is real and imagined and we program our future with intentions and pretense exercises, we can do the same thing by returning to the time of the wound and changing the experience of the part of us that holds on to the pain.

Again, the only reason this is possible is because we have attained the level of empowerment that enables us, as adults, to intervene. We step into the original scene of the wound; and on behalf of the Inner Child—we protect, retrieve, and rescue him or her from the hurtful experience. And if you think about it, it stands to reason that as we set our intentions for our heart's desires, we flush out the trailers that sabotage our efforts to succeed. When we attract more Light, we also illuminate our shadow self and the wounded parts that inadvertently sabotage our efforts to succeed. But we can repair that wound and invite that essence back into the vibration of our force field where it can be safe if we give a face to those saboteurs that run rampant with their negative statements and destructive behaviors; if we learn how to relate to those wounded ones with care and love. Not only does this halt the sabotage, it also augments the magic with which we can manifest. Bring a child's imagination and wonderment into any intention, and the vibrational frequency increases tenfold.

BRINGING IT ALL TOGETHER—The Seven Layers Of Healing

Each area of concern ends with targeted tapping sequences that systematically enable you, as the adult, to help the Inner Child heal, so it can also learn and experience the magic of the law of attraction. As you saw in Section Three, each Layer uses interactive tapping™ sequences to accomplish the task stated. Because this process takes you through a step-by-step process, each Layer respectively uses the pronouns appropriate to the task at hand. You 1) identify the contrasting feelings; 2) separate from and externalize that feeling so, as the adult, you can 3) respond to and, therefore, heal the contrasting emotion by relating to the feeling as an emotional expression of the child within that is afraid. For your convenience, the tapping chart that was used in Sections One and Two is once again provided. Each module is designed to target the area of concern that most appeals to you. So that each module stands on its own there is redundancy. You will find that you will know exactly which exercises, meditations, and interactive tapping™ sequences most benefit you. Trust yourself and discern accordingly.

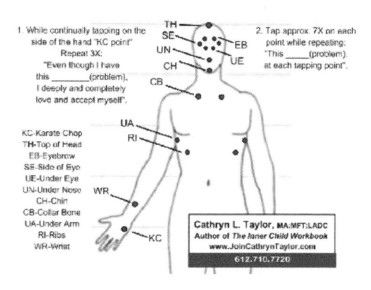

Module 1:
Attracting
Intimate Relationships

To attract an intimate relationship with another you first have to establish an intimate relationship with yourself, which can only occur if you have a connection to Source Energy.

A Word From Abraham

The following, excerpted again from the video, *The Secret Behind the Secret,* sheds an inspirational, "Abraham" light on this subject.

Moderator: "What would you most value in a friendship? "

Abraham's Response: "NOTHING! You should look to your connection to Source, and in your connection to Source, you will be self-sufficient. Then you radiate value to all around you.

Moderator: "But we have loneliness … "

Abraham's Response: "But loneliness is a reflection of not allowing the full essence of who you are to flow through you. We would not ask anything from another to fill any void within you. Any void can only be filled by allowing that which needs to be filled to be filled by Source. Sometimes you look to others, for example, someone who loves you, and they hold you as their object of intention, and oh, it does feel so delicious because in their love for you, they are connected to Source energy, and they are flooding it all over you. And it feels so good, but now you need their undivided attention. If they give their attention to someone else or something else, then you feel like a puppet, and someone has let go of the string. Where, if you are interested in the feeling of love, rather than being loved by someone else, now you are self–sufficient. Now you are connected to this eternal string. You see?"

Excerpt from the video, *The Secret Behind the Secret,* Hay House. www.abraham-hicks.com

Establishing A Connection Between You And Source Energy

It is important first to establish what Source Energy is. It is the energy of the Divine. It is the energy of pure love. It is the energy that comes from your Higher Self— that spiritual essence connected to "all that is." Some call it God, others refer to the energy as Buddha or Allah, the universal source, or simply Spirit. Irrespective of how you name it this energy is what will fill your Soul. The meditation below provides an avenue to experience this connection. As with any relationship which is vital, it is not only necessary to establish this connection; you must also be willing to nourish and nurture it.

EXERCISE: MEDITATION––CONNECTING WITH SOURCE ENERGY

Close your eyes and get into a meditative position. As you take a deep breath, allow your awareness to float up above your head approximately 60 feet—into the grid of unconditional love. It is here where you can reconnect with the essence of your spiritual self as you merge with your Source energy. Do so now. Feel what it is like to have that union—with no sense of separation—no sense of longing.

See colors—listen as you allow a sound to emerge from the center of your being. Begin then to express that tone in sound as the beam of light travels back down your spinal column, through your physical form to the very center of Mother Earth. Connect with the beat of her heart. Unify your pulse with Mother Earth's as you notify her of your intention to share all healings with her in exchange for her anchoring your hearts' desires into the physical plane—into your day-to-day life.

Feel that vibration of sound as it begins to resonate within every chakra. Begin with your root chakra right at the base of your spine. Then allow that resonation to travel up to your second chakra, in the pelvis, the belly, the reproductive area of your body where you give birth to ideas and desires.

Take another deep breath and continue to travel up to the center of your solar plexus—the area right below your belly button—feel the vibration tingling in this center—breathe it—radiate with it. It is here where your Inner Children reside.

Breathe in comfort and compassion, love and joy. With another deep breath bring that vibration to the center of your heart. Feel your breath radiate divine love as it magnifies the adamantine particles held within every fiber of your ever-beating heart. As that vibration rings with sound and color expand this sensation. Bear witness as it filters into your throat—your vocal chords—creating a pulsation of honesty as you commit to speaking your truth. Breathe it. Feel it. Express it through sound.

Bring this sensation further up into the center of your third eye—right into the center of your forehead. Again, feel the pulsation of energy. See the color or radiance. Allow the sound of your innermost truth to emerge. Then bring your focus to your crown chakra as you allow the energy to travel through that portal of entry extending your consciousness all the way back up to the grid of unconditional love, sixty feet above your head. It is within this infusion of Source Energy that all your dreams and wishes can manifest. Hold this vibration. It is this sensation that all of your dreams and wishes can come true.

Attracting The Mate You Desire

To attract your ideal mate you have to give vision to that which you want to attract.

JOURNAL EXERCISE: ATTRACTING AND BEING THE MATE THAT YOU DESIRE

Now that you are connected to your Source take a moment to write your hearts' desire in your ideal relationship. Be specific.

Make a list in your journal of adjectives that describe them.

What does he and she do for a living? What are their important values, common interests, etc.? Include any aspect of your ideal partner which holds importance for you.

Once you have this clear in your mind's eye, describe your ideal mate as if you are already in a relationship with him or her. Even if it is your actual mate, describe him or her as if he or she is exactly as you would like him or her to be.

You have created your vision for your ideal mate. However, before you can attract the mate you want, you have to determine the kind of mate YOU want to be This step is imperative and often ignored. We become so focused on what we want from the other person we do not pay attention to what we have to offer. What message are you sending out to the Universe that you want the Universe to match? Remember, you attract back that which you transmit.

JOURNAL EXERCISE: WHAT KIND OF MATE DO YOU WANT TO BE?

To take it one step further and to get clarity take a moment to think about the following journal questions. Then record your responses in your journal.

What kind of mate do I want to be? What attributes do I want to enhance or acquire which would resonate with the kind of partner I would like to attract?

If I look at my recent relationships, what did they reflect about me?

What did they mirror in me? What patterns emerged?

In your review of past relationships can you detect a theme? If so, what is that theme? What dynamics do you continue to create and attract in your pursuit of a loved one?

Now record your thoughts on the above. Record any themes you see in your intimate relationships. Do these words, or similar ones, sound familiar? **"No matter what I do, I always am abandoned… I never feel safe … Everyone always betrays me … this always happens to me!** Modify the words according to your personal experience, but know that statements such as these suggest a possible Soul theme, and it is in your best interest to identify that theme so you can use the methods offered in this material. They will give you what you need to alter and dissolve that out-dated pattern that vibrationally keeps attracting that which you do not want.

You now have an idea of what you would want to neutralize within your Illuminated Adult Self to clear out old patterns. You accomplish this by applying the interactive tapping™ sequences to dissolve what you have discovered.

You will want to first clear the Adult Self. Below is the standard tapping sequence offered throughout this material that will help you begin to feel empowered and be equipped to design your strategy for healing.

EXERCISE: TAPPING SEQUENCE ON INTIMATE RELATIONSHIPS

On a scale from 1 (low) to 10 (high) determine your level of intensity. Now, while tapping on your karate point repeat the following statements:

Even though I have attracted relationships which have carried this specific pattern in the past, I love myself fully and completely and am ready to attract something new.

Even though I have attracted many relationships that carried this theme, and at times have lost trust in myself, I choose now to release that pain and to try something new. I love myself and those aspects within me enough to take this risk of trying something new.

Even though I have a lot of history where this pattern has been repeated and it has tripped me up over and over and over again, I love myself and that part of me enough to take the risk to try something new.

Once you have the setup phrase or the psychological reversal intact, you are ready to begin to neutralize the disturbance associated with this situation. Gently tap on the respective endpoints 5-6 times while repeating what are called *the reminder phrases*. Refer back to the graphic in Section Two if necessary. It will remind you of exactly where to tap.

Neutralizing the Negative

Eyebrow: I'm always afraid of what might happen.

Side of the Eye: I have lost so much trust in myself.

Under the Eye: I feel the doubt and fear in my vibration every day.

Upper Lip: I have so much history—how can I ever trust myself or another again?

Under the Lip: I don't feel safe trusting.

Collarbone: I'm afraid to let go of my fear.

Under the Arm: Afraid to feel any other way.

Rib: So many of my relationships have gone bad…

Head: What if I can't let go of my fear?

Check your intensity level here and keep doing rounds clearing the negative until you experience a shift. Once the intensity lessens to at least a level of 1 or 2—proceed.

This next round moves through the Fear to Possibility of Change to Conviction

Eyebrow: Maybe it is safe to trust things can be better than ever before.

Side of the Eye: Maybe it is time to take a risk and try something new.

Under the Eye: Maybe I am ready to be the mate I have always longed to be.

Upper Lip: Maybe, with trust in my Higher Source, I can rely more on myself.

Under the Lip: Maybe my connection to my Higher Source can keep me secure.

Collarbone: I am ready to try something new.

Under the Arm: I choose to trust my Higher Source and believe I can be who I want to be.

Rib: I am ready to attract that which I so desire because …

Head: … I am ready to believe in myself and my connection to Source.

EXERCISE: MEDITATION ON YOUR IDEAL MATE

Now, take a moment to participate in the following meditation.

Close your eyes and imagine you are walking along the trail in a wooded area. The sun is shining down through the trees and lightly touches your face—warming you with a summer day glow. You are aware of the presence of a power greater than you—it is in nature—it is all around you. Once again you tune into the vibration of Mother Earth and notify her of your intention to align your heartbeat to hers. Feel connected to the new person you want to be in relationships. You are vibrating with that essence of your illuminated lover within. You are who you want to be, and it is from this vibration you can now send your intention to the Universe. It is this frequency of energy which attracts that which you so desire.

Now, as you continue your journey, look ahead on the path before you. At a distance you see the results of your intentions emerging. You see this being coming forth… the one that your new vibration has attracted. You recognize this person … it is your ideal mate walking towards you.

If your ideal mate appears as a person you already know, see them in the Light of their most Divine Self. You may be attempting to bring forth the highest form of a relationship with a person with whom you are already involved. And therefore his or her approaching you feels familiar and fine. If you don't know the person approaching you then you are in the process of manifesting your intention to attract your ideal mate. Either way, this person who is now coming towards you, is your ideal mate. He or she is now standing before you. How do you feel? Record your thoughts and experiences.

Now to go deeper, use the following exercise to determine the layers of feelings the different parts within you might be experiencing.

EXERCISE: DETECTING YOUR FUTURE SELF

Reflect back on your experience of the above meditation. Make a list of the five predominant feelings you have in response to this meeting. List them in order of those which are most congruent with your ultimate goal and those which hold the most contrast to that which you desire to attract.

1. Example—anticipation
2. Example—possibility, hope
3. Example—disbelief, mistrust
4. Example—anxiety, fear
5. Example—despair

The contrasting emotions are the feelings of your children within. Any time you begin to look at relationships you invite the aspect of you who fears abandonment and betrayal onto center stage. Few make it through childhood without some wounding experiences which get repeated in adulthood. These wounds will be evident in any endeavor you choose to pursue.

And So Emerges Inner Child Work

In response to your childhood experiences, your wounded Inner Child developed belief systems and knee-jerk reactions to getting close. Intimacy became equated with pain and risk! Each reaction has a voice. Each voice has a face. These faces express the emotional responses you have to others in your world. At any given time your emotions tell you if you are in alignment with your Highest Self or in conflict with it. Any negative emotion indicates that you are seeing a situation differently than your Higher Self. Your *emotional guidance scale (Abraham's term)* is useful to confer if you want to determine if you are in or out of alignment with your Higher Self. Obviously, the best position is to be able to hold the vibration that will bring you what you desire is to be in alignment.

The list you just made is your personal *emotional guidance scale* from which you can work. It reveals the congruent feelings you will want to augment and the contrasting or challenging feelings you will want to neutralize. In other words, you will tap on those emotions that resonate with your heart's desire to increase their frequency, and you will tap on those feelings you find challenging to neutralize them and move from resistance to allowance.

And, again, according to the *Teachings of Abraham ...*

Within only a few seconds of focusing your attention on a subject, you activate the vibration of that subject within you, and immediately the Law of Attraction begins to respond to that activation. Within 17 seconds of focusing on something, a matching vibration becomes activated... and if you manage to stay purely focused upon any thought for as little as 68 seconds, the vibration is powerful enough that its manifestation begins.

(Ask, and it is Given by Esther and Jerry Hicks, Page 109. Hay House)

As you are beginning to see, the Inner Child who is fearful of this attraction will sabotage your efforts to succeed. The vibration of this wounded one will emit will attract that which vibrationally matches his or her fears. The following illustrates this point.

A BIRD'S EYE VIEW OF SABOTAGE

Mary flipped on her television and tuned right into Oprah's show. She was so excited. She had heard the show was going to feature practitioners from the movie her friend had given her for Christmas. She watched in amazement. She felt pride that something so well known to her was featured on the Oprah show! She had flirted with these concepts. In fact, she had even had some success with them. She had attracted more contracts when she began applying these principles to her business, and she had manifested a cruise which she had wanted to take for a long time.

But now Mary wanted to apply these principles to something close to her heart. She wanted to attract the relationship she so desperately desired. She created her affirmations and faithfully recited them every day. Every moment she thought of a relationship she would envision her true love walking into her life.

And then he did. Mary did meet the man of her dreams. But instead of embracing him she fumbled with her words and became so frightened she stopped returning his phone calls. Mary was plagued with guilt and shame. What had she done wrong? Why would she now reject the very thing she had for so many years wanted? Why were her fears of abandonment and inability to trust so strong?

No matter what your experience is with intimate relationships—it begins with your experience as an infant because it is at this time in your life when you first develop your blueprint for closeness. This part within you will need your attention and healing if you are to be successful in attracting the relationship you so desire.

Where Challenges To Intimacy Begin

The first developmental stage in childhood is infancy. The task in infancy is to develop a sense of trust and safety in relation to our environment. The task is accomplished through the relationship we have with our mother or primary caretaker. From her we learn, body to body, what it means to be safe.

If she transmits acceptance, calmness, and security, we internalize that experience to the depth of our physical being and trust it is safe to exist, develop, and take form. When we experience this sense of safety and trust, we develop the capacity to experience mastery in every area of life. However, if our primary caretaker is tentative about her mothering skills, ambivalent about motherhood, distracted from her maternal tasks because of an external life crisis which demands her attention, we internalize unrest, feel unsafe, and relate to our environment in a tentative and ambivalent manner.

As infants, we cannot assess when our mother's reactions are in response to us and when they are in response to external circumstances. We self-reference every event and organically assume responsibility for all reactions around us. These reactions become the blueprint which ultimately dictates the degree of safety we feel in trusting others and in allowing ourselves to become attached to them. If in infancy, we are not safe to trust, we cannot bond. If we cannot bond, we cannot successfully attach. This inability results in a longing. We long for that attachment. Until this is satisfied within we will project out to the Universe that longing, and in return, that is what we will attract.

EXERCISE: A LOOK AT INTIMACY THROUGH THE EYES OF THE INNER CHILDREN

The following is an overview of the seven developmental stages and how the experiences of those stages may appear in adulthood when experiencing intimacy in your close relationships.

Respond to the statements according to you feel at this present moment. Rate them from 1, for not all, and 5, for very much. These are behaviors which you exhibit in your adult life today. The origin of this behavior, however, rests in childhood.

Infant Self (Birth to 18 months)—The unfinished task from infancy that is brought into your intimate relationships is your ability or inability to bond with, and be present with, your loved one. This even extends to your being able to track if you are indeed interested in a new person enough to pursue an intimate relationship. Not being able to form intimate connections is directly related to having never been able to establish a safe relationship with your central caretaker.

_____1. I have difficulty determining if I am interested in someone new.

_____2. My relationships with family members feel stagnant and confined.

_____3. Many of my relationships lack depth and trust.

_____4. I have difficulty initiating contact in new relationships.

Toddler (18 to 36 months)—The "toddler" goal that is evident in intimate relationships is how well you set and accept the boundaries related to loved ones…how do family members and/or your intimate partner respond when you say No to them? Is it well-received? How do you deal with hearing No? Again, determine if you can say No or Yes without resentment or engulfment.

_____1. I dislike having to say No to a friend or loved one.

_____2. I would rather not ask for a favor than risk being told No.

_____3. I fear if I say yes once, I will be obligated to say yes the next time.

_____4. If I do not know what I feel or want, I remain quiet and simply go along.

Young Inner Child (3-6 years)—The goal from this stage of development with respect to intimate relationships is for you to begin to examine the differences in value systems between you and your loved ones and you and an intimate partner. You will want to explore ways in which both parties operate in the day-to-day activities. You will want to begin the on-going process of making adjustments and attempting to find an approach which incorporates both styles of operation. This step is also when you make peace with what your loved ones can and cannot offer. You realize you can either get stuck in judgments—theirs or yours—or you can to use the judgments and projections as mirrors for personal growth.

_____1. It is difficult for me to articulate what I feel about something.

_____2. If I state an opinion which is challenged, I wish I had remained silent.

_____3. If another's opinion differs from mine, I assume theirs is wrong.

_____4. When I give in and agree with others, I feel I give them my power.

Grade School Self (6-12 years)—You will find you still want to fit in with your family, but the stirrings of breaking away are under the surface…and fitting in with peers will begin to have more dominance. You might notice there are silent bargains maintained enabling you to fit in with the "in" crowd rather than break the molds. A compromise of your authentic self will take precedence over risking the loss of peer approval. Unfortunately, the price paid is your authenticity. Your need for approval can also be based on being counted on for "being there for others and doing for others" at the expense of self—which is a perpetuation of the theme of the codependent bargain which now gets projected onto intimate relationships.

Love becomes defined by how much you are needed and by the degree to which you feel accepted and revered.

_____1. I would like to be more acknowledged by those I love.

_____2. I feel invisible and unseen by those who I consider close to me…

_____3. If I disagree with my partner, I stay silent rather than risk disapproval.

_____4. Even if I have strong feelings, I will still agree with others.

The same issues that were presented in the first three stages of development get revisited.

Young Inner Teen (12-15 years)—This aspect of self emerges in our close relationships when we begin to risk new ways of being with those we love. If we feel shy and quick to pull back into the old patterns due to our self-consciousness our inner teen needs attention. In our primary relationship, we can move into wanting to experiment with more authenticity but might still be very cautious. We may not want to "rock the boat" for fear of losing the relationship.

_____1. I proceed with great caution when I exhibit a new behavior with others.

_____2. I get nervous when I attempt to break away from my family's ideas.

_____3. I figure nothing is going to change anyway so why try to be different.

_____4. I would rather avoid family members that are different than me.

Adolescent (15-17years)—As we embrace the tasks from this stage of development we might witness that we are more brazen and risky with speaking our truth and being real…despite the possibility of losing them. The same is true in our primary relationship…we have to speak our truth irrespective of the risk because to remain in the relationship in a non-authentic manner is intolerable.

_____1. Even though my loved ones and I disagree, I speak up nonetheless.

_____2. Even if I agree, I like to disagree with someone just for the fun of it.

_____3. I find myself in situations where my values stand out.

_____4. I would rather keep my feelings to myself than risk losing a close friend.

Young Adult Self (17-21 years)—Having mastered communication and compassion we are now able to experience authentic and vital relationships with those we love. They are not always peaceful or without tension, but they are real and laced with a commitment to obtain and maintain an integrity which promotes trust and growth.

_____1. I have few relationships based on mutual trust.

_____2. It is challenging to confront differences in my relationships with others.

_____3. When someone challenges me, I have a hard time defending myself.

_____4. I am uncomfortable with others who "agree to disagree."

Take a moment to review your responses. What can you learn from how you are responding today? See if you can tune into the specific age groups and determine the source of his or her fears. The more you become familiar with the face of your wounded ones the more effective the application of the *Seven-Layer Healing Process* will be.

Seven-Layer Healing Process
APPLIED TO ATTRACTING INTIMATE RELATIONSHIPS

Intimate Relationships—Before You Begin

The *Seven-Layer Healing Process* is useful if clearing the Adult Self of a current issue does not bring full resolution. As you read in the introduction, if you cannot clear a situation that is current it is because the situation has triggered a residual issue from your past. This trigger offers you an opportunity to clear the disturbance in all dimensions of time and consciousness. This modality invites you to identify the aspect of you who has gotten triggered then systematically takes you through the process of healing the unresolved issues so this part can let go and you can begin to attract that which you so desire.

The following material provides a progression of interactive tapping™ sequences which will equip you to work with the aspect of you who carries your abandonment and inability to trust. As you discovered in the introductory material, this most often begins with the stage of development of infancy. This process will assist you in neutralizing those fears and replacing them with faith, hope, and trust.

Please Note: Included in the Kindle format is the mp3 of this process. This audio is a variation of the tapping script for the Tapping Sequences for Intimate Relationships. You may prefer one over the other, or you may want to use examples from each to customize your own setups and sequences. However, the following script leads you through the process in its entirety.

Interactive Tapping™ Sequences For Attracting An Intimate Relationship

The following section reviews the Seven Layers of Healing and then offers the interactive tapping™ setup phrases and sequences to work with them. Feel free to experiment with using one sequence a day or just pick a time and move through the Layers all at once. I have presented it in a daily fashion for simplicity. For some, working with one aspect a day augments the depth of the work. Others may want to intensify the experience by going through this process at one sitting.

There is no right or wrong way to proceed. Honor whichever style appeals to you. If you are doing this on a day-to-day basis, then you will want to begin each day with clearing the adult. If you do it in one sitting then once you have cleared the Adult Self it is unnecessary to repeat this with each Layer unless you feel the need to do so.

1ˢᵀ Layer--Empowering and Clearing the Adult Self

Discussion: These first sequences neutralize any disturbances which are currently in the Adult Self. The wording does not deal directly with a relationship, but rather addresses general irritations so you can enter this work as clear as possible. You begin this part of the process by neutralizing the Adult Self because it is this part of you who will orchestrate the layered healing. It is, therefore, essential that he or she is cleared of any current, distracting emotions or thoughts.

Again, the process begins with three setup phrases. I use the setup phrases to identify the ambivalence and contrasting feelings of any issue. In the statements presented in the previous section, you established that you have this sabotaging voice. The setup phrases position this sabotage against a positive affirmation.

The script is divided into three sections. You first neutralize the negative thoughts and feelings—then introduce the possibility of change and finish with a strong infusion of your conviction to a new way of relating to the part of you who is sabotaging your efforts to successfully attract your right livelihood.

Stay with each series of sequences until you feel ready to move to the next one. You will intuitively feel an energetic shift when you are done with the negative and your psyche is ready to consider something new.

The second set of sequences usually does not take as long—it just softens the psyche, so it is ready to claim the right to feel convicted about the new approach.

The last set should leave you feeling strong and energized in your new conviction. You will then be ready to proceed to my *Seven-Layer Healing Process* which will work with each piece of this dynamic more fully.

Again, the setup phrases position your disturbance against an affirmation thus preparing your psyche to accept the neutralization process which will follow.

Again feel free to refer to the graphic in Section Two to refresh your memory on exactly where to tap.

Interactive tapping™ Sequences: Begin by tapping on the karate point while stating the following:

Even though there may be some things I am not totally in harmony with today ... I choose, for this time, to suspend those feelings so I can now focus entirely on the exercises for the layers of this work.

So, even though I may need to neutralize some general irritations ... I am going to do that before I do this work because I love myself fully and completely and I am committed to clearing this up so I can attract the mate of my choice.

So even though I may not be in total harmony, I am willing to suspend any contrasting feelings I have at this time so that I can be as clear and as open to doing this work because I love myself enough to respond.

Next, you will do the general neutralizing. It involves stating reminder phrases while you tap on the designated endpoints.

Neutralizing the Negative

Eyebrow: Generally disturbed … A little bit antsy … Clear out any anger.

Side of the Eye: Clear out all distraction.

Under the Eye: Any frustration.

Upper Lip: A little bit fatigued.

Under the lip: But choose to feel empowered to do this work.

Collarbone: Am excited to do this Layer of work.

Under the Arm: Have committed to showing up to do this work.

Rib: Am getting jazzed to meet this Inner Child and to help it heal.

Head: I ask my Higher Guidance to help clear this disturbance.

That completes the sequences and gives you an example of how you would neutralize anything currently in your day-to-day life. Continue to tap on each of the endpoints until you move through any resistance to being responsive to your efforts to help it heal.

Note: Sometimes the Adult Self has antagonistic feelings towards the Inner Child, and these would need to be neutralized before you can be effective. This need is especially true for this Inner Child because if our childhood experiences were that it was not safe to trust, feel, or speak the truth, then we would have learned it was not safe to exist or even have needs. In adulthood, we can detest that part of us who we judge as "needy." We need to heal this relationship before we can have a satisfactory relationship with another.

2ND LAYER--EXTERNALIZING THE PAIN

Discussion: In the exercises in the first section, you were able to put a face to the part within you who fears closeness, is unable to trust and has most likely lost faith. Now is the time to begin to separate from him or her or "externalize" these feelings. When we externalize the disturbance, we set up a dyad between the part of us who carries the wound and the part of us who can respond to the wound.

You will be using the pronoun "he" or "she" to begin the separation process. This step is crucial in that it is this very separation that allows us to interact and the interaction between the wounded one and the Healer within you is what creates the healing.

If you are confident your Adult Self is clear, take a moment to review your responses to the exercises in the workbook. Get in touch with one of your contrasting feelings about attracting healthy, intimate relationships. Know that this is the voice of a wounded one who holds onto all of your issues on attracting your ideal mate. You want to introduce the possibility that you can respond to this wounded one … that you can help it heal its' pain and fear related to your being intimately involved with others. You will be inviting him or her to partner with you to manifest what you deserve. Again, you want to externalize these feelings so you can prepare to respond to them.

Interactive tapping™ Sequences: State the setup phrase while tapping on the karate point.

Even though a part of me feels fearful of opening up and trusting again, I know this is only a part of me, and I love myself and this wounded one enough to be willing to respond to his or her pain.

Even though a part of me is fearful of trusting, and steps in there and sabotages my efforts to feel safe with others … I now choose to work with that part of self … to help him or her heal … because I love that part of self and I understand that its' efforts are in response to its' fears.

Even though a part of me is trying to distract me from my ultimate goal .... I am ready to respond to his or her needs because I love myself and that part of me enough to heal.

That completes the setup phrases. You are now ready to proceed with the reminder phrases. Continue to repeat the reminder phrases until you move through any resistance to your being willing to respond toW this part of you.

Neutralizing the Negative

> *Eyebrow: He or she experiences such distrust.*
> *Side of the Eye: So fearful ... and unable to feel safe.*
> *Under the Eye: Has been so abandoned ... has so much fear.*
> *Upper Lip: He or she is afraid to open up and trust.*
> *Under the Lip: He or she just cannot feel safe enough to trust.*
> *Collarbone: So wounded ... so afraid to reach out and trust.*
> *Under the Arm: This little one cannot imagine not being left.*
> *Rib: So much fear.*
> *Head: Wonder if I will ever be able to heal this fear.*

Introducing the Possibility of Change

> *Eyebrow: Maybe he or she doesn't have to feel so bad?*
> *Side of the Eye: Maybe I can help him or her to feel trust.*
> *Under the Eye: Maybe I can help to restore his or her faith.*
> *Upper Lip: Maybe I can help him or her to feel enough to let go.*
> *Under the Lip: Really want to help him or her let it go.*
> *Collarbone: Maybe he or she can let it go ... maybe it wasn't that bad.*
> *Under the Arm: Maybe he or she can let it go ... maybe I can forgive myself and help him or her to let it go.*
> *Rib: I don't want this little one to feel so much fear.*
> *Head: I really want to help him or her let it go.*

Conviction to Change

Eyebrow: I'm going to help … help him, or her let go of this fear.

Side of the Eye: I am so glad to release this lack of trust and faith.

Under the Eye: Help him or her let go so he or she can feel safe.

Upper Lip: I can feel compassion and help him or her grieve.

Under the Lip: I really can feel compassion for him or her.

Collarbone: Every cell in my body feels the compassion I need.

Under the Arm: The compassion to feel forgiveness for myself and him or her…

Rib: Every cell vibrates with compassion and joy. Every cell now invites him or her to trust.

Head: I can invite him or her to replace this fear with trust.

Continue to work with these sequences until you feel complete with this initial clearing and are prepared to proceed.

3ʀᴅ LAYER--THE INTERACTIONS

Discussion: This step is the heart of Inner Child work. Once you have separated from this part of yourself, you can truly begin to relate to him or her and respond to its fears of attracting love and feeling trust. This fact is the true essence of building a trusting relationship between your most illuminate and nurturing self and the wounded Inner Child or aspect of your Soul. It is essential to ascertain the issues this Inner Child has with trusting you to make him or her feel safe. Before you can clear feelings from the past, it is necessary to clear issues he or she may have with you in relationship to your abandoning him or her and violating his or her trust. This little one may even feel betrayed by you … all of these feelings need to be flushed out so you can be effective in your approach. By responding to his or her pain and operating on its behalf, you enhance the experience of deservedness and nourish a sense of importance. This is true of the Inner Child as well as an aspect of your Soul's past.

You are again doing a form of "surrogate tapping"… tapping on behalf of another. In this sequence, you are using the word "you."

Referring to the wounded one in second person creates the feeling that he or she is finally being heard—that finally, someone notices that the fear of being abandoned needs to be addressed so safety can be established or restored.

Again, if you have taken a break then begin your sequences by doing one round where you get the Adult Self ready to be present for this work. Then take a moment to reconnect with the wounded one from whom you separated in the previous sequence. Invite him or her to sit beside you or even to jump upon your lap. Further, explain that you are going to be tapping on different endpoints on your body and face while speaking certain phrases—acknowledge it may look a little weird but you are doing this to help him or her feel better, so he or she does not have to feel so much pain. *(It is necessary to do this step every time you begin a piece of work because you may be dealing with a different Inner Child.)*

Interactive tapping™ *Sequences: When you feel ready, begin to state the following setup phrases while tapping on the karate point.*

Even though you are fearful of opening up and trusting again, I love myself enough to be willing to respond to your pain.

Even though my desire to find my ideal mate illuminates your fears, I am willing to work with your lack of trust so you can climb aboard and together we can heal.

So even though I want to attract a mate who now matches my most illuminated self … I know this puts you at risk and I am willing to soothe these fears so together we can heal.

Reword this in whatever way speaks to you but say the setup phrases, so you set your psyche up to begin to do this interactive process.

These next sequences begin with the neutralization process; move into the possibility of change and completes this Layer with the conviction to resolve this Inner Child's fears of being abandoned, fears of trusting and not feeling safe.

Use these as suggestions, but you may need to work with this in a little more personal manner ... so do not be shy to make up your own reminder phrases that suit your needs more specifically. Again, you will be using the pronoun, "you."

Neutralizing the Negative

Eyebrow: Afraid, so afraid to trust...

Side of the Eye: So many triggers... you carry so much fear...

Under the Eye: I am here to help you heal...

Upper Lip: I promise to help you feel safe...

Under the Lip: I know you are afraid to trust, but I vow to help you feel safe...

Collarbone: You witnessed so much... so much fear and mistrust...

Under the Arm: So afraid to feel trust...

Rib: All these years ... so many triggers for your fear and mistrust...

Head: So much fear ... so afraid to trust.

Introducing the Possibility of Change

Eyebrow: But maybe you can trust me.

Side of the Eye: Maybe you will let me help you heal.

Under the Eye: Maybe you will learn to trust me.

Upper Lip: Just take the risk and see if this works.

Under the Lip: I invite you to come along.

Collarbone: I promise you I will not let you down.

Under the Arm: I just invite you to work with me.

Rib: Please look ... I really have healed.

Head: I do deserve your trust, and I am willing to show up. I am really excited to work with you on this. I won't let you down.

Conviction to change

> *Eyebrow: I really feel a connection to you.*
>
> *Side of the Eye: I guarantee you I am trustworthy and can help you heal.*
>
> *Under the Eye: I can to help you heal. I am willing to come back to your time.*
>
> *Upper Lip: I can come to you. I can teach you how to neutralize your fears.*
>
> *Under the Lip: I am so excited that you are willing to try.*
>
> *Collarbone: I am so excited we get to work on this together.*
>
> *Under the Arm: I am so excited you have shown up.*
>
> *Rib: I am so excited that together we can heal.*
>
> *Head: I am so excited that together you and I can heal.*

While repeating your reminder phrases, do sequential rounds on the endpoints until you move through any resistance this wounded one holds. Stay with it until he or she can be responsive to your efforts to help it heal. You will sense this part moving from doubt, fear or betrayal, into perhaps even anger that it took you so long, then into a willingness to believe and finally into an eagerness to try the tapping for him or herself. If new feelings emerged in response to these reminder phrases tap on them as well. Customize your sequences until you feel completely clear then move on to Layer Four.

4ᴛʜ LAYER--THE TEACHING STEP: HEALING THE INNER CHILD AND SOUL

Discussion: In this next sequence, you shift into a meditative state and begin to teach your Inner Child or wounded one the technique for this neutralizing process. Remember, if necessary begin your work by doing one round where you get the Adult Self clear enough to be fully present for this work. When you feel ready to proceed, take a moment to reconnect with the Inner Child with whom you worked in the previous Layer. Always invite him or her to sit beside you or even to jump upon your lap. Then explain how you want to teach him or her how to do this process so he or she can feel safe enough to trust you. It is this relationship you must first heal—It is this part of you that sabotages your efforts to attract the mate that you desire.

In your mind's eye, ask your wounded one to take you back to the time when he or she first developed the fear of being abandoned which eroded the ability to feel safe enough to trust. Be prepared that this little one might even begin by taking you back to an experience in which you were the cause of its fear. If that occurs—neutralize that first and end the sequence with an apology. Every time you collapse into the fear and act from this part of you, it is experienced by this Inner Child as abandonment. As you progress in your work, you will be able to recognize this more easily and respond more quickly. But this internal relationship between you and your Inner Child needs to be healed before you can ever hope to transmit a positive vibration to the Universe to which it can respond.

Exercise: Resolving the Past

When you feel ready, proceed to inquire about past situations where this little one felt abandoned or experienced a lack of trust and faith.

1. Who was involved?

2. What did he or she hear or witness that resulted in so much fear, sadness, and pain?

3. Spend time really exploring this past situation, so you will be able to more effectively respond.

4. When you feel you have enough information, close your eyes and imagine you return to the scene where the wounding took place.

5. Observe it for a minute then freeze the scene and pull your wounded one to the side.

6. Invite him or her to either sit on your lap or sit cross-legged in front of you. Build on the experience of that last sequence when this little one watched as you tapped, and explain that,

in this round, you are going to tap along to show him or her how it is done.

All you want is for your Inner Child to repeat what you say and tap where you tap. Explain this, so your little one understands you are stating these sequences as if you are him or her (using the word "I") and you are asking that he or she repeats the phrases after you speak them while tapping where you tap.

In this first round imagine that both you and your Inner Child are tapping on the karate point as you state the setup phrase on his or her behalf. Then envision him or her tapping with you and repeating after you if he or she is willing. If not, just imagine the little one tapping along to your words. Again, determine if these statements need to be tweaked and customized to meet your specific needs.

Interactive tapping™ Sequences: When you feel ready, begin to state the following setup phrases while tapping on the karate point.

Even though I am really afraid to trust once again because I have been so badly hurt in the past, I know you love me, and I love myself enough to trust you to help me heal.

Even though this is really scary for me and I am afraid to revisit this hurt, I feel safe enough with you that I trust it will be okay.

So even though moving ahead causes such great fear I am willing to experiment with this because I trust you enough to believe that you will keep me safe.

These are only examples of your setup statements. Again, customize them to meet your needs. When you feel you have adequately addressed where your Inner Child is and where, as the Adult Self, you want to take him or her, move into the neutralization sequences. I provide examples, but you are going to want to experiment with designing your own sequences and inserting your own words because this is really the Healing Layer of this entire process.

As you will see the sequencing gradually helps you identify the origin of the disturbance and then assists you in moving into the possibility of letting that go ... the possibility that something really can be different … that this wound really can be healed. The sequences then end with the conviction that it is safe to let it go and once again feel faith and trust. Follow this to get a feel for this Layer but, again, when it feels right to do so, experiment with your own words as well.

Neutralizing the Negative

Eyebrow: So much pain in this scene … just remember feeling so unsafe … so wounded and unable to trust.

Side of the Eye: Seldom felt safe.

Under the Eye: Always feared being left … afraid I would not survive.

Upper Lip: I remember the pain … I am so afraid to once again open up and trust.

Under the Lip: Seldom felt safe … so afraid to let go and feel trust.

Collarbone: I was so abandoned … left alone to fend for myself.

Under the Arm: Wish they could have just loved me for who I am.

Rib: So much fear … will I ever be able to trust?

Head: Wish I wasn't so afraid … just don't know if it is safe to trust.

Another round …

Eyebrow: All I ever heard was that I had too many needs.

Side of the Eye: Never felt safe … always feared being left.

Under the Eye: So afraid of being left and fear I will not survive.

Upper Lip: What if I'm not good enough to be loved.

Under the Lip: That's how I feel … when I look back.

Collarbone: Just wish I felt safe.

Under the Arm: I get so afraid of being rejected and abandoned.

Rib: So afraid to trust.

Head: Just so afraid if I trust I will again be left.

Introducing the Possibility of Change

Eyebrow: Maybe this can change…

Side of the Eye: Maybe I can finally feel safe.

Under the Eye: I have always felt the fear of being left.

Upper Lip: But maybe it is safe to trust.

Under the Lip: Maybe I can let this tension go.

Collarbone: Maybe my Adult Self is really here to help me heal this pain.

Under the Arm: Maybe I can let go of my need for Mom and Dad's love.

Rib: Maybe I don't have to carry this tension that I did not deserve.

Head: Maybe I can let go. Maybe it is safe to trust.

Conviction to Change

Eyebrow: I am going to let go and let my Adult Self in…

Side of the Eye: I am going to let go … let go of the past.

Under the Eye: I am willing to let this go and trust my Adult Self.

Upper Lip: I am willing to let go and let God.

Under the Lip: I know I have carried this for so long.

Collarbone: But I am willing to let this fear go…

Under the Arm: … and truly believe my Adult Self is different than my parents.

Rib: I am willing to give it a try.

Head: I feel really good about joining forces with the Adult Self … I am ready to take the risk of letting it go.

Again, this gives you suggestions on how to move through this phase of addressing your Inner Child's pain. I really encourage you to continue to work with these sequences and to keep going through this process. Keep in mind there is no right or wrong way to implement this healing. Continue to work with this Inner Child until he or she is ready to let go and can fully begin to trust you. But keep in mind that this healing will happen progressively. Each time you work with your

Inner Child in this way the trust will grow. But it will not, and does not have to, all happen at once. Accept the Inner Child for where he or she feels at each juncture. As with any issue, you will sense this part moving through the stages of grief, tension, and fear, acknowledging how badly he or she wanted to feel safe and to trust. At points, the anger will emerge regarding the experience of not feeling safe. It is common for your Inner Child to finally embrace the collapse into the total despair of fear and abandonment.

The idea here is to walk this part of you through all of its feelings until it is willing to trust you enough to feel safe. Your little one really does want to trust you will take care of him or her and doesn't want to sabotage your efforts to have an intimate relationship. This wounded one just wants to know that you will still be mindful of his or her needs even if you get involved with someone else. He or she needs to experience you will not abandon yourself, or him or her, when you enter into a relationship. He or she needs to believe you can set limits, you will not lose yourself, and you can keep him or her safe even if you enter into a relationship with another.

Continue to explore your Inner Child's experience around this issue. Tap and neutralize those feelings from every angle, and eventually, you will win back his or her trust. But it is important to be patient. This often takes more than one sequence and more than one day. But this will give you a start. When you feel you have healed this part enough to proceed to the merger that takes place in Layer Five then do so. If you cannot move the pain consider setting up a one-to-one session, and we will see what we can do. You may be inspired to access the Divine and assess if this issue is anchored in a past life. If so, work the first Four Layers from that multidimensional angle. The Fifth Layer addresses the merger with your Inner Child only. If you do discover this is past-life oriented, the process is not to merge, but rather to send that past part of your Soul back to its original source.

5ᵗʰ Layer—The Step of Integration and Merger

Discussion: This Layer is perhaps one of the most empowering Layers. As mentioned above, the following process is used only for the integration of an Inner Child. With an aspect of your Soul, you want to just send it back into the Light so that energy that was tied up in the wound can be freed. But with an aspect of your personality from this lifetime (the Inner Child) you want to partner with him or her and build a bonding, cooperative relationship.

Combining the neutralization process with the pronoun, "we," enables you to begin to set up the merger and integration. Partnering with the Inner Child in this manner empowers him or her to return to your force field in a healed state and empowers you to help your Inner Child reclaim the spontaneity and magic that was lost in the wounding experience. When you bring this magic back, the essence of the believability and trust we all have as children returns as well. If you then infuse your desire to attract the relationship of your choice with this vibration, you experience magic ten-fold! The result will mirror this very relationship you have taken the time to heal.

Keep in mind you can only feel as safe with others as you feel safe within yourself. You can only trust others to the degree you trust yourself. If you are secure in knowing no matter what happens you will not abandon this Inner Child he or she will trust you and not feel the need to sabotage your efforts to find love.

If you have taken a break then begin your Fifth Layer of exercises by doing one round where you get the Adult Self clear enough to be present for this work. You may also want to add another round to make sure your Inner Child has remained clear. When you feel ready to proceed the sequence will go something like the example below.

State the setup phrase while tapping on the karate point. For this Layer, you will be using the pronoun "we" because you are stating the sequences in a way that promotes the Inner Child and Adult Self saying them in unison.

Interactive tapping™ Sequences: When you feel ready, begin to state the following setup phrases while tapping on the karate point.

Even though we have both experienced a lot of betrayals and have ample reason to not feel trust—and we have both experienced a lot of tension about not feeling safe, being left feeling unsure we would survive—we are so excited we have found each other again and we love ourselves and each other enough to trust we can manifest the relationship our heart desires.

Even though we both have experienced so many disappointments, betrayals, and reasons to not trust we are so excited we have come together and are now able to feel safe enough with each other so we can heal.

So even though we have so many experiences of abandonment, so many reasons to not trust—we are so excited we have found each other— we have come home to each other and are ready to heal.

The following is an example of the sequences you could use to augment this layer. It is really not so much of a process of neutralization as an infusion of what you have affirmed. But just to be on the safe side I have provided one round to help you clear any resistance to come together in this fashion. Add more if you feel it would be useful.

Again, prepare to tap by beginning with the corner of your eyebrow.

Tapping in the Merger

Eyebrow: We are so excited to come together and heal.

Side of the Eye: We are just buzzing with enthusiasm and trust for each other.

Under the Eye: So excited we are going to finally manifest our heart's desire.

Upper Lip: With the love of each other and the love of God we deserve all we desire.

Under the Lip: We are so excited to come together to heal.

Collarbone: So excited we are together to heal, to attract the relationship we deserve.

Under the Arm: We are so full of energy, love, and Light, we send this out to the entire world.

Rib: We are so excited we have done such good work.

Head: We are so proud of each other and love each other so much that we are ready to attract another who mirrors our love.

Now just keep going with that until you are really, really buzzing and when you feel ready to proceed—move onto Layer Six.

6ᵀᴴ Layer—Rewiring your Brain; Reprogramming your DNA; Reconfiguring the Electromagnetic Field

Discussion: This implementation of this Layer was inspired by the New Brain Science, most specifically the work of Dr. Richard Hanson, and Margaret Ruby's work on reprogramming the DNA. www.possibilitiesdna.com/margaret.html

You use meditations and interactive tapping™ sequences to first rewire the brain by building new neuro-pathways between the amygdala and the prefrontal cortex. You then clear the energetic disturbance from your electrical system in your body, ask your body for its forgiveness, and then give it permission to release. This reprograms the DNA in every cell so it can hold your new vibration and enables you to reconfigure the electromagnetic field around you.

I encourage you to experiment with the wording as much as your imagination will allow. Just keep tapping and saying affirming statements. I have included suggestions, but please experiment. Try it on every feeling you think you have stored in your body about the Divine work you should be doing and the right livelihood you want to attract.

Before you begin, however, do one round to clear any current trigger in your Adult Self and to neutralize any current disturbance that may be getting in the way of giving your body permission to release. State each setup phrase while tapping on the karate point.

The interaction is between you and your body so imagine you are speaking directly to it.

Interactive tapping™ Sequences: State the setup phrase while tapping on the karate point. Imagine you are speaking directly to your body.

Even though I have needed you to store my pain, I am now strong enough to process my pain myself—so I invite you to release the tension and the stress. I invite you to let it go.

So even though you, my dear body, have held so many feelings of tension related to my fear of abandonment and not feeling safe I just, for so long, was unable to deal with these feelings myself, I now forgive myself and love myself completely and profoundly because I did not know what else to do.

In turn, I ask you to forgive me as well. I humbly apologize for needing you to hold this disturbance for me and now give you total permission to release it. I firmly commit to you that I will now neutralize and dissolve all disturbances related to my lack of trust and my inability to feel safe. *Thank you, Thank you. Thank you.*

Repeat this sequence until you feel you have moved through all the resistance your body is holding for you. Give your body permission to release what it has held. Reassure it that you are now completely willing to deal with what comes your way with the tools you have acquired. When replenishing your body with a new vibration, you are acknowledging that the DNA has been reprogrammed. You infuse every cell with the new vibration of your intention.

To accomplish this task I suggest you tap on what is called your sore spots. They are several inches from your collarbone. These are tender spots and can be found by slowly tapping and putting pressure on this area of your body. You will know by the tenderness you feel that you have hit the right spot. As you tap on these two sore spots, begin to tell the story of your new intention.

Continue to do this technique for at least 68 seconds. As you read in the previous section, according to the teachings of Abraham, this amount of attention is enough for your intention to take form and to begin gathering reciprocity from the Universe which will then match its vibration and begin the process of materializing your intent.

In a narrative fashion, state something like this:

I now envision compassion and safety in every area of my life. All my needs and wants are fully realized in the presence of the Light. I am so fortunate to experience such acceptance and unconditional love. I feel so safe and am willing to respond with love. Every area of my life is enriched with this sense of acceptance. This acceptance radiates out to all I attract. I love what I do. I love the rewards my actions bring back. I radiate in unconditional love, and this vibration attracts the perfect people into my life. I am now safe to relate. I am safe to be present in my body. I trust I can cope, so my body does not have to take on my pain.

I am rich with experiences of love and Light and see the magic of the Universe everywhere I look. I truly am a worthwhile being, and I exude that worthiness in every act! I am perfect in mind, body, heart, and Soul! I deserve to be loved. I trust enough to attract love into my life.

Then complete this infusion by tapping on the endpoints while stating reminder phrases which *anchor this into* your body, mind, heart, and Soul. I have provided an example of one round. Add other rounds as you see fit.

Eyebrow: My body has held onto all of this fear and mistrust.

Side of the Eye: All of this fear of abandonment, betrayal, and mistrust my body has stored because I didn't know how to process it.

Under the Eye: My body has held onto this fear and mistrust … this lack of safety and fear.

Upper Lip: But I now give my body permission to let go.

Under the Lip: I release all of this mistrust—fear of abandonment and my inability to feel safe.

Collarbone: My body is now programmed with faith and trust.

Rib: Every cell now holds this new DNA vibration of compassion and love.

Under the Arm: My body forgives me and vibrates with unconditional love.

Head: I am so glad my body can finally let go and vibrate with safety and trust.

7ᵀᴴ LAYER—GIVING BACK TO THE WORLD

Discussion: Now you get to share this with the world. It needs an infusion of compassionate, unconditional regard. Take all you have neutralized and realigned and send this energy into the Universe as an offering for planetary healing. This gesture dissolves isolation and contributes not only to increasing the Light on the planet but also to the healing of Mother Earth. It reinforces the fact that you are part of something bigger than yourself and a valuable agent of change for humanity. You have shared the gift with your Inner Child or Soul Fragment. You now have an opportunity to share it with the world.

Again, I encourage you to experiment with the wording as much as your imagination will allow. Just keep tapping and saying affirming statements. I have included a sample but please experiment and try it on everything. Make sure, however, you use this only after you have moved to a low intensity on the scale from 1—to 10—or have neutralized your way *up* your emotional guidance scale—because you want the energy you send out into the world to be as pure as possible. As always, before you begin, I suggest you do one round to clear any current triggers in your current day self, body, mind, heart, and Soul! Begin to tap as you enter into a meditative state. When you feel ready tap again on your sore spots while you say something like:

Interactive tapping™ Sequences:
(Click here for the audio version)

I feel so fortunate to have done this work. I now envision the cylinder of Light running from the center of Mother Earth to the grid of unconditional love about 60 feet above my head.

I am so full of Light and high energy. From this highest place within myself, I now offer 10% of this healing back to heal the planet and the Universe for their use in healing wherever the energy needs increasing.

I feel so fortunate I have been able to complete this work and am so grateful I am now in a position to truly share this gift with the rest of the world. I love feeling safe, and I love contributing this sense of safety to the world. Thank you, God, Goddess, Higher Power, Angels, Masters and all above for your support and direction. Thank you for your support in my feeling safe. Thank your Soul fragments for having the courage and fortitude to call me back—and thank you my dear little ones for having the patience to await my return.

I love that we are healed and can now hold the Light which allows us to attract the relationship we so desire. We can now contribute to this world in a supportive, safe way. Thank you, Thank you. Thank you.

This sequence. again, is but an example. As you work in this fashion, the inspiration will come to you, the words will come to you, and this last sequence will simply augment your ability to attract the relationship of your desire into your life.

GENERAL TAPPING INSTRUCTIONS AND PROGRESSIONS

When you begin the tapping sequence, you just keep restating the above examples and do as many rounds as it takes to envision and implant this new expression. Experiment with it and feel free to alter it as your experiences shift.

As the energy shifts, you might want to imagine you progressively moving up Abraham's *Emotional Guidance Scale. (Ask and It Is Given* by Esther and Jerry Hicks, page 114) In other words, you move through the Five Layers of grief … up from the despair of being alone and unsafe, to the anger that no one was there to take care of your needs, to the frustration of being abandoned, to the irritation that you had to fear you would not survive, to the possibility that things can change, to the belief and appreciation that you are finally safe. You adjust the setup phrases and reminder phrases accordingly.

Module 2:
Attracting Abundance

A Word From Abraham

I begin with an excerpt from *"The Secret behind the Secret."* featuring the *"Teachings of Abraham,"* Channeled by Esther Hicks.

Interviewer: There are things out there that we all want—whatever it is, health, money, whatever—we all have our heart's desire—how, in concrete terms, can we head towards these things we want?

Abraham's response:

When you think about it, every subject is really two subjects. What is wanted and the lack of it or absence of it. When you identify a desire such as money, you pick up the stick with money written on it; on one end is more money and on the other end of the stick is the lack of it. You are vibrating somewhere along this stick.

You have been having the experience of not enough money. You have been worrying about it. You have been talking about it, and you are now, from your awareness of not having enough money, asking for more money. But you are not a vibrational match to more money; you are a vibrational match to not enough money.

You can tell what end of the stick you are on by the way you feel about money. So if you think about money and it makes you feel free, and it makes you feel exhilarated and adventurous, then you are on the vibrational end of the stick that matches dollars. That is why rich people get richer. They feel prosperous. They see money coming towards them. They do not hold money away from themselves.

People who do not have enough money are not allowing money to come to them. So the key to moving up the stick is to find a way to feel more prosperous. Stand where you are because you cannot do anything else, but try to play down the "not enough money" and play up how well things are going.

WHERE IT ALL BEGINS: From Developmental Tasks To Adult Patterns To Spiritual Lessons

EXERCISE: HOW THE STAGES OF DEVELOPMENT FROM CHILDHOOD IMPACT YOUR ABUNDANCE

The following interfaces the tasks from each developmental stage of childhood (with which you have already worked with) into your ideas about money and abundance.; here are a few sentences that describe the goal you were mastering at each stage of development, and then a series of four questions gives you a thumbnail view of how these tasks (if not mastered) may manifest in your current, Adult behavior (as an adult) or feelings regarding abundance. They will further assist you in being able to identify where you are stuck and how you might proceed with the next step—which is to neutralize contrasting feelings that crop up in response to attracting the abundance you deserve.

Infant (Birth to 18 Months)—The goal here is to give birth to a vision of the kind of wealth you want to have. What does wealth look like? What kind of person would you be if you were wealthy? You need to create a vision of wealth so that the seed can be planted. You will want to define what is feasible and within reach of your vision of self, so you can indeed evolve into the wealthy and prosperous person you deserve to be. Ponder those thoughts and record your responses in your journal. Use the statements below to further your exploration.

They may reflect where you are stuck, or they may inspire additional thoughts. Your responses will help you identify which part of self needs your attention.

_____1. I have difficulty conceiving of myself as a wealthy person.

_____2. Abundance seems out of my immediate reach.

_____3. I am so familiar with struggling I can't imagine having money.

_____4. I have great wealth; I just don't know what to spend it on.

Feel free to modify these statements to accommodate what is true for you. Again, I encourage you to record your thoughts and feelings as you design the profile of the saboteur within that blocks you from attaining all the prosperity you desire and deserve.

Toddler (18 to 36 months)—The adult issue that may emerge here is your need to set appropriate limits on your spending ... to see where you need to set limits with your budget or possibly determine where you have been *too* restrictive. Ask yourself if you see the world from a perspective of scarcity or prosperity. If you owe and borrow against tomorrow, you might examine whether that action reveals scarcity or lack of faith, implying that you receive what you ask for. Use those thoughts to stimulate responses in your journal. Use the statements below to further your exploration. Ponder your answers. They may reflect where you are stuck, or they may inspire additional thoughts. Your responses will help you determine which part within needs your attention.

_____1. I devise a budget plan but then do not stick to it.

_____2. I wish I could spend money wisely—but I don't.

_____3. I don't attract a lot of money. I am afraid it might change me.

_____4. If I do get money, I feel a need to spend it right away.

Feel free to modify these statements to accommodate what is true for you. Again, I encourage you to record your thoughts and feelings as you design the profile of the saboteur within that blocks you from attaining all the prosperity you desire and deserve.

Young Inner Child (3-6 years)—The goal originating from this stage is to balance what you have with what you don't have … to mix your spiritual affirmations for wealth with a concrete plan of action. It is also effective to examine your definition of prosperity and abundance. Value shifts may occur that enable you to feel abundant with what you have as opposed to what you dream of having. You can become more realistic as you deal with judgments towards self or others and give up the comparison game of being better or worse off than others. Use these thoughts to promote responses in your journal. Use the statements below to further your exploration. Ponder them. Let them reflect where you are stuck, or inspire additional thoughts. Your responses will help you know which part of self needs your attention.

_____1. I am uncomfortable attracting more money than I need.

_____2. I feel everyone else has more of everything than I.

_____3. I don't like to be around people who have a lot of money.

_____4. When I am well off, I feel uneasy being around someone who is not.

Feel free to modify these statements to accommodate what is true for you. Again, I encourage you to record your thoughts and feelings as you design the profile of the saboteur within that blocks you from attaining all the prosperity you desire and deserve.

Grade School Self (6-12 years)—The challenge extending from this stage is to determine if your financial goals are based on your value system or on an external one. You may find you base your financial goals on your need for recognition, so you set goals that are in alignment with society's values and not your own. You may discover you spend money on things that will win approval from others as you try to *keep up with the Jones* so that you can fit in with friends, neighbors, and family. It is important to keep in mind that this is a phase and not become too judgmental of yourself as you explore these tendencies. Use these thoughts to promote responses in your journal. Use the statements below to further your exploration. They may reflect where you are stuck or inspire additional thoughts.

Your response will help you identify which part of self needs your attention.

_____1. It is important to me to *keep up with the Jones.*

_____2. My job pays well, and I like others to know this.

_____3. I feel less prosperous than most around me.

_____4. I feel abundant but keep it quiet rather than risk rejection or criticism.

Feel free to modify these statements to accommodate to what is true for you. Again, I encourage you to record your thoughts and feelings as you design the profile of the saboteur within that blocks you from attaining all the prosperity you desire and deserve.

The same issues from the first three developmental stages are revisited in adolescence.

Young Inner Teen (12-15 years)—You may begin to play with the concepts of *wealth* and *prosperity*, but you do not quite know how to put those principles into practice. You can shift from manifesting abundance based on horizontal principles to manifesting wealth according to your higher wisdom and inner knowingness. The young inner teen carries the same themes as three-to-six-year-old. The developmental task of moving from shame to self-regard which is first experienced in response to your family morphs into the task of moving from self-consciousness to self-confidence experienced in response to your peers.

Keep this in mind as you use these thoughts to stimulate responses in your journal. Use the statements below to further your exploration. They may reflect where you are stuck, inspire additional thoughts; help you identify which part of self needs your attention.

_____1. I feel inadequate when it comes to managing my money.

_____2. I don't have much passion for life or love.

_____3. I believe if I do what I love, the money will follow.

_____4. I avoid people who obviously have significantly more or less money than I.

Feel free to modify these statements to accommodate to what is true for you. Again, I encourage you to record your thoughts and feelings as you design the profile of the saboteur within that blocks you from attaining all the prosperity you desire and deserve.

Adolescent (15-17 years)—The challenges you carry at this stage of your exploration reflect the unresolved tasks from when you were a toddler. Knowingly or unknowingly you revisit how well you set boundaries in your relationship to money and abundance. You begin to examine where you need to address potential overspending and where you need to deal with your rigidity in response to your financial goals. As you carry your adolescent issues into manifesting abundance, you may find you become more willing to risk everything for the chance to "do what you love and hope that the money follows." You may become unwilling to *prostitute* yourself. As in toddlerhood, you are carving out your sense of self and independence. Your focus shifts to wanting to stay true to your unique passion and path. You become more committed to attracting the money and prosperity from a more authentic place that is in alignment with your truest self and your own unique values.

Again, use these thoughts to promote responses in your journal. Use the statements below to further your exploration. They may reflect where you are stuck, or they may inspire additional thoughts; your response will help you know which part of self needs your attention.

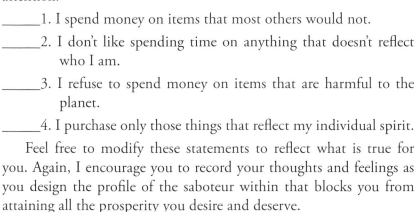

_____1. I spend money on items that most others would not.

_____2. I don't like spending time on anything that doesn't reflect who I am.

_____3. I refuse to spend money on items that are harmful to the planet.

_____4. I purchase only those things that reflect my individual spirit.

Feel free to modify these statements to reflect what is true for you. Again, I encourage you to record your thoughts and feelings as you design the profile of the saboteur within that blocks you from attaining all the prosperity you desire and deserve.

Young Inner Adult (17-21 years)—By the time you begin to explore your relationship with money through the eyes of your young adult, you have experienced some mastery with regard to your lessons regarding abundance. You begin to trust that your "needs and wants" will be met with ease and enthusiasm. You welcome the opportunity to revise old beliefs about trusting the Universe, about feeling safe with the Universe, as you explore your place in the financial world. You begin to think about the future in a more responsible way. You may find yourself interested in investments or long-term financial goals. You begin to experience a maturity with respect to your relationship to your abundance. Whatever you discover that conflicts with this trajectory hold seeds of the unfinished business from your young inner adult.

Again, use these thoughts to stimulate responses in your journal. Use the statements below to further your exploration. They may reflect where you are stuck. They may inspire additional thoughts; help you know which part of self needs your attention.

_____1 .I believe abundance is a direct extension of the Universal energy.

_____2. I feel abundant in my life but know there is room for improvement.

_____3. I do what I love—I just wish the money would follow.

_____4. When I look at the world, I wish I saw more abundance and prosperity.

Feel free to modify these statements to accommodate what rings true for you. Again, I encourage you to record your thoughts and feelings in your journal as you design the profile of the saboteur within that blocks you from attaining all the prosperity you desire and deserve.

Now review your responses to give form to the cherished saboteur™ that blocks your efforts to succeed with antiquated beliefs or old fears. You will reference this exploration later when you begin to apply the *Seven-Layer Healing Process* to heal this old wound.

Working With The Resistance

The next set of exercises help you flush out the saboteur and begin the process of working with him or her.

Exercise: Meditation on your Cherished Saboteur™

This journal meditation will help you give form to the part of you that might be sabotaging your efforts to attract the abundance you so desire. Begin by taking a deep breath and allowing yourself to relax into a deeper state of consciousness. Invite your Guardians and Higher Teachers in to assist you. When you feel ready—read each question, contemplate your response, and then record it in your journal. Work with it and use these questions to reveal whatever needs to emerge.

Then begin by visualizing the word *money*. Let yourself bring up any reaction you have to that word.

1. What does that word "money" provoke in you?

2. Does it excite you or frighten you?

3. Go back to when you were a child.

4. What do you remember hearing about money when you were growing up?

5. See if you can retrieve a representative scene that portrays the manner in which money was dealt with in your family.

6. Was it a source of tension … of arguments?

7. Which Inner Child carries this theme for you and what does he or she need from you now to trust that you will be able to deal with money and abundance without putting him or her at risk?

The above gives you a profile of the Inner Child that may be sabotaging your efforts to succeed. Take a few moments to interact with this part of you. See what he or she needs from you. It will be this Inner Child with whom you will be working when you proceed with the *Seven-Layer Healing Process.* Keep in mind that the source of your resistance is the fear of your Inner Child.

EFT Sequence for Clearing Resistance

This next section leads you through the tapping sequences that will help your Adult Self become clear. As was mentioned in the introduction, if what you want to manifest is in alignment with your higher purpose, then these sequences will clear the sabotage resulting from current stressors. If you do not see results or do not feel clear after doing these sequences, then this would most likely indicate your issues are Inner Child based and it would be beneficial to continue with the *Seven-Layer Healing Process.*

When you feel ready to proceed, tap on the karate point as you state the setup statements.

Even though I have a part of me that wants to hang onto the old patterns ... and is afraid to let go and trust that I will be able to manage my finances while staying connected to my Source, I love myself and that part of me fully and completely.

Even though I have had some challenging experiences around money, and God knows I have been stressed with respect to attracting abundance into my life, that little one who is holding onto this now allows me to help him or her let it go. That part of me knows I have enough love for both of us to warrant the release of tension so we can heal.

Even though I may have a variety of voices within me that all speak of fear and doubt, I have earned their trust, and they are now willing to follow my lead because they know I love myself and them enough to help us all heal.

In the above statements, you established that you have this sabotaging voice and then positioned it with the positive affirmation. The following sequences will help you move from the sabotage to the conviction of change. As before, the following process is divided into three sections. You first neutralize the negative thoughts and feelings then introduce the possibility of change. The second section usually does not take as long; it just softens the ego, so it is ready to claim your right to feel convicted about the new approach. The last section should leave you feeling healthy and energized in your new conviction. If this does not clear the issue, then proceed to the *Seven-Layer Healing Process* that will work with each piece of this dynamic more fully.

Neutralizing Negativity

Eyebrow: Hangs onto old feelings.

Side of the Eye: Old feelings of fear/doubt.

Under the Eye: Fear, doubt, and anxiety.

Upper Lip: So much tension.

Under the Lip: Can't imagine trusting again.

Collarbone: Can't let go.

Under the Arm: Afraid to trust and allow abundance to flow.

Rib: What if it all falls apart again.

Head: So much fear and mistrust; what if it falls apart again.

Introducing Possibility of Change

Eyebrow: Maybe things have begun to change.

Side of the Eye: Maybe I can take a deep breath and try to trust.

Under the Eye: Maybe I can see some reason to hope.

Upper Lip: Maybe I do need to take this risk.

Under the Lip: Maybe it is worth my attempting to trust.

Collarbone: Perhaps I can turn it over and let God lead the way.

Under the Arm: Maybe I can try just one more time.

Rib: Maybe I can believe and have faith and trust.

Head: Maybe I can take this risk; believe; have faith and trust.

Conviction to Change

Eyebrow: I choose to believe I can attract all I need and want.

Side of the Eye: I am so ready to attract all my desires.

Under the Eye: I love this feeling of being abundant.

Upper Lip: I love knowing I can intend and trust.

Under the Lip: I love this vibration of harmony and wealth.

Collarbone: I love attracting all my desires.

Under the Arm: It is so exhilarating to let go and let God.

Rib: I know I can finally trust.

Head: I am so grateful I can finally trust.

Again, continue to work with each of these sections until you feel the shift from sabotage and doubt to conviction and trust. To build on what you just experienced, move on to the next couple of exercises.

EXERCISE: A 1,000,000 WISH

Take out one of your personal checks. Fill it out for the amount of a million dollars or any amount you wish to attract. On the back, where you list the deposits, make your wish list of how you want to spend your million dollars. Put this check in your pocket. Take a trip to your local mall; imagine you begin to spend this money energetically. Notice all of the things you can purchase without fear. Each day spend a little bit more until you have successfully spent the entire million dollars. Notice how you feel as you do this exercise! Feel free to combine this exercise with the following exercise.

EXERCISE: THE MIRROR EFFECT

Either look at yourself in the mirror or use a friend as your mirror and speak about the abundance that is coming into your life. Speak about it with as much detail as possible. Color it with emotion. Enumerate all of the things you purchased with your millions of dollars. Be sure to talk for at least 68 seconds, for as before, according to the *Teachings of Abraham,* this amount of time is enough to send your vibrational message out to the Universe so it can begin to bring to you your financial match.

Once you feel complete, take a few moments to write about your experience in your journal. Sit with this for awhile. Then determine to proceed with the *Seven-Layer Healing Process.*

Seven-Layer Healing Process Applied To Attracting Abundance

ATTRACTING ABUNDANCE—*An Interactive Tapping™ Overview*

As you witnessed in the above exercises if you are having difficulty attracting money there is a reason and that reason, once identified, can be neutralized and resolved. Let the interactive tapping™ sequences do the work for you. Use these as a guide but always feel free to create your own.

If you are doing this on a daily basis, then you will want to begin each day with empowering your Adult Self before you work with the Layer of that day. If you do it in one big swoop, then once you have cleared the Adult Self, it is unnecessary to repeat this with each Layer unless you feel the need to do so. There is no right or wrong way to proceed. Honor whichever style appeals to you.

These first sequences neutralize any disturbance that is currently in the Adult Self. They do not necessarily refer to abundance but rather it addresses general irritations. Clearing these enables you to begin this work with a clear mindset.

This process begins by neutralizing the Adult Self. It is this part of you that will orchestrate the layered healing, so it is, therefore, essential that he or she is cleared of any distracting emotions or thoughts. The setup phrase positions any disturbance with an affirmation, thus preparing your psyche to accept the neutralization process that will follow.

INTERACTIVE TAPPING™ Sequences For Attracting Abundance

1ST LAYER: EMPOWERING AND CLEARING THE ADULT SELF

Begin by tapping on the karate point while stating the following:

Even though there may be some things I am not totally in harmony with today … I choose for this time to suspend those feelings, so I can now focus entirely on the exercises for the layers of this work.

So even though I may need to neutralize some general irritations … I am going to do that before I do this work because I love myself fully and completely, and I am committed to clearing this up.

So even though I may not be in total harmony, I am willing to suspend any contrasting feelings I have at this time, so that I can be as clear and as open to doing this work because I love myself enough to succeed.

You will next state reminder phrases while you tap on the designated endpoints, to neutralize whatever emerges. If you are reading this in its Kindle format again, this loosely follows the tracks on the mp3.

Neutralizing the Negative

Eyebrow: Feel generally irritated.
Side of the Eye: Have some disturbances right now.
Under the Eye: May feel a little tired, not quite up for this.
Upper Lip: Don't feel completely attentive today.
Under the Lip: But would like to get this issue cleared up.

Collarbone: Have some irritation about some events that have happened today.

Under the Arm: But am willing to let those go.

Rib: Any disturbance I have from the last 24 hours …

Head: I am now willing to let go.

One more round…

Eyebrow: Generally disturbed … A little bit antsy … Clear out any anger.

Side of the Eye: Clear out all distraction.

Under the Eye: Any frustration.

Upper lip: A little bit fatigued.

Under the lip: But choose to feel empowered to do this work.

Collarbone: Am excited to do this Layer of work.

Under the Arm: Have committed to showing up to do this work.

Rib: Am getting excited to meet this Inner Child and to help this Inner Child heal.

Head: I ask my Higher Guidance to be of assistance, so that I can move forward, clear this disturbance, and at last heal.

That completes the sequences and gives you suggestions of how you would neutralize anything that is currently in your daily life. Continue to tap on each of the endpoints until you move through any resistance that might crop up in your efforts to heal the inner saboteur.

2ND LAYER: THE SEPARATION STEP

Discussion: In the exercises in the first section, you were able to put a face to your wounded one. Now is the time to separate from the feelings of the wounded one and *externalize* the challenging feelings. When you *externalize* the disturbance, you set up a dyad between the part of you that carries the wound and the part of you that can respond to the wound.

You will be using the pronouns "he or she" to begin the separation process. This is a crucial step because this very separation allows us to interact, and the interaction between the wounded one and the Healer within you creates the healing.

When you are sure your Adult Self is clear, get in touch with one of your contrasting feelings about abundance. Know that this is the voice of a wounded one that holds on to all of your issues related to attracting abundance in your life. You want to introduce the possibility that you can respond to this wounded one … that you can help it heal its' pain around money and abundance. You will be inviting it to partner with you to manifest what you deserve. Again, you want to externalize these feelings to be able to respond to them. (Note: sometimes as the Adult Self you have antagonistic feelings towards the Inner Child, and these feelings need to be neutralized before you can more effectively move forward. Do so with your tapping. Acknowledge the animosity in one round and then release it and let it go in the next.

State the setup phrase while tapping on the karate point:

Even though a part of me feels really fearful of attracting abundance into my life … and it is not sure it can trust me to set the appropriate limits that will ensure its safety … as the adult, I know this is only a part of me, and I love myself and this wounded one enough to be willing to respond to his or her pain.

Even though a part of me is really shy about trusting so he or she takes center stage and sabotages my efforts to attract abundance into my life … I now choose to work with that part of self … to help him or her heal … because I love that part of self and I understand that this little one's efforts are in response to fear.

Even though a part of me is trying to distract me from my ultimate goal …. I am ready to show up for this work … I am ready to respond to his or her needs because I love myself and that part of me enough to heal.

That completes the setup phrases. You are now ready to proceed with the reminder phrases. Continue to repeat the reminder phrases until you move through any resistance that might crop up in your efforts to heal the inner saboteur.

Neutralizing the Negative

Eyebrow: He or she feels really scared.

Side of the Eye: Does not want to allow me to attract my heart's desire.

Under the Eye: Really frightened about bringing in money.

Upper Lip: Just as scared of being exposed.

Under the Lip: This part is just so judgmental about abundance and money ...

Collarbone: ... really is judgmental and scared.

Under the Arm: So much fear ... so much mistrust of me.

Rib: Really scared ... doesn't want to let me bring the money in.

Head: This part of me wants to sabotage all of my efforts to succeed.

One more round...

Eyebrow: So much fear and doubt.

Side of the Eye: So much fear... so much doubt.

Under the Eye: Really scared to allow me to attract that which I deserve.

Upper Lip: Doesn't feel deserving or worthy of abundance in this life.

Under the Lip: Has seen people really misuse money ... has been hurt by their efforts and their greed.

Collarbone: Doesn't want money in my life ... doesn't want prosperity or abundance or greed.

Under the Arm: So afraid that I might abandon him or her if I really become abundant and gain profit.

Rib: So much distrust and so much fear.

Head: So much distrust and fear of greed.

This series of sequences completes this initial clearing and prepares you to proceed. The next set of sequences introduces the possibility that the Adult Self can really respond to this Inner Child ... you are still going to be using the pronouns "he or she." You are still working on separating and empowering the Adult Self so you can be separate enough to respond (as the Healer) to this wounded self.

Introducing the Possibility of Change

Eyebrow: Maybe if I work with this part of self, he or she will allow me to help him or her let go.

Side of the Eye: Maybe he or she can begin to trust me.

Under the Eye: Maybe he or she can let go.

Upper Lip: Maybe I have healed enough to warrant winning his or her trust.

Under the Lip: Maybe he or she can watch as I manage my finances and not be so afraid I will get greedy and forget to protect that little one within.

Collarbone: Maybe I can help him or her heal.

Under the Arm: Maybe he or she will let me stand by his or her side.

Rib: Maybe he or she will come and assist me in this process.

Head: Maybe I can help him or her heal.

Again, do as many rounds as it takes for you (as the Adult Self) to really solidify this belief in the possibility that this pattern can change, and you can be the active agent orchestrating that change. The following sequences anchor in that conviction. You have indeed mastered the ability to respond to the wounded one instead of collapsing into his or her fears.

Conviction of Change

Eyebrow: He or she really can begin to trust me.

Side of the Eye: I do manage my money well.

Under the Eye: I have mastered what I need—to win his or her trust.

Upper Lip: I can address the needs and keep my little one safe.

Under the Lip: I am excited to do this work … I am excited to walk my Inner Child through this process.

Collarbone: I can do this … together we can heal!

Under the Arm: I am really excited to begin to work with this part of self.

Rib: I am very excited to bring him or her forth.

Head: I am now ready to bring my little one forth, so together we can heal.

Continue to work with these sequences until your Adult Self is buzzing with enthusiasm and is really convinced it can respond to this wounded self and help it heal. When you feel ready ... move on to the interactive step.

3ʀᴅ Lᴀʏᴇʀ: Tʜᴇ Iɴᴛᴇʀᴀᴄᴛɪᴏɴ

Discussion: This step is really the heart of the Inner Child work. Once you have separated from this part of yourself, you can truly begin to relate to your Inner Child and respond to its fears of being abundant. This response is the true essence of building a trusting relationship between your most illuminate, nurturing self and the wounded Inner Child or aspect of your Soul. It is sometimes useful to ascertain whether this Inner Child has any issues with trusting you, in current time, to set appropriate boundaries around money and abundance. This Inner Child may even feel betrayed by you. Because of your own addictions or stages of immaturity and irresponsibility, your little one may have lost trust in you. All of these feelings need to be flushed out before you can be effective in your approach.

If you do uncover current issues simply tap them out as you have done in previous sections. Establish your setup phrase by determining where the little one is at and where, as the Adult, you want to take him or her. Play with the wording but state the setup phrase at least three times. Then do your rounds of reminder phrases ... neutralize the negative or challenging feelings ... introduce the possibility of change ... and end with a conviction to establish something new. Once the current distractions have been resolved you are in a position to help your wounded one address the issues of the past.

You will be doing a form of *surrogate tapping* ... tapping on behalf of another. In this sequence, you are using the word *you*. Addressing your wounded one directly creates a sense of accountability. The Inner Child feels seen, heard, and assisted, perhaps for the very first time. By responding to his or her pain and operating on its behalf, you give the Inner Child the experience of deservedness and nourish a sense of importance.

Again, if you have taken a break from your work begin your sequences by doing one round where you get the Adult Self ready to be present for this work. Then take a moment to reconnect with the wounded one from whom you separated in the previous sequence. Invite him or her to sit beside you or even jump upon your lap. Explain you are going to be tapping on your face and body while speaking certain phrases. Acknowledge it may look a little weird. You are doing this though to help him or her feel better so that he or she does not have to feel so much pain.

When you feel ready, begin to state the following setup phrases while tapping on the karate point:

Even though the circumstances surrounding attracting abundance into my life trigger your old fears and wounds (substitute any feeling that fits) and sometimes causes you great pain, I love you and myself enough to begin to work with your original wound, so we can work together to manifest what we deserve.

Even though my desires illuminate your fears, I am willing to work with you so that you can climb aboard and together we can heal.

So even though I want to bring forth great abundance, because I do know we deserve it, I am sensitive to the fact that this puts you at risk, and I am willing to soothe your fears so that you can feel safe enough so that together we can heal.

Reword this in whatever way speaks to you, but state the setup phrases in such a way that you are able to set your psyche up to begin to orchestrate this interactive process. These next sequences begin the neutralization process and then move into the possibility of change. Use these as suggestions, but keep in mind that you may want to work with this in a more personal manner … so do not be shy to make up your own reminder phrases that suit your needs more specifically. Again, you will be using the pronoun "you."

Neutralizing the Negative

Eyebrow: You have so much fear. You are so afraid of being left behind.

Side of the Eye: You are really full of mistrust … and it's based on what you experienced as a child.

Under the Eye: You are so full of doubt … so full of fear.

Upper Lip: Scared I will leave you behind.

Under the Lip: Don't trust me to bring you along.

Collarbone: So much fear … so much mistrust.

Under the Arm: All you have seen is greed, failure, or tension around money.

Rib: So much fear … do not know what to do.

Head: So much fear and doubt that I will leave you behind.

Possibility of Change

Eyebrow: But maybe by now I have done enough to earn your trust.

Side of the Eye: Maybe you have witnessed me managing my current affairs.

Under the Eye: All I need is for you to be willing to work with me, to try this silly technique.

Upper Lip: Maybe showing up for you will be enough for you to be ready to try.

Under the Lip: I invite you to come along.

Collarbone: I promise you I will not let you down.

Under the Arm: I just invite you to work with me.

Rib: I want you to recognize that I have really healed and am now trustworthy with the affairs that have to do with attracting abundance into our lives.

Head: I do deserve your trust, and I am willing to show up. I am really excited to work with you on this.

Conviction of Change

Eyebrow: I really feel a connection with you.

Side of the Eye: I guarantee you I am trustworthy and can help you heal.

Under the Eye: I really want to help you heal.

Upper Lip: I am willing to come back to your time ... to teach you how to neutralize your fears.

Under the Lip: I am so excited that you are willing to try.

Collarbone: I am so excited we get to work on this together.

Under the Arm: I am so excited you have shown up.

Rib: I am so excited that together we can heal.

Head: I am so excited that together you and I can heal.

While repeating your reminder phrases, do sequential rounds on the endpoints until you move through any resistance this wounded one holds. Stay with it until he or she can be responsive to your efforts to help it heal. You will sense this part moving from doubt, fear or betrayal, into perhaps even anger that it took you so long, then into a willingness to believe, and finally into an eagerness to try it for him or herself.

4ᴛʜ Layer: The Teaching Step: Healing the Wound

Discussion: **In this next sequence, you shift into a meditative state and begin to teach your Inner Child or wounded one the technique for this neutralization process. If you have taken a break from your work, remember to begin by doing one round where you get the Adult Self ready to be present for this work. When you feel ready to proceed, take a moment to reconnect with the Inner Child with whom you worked in the previous sequence. Always invite him or her to sit beside you or even to jump upon your lap. Then explain how you want to teach him or her how to do this process so that he or she can feel safe enough to join you in allowing wealth and abundance to flow into your life.**

Exercise: Taking your Inner Child back to the Original Wound

In your mind's eye, ask your wounded one to take you back to the place where he or she first developed fears about abundance or having money in his or her life. As always do not be alarmed if he or she first takes you back to an experience in which you were the cause of its fear. If that occurs, as before, neutralize that situation first and end the sequence with an apology. Then proceed to inquire about past situations where this fear originated. Record your responses in your journal.

1. *Who was involved?*

2. *What did he or she hear or witness that resulted in so much fear, sadness, or judgment?*

3. *Refer to the experience of that last Layer when he or she watched as you tapped. Imagine you return to the scene where the wound took place. Observe it for a minute; then freeze the scene and pull your wounded one to the side. Invite him or her to either sit on your lap or sit cross-legged in front of you.*

4. *Explain that in this first round you are going to tap with him or her. All you want is for your Inner Child to repeat what you say and tap where you tap.*

5. *Explain to your little one that you will be stating these sequences as if you are him or her (using the pronoun "I"), and you are asking that he or she repeats the phrases after you speak them while tapping where you tap.*

Begin by tapping on the karate point as you state the setup phrases:

Even though I learned at a very young age that money was the root of all evil, that it was bad and could cause great pain ... and actually I have seen nothing but bad happen when it comes to money ... I know you love me, and I love myself enough to trust you can help me heal.

So even though as I return to this fearful scene and I watch as I see money destroy my trust, I am ready to have you help me heal because I know you love yourself and me enough to show up.

Even though I had very few good experiences regarding money and many I did have were wounding experiences that left me in doubt ... I now allow you to help me deal with that pain ... and let go of that pain ... because I love myself and trust that you love me enough that it is safe to heal.

That completes the setup statements. We will now move into the neutralization sequences. I will give you an example of it, but you are going to want to experiment with this because it is really the Healing Layer of this entire process.

I will be doing the sequencing where I gradually identify the origin of the disturbance and then move into the possibility of letting that go ... the possibility that something can be different ... that it really can be healed. We will then end with the conviction that it is safe to let it go. Follow this to get a feel for the flavor of these sequences, but experiment on your own with your own words as well.

Neutralizing the Negative

Eyebrow: So much pain in this scene ... just remember Mom and Dad had so much tension around money.

Side of the Eye: Never had enough.

Under the Eye: Money was always, always an issue.

Upper Lip: So many fights ... got tired of hearing them yell.

Under the Lip: Never had enough money.

Collarbone: So frightened we wouldn't survive.

Under the Arm: Wish they wouldn't fight so much about it.

Rib: So much lack ... just never had enough.

Head: Wish I didn't have to worry about money.

Another round...

Eyebrow: All that I heard was that there was not enough.

Side of the Eye: Money was used to buy my love.

Under the Eye: It was used as a substitute.

Upper Lip: But it was never enough.

Under the Lip: Just so afraid it will destroy what I have.

Collarbone: I was told that money is the root of all evil.

Under the Arm: I get so angry that there is so much focus on this.

Rib: So afraid to trust.

Head: Just so scared to allow this to come in.

Possibility of Change

Eyebrow: Afraid it will compromise values, and I will once again be alone.

Side of the Eye: I am always abandoned when money comes into my world.

Under the Eye: I have always been abandoned because of their greed.

Upper Lip: But maybe I can let go ... maybe it doesn't have to be this way.

Under the Lip: Maybe I can let this tension go.

Collarbone: Maybe my Adult Self is really here to help me heal this pain.

Under the Arm: Maybe I can let Mom and Dad go.

Rib: Maybe I don't have to carry this tension that was not even mine.

Head: Maybe I can let it all go.

Conviction of Change

Eyebrow: I am going to let go and let God!

Side of the Eye: I am going to let go of the past.

Under the Eye: I am willing to let this go and trust my Adult Self.

Upper Lip: I am ready to let go and let God.

Under the Lip: I know I have carried this for so long.

Collarbone: But I am willing to now let it go.

Under the Arm: I am willing to trust that my Adult Self might be different than my parents.

Rib: I am willing to give it a try.

Head: I feel magnificent about joining forces with my Adult Self … I am ready to let it go.

Again, this sequence gives you an example of how to move through this Layer. I really encourage you to continue to work with this and keep going through this. Bear in mind that there is not a right or wrong way with this. Just keep working with the Inner Child until you sense he or she is ready to let go.

And you *will* sense it. You will sense this part moving through the stages of grief, tension, and fear into a total despair of helplessness—considering that this part acknowledged its attempt to please and felt the anger when its attempt did not keep him or her feel safe.

You may want to look back in the introduction section of *Abraham's Emotional Guidance Scale*. Take this as far up that scale as you can … the ideal is to escort this part of you through all of its feelings until it is once again willing to trust you will keep it safe. He or she really does want to trust that you will not abandon him or her when money becomes limitless. Discover your Inner Child's experience around this issue; then tap and neutralize those feelings until you have won this little one's trust.

Sometimes this takes more than one sequence and more than one day. But this will give you a start. If you feel you have healed this part enough to proceed to the next step, then do so. If you cannot get past the pain, consider setting up a one-to-one session for additional help and facilitation.

5ᵀᴴ Layer: The Step of Integration and Merger

Discussion: This Layer is perhaps one of the most empowering Layers. Again, the following process is used only for the integration of an Inner Child. With an aspect of your Soul, you want to just send it back into the Light to free energy. (For further assistance, refer to my book, *Which Lifetime Is This Anyway?* for a Ten-step Formula on dealing with the aspect of your Soul.) But with an aspect of your personality from this lifetime (the Inner Child), you want to partner with him or her and build a bonding, cooperative relationship.

Combining the neutralization process with the pronoun "we" enables you to set up the merger and integration. Partnering with the Inner Child in this manner empowers him or her to return to your force field in a healed state and empowers you and your Inner Child to reclaim the magic that was lost in the wounding experience. When you bring this magic back, that essence of the believability you had as a child returns as well. If you then infuse your desire for abundance with this vibration, you experience magic ten-fold!

If you have taken a break, then remember to begin your Fifth Layer by doing one round where you get the Adult Self ready to be present for this work and another round to make sure your Inner Child has remained clear. When you feel ready to proceed, the sequence may look like the one below.

State the setup phrase while tapping on the karate point:

Again, for this Layer, you will be using the pronoun "we" because you are orchestrating the sequences as if the Inner Child and the Adult Self are saying them in unison. When you feel ready, begin.

Even though we have both experienced a lot of disappointment around money and not having enough, and we both have experienced a lot of tension about this in our lives, we are so excited we have found each other again. We love ourselves and each other enough to trust and to manifest the abundance we deserve.

Even though we both have experienced a lot of bumps on the road to abundance, we are so excited we have come together and are now ready to heal.

So even though we have had a lot of disappointments, starts and stops about attracting what we deserve, we are so excited we are together and are ready to heal.

This is an example of the setup phrases. Please feel free to customize them, and make them fit your particular situation. Below are suggestions for sequences you could use to augment this Layer. It is really not so much of a neutralization process as it is an infusion of what you have affirmed.

Again, begin with the corner of the eyebrow.

Affirming the Merger

Eyebrow: We are so excited to come together and heal.

Side of the Eye: We are buzzing with enthusiasm and trust for each other.

Under the Eye: So excited we are going to finally manifest our heart's desire.

Upper Lip: Through the love of each other and the love of God we know we deserve all we desire.

Under the Lip: We are so excited to come together to heal.

Collarbone: So excited we are together to heal … to attract all we deserve.

Under the Arm: We are so full of energy, love, and Light … we send this out to the entire world.

Rib: We are so excited we have done such good work.

Head: We are so proud of each other and love each other so much that we are ready to attract all we desire and deserve.

Now just keep going with that until you are really, really buzzing. When you feel that momentum of conviction, move on to Layer Six to complete the transformation.

6ᵀᴴ Layer: Rewiring your Brain; Reprogramming your DNA; Reconfiguring the Electromagnetic Field

Discussion: This implementation of this Layer was inspired by the New Brain Science, most specifically the work of Dr. Richard Hanson, and Margaret Ruby's work on reprogramming the DNA. www.possibilitiesdna.com/margaret.html

You use meditations and interactive tapping™ sequences to first rewire the brain by building new neuro-pathways between the amygdala and the prefrontal cortex. You then clear the energetic disturbance from your electrical system in your body, ask your body for its forgiveness, and then give it permission to release. This reprograms the DNA in every cell so it can hold your new vibration and enables you to reconfigure the electromagnetic field around you.

I encourage you to experiment with the wording as much as your imagination will allow. Just keep tapping and saying affirming statements. I have included an example, but please experiment. Try it on every feeling you think you have stored in your body about the Divine work you should be doing and the right livelihood you want to attract.

Before you begin, however, do one round to clear any current trigger in your Adult Self and to neutralize any current disturbance that may be getting in the way of giving your body permission to release. State each setup phrase while tapping on the karate point. The interaction is between you and your body so imagine you are speaking directly to it.

Meditation Tapping: While tapping on your karate point, imagine speaking to your body.

Even though you (my dear body) have held so many feelings of tension related to scarcity and lack, and we have held so many other issues around abundance for so long, I am sorry I was unable to deal with them on my own. But I now truly want to forgive myself because I understand I simply did not know what else to do at the time.

In turn, I ask you (my dear body) to forgive me as well. I humbly apologize for needing you to hold this disturbance for me for so long. And I now give you total permission to release it fully and completely. I vow to neutralize and dissolve all disturbances related to this situation. You no longer have to carry my pain. I am willing to do for myself what you have so graciously done for me all these years. I ask you to trust me enough to release it and let it go. Thank you. Thank you. Thank you.

Repeat this setup at least three times or until you feel you have moved through all of the resistance your body is holding for you. You'll sense when you feel truly in alignment with giving your body permission to release what it has held. Reassure your body you are now completely willing to deal with what comes your way with the tools you have acquired. When replenishing your body with a new vibration, you are acknowledging that the DNA has been reprogrammed and you are infusing every cell with the new vibration of your intention.

Now begin to tap on the two sore spots right on your chest (near the collarbone but not on the collarbone) to infuse your body with this new vibration of energy. State your new intention much like an affirmation. Imagine bringing significant amounts of abundance into your force field and your daily life. Once you have this image firm in your mind's eye, hold this vibration for 68 seconds. As has been discussed, according to the Teachings of Abraham, this length of focus is enough for your intention to take form and begin attracting reciprocity from the Universe. It will match it and begin the process of materializing your intent. The following is an example of how the narrative of your infusion might flow. Repeat it while tapping on the sore spots.

I now envision harmonic wealth in my life. All my needs and wants are fully realized in the presence of the Light. I am so fortunate to experience such abundance! Every area of my life is enriched with this sense of prosperity. I experience abundance in my relationships with all those in my life. I experience abundance in my career and my right livelihood. I experience an abundance of energy and physical health. I am abundant in my thinking ... in my heart! I am rich with experiences of love and Light and see the magic of the Universe everywhere I look. I am truly an abundant being, and I exude that abundance in every act! I am abundant in mind, body, heart, and Soul!

Sometimes I complete this infusion by tapping on the endpoints while stating reminder phrases that anchor this into my body, mind, heart, and Soul. You can even restate the above and move from endpoint to endpoint. When you feel ready to give back complete your process with the Final Layer of healing.

7ᵀᴴ LAYER: GIVING BACK TO THE WORLD

Discussion: You are now ready to share a portion of your healing with the world. It too needs an infusion of abundant thinking ... especially now! You do this by taking all you have neutralized and realigned and sending this energy into the Universe as an offering for planetary healing. This activity contributes to the healing of Mother Earth, dissolving separateness and spreading the Light on the planet. It reinforces the fact that you are part of something bigger than yourself. You are a valuable agent of change for humanity. You have shared the gift with your Inner Child and/or the fragment of your Soul. You now have an opportunity to share it with the world.

Again, I encourage you to experiment with the wording as much as your imagination will allow. Just keep tapping and saying affirming statements. I have included an example, but please experiment and try it on everything.

Before you begin, I suggest you do one round as always to clear any current trigger in your body, mind, heart, and Soul! Enter into a meditative state and when you feel ready, begin to tap again on your sore spots while you say something like the affirmation below:

I feel so fortunate to have done this work. I now envision the cylinder of Light running from the center of Mother Earth to the grid of uncon-ditional love about 60 feet above my head. I am so full of Light and expanded energy from this highest place within myself, I now offer 10% or more of this healing back to the planet and the Universe for their use in healing wherever the energy needs to be directed. I feel so fortunate I have been able to complete this work. I am so grateful I am now in a position to "Share this Gift." Thank you, God, Goddess, Higher Power, Angels, and Masters for your support and direction. Thank you … aspects of my Soul … that may have emerged from other times … thank you for having the courage and fortitude to call me back, and thank you, my dear little ones … you (the children within me) … for having the patience to await my return. I love that we are healed and can now hold the Light that allows us to attract abundance and wealth into all areas of our life. And I love that we can contribute to Mother Earth so that our planet can be abundant as well. Thank you. Thank you. Thank you.

This, again, is an example. As you work in this fashion, the inspiration will come to you… the words will come to you; this above sequence augments your ability to attract abundance and wealth into your life and can be used as often as you deem appropriate.

Module 3: Attracting Right Livelihood

A Word From Abraham

Reduce your workload by 30% and increase your fun load by 30%, and you will increase your revenues by 100%. And you will increase your productivity by 10,000%. (If there could be such a percentage.) More fun, less struggle—more results on all fronts—Abraham.

Excerpted from the workshop in Salt Lake City, UT on Saturday, September 9th, 2000 # 235

Resolve Shame And Guilt! Embody Compassion! Manifest Divine Right Livelihood!

The more disruptive feeling that eclipses our ability to attract the career or right livelihood we desire and deserve is our shame and our guilt. When you befriend the Inner Child that carries your shame, guilt, and even judgment, and projection, you learn to relate to this wounded self with compassion and love; you learn to give him or her permission to feel accepted unconditionally. You partner with perhaps the most wondrous, curious, courageous part of you.

Most often this is your young Inner Child between the ages of three to six.

Remember the last time you were around a three-to-six-year-old? Their thirst for adventure; their ability to believe in magic; their utter commitment and expectation to be astonished by everything they encounter—it is amazing! Their resistance to believing is zero! They have no idea about doubt or skepticism! They just believe! To bring back into your life that "passion for allowing" is truly breathtaking! Mix that passion with the wisdom of your Adult Self and you'll see that your ability to manifest your divine right livelihood increases ten-fold!

EXERCISE: MEET YOUR YOUNG INNER CHILD (3-6)

Magic is Passion. Passion Creates Manifestation. Where is your passion? When was the last time you felt that fire in your belly and were willing to jump off the cliff for something in which you believed?

Look through the eyes of your younger self; then take a moment to make a list of five expressions of magic in your world.

1. _____
2. _____
3. _____
4. _____
5. _____

If you find this exercise a challenge …if you cannot relate to your passion and your attempts to manifest your right livelihood are thwarted … you are most likely disconnected from your Authentic Self and this Inner Child.

When Does Resistance Begin

I begin with a quote from the *Teachings of Abraham*. Each morning I receive an email with a morning quote. This one is relevant to our relationship to employment!

Is it an employment 'opportunity' or bondage? Because what you really want is freedom; many of you equate working for other people as bondage. But if you would realize that the corporation, as an entity, is not so different from the individual, it might be easier to understand the employer's decisions. Long before the buildings or the workers, the visionary of the corporation had an idea for something that began summoning Energy.

So years later, maybe you are hired as a part of that team and, without realizing it, you are now the beneficiary of that continuing flowing Energy. When you step into one of those employment positions, Life Force is summoned through you because of the vision of the founder— unless you're bucking the current. Most get into that fast-moving stream and paddle against the current—and then complain about it being a hard ride—where they could get into their canoe and easily paddle with the fast-moving current. You can soar and thrive in any environment as long as you are not seeing things that you are using as your reason to paddle against the current.

And so, it doesn't really matter what others are deciding. The question is: 'As I am choosing to stand here, it's a way for dollars to flow through me in exchange for the effort I am offering. Am I predominantly letting the Energy flow through me, or not? Am I letting it in?

Abraham (Excerpted from the workshop in Albuquerque, NM
On Tuesday, August 1st, 2000 #218)

If you are reading this Module then there is most likely some discontent with respect to how you *earn* your living. What is the source of this dissonance (experienced as resistance) and when did it begin?

We first experienced our resistance and fear of joy when we entered the third stage of childhood development because it is at that time we begin to work with the positive and negative aspects of who we are. It was also the time in our life when we first observed the fact that we were rewarded when we were good (acting like the adults in our life expected and wanted us to act). Likewise, we began to be aware of the fact that we were punished when we were bad (acting in ways that were unacceptable to these adults).

The rewards may have been in the form of praise; you may have been given special food, toys, or outings. Punishment may have been emotional. You may have been humiliated or teased. Your parents may have ignored you. Perhaps you were punished physically … spanked, slapped, or sent to your room. Fearing punishments and desiring rewards, you quickly learned what was acceptable and unacceptable.

The developmental task during the ages of three to six was to learn how to negotiate between the good and bad; right and wrong; and positive and negative aspects of self. You had developed enough cognitive ability to determine what was acceptable and unacceptable; therefore you could calculate which behaviors brought rewards and which resulted in punishment. You began to make choices accordingly. You began to compromise who you were as a way to avoid risking rejection or judgment. By the age three, you were also figuring out how to relate to other people. You began to calculate what to do to get what you needed.

Sometimes this worked. But unfortunately, if you were raised in a dysfunctional home, most often your needs were ignored or even ridiculed. You may have been the object of anger because you even *had* needs. The words you heard others use to describe you became the words you adopted to describe yourself.

If you were told you were bad, you would begin to believe you were bad. If you were told you were stupid, you would begin to believe you were stupid. If you were teased or told to shut up anytime you were curious and asked a question; you learned it was not safe or wise to inquire about anything. If you felt ashamed, humiliated, or teased about your body; if you were violated; if your physical boundaries were not honored—you most likely grew up believing you had little right to physical or emotional privacy and that your body was bad—perhaps even evil.

It is for these reasons that this stage of development is the origin of shame and guilt. These beliefs are the foundation for who you became as an Adult. And these beliefs are the source of your ability to attract or repel the career of your choice.

How Patterns Are Carried Into Adulthood—This stage of development sets the arena in adulthood for our ability to negotiate with the positives and negatives of any life situation. This negotiation process evolves into our capacity to know how to make the necessary adjustments to survive. As Adults, if we are to successfully discern our strengths and challenges, we have to have developed a healthy relationship with our humanness. This includes developing the ability to relate to ourselves with compassion. We have to be able to assess our positive and negative qualities and blend the good with the challenging if we want to create, accept, and revere our Authentic Self. This solidified-self empowers us to negotiate our differences with others and to reach an acceptable compromise without feeling overpowering or disempowered. To be successful in our Adult activities, we also need to have developed the ability to assess our internal value system as it compares to an external one.

For example, in your career or job, you may be able to determine what aspects of the company resonate with your values and where you need to make adjustments to fit in. If so, you can then draw on what you learned in this third stage of development to determine how to make these adjustments without losing your integrity or sense of self. If the mastery of your ability to assess right and wrong or good and bad was thwarted, your adjustments in Adulthood would be faulty. They will be based on shame and laced with fear of what others may think or do instead of being based on a viable, internal sense of self.

The same can be said in your relationships with others.

This blending that requires compromise is built on a clear understanding and acceptance of the person we are ... identifying where we can bend and where we need to stay true to ourselves so that we do not violate our own value system. This negotiation and adjustment phase involves sorting out what is going to work for us and what is going to have to be altered.

With respect to relationships that involve our right livelihood, this emerges as our need and ability to begin to speak our truth and attempt to work things out with others in a negotiating manner. It is in this adjustment phase of our professional relationships where we juggle our values with the other person's values or the value system of the organization or the corporation, and try to mediate an agreement or at least peaceful coexistence.

This developmental stage represents all of the basic tasks we need to master so that we can find balance in our professional lives. This ongoing challenge invites us to experiment with staying centered in our professional persona as we encounter the issues of judgment and projection; shame, blame, and guilt that can erupt in any professional environment. Our collapsing into the patterns that can result from this stage ultimately brings us face to face with the *cherished saboteur*™ that I referred to in the introduction.

The Cherished saboteur™

We all have one central character within us that sabotages our best efforts to succeed. When we come up against this relentless part of self, a self that feels bigger than even our most desired goals ... we have come into relationship with what I call the Cherished saboteur™. The foundation of this saboteur is embedded in the co-dependent bargain™. In every endeavor we pursue, we encounter this resistance towards loyalty that springs from our original co-dependent bargain™. This part of self knows nothing else.

This cherished saboteur™ is ingrained in our state of being to such a degree we often come to believe it is our true self. Its patterns give rise to our righteous indignation as we defend this saboteur's legitimacy. It's tricky. It can shape-shift, change forms, and jump from one area of our life to another ... always leaving us with that one thread in our perfect tapestry that needs to be rewoven ... that one brick in our successful fortress that needs to be replaced ... that core issue that is embedded in the continual reenactment of our co-dependent bargain™.

THE CO-DEPENDENT BARGAIN™ IN MORE DETAIL

Our codependent bargain™ was made in this lifetime with the parent we identify as the one who could have loved and protected us but didn't. We assume they didn't love us because of our deficiency which became the source of our shame. In response to this shame and our perceived *lack,* we enter into this unconscious agreement to *earn* their love in hopes they will finally love us enough to keep us safe.

When our co-dependent bargain™ doesn't work, we feel the tension. This tension is uncomfortable and must be discharged. We discharge it by developing compulsive, perfectionistic behaviors that can easily set the stage for our addictions. However, irrespective of how we respond excessively in our life, that behavior is usually fueled by this unconscious, ineffective, and yet unmet, bargain.

Because this bargain is unconscious, we engage in this dynamic over and over.

Our perpetual belief that permeates every interaction and relationship dictates that if we can just figure out what needs to be changed or fixed, then things will be the way we need them to be, and we will feel safe, loved, and protected. This act is a response to the *bargaining* stage of grief. It is an attempt to deal with the first stage of grief, the anxiety and panic we feel in response to not feeling safe and fearing abandonment.

It never works. No matter how much we try to be perfect; no matter how much we try to fix things and make them better, we always fail because the source of the dysfunction is not us, unfortunately. It is the dysfunction in the parental system or our caretaker's addiction, negligence, or inabilities to provide for us. As children, we did nothing to deserve being unloved. Therefore, we can never be *good enough* to impact or change what is wrong in order to make things get better. We get caught in the vicious cycle of attempting to be perfect, fail, and then act out compulsively or addictively to discharge the energy of that failure.

This cycle keeps us active in our compulsions and addictions as well as disconnected from our authentic self and Source. This cycle is the source of our saboteurs, of those behaviors that derail us and keep us from coming fully into the commitments and intentions of the life we deserve to live. It is the essence of our DNA make–up, the root of our energy disturbances and energetic imbalances. It is this biochemical response that reinforces this pattern over and over and continually bombards the receptor sites with the peptides that disarm us.

EXAMPLE OF A CLASSIC CO-DEPENDENT BARGAIN™:

An unconscious bargain a child might make with his or her parents is, *"Mom/Dad if I am really good and do not make a sound, then will you love me enough to make me feel safe?"*

As an adult, that same co-dependent bargain™ might look like this … " _____ (Fill in any name that is appropriate …) If I take care of all of your needs and make sure everything is just right, then will you love me enough not to leave me?"

The co-dependent bargain™ is always unconscious until it is made conscious through your inner work. It is always a bargain the other person could not respect because it is founded on the principle that you agree to be perfect in some aspect of your behavior, and perfection is a myth. The end result is the shame that is the under-belly of this stage of development.

HOW YOUR YOUNG INNER CHILD'S (3-6) EXPERIENCE IMPACTS THE MANIFESTATION OF YOUR RIGHT LIVELIHOOD?

What erupts between the ages of three and six has its foundation in the first two stages of development and evolution in the subsequent stages. Each stage creates a blueprint for the worthiness that later translates into attracting the kind of work that mirrors the way you feel about yourself. Being in alignment with what you do requires passion. Passion is energy… passion is sexuality and sensuality. The following Journal Meditation will give you a bird's eye view of your blocks on your passion and right livelihood.

EXERCISE: BIRDS EYE VIEW

1. Imagine you are standing in front of a mirror, and you look deep into the center of your eyes … right there, before you, you can see into the eyes of your Soul.

2. Ask your higher self to show a picture of how you can contribute to the world through your divine right livelihood.

3. Envision embodying your passion for what you do and what you have to offer the world.

4. Once you have that vision, ask who within would be moved out of their comfort zone if you were to manifest this.

5. Pause and see who comes forward. Once you have a glimpse of this part of you, ask what he or she needs to feel safe. Make a list of the feelings that become apparent.

Record your experiences in your journal.

Healing Your Shame With Interactive Tapping™

Interactive tapping™ can then help neutralize the contrasting emotions and bring harmony to what you intend to attract. In the previous journal exercise, you gave form to your desire … a face to the aspect of you that is resisting or is ambivalent regarding the manifestation of that desire.

REMEMBER … When we take action towards our desires, we push our wounded ones beyond their comfort zone. They make themselves known to us by their sabotage. Once that sabotage is identified, we are in a position to respond to their needs instead of collapsing into them.

HOWEVER … Until we have strengthened the illuminated Adult Self within us enough to respond, there can be no beneficial interaction. If we cannot stay separate enough to respond to our wounded ones, we simply collapse into their vibration and come to believe that this is all there is or that this is all we are.

When we send that compromised vibration out to the Universe, it begins to bring us a vibrational match to the wound and not the most illuminated desire.

Our tapping will again begin with the three setup phrases to identify the ambivalence and contrasting feelings regarding your career or employment. In the Journal Meditation, you identified your sabotaging voice. The setup phrases position this sabotage with a positive affirmation. The following formula will help you move from the sabotage to the conviction of change.

This method is divided into three sections. You first neutralize the negative thoughts and feelings, then introduce the possibility of change, and finish with a strong infusion of your conviction—to a new way of relating to the part of you that is sabotaging your efforts to successfully attract your right livelihood.

Suggestion: Setup phrase stated while tapping on the karate chop point:

Even though I feel so much shame and humiliation about this situation, and so very, very humiliated, I love myself completely and profoundly.

Even though my shame and humiliation prevent me from attracting the career I so desire, I love myself completely and profoundly.

Even though I feel unworthy of attracting the career I want and I judge myself ruthlessly about this, I love myself completely and profoundly.

The following are the reminder phrases that you say after the psychological reversal. Say these while you are sequentially tapping on the different meridian points. Refer to the graphic provided to refresh your memory on where to tap.

Neutralizing the Negative

Eyebrow: Feel so much shame.

Side of the Eye: So humiliated and ashamed.

Under the Eye: Just don't want this shame.

Upper Lip: Feel judgment no matter what I do.

Under Lip: Feel critical; don't know what to do.

Collarbone: Just can't let go of this shame.

Under the Arm: Can't imagine not feeling this shame!

Rib: So much shame ... so much humiliation ...

Head: What am I going to do with all this judgment and shame?

Introducing the Possibility of Change

Eyebrow: Maybe I do not have to feel so much shame.

Side of the Eye: Maybe I can move beyond this humiliation and fear.

Under the Eye: Wonder if I can move beyond this shame!

Upper Lip: Maybe I can manifest the career of my choice.

Under the Lip: Maybe I do not have to drown in this shame.

Collarbone: Maybe, just maybe I can let go and allow everything to just flow.

Under the Arm: Maybe I can imagine not feeling this shame!

Rib: Maybe I am ready to let go of this fear, judgment, and shame.

Head: Wouldn't it be wonderful to let go of this doubt, fear, and shame.

Conviction to Change

Eyebrow: I choose to let go of this doubt, fear, and shame.

Side of the Eye: I am so ready to release these doubts, claim what is mine by divine right.

Under the Eye: I trust God and my Higher Self.

Upper Lip: I am ready to claim my passion, my inspiration, and my heart's desire!

Under the Lip: Feel so full of passion, inspiration, and desire!

Collarbone: I am ready to claim my heart's desire.

Under the Arm: I embody the passion and inspiration to manifest the career of my choice!

Rib: I can manifest the career of my choice!

Head: I now stand in the vibration of my heart's desire.

Now that you have given birth to your intention and have brought Light to the aspect of you that wants to manifest it, you have also brought Light to the shadow self that might want to sabotage your efforts. Use the following to flush out that voice, so that you can begin to neutralize his or her fears. You may relate to this voice as your three-to-six- year-old, or it may be housed in another developmental stage. Just concentrate on his or her voice and his or her concerns. The specifics will evolve.

WEEDING OUT PROCESS

I originally came across this exercise in a book written in the 80's by Sondra Ray. Since then I have used this or a version of it in a multitude of ways. It never fails to weed out my saboteurs and those within me that resist change.

Instructions: Write your intention in a few words. Right underneath it, record the first negative thought you have that would undermine your efforts. Continue writing your intention followed by your first sabotaging thought. At the end of this exercise, you will have the duality of your experience when you try to attract your right livelihood.

This process will reveal the natural ambivalence that emerges anytime we are trying to move forward. I envision my ambivalence as being on a teeter-totter. On one side is the desire, and on the other is the sabotage… each is constantly vying for attention. Once you have this duality clear in your mind, you can neutralize the sabotage with the tapping sequences presented in the *Seven-Layer Healing Process.*

Suggestion:

Affirmation: *I am now working in the field of my choice, attracting the salary I deserve.*

Negation: *Sure you are! What makes you think you can do it this time.*

Write at least ten separate statements flushing out your polarity around creating your divine right livelihood. These statements will give you the reminder phrases that you can use to neutralize the sabotaging thoughts that interfere with your adult's ability to attract the career of your choice. Once you have those phrases, use the formula below to create your tapping sequences … customizing them to your own unique needs.

The above helps you flush out the sabotaging voice, and use the EFT sequences to neutralize this distraction. The following will enable you to zero in on whether there was a specific theme to your sabotage that correlates to a developmental stage.

How The Stages Of Development In Childhood Impact Your Ability To Attract Your Right Livelihood:

Even though your shame regarding attracting your right livelihood may have originated during the three-to-six-year-old time in your life, there may be other issues regarding this attraction that originated during your development in the other stages of your childhood.

The following applies the respective tasks from each of the developmental stages to your ideas about right livelihood. There are few sentences that describe the task you were to master during that stage of development. The series of eight questions that follow give you a thumbnail view of how these tasks—if not mastered—may appear in your current adult life today. They will shed Light on or provoke thoughts about your behavior or feelings regarding the relationship between your passion and your desire for right livelihood.

The first four statements reflect adult issues that may be related to your passion during that particular stage of development. The second set of four statements suggests how those age-related issues may impact your pursuit of right livelihood. They will help you identify your feelings and attitudes about expressing your passion for a career or job of your choice ... where you are stuck, how you neutralize your contrasting feelings, and whether you allow yourself to passionately attract the right livelihood you so desire.

Read the description; then respond to the statements accordingly. If a statement triggers a response but does not quite fit your situation, use it to modify the statement, so that it does. What you end up with will provide you with your customized setup phrases for your EFT sequences.

Infant (Birth to 18 months)—Every time you pursue a goal, you progress through the same developmental stages you did as a child. If you are trying to attract your right livelihood the first time you envision that which you want to attract, you are *giving birth* to your vision. You have to have the passion that fuels your desire to give form to what you want to do before you can execute a plan to attract it.

Your ability or challenge in doing this will reflect what you experienced in infancy. Did you feel safe enough to feel the right to exist? Did you develop trust in knowing your needs would be met?

You may not have a cognitive memory of this ... in fact, until the age of about three, we do not even have the cognitive ability to comprehend experiences ... but your body remembers. And your behavior and reactions to even being able to determine and *give form* to what you want are directly related to your experience as an infant. On determining, and then attracting your right livelihood, the goal is to give birth to a vision of what *following your bliss* would mean.

1. How does your passion get blocked or manifested?

2. Can you give birth to your creativity through passionate expression?

3. Have you learned to block your passion and therefore your ability to create your heart's desire?

Use the statements below to further your exploration. They may reflect where you are stuck or they may inspire additional thoughts; your response will help you decipher which part of self needs your attention. Again, if these statements do not quite resonate, rework the statement to accommodate your experience; then record your response, thoughts, and feelings in your journal.

Regarding your passion ...

_____1. I find it hard to express my creative ideas.

_____2. I am a creative person but don't do much with my talent.

_____3. My sexual expression is more physical in nature than emotional.

_____4. I have difficulty initiating sexual or passionate contact.

Regarding your relationship with a career ...

_____1. I have difficulty trusting the value of my ideas.

_____2. If offered a position in a new job I can't decide what to do.

_____3. The thought of being in business for myself terrifies me.

_____4. I experience great anxiety when beginning a new position.

Do any of these statements fit? Did they provoke thoughts? If need be, modify these statements to match what is true for you. Play with the statements; then record your thoughts and feelings in your journal. It is this process that will assist you in designing the profile of the saboteur within that blocks you from attaining the right livelihood you desire and deserve. Once you have his or her profile, you will have the issues that need to be neutralized in my *Seven-Layer Healing Process* to dissolve them and get on with manifesting what you want to do and be!

Toddler (18 to 36 months)—The adult issue that originated during your second stage of development is related to how well you set boundaries with yourself, coworkers, and those of authority. You will want to explore what your goals are versus the goals you are pursuing based on the value of others. Where do they energetically end and you begin? Often people find they are uncomfortable with their passion. They have learned to put out the fire.

Ponder how has your childhood experience resulted in your feeling ambivalent about creating the career of your choice … the divine right livelihood you deserve? Did you learn it was not good to be too visible … too exuberant … too live? If so, it will not only be reflected in your inability to embrace your sexuality but also in your drive to do what you enjoy doing. For some, even *feeling* your passion may feel too threatening. Following your bliss may feel too selfish and self-absorbed. With this encroachment, you never seize the opportunity to experience your passion, let alone use it as a foundation upon which you create and attract your right livelihood.

Use the statements below to further your exploration. They may reflect where you are stuck or inspire additional thoughts. Your response will help you assess which part of self needs your attention. Again, if these statements do not quite resonate, rework the statement to reflect your experience. Then record your response, thoughts, and feelings in your journal.

Regarding your passion …

_____1. I have a hard time saying *no* to sexual advances.

_____2. I have creative ideas but not enough discipline to manifest them.

_____3. If I give in once, I fear I will feel obligated to respond every time.

_____4. I have no idea what I like or want sexually, so I remain quiet.

Regarding your relationship with a career …

_____1. I find it hard to say *no* to my employer.

_____2. I would rather not ask for special treatment than risk being told *no*.

_____3. If my boss is angry or in a bad mood, I assume I made a mistake.

_____4. If a coworker asks me to do something I do it even if I don't want to.

Again, play with these statements and modify them to match what is true for you. Use these thoughts and feelings to further design the profile of the saboteur within that blocks you from attaining the right livelihood you desire and deserve. Look for evidence of your ambivalence ... who inside wants to move forward and who inside is afraid of that expansion. Make a note of issues regarding boundaries and discernment. Explore your ability to say and hear *no*. This exploration will help you bring focus to the tapping sequences that will be used to neutralize your inner toddler's fears and free your inner adult to manifest with clarity and passion.

Young Inner Child (3 to 6 years)—This stage was covered in more detail at the beginning of this material, but, for the purpose of this exercise, it is useful to remember the primary goal of this stage is to balance what you have with what you don't have——to mix your spiritual intentions for right livelihood with a concrete plan of action.

It is also effective, at this point, to examine your definition of right livelihood. Value shifts may be necessary to accommodate feeling more in sync with what you are doing as opposed to what you dream of doing. You will be invited, through your exploration, to become more realistic as you deal with judgments towards self or others. You will also be encouraged to give up the comparison game of being better or worse off than others.

But perhaps the most relevant in the pursuit of your right livelihood during this phase is that you come face to face with any residual shame or guilt you brought from childhood to adulthood. If you were shamed, humiliated, ridiculed, or abused, as a child, you carry this self-image into your behavior as an adult.

Guilt, on the other hand, is the result of being told that what you *did* was wrong or not good enough. We can feel guilty in response to what we have done ... the professional actions were taken that lacked integrity. Shame is feeling bad about who we are. It emerges as our not feeling good enough or worthy enough to pursue our professional dreams.

Shame is the most lethal of all emotions.

It reduces us to the smallest part of us riddled with every self-in-criminating accusation we have ever experienced. We can change what we do or how we act. But we cannot change the core of the person we are. Both of these emotions may emerge in the way you feel about how you presently make a living or how you experience not having pursued your dreams when you had the chance.

The antidote for either emotion is compassion. Once you can identify and give a face to the Inner Child that carries your shame and guilt, you can compassionately respond to your wounded one and begin the healing process.

This modality encourages you to identify these issues because they will emerge as sabotage. The exercises and meditations invite you to uncover the underlying issues which can then be neutralized with your tapping sequences.

Use these thoughts to stimulate responses in your journal. Use the statements below to further your exploration. They may reflect where you are stuck, or they may inspire additional thoughts … as before, whichever occurs … your responses will help you know who inside needs your attention.

Regarding your passion …

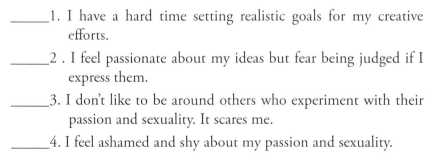

_____1. I have a hard time setting realistic goals for my creative efforts.

_____2 . I feel passionate about my ideas but fear being judged if I express them.

_____3. I don't like to be around others who experiment with their passion and sexuality. It scares me.

_____4. I feel ashamed and shy about my passion and sexuality.

Regarding your relationship with a career ...

_____1. I worry a great deal about what my coworkers and boss think of me.

_____2. I don't think many of my coworkers are as competent as I.

_____3. I can be rigid and somewhat inflexible. If I agree to do something, no matter what arises, I stick to it until it's done.

_____4. I feel irritated when others do not seem to value integrity.

Feel free to modify these statements to match what is true for you. You are flushing out your judgments ... your fears. You are exploring your relationship with your passion because it is your level of comfort with your passion that will fuel your desires. Again, I encourage you to record your thoughts and feelings as you design the profile of the saboteur within that blocks you from attaining the right livelihood you desire and deserve.

Grade School Self (6 to 12 years)—The challenge at this stage is to determine if your professional goals are based on an internal or external value system. You may find that you may base your professional goals on your need for recognition, so you set goals that are in alignment with society's values and not our own. You may discover that you seek employment that wins the approval from others rather than one that is inspired by your own passion because you want to fit in with friends, neighbors, and family. This is referred to as external instead of internal referencing. Your choices are based on the values of others rather than identifying and trusting the values within.

It is important to keep in mind that this is a phase. Try not to become too judgmental of yourself as you explore these tendencies. There are issues of false loyalty and the need to find a group of like-minded individuals that may supersede your need for authenticity in your career. Use these thoughts to stimulate responses in your journal. Use the statements below to further your exploration. Again, modify as necessary as they may reflect where you are stuck or to inspire additional thoughts. Whichever occurs, your response will help you identify what needs your attention.

Regarding your passion …

_____1. I have a hard time setting realistic goals for my creative efforts.

_____2. I feel passionate about my ideas but fear judgment if I express them.

_____3. I don't like to be around others who experiment with their sexuality.

_____4. I feel awkward with respect to my passion and my sexuality.

Regarding your relationship with a career …

_____1. I want more acknowledgment from those with whom I work.

_____2. I feel overlooked by my superiors.

_____3. I think about going into business for myself but am afraid I wouldn't succeed.

_____4. I dread giving presentations and sabotage promotions because of this.

Hopefully, you felt free to modify these statements to reflect what was true for you. That exercise in itself will help you establish the unique profile of your saboteur. Again, I encourage you to record your thoughts and feelings as you design the profile of the saboteur within that blocks you from attaining the right livelihood you desire and deserve.

The unmastered tasks from the first three stages of development are revisited in the three stages of adolescence.

Young Inner Teen (12-15 years)—The patterns that follow us into adulthood from this first adolescent stage carry the threads of the unmastered tasks from the three to six-year-old stage of development because the same issues of shame, guilt, and projection are reflected in what evolves as the battle between our sense of self-consciousness versus self-confidence.

This battle emerges in adulthood when you begin to entertain thoughts such as _creative life work_ or _right livelihood._ However, it is also common that you do not quite have the self-confidence to know how to put those principles into practice. Once you identify and resolve these issues, you can shift from manifesting right livelihood based on horizontal principles or the values of others to manifesting it according to your higher wisdom and inner knowingness.

Again, use these thoughts to stimulate responses in your journal. Use the statements below to further your exploration. Modify the statements if necessary. They may reflect where you are stuck or inspire additional thoughts. Whichever occurs, your response will help you know which part of self needs your attention.

Regarding your passion ...

_____1. I feel awkward with my sexuality.

_____2. My passion for life and love frightens me.

_____3. I would rather eat, smoke, or drink than let my passion emerge.

_____4. I avoid people who have different sexual preferences than I.

Regarding your relationship with a career ...

_____1. I feel very cautious when I try a new behavior at work.

_____2. I get nervous if I do something at work that draws attention to me.

_____3. If I don't like something, I keep quiet. Why buck the system?

_____4. I have some ideas that excite me, but I don't share them with anyone.

Feel free to modify these statements to accommodate to what is true for you. Again, I encourage you to record your thoughts and feelings as you design the profile of the saboteur within that blocks you from attaining the right livelihood you desire and deserve.

Adolescent (15 to17 years)—The issues that are related to manifesting right livelihood which originated first in your toddler years and then are now revisited in this second stage of adolescence have to do with how much you are willing to take a risk with respect to your career choice. You will find that you fall somewhere on the continuum of being too risky and rebellious on one end or too passive and not willing to take chances at all on the other. Because these stages have to do with *carving out a sense of individuality* you want to assess how willing you are to risk everything for the chance to do what you love as you hope the money will follow. You may discover that you are less willing to *prostitute* yourself. You are aiming to stay true to your unique passion and path and see the career of your choice coming from your Divine Source. I refer to this as your beginning to see yourself as an *employee of the Universe*.

What can eclipse this aim is rebellion. Most often it is related to feeling stuck in doing what is not in alignment with our true passion. However, often due to financial reasons that feel beyond our control, we feel stuck and unable to move. We, therefore, rebel against what we are currently doing but feel blocked to take action in doing something that would take us closer to a more inspired goal. This internal unrest can also manifest as sexual rebellion. Keep in mind your connection to your sexuality directly reflects your connection to the very passion that could ultimately fuel your ability to attract the career of your choice.

Again, use these thoughts to stimulate responses in your journal. Use the statements below to further your exploration. They may reflect where you are stuck or inspire additional thoughts. Whichever occurs, your response will help you assess which part of self needs your attention.

Regarding your passion …

_____1. I like to experiment with sexual alternatives even if they offend others.

_____2. I have creative talents but do not express them.

_____3. I find my sexual values are unique and often stand out.

_____4. I am a person with great passion and will compromise it for nothing.

Regarding your relationship with a career ...

_____1. I am determined to speak my mind—even if it gets me into trouble.

_____2. Even if I agree, I like to disagree with my coworkers, just for fun.

_____3. I enjoy testing company rules.

_____4. I have strange ideas, and I enjoy shocking others with them.

Feel free to modify these statements to more accurately identify what is true for you. Again, I encourage you to record your thoughts and feelings as you design the profile of the saboteur within that blocks you from attaining the right livelihood you desire and deserve.

Young Adult (17 to 21 years)—By this stage of development, you have hopefully begun the process of sorting out who you want to be as an adult and what you want to do for your livelihood. Just as you spent infancy learning how you fit into your family, now you take a lifetime to negotiate how you fit into society as a whole. These processes of negotiation will shapeshift with each decade and with each career experience.

You may also notice that you begin to look at your life through the lens of your gender. It is the foundation upon which your internal masculine and feminine traits are built. Again, the process spans decades. The inner female dictates your ability to create; the inner male dictates your capacity to execute that which you envision. The interplay between these two parts within you determines your success at attracting and accepting that which you want. Balancing these contrasting sides of your personality emerge in your sexual identity; your financial and professional success; the quality of your intimate relationships ... in every aspect of who you are.

Use these thoughts to stimulate responses in your journal. Use the statements below to further your exploration. Modify them as needed for they can reflect the strengths upon which you can build and the challenges that will need to be addressed.

Regarding your passion …

_____1. I believe sexuality is an extension of the Universal Source.

_____2. Sexuality is sacred, but few partners feel the same

_____3. If my creative projects are challenged, I feel they have little worth.

_____4. I know I am passionate about life but am afraid to express it.

Regarding your relationship with a career …

_____1. I wish I enjoyed what I do for a living, but I don't.

_____2. I don't know what I want to do when I grow up.

_____3. If an evaluation challenges my image, I feel deflated.

_____4. If I had more training, I could go into business for myself.

Again, I encourage you to record your thoughts and feelings as you design the profile of the saboteur within that blocks you from attaining the right livelihood you desire and deserve.

Now review your responses; then use the meditation below to meet the cherished saboteur™ that blocks your efforts to succeed with their antiquated beliefs or old fears. You will reference this exploration later when you begin to apply the *Seven-Layer Healing Process* to heal this old wound.

MEDITATION: MEET YOUR SABOTEUR THAT CARRIES YOUR FEAR AROUND PASSION AND SUCCESS.

This journal meditation will prepare you to work with the part of you that might be sabotaging your efforts to attract your right livelihood. As is evidenced in the work you did above, you may find the issues were rooted in the fifteen-to-seventeen-year-old stage of development, or they may have been carried into your experience from an earlier age.

When you feel ready, read each question; contemplate your response; then record it in your journal. Work with it and use these questions to trigger whatever needs to emerge.

1. Begin by imagining the word *passion*. Passion is what fuels your ability to attract right livelihood. It is that fire in your belly that invites you to *follow your bliss*. It is that feeling within you that inspires you to take risks you would not ordinarily take ... dream dreams you would not usually allow yourself to dream.

2. What thoughts or feelings does the word *passion* provoke in you?

3. Do you feel excited or frightened?

4. Pause, take a deep breath then go back to when you were a child.

5. What did you witness with respect to your parents living their dreams?

6. How were you treated when you expressed your enthusiasm and passion? Were you revered ... quieted ... shamed?

7. See if you can retrieve a representative scene that portrays the manner in which passion was dealt with in your family.

8. Was it allowed ... encouraged ... ignored ... denied?

9. Which Inner Child carries this theme for you and what does he or she need from you now to trust that you will be able to deal with the passion that resides within you without feeling at risk?

The above gives you a profile of the Inner Child that may be sabotaging your efforts to succeed. Take a few moments to interact with this part of you. See what he or she needs from you. It will be this Inner Child with whom you will be working when you proceed with the *Seven-Layer Healing Process*. Keep in mind that the source of your resistance was the fear of your Inner Child. The following key points are beneficial to keep in mind as you move forward.

Key Points Relating To The Sabotage Of Your Joy!

1. *The source of shame is perfectionism.*

2. *The source of guilt is unreasonable expectations of self and others.*

3. *The antidote for shame and guilt is acceptance and compassion.*

4. *As we can heal ourselves of our imperfections, we accept the imperfections in others as well.*

5. *When we can trust and feel love for ourselves, we can right the wrongs of what we have done; we can make peace with who we have been!*

6. *Everyone's relationship to passion and career falls somewhere on the continuum between passivity and rebellion. Try to identify where you are on this continuum and proceed accordingly.*

It is now time to heal that little one who needs your attention, compassion, and love.

Seven-Layer Healing Process Applied To Attracting Right Livelihood

RIGHT LIVELIHOOD—Overview

The *Seven-Layer Healing Process* is useful if clearing the Adult Self of a current issue does not bring full resolution. As you read in the introduction, if you cannot clear a situation that is current, it is because the situation has triggered a residual issue from your past. This trigger offers you an opportunity to clear the disturbance in all dimensions of time and consciousness. The process invites you to identify the aspect of you that has gotten triggered and then systematically takes you through the process of healing the unresolved issues so that wounded part of you can learn to let go.

The following material provides a method for dealing with the aspect of you that carries your shame and your guilt … your judgment … your projection. As you discovered in the introductory material, this most often begins with the stage of development of the three-to-six-year-old because it is at that time of your childhood when you are first able to cognitively experience shame and guilt. Whatever was not mastered at that stage of development is revisited between the ages of fifteen and seventeen because the tasks which emerge for mastery at each of these stages carry a similar thread.

When you neutralize these judgments and fears that result from your shame and replace them with compassion and self-acceptance, perhaps you partner with the most wondrous and courageous part of you and connect to the most magnificent, passionate vibration possible. Mix that passion with the wisdom of your Adult Self and your ability to manifest increases ten-fold. This ability is a direct expression of the interplay between your second and third-eye chakra energy centers.

The second chakra is your reproductive center. It holds your passion. When expressed horizontally in relation to a loved one, it is experienced as sexual energy. But when it is channeled vertically in conjunction with your Higher Self, it is a pure creative expression. This connection is achieved when you weave the passionate energy of your second chakra with the insight of your third-eye energy center (or sixth chakra) which houses your wisdom and your connection to your Highest Self. This combination of passion and wisdom fuels the vibration that enables you to create that which you were destined to do.

But first, you have to resolve the vibration of your perfectionism and shame … your judgments and projections. Most have a tendency to project these feelings out onto others. This, in turn, sends out a vibration to the Universe to which it responds. In other words, when you greet the world with judgment and criticism, it returns that same energy. You begin to identify situations in which you are shamed, judged, and criticized. It is difficult to attract that perfect right livelihood in the climate of this negative and often crippling energy. The following will assist you in changing that pattern and guide you through the seven-layered process that will neutralize your fears and replace them with hope, trust, and harmony.

Interactive Tapping™ Sequences For Attracting Right Livelihood

The following section reviews the Seven Layers of Healing and then offers the interactive tapping™ setup phrases and sequences to work with them. Feel free to experiment with using one sequence a day, or just pick a time and move through the Layers all at once. I have presented it in a daily fashion for simplicity. For some, working with one aspect a day augments the depth of the work. Others may want to intensify the experience by going through this process at one sitting.

There is no right or wrong way to proceed. Honor whichever style appeals to you. If you are doing this on a daily basis, then you will want to begin each day with empowering your Adult Self before you work with the Layer of that day. If you do it in one big swoop, then once you have cleared the Adult Self, it is unnecessary to repeat this with each Layer unless you feel the need to do so.

1ST LAYER: EMPOWERING AND CLEARING THE ADULT SELF

These first sequences neutralize any disturbance that is currently in the Adult Self. This is not necessarily about right livelihood but rather relates to the general irritations that need to be neutralized so you can enter this work with a clear mindset. You begin this part of the process by neutralizing the Adult Self because it is this part of you that will orchestrate the layered healing. It is, therefore, essential that he or she is cleared of any current, distracting emotions or thoughts.

The process begins with three setup phrases. I use the setup phrases to identify the ambivalence and contrasting feelings of any issue. In the statements presented in the previous section, you established that you have this sabotaging voice. The setup phrases position this sabotage with a positive affirmation.

It is divided into three sections. You first neutralize the negative thoughts and feelings and then introduce the possibility of change. You finish with a strong infusion of your conviction—a conviction to a new way of relating to the part of you that is sabotaging your efforts to successfully attract your right livelihood.

Stay with each series of sequences until you feel ready to move to the next one. You will intuitively feel an energetic shift when you are done with neutralizing the negative responses and your psyche is ready to consider the possibility of experiencing something new. The second set of sequences usually does not take as long. It just softens the psyche, so it is ready to claim the right to feel convicted about the new direction.

The last set of conviction sequences should leave you feeling strong and energized by your new conviction. You will then be ready to proceed with the *Seven Layers Process* that will work with each piece of this dynamic more fully.

Again, the setup phrases position your disturbance with an affirmation, thus preparing your psyche to accept the neutralization process that will follow. Refer to the graphic provided in Section Two to refresh your memory on the exact places to tap.

Begin by tapping on the karate point while stating the following:

Even though there may be some things I am not in total harmony with today … I choose for this time to suspend those feelings so I can now focus entirely on the exercises this work.

So even though I may need to neutralize some general irritations … I am going to do that before I do this work because I love myself fully and completely and I am committed to clearing this up.

So even though I may not be in total harmony, I am willing to suspend any contrasting feelings I have at this time. I want to be as clear and as open to doing this work as I can be because I love myself enough to respond.

Next, you will do the general neutralizing. It involves stating reminder phrases while you tap on the designated endpoints.

Neutralizing the Negative

Eyebrow: Generally disturbed … A little bit antsy … Clear out any anger.

Side of the Eye: Clear out all distraction.

Under the Eye: Any frustration.

Upper Lip: A little bit fatigued.

Under the lip: But choose to feel empowered to do this work.

Collarbone: Am excited to do this Layer of work.

Under the Arm: Have committed to showing up to do this work.

Rib: Am getting jazzed to meet this Inner Child and to help this Inner Child heal.

Head: I ask my Higher Guidance to be of assistance so that I can move forward and clear this disturbance and finally heal.

That completes these sequences. This sequence is just an example of how you would neutralize anything that is currently in your daily life. Continue to tap on each of the endpoints until you move through any resistance that crops up in your efforts to heal the inner saboteur. Refer back to the exercises and sequences in the previous section for Layer One if you need more direction.

Note: Sometimes the Adult Self has antagonistic feelings towards the Inner Child, and these would need to be neutralized before you can be effective.

2ND LAYER: EXTERNALIZING THE PAIN

In the exercises in the first section, you were able to put a face to your wounded one. Now is the time to separate from him or her or *externalize* these feelings. When we externalize the disturbance, we set up a dyad between the part of us that carries the wound and the part of us that can respond to the wound.

You will be using the pronoun "he or she" to begin the separation process. This step is crucial because this very separation allows us to interact; the interaction between the wounded one and the Healer within you creates the healing.

If you are sure your Adult Self is clear, take a moment to review your responses to the exercises in the workbook. Get in touch with one of your contrasting feelings about right livelihood. Know that this is the voice of a wounded one that holds on to all of your issues about attracting right livelihood in your life. You want to introduce the possibility of change that you can respond to this wounded one … that you can help it heal its' pain and fear about attracting the career of your choice. You will be inviting your little one, once healed, to partner with you to manifest what you deserve. Again, you want to externalize these feelings, so you can prepare to respond to them.

State the setup phrase while tapping on the karate point.

Even though a part of me feels really fearful of attracting right livelihood into my life … and it is not sure it can trust me to set the appropriate limits that will ensure its safety … as the adult, I know this is only a part of me, and I love myself and this wounded one enough to be willing to respond to his or her pain.

Even though a part of me is really shy about trusting, and comes forward to sabotage my efforts to attract right livelihood into my life, I now choose to work with that part of self … to help him or her heal… because I love that part of self and I understand that these efforts are in response to fear.

Even though a part of me is trying to distract me from my ultimate goal …. I am ready to respond to his or her needs because I love myself and that part of me enough to heal.

That completes the setup phrases. You are now ready to proceed with the reminder phrases. Continue to repeat the reminder phrases until you move through any resistance that crops up in your efforts to heal the inner saboteur.

Neutralizing the Negativity

Eyebrow: He or she feels so much shame.

Side of the Eye: So humiliated and shamed.

Under the Eye: Just don't know how I can live with all of his or her shame.

Upper Lip: He or she just feels so much shame, no matter what I do, he or she feels shame.

Under the Lip: Feels so much judgment, humiliation, and shame.

Collarbone: Just can't let go of the shame.

Under the Arm: he or she cannot imagine not feeling this shame.

Rib: So much shame and humiliation.

Head: What am I going to do if this shame just does not go away?

Introducing the Possibility of Change

Eyebrow: Maybe he or she doesn't have to feel so bad.

Side of the Eye: Maybe I can help him or her not feel quite so humiliated.

Under the Eye: I really do want to help him or her let go of this shame.

Upper Lip: he or she felt a lot of shame, but maybe I can help let it go.

Under the Lip: Really want to help him or her let it go.

Collarbone: Maybe he or she can let it go, maybe it wasn't that bad.

Under the Arm: Maybe he or she can let it go, maybe I can forgive myself and help him or her let it go.

Rib: I don't want him or her to feel so much shame and humiliation.

Head: I really want to help him or her … he or she can let it go.

Conviction to Change

Eyebrow: I'm going to help … help him or her let go.

Side of the Eye: I am so glad to release this humiliation and shame.

Under the Eye: Help him or her let go of the humiliation and shame.

Upper Lip: I can feel compassion and help him or her grieve.

Under the Lip: I really can feel compassion for him or her.

Collarbone: Every cell in my body feels the compassion I need.

Under the Arm: The compassion to feel forgiveness for myself and him or her.

Rib: Every cell vibrates with compassion and joy.

Head: I can invite him or her to replace this shame with joy.

These sequences complete this initial clearing and prepare you to proceed.

3ʳᵈ Layer: The Interaction

This step is really the heart of the Inner Child work. Once you have separated from this part of yourself, you can truly begin to relate to him or her and respond to the fear of attracting the career of your choice. This is the true essence of building a trusting relationship between your most illuminate, nurturing self and the wounded Inner Child or fragment of your Soul. Sometimes it is useful to ascertain whether this Inner Child has any issues with trusting you to set appropriate boundaries around your current issue. Before you can clear feelings from the past, it is necessary to clear issues he or she may have with you in present time.

You are again doing a form of *surrogate tapping…* tapping on behalf of another. In this sequence, you are using the pronoun "you." This creates that internal experience for the wounded aspect that finally someone notices he or she feels the fear of exposure that might come from the Adult's attracting right livelihood. It reassures this fragile self that as the Adult you understand he or she needs help in learning to trust that safety can be returned. This part of you, again, may even feel betrayed by you. All of these feelings need to be flushed out if you are to be effective in this interaction. By responding to the pain and operating on his or her behalf, you enhance the experience of deservedness and nourish a sense of importance. This is true of the Inner Child as well a fragment from your Soul's past.

Again, if you have taken a break, then begin your sequences by doing one round where you get the Adult Self ready to be present for this work. Then take a moment to reconnect with the wounded one from whom you separated in the previous sequence. Invite him or her to sit beside you or to even jump up on your lap. Explain to your Inner Child that you are going to be tapping on your face and other endpoints on your body while speaking certain phrases. It may look a little weird, but, you are doing this though to help him or her feel better, and not experience so much pain.

(It is necessary to do this step every time you begin a new piece of work because you may be dealing with a different Inner Child.)

When you feel ready, begin to state the following setup phrases while tapping on the karate point.

Even though the circumstances of my attracting the exact right career into my life trigger your old fears and wounds, (substitute any feeling that fits) and sometimes causes you great pain, I love you and myself enough to work with your original wound, so together we can manifest what we deserve.

So even though my desires illuminate your fears, I am willing to work with you so that you can climb aboard and together we can heal.

I really do want to bring forth the right career for us because I know, we deserve it … I know this puts you at risk, and I am willing to soothe your fears, so together we can heal.

Reword this in whatever way speaks to you, but say the setup phrases, so that you set your psyche up to begin to do this interactive process. These next sequences begin with the neutralization process; move into the possibility of change, and complete with the conviction to resolve this Inner Child's fears. Use them as examples, but understand that you may need to work with this in a little more personal manner as well, so don't be shy to make up your own reminder phrases that suit your needs more specifically.

Again, you will be using the pronoun "you."

Neutralizing the Negative

Eyebrow: Afraid; feel so much shame and fear…

Side of the Eye: So many triggers… you carry so much fear…

Under the Eye: I am here to help you heal…

Upper Lip: All of your shame, judgment, and fear…

Under the Lip: So afraid, so humiliated, and crushed…

Collarbone: You witnessed so much… so much shame and fear…

Under the Arm: Shame, judgment, humiliation, and fear…

Rib: All these years … so many triggers for your shame and fear…

Head: All of your judgment … shame and fear…

Introducing the Possibility of Change

Eyebrow: But maybe you can trust me.

Side of the Eye: Maybe you will let me help you heal.

Under the Eye: Maybe you will learn to trust me.

Upper Lip: Just take the risk and see if this works.

Under the Lip: I really want you to come along.

Collarbone: I promise you I will not let you down.

Under the Arm: I just invite you to work with me.

Rib: I want you to recognize that I have really healed.

Head: I do deserve your trust, and I am willing to show up. I am really excited to work with you on this.

Conviction to Change

Eyebrow: I really feel a connection with you.

Side of the Eye: I guarantee you I am trustworthy and can help you heal.

Under the Eye: I want to help you heal. I am willing to come back to your time.

Upper Lip: I can come to you. I can teach you how to neutralize your fears.

Under the Lip: I am so excited that you are willing to try.

Collarbone: I am so excited that we can work on this together.

Under the Arm: I am so excited you have shown up.

Rib: I am so excited that together we can heal.

Head: I am so excited that together you and I can heal.

While repeating your reminder phrases, do sequential rounds on the endpoints until you move through any resistance this wounded one holds. Stay with it until he or she can be responsive to your efforts to heal. You will sense this part moving from doubt, fear, or betrayal, into perhaps even anger that it took you so long, then into a willingness to believe, and finally into an eagerness try the tapping and experiment with letting go.

If new feelings emerged in response to these reminder phrases, tap on them as well. Customize your sequences until you get completely clear.

4ᵀᴴ LAYER: THE TEACHING STEP: HEALING YOUR INNER CHILD AND SOUL

In this next sequence, you shift into a meditative state and begin to teach your Inner Child or wounded one the technique for this neutralization process. If necessary, remember to begin your work by doing one round where you get the Adult Self clear enough to be fully present for this work. When you feel ready to proceed, take a moment to reconnect with the Inner Child with whom you worked in the previous sequence. Always invite him or her to sit beside you or even jump up on your lap; then explain how you want to teach him or her how to do this process, so he or she can feel better in response to allowing right livelihood to flow into your life.

In your mind's eye, ask your wounded one to take you back to the place where he or she first developed fears about expressing his or her passion about being worthy of receiving what he or she wants. Be prepared that this little one might even begin by taking you back to an experience in which you were the cause of its fear. If that occurs, neutralize that first; then end the sequence with an apology.

Then proceed to inquire about past situations where he or she developed this fear.

Who was involved?

What did he or she hear or witness that resulted in so much fear, sadness, or judgment?

Spend time exploring this past situation, so you will be able to more effectively respond. When you feel you have enough information, close your eyes and imagine you returning to the scene where the wound took place. Observe it for a minute then freeze the scene and pull your wounded one to the side. Invite him or her to either sit on your lap or sit cross-legged in front of you. Build on the experience of that last sequence when this little one watched as you tapped. Explain that in this round you are going to tap along to show him or her how it is done.

All you want is for your Inner Child to repeat what you say and tap where you tap. Explain this, so your little one understands you are stating these sequences as if you are him or her (using the word *I*), and you are asking that he or she repeats the phrases after you speak them while tapping where you tap.

In this stage, imagine that both you and your Inner Child are tapping on the karate point as you state the setup phrase on behalf of your Inner Child. He or she will tap with you and can repeat after you if he or she is willing. If not, just imagine the little one is tapping along to your words. Again, determine if these statements need to be tweaked to customize them to your specific needs.

Even though I learned at a very young age that following my dreams was for someone else and that having great hope of getting what I want was dangerous, I know you (referring to the adult you) love me, and I love myself enough to trust you to help me heal.

Even though I stand back in this fearful scene and I watch as my parents criticize each other and sometimes belittle me, I am ready to have you help me heal because I know you love yourself and me enough to show up.

So even though I was always told not to be too confident, it was conceited to act that way, and I had many wounding experiences that left me in doubt ... I now allow you to help me deal with that pain ... and let go of that pain ... because I love myself and trust you love me enough to heal.

The above sequences give you examples of your setup statements. Again, customize them to your needs and when you feel complete, move into the neutralization sequences. I provide samples, but you are going to want to experiment with this because this is the Healing Layer of this entire process.

The sequencing gradually helps you identify the origin of the disturbance and then move into the possibility of letting that go ... the possibility that something really can be different ... that this wound really can be healed. The sequences then end with the conviction that it is safe to let it go. Follow this to get a feel for this stage but if it feels right to do so, experiment with your words as well.

Neutralizing the Negative

Eyebrow: So much pain in this scene ... just remember Mom and Dad had so much of their own shame and criticized each other every step of the way.

Side of the Eye: Seldom felt safe.

Under the Eye: Always feared being shamed.

Upper Lip: So many fights ... got tired of hearing their blame and shame.

Under the Lip: Seldom felt safe ... blame and shame turned on me.

Collarbone: So frightened of their judgments…

Under the Arm: Wish they could just love me as I am.

Rib: So much shame … got put out as blame.

Head: Wish I didn't have to worry so much about being judged and shamed.

Another round …

Eyebrow: All that I hear is that I am not good enough.

Side of the Eye: Never felt safe … always felt judged.

Under the Eye: So afraid of their judgments and always felt ashamed.

Upper Lip: Just never felt I was good enough.

Under the Lip: Always felt blamed … like it was my entire fault.

Collarbone: Just wish they would leave me alone.

Under the Arm: I get so angry that I always feel blamed.

Rib: So afraid to trust.

Head: Just so afraid to bring attention to me.

Introducing Possibility of Change

Eyebrow: Maybe this can change…

Side of the Eye: Maybe I can finally feel safe.

Under the Eye: I have always felt the fear of not being good enough to be loved.

Upper Lip: But maybe I am finally good enough. Maybe it is safe to trust.

Under the Lip: Maybe I can let this tension go.

Collarbone: Maybe my Adult Self is here to help me heal this pain.

Under the Arm: Maybe I can let Mom and Dad go.

Rib: Maybe I don't have to carry this tension that was not even mine.

Head: Maybe I can let go. Maybe it is safe to trust.

Conviction to Change

Eyebrow: I am going to let go and let my Adult Self in…

Side of the Eye: I am going to let go … let go of the past.

Under the Eye: I am willing to let this go and trust my Adult Self.

Upper Lip: I am willing to let go and let God.

Under the Lip: I know I have carried this for so long.

Collarbone: But I am willing to let it go.

Under the Arm: I am willing to trust that my Adult Self might be different than my parents.

Rib: I am willing to give it a try.

Head: I feel really good about joining forces with the Adult Self… I am ready to let it go.

Again, this gives you an example of how to move through it. I encourage you to continue to work with this and keep going through this process. Keep in mind there is no right or wrong way with this. Just keep working with the Inner Child until he or she is ready to let go and can fully begin to trust you.

As with any issue, you will sense this part moving through the stages of grief, from tension, and fear—into total despair of helplessness. He or she will ultimately acknowledge the effort that was made to please and experience anger when those efforts failed to keep him or her safe.

The idea is to work with this part of you through all of its feelings until it is once again willing to feel safe. He or she does want to trust you will not abandon him or her if you find the right job or the perfect career. Continue to explore what your Inner Child's experience is around this issue; then use the tapping to neutralize those feelings until you have won his or her trust.

Sometimes this takes more than one sequence and more than one day. But this will give you a start. If you feel you have healed this part enough to proceed to the next step, then do so. If you cannot get past the pain, consider setting up a one-to-one session, and we will see what we can do. You may be inspired to access the Divine and assess whether this issue is anchored in a past life. If so, approach the first four layers from that angle. Layer Five continues this process for the Inner Child only. If you do discover this is past-life oriented, the task is not to merge, but rather to send that past part of your Soul back to its Source.

5ᵀᴴ Layer: The Step of Merger and Integration

This Layer is perhaps one of the most empowering Layers. As mentioned above, the following process is used only for the integration of an Inner Child. With a fragment of your Soul, you want to just send it back into the Light to free the energy. But with an aspect of your personality from this lifetime (the Inner Child), you want to partner with him or her and build a bonding, cooperative relationship.

Combining the neutralization process with the pronoun "we" enables you to set the stage for the merger and integration. Partnering with the Inner Child in this manner empowers him or her to return to your force field in a healed state and empowers you and your Inner Child to reclaim the magic that was lost in response to the wounding experience. When you bring this magic back the essence of the believability you had as a child returns as well. If you then infuse your desire for right livelihood with this vibration, you experience magic ten-fold!

If you have taken a break, then begin your Fifth Layer of exercises by doing one round where you get the Adult Self clear enough to be present for this work. You may also want to add another round to make sure your Inner Child has remained clear. When you feel ready to proceed, the sequence may look something like the example below.

State the setup phrase while tapping on the karate point. For this Layer, you will again be using the pronoun "we" because you are stating the sequences as if the Inner Child and the Adult Self are saying them in unison. When you feel ready, begin.

Even though we have both experienced a lot of disappointment about our career and have often felt not good enough, and we have both experienced a lot of tension about this in our lives, we are so excited we have found each other again, And we really do love ourselves and each other enough to trust that we can manifest the right livelihood we deserve.

Even though we both have experienced a lot of bumps in the road in response to following our bliss and doing what we passionately want to do to attract the right work, we are so excited we have come together and are now ready to heal.

So even though we have had a lot of disappointments, starts, and stops with respect to attracting what we deserve ... we are so excited we are now together and are ready to heal.

This is an example of the setup phrases; please feel free though to customize them. Make them fit your particular situation. The following is an example of the reminder phrases you could use to augment this Layer. It is not as much of a process of neutralization as an infusion of what you have affirmed. But just to be on the safe side, I have provided one round to help you clear any resistance to coming together. Add more if you feel it would be useful.

Again, prepare to tap by beginning with the corner of your eyebrow.

Eyebrow: We are so excited to come together and heal.

Side of the Eye: We are just buzzing with enthusiasm and trust for each other.

Under the Eye: So excited we are going to finally manifest our heart's desire.

Upper Lip: With the love of each other and the love of God, we deserve all we desire.

Under the Lip: We are so excited to come together to heal.

Collarbone: So excited we are together to heal ... to attract all that we deserve.

Under the Arm: We are so full of energy, love, and Light and want to send this energy out to the entire world.

Rib: We are so excited we have done such good work.

Head: We are so proud of each other and love each other so much that we are ready to attract the career that matches our talents and our gifts.

Now just keep going with that until you are really, really buzzing, and when you feel ready to proceed, move on to Layer Six.

6ᵀᴴ LAYER: REWIRING YOUR BRAIN; REPROGRAMMING YOUR DNA; RECONFIGURING THE ELECTROMAGNETIC FIELD

Discussion: This implementation of this Layer was inspired by the New Brain Science, most specifically the work of Dr. Richard Hanson, and Margaret Ruby's work on reprogramming the DNA. www.possibilitiesdna.com/margaret.html

You use meditations and interactive tapping™ sequences to first rewire the brain by building new neuro-pathways between the amygdala and the prefrontal cortex. You then clear the energetic disturbance from your electrical system in your body, ask your body for its forgiveness, and then give it permission to release. This reprograms the DNA in every cell so it can hold your new vibration and enables you to reconfigure the electromagnetic field around you.

I encourage you to experiment with the wording as much as your imagination will allow. Just keep tapping and saying affirming statements. I have included an example, but please experiment. Try it on every feeling you think you have stored in your body about the Divine work you should be doing and the right livelihood you want to attract.

Before you begin, however, do one round to clear any current trigger in your Adult Self and to neutralize any current disturbance that may be getting in the way of giving your body permission to release. State each setup phrase while tapping on the karate point. The interaction is between you and your body so imagine you are speaking directly to it.

Even though I have needed you to store my pain, I am now strong enough to process my pain myself … so I now invite you to release the tension and the stress. I invite you to let it go.

So even though you, my dear body, have held so many feelings of tension related to my not doing what I wanted to be doing because, for so long I was unable to deal with these feelings myself, I now forgive myself and love myself completely and profoundly. I do understand I did not know what else to do and I can forgive myself for not knowing what I did not know.

In turn, I ask you to forgive me as well. I humbly apologize for needing you to hold this disturbance for me. I now give you total permission to release it. I firmly commit to you that I will now neutralize and dissolve all disturbances related to this situation. Thank you. Thank you. Thank you.

Repeat this sequence until you feel you have moved through all the resistance your body is holding for you. Give your body permission to release what it has held. Reassure it that you are now completely willing to deal with what comes your way with the tools you have acquired. When replenishing your body with a new vibration, you are acknowledging that the DNA has been reprogrammed. You infuse every cell with the new vibration of your intention.

Now begin to tap on the two sore spots right on your chest (near the collarbone but not on the collarbone) to infuse your body with this new vibration of energy. State your new intention much like an affirmation. Imagine bringing in your Divine Right Livelihood, right into your force field and into your daily life. 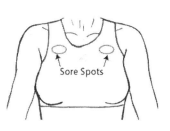 Once you have this image firm in your mind's eye, hold this vibration for 68 seconds. As has been discussed, according to the *Teachings of Abraham,* this length of focus is enough for your intention to take form and begin attracting reciprocity from the Universe. It will match it and begin the process of materializing your intent. The following is an example of how the narrative of your infusion might flow. Repeat it while tapping on the sore spots.

In a narrative fashion, state something like this:

I now envision compassion and passion in every area of my life. All my needs and wants are fully realized in the presence of the Light. I am so fortunate to experience such acceptance and unconditional love. Every area of my life is enriched with this sense of acceptance. This acceptance radiates out to all I attract. I love what I do. I love the rewards my actions bring back. I radiate in unconditional love, and this vibration attracts the perfect places and things that promote the right livelihood of my choice.

I am rich with experiences of love and Light and see the magic of the Universe everywhere I look. I am truly a worthwhile being, and I exude that worthiness in every act! I am perfect in mind, body, heart, and Soul!

I then complete this infusion by tapping on the endpoints while stating reminder phrases that *anchor in* my body, mind, heart, and Soul. I have provided an example of one round. Add other rounds as you see fit.

Eyebrow: My body has held on to this shame, guilt, or judgment.

Side of the Eye: All this shame, guilt, or judgment my body has stored because I didn't know how to deal.

Under the Eye: My body has held on to this shame, guilt, or judgment for so very long.

Upper Lip: But I now give my body permission to let go.

Under the Lip: I release all of this shame, guilt, judgment, and fear.

Collarbone: My body is now programmed with health and love.

Rib: Every cell now holds this new DNA vibration of compassion and love.

Under the Arm: My body forgives me and vibrates with passion and love.

Head: So glad my body can finally let go and vibrate with passion and love.

GENERAL TAPPING INSTRUCTIONS AND PROGRESSIONS

When you begin the tapping sequence, you just keep restating the above examples and do as many rounds as it takes to envision and implant this new expression. Experiment with it and feel free to alter it as your experiences shift.

As the energy shifts, you might want to imagine you progressively moving up Abraham's *Emotional Guidance Scale (Ask and It Is Given* by Esther and Jerry Hicks, page 114). In other words, you respectively move up from shame (in despair) to anger; frustration; irritation; possibility; hope; belief; and appreciation. You adjust the setup phrase and reminder phrases accordingly.

Example: Even though a part of me still feels ashamed, maybe I can envision feeling _____

Then graduate to the proclamation! *I am now feeling more hopeful...* and lastly, move to: *"I am infused with hope and Divine faith!" Tap until you feel the buzz...* once you feel the buzz, then according to Quantum Physics the neurons begin to fire the picture, and the DNA begins to manifest accordingly.

7TH LAYER: GIVING BACK TO THE WORLD

Now you get to share this healing with the world. It, too, needs an infusion of compassionate, unconditional regard. Take all you have neutralized and realigned and send this energy into the Universe as an offering for planetary healing. It dissolves isolation and contributes not only to the increasing of the Light on the planet but also to the healing of Mother Earth. It reinforces the fact that you are part of something bigger than yourself and a valuable agent of change for humanity. You have shared the gift with your Inner Child and the fragment of your Soul. You now have an opportunity to share it with the world.

Again, I encourage you to experiment with the wording as much as your imagination will allow. Just keep tapping and saying affirming statements. I have included a sample, but please experiment and try it on everything. However, make sure you use this only after you have moved to a low intensity on the scale from 1-10 or have neutralized your way up your emotional guidance scale because you want the energy you send out into the world to be as pure as possible.

Before you begin, I suggest, as always, you do one round to clear any current trigger in your current self, body, mind, heart, and Soul! Begin to tap as you enter into a meditative state. When you feel ready to begin, tap again on your sore spots while you say something like the example below:

I feel so fortunate to have done this work. I now envision the cylinder of Light running from the center of Mother Earth to the grid of unconditional love about 60 feet above my head.

I am so full of Light and High Energy. From this highest place within myself, I now offer 10% or more of this healing back to heal the planet and the Universe for their use in healing wherever the energy needs to be spread.

I feel so fortunate I have been able to complete this work and am so grateful I am now in a position to Share this Gift. Thank you, God, Goddess, Higher Power, Angels, Masters, and all above for your support and direction. Thank you, Soul fragments for having the courage and fortitude to call me back and thank you my dear little ones for having the patience to await my return.

I love that we are healed and can now hold the Light which allows us to attract the career of our choice so that we can contribute to this world in a supportive, safe way. Thank you. Thank you. Thank you.

This meditative sequence is again an example. As you work in this fashion, the inspiration will come to you… the words will come to you; that last sequence will simply augment your ability to attract your right livelihood into your life.

Module 4:
Attracting Reciprocal
Partnerships

E qual partnerships are built on a good match and a fair exchange … on reciprocity … on an ability to state your needs … the capacity to hear your partner's needs … the fortitude and skill to take these respective needs and negotiate a solution that responds fairly to both of your positions.

Reciprocity requires accountability! Accountability depends on having a strong connection to Source Energy—one which provides the foundation for our self-worth and safety. We can only hold ourselves accountable if we feel safely embedded in the arms of our Higher Source. Without this connection, we build our expectations on projections fueled by our antiquated co-dependent bargain™ … the belief that dictates we have to act in a certain manner in order to earn and ensure love and safety. We develop a *"false loyalty"* to the belief that then becomes the blueprint for our partnerships in adulthood. It becomes the foundation of our expectations for self and others.

A Word From Abraham

"Every thought radiates a signal."

"Every thought attracts a matching signal back."

"We call that process The Law of Attraction."

"You get what you think about."

You came forth to have a glorious experience and left to your own devices—you would. In other words, you are born seeking joy; you are born knowing you are supposed to feel joyful. And it turns a little topsy-turvy.

You are influenced by others to believe—if it feels good—it isn't. If there are struggle and suffering in it, there is probably virtue. You get crosswise in your guidance system … and that really is what we are wanting to help you rediscover… we want you to reactivate within yourself your awareness of your own guidance system … and remember who you are, so you can figure out which way you are headed and which way is the right way for you.

There is no one right answer, but there is certainly guidance coming forth from your broader perspective that would let you find the path to that which you are about. You did not come to live identical lives; you came forth to live diversity, variance, and difference… and to stimulate within each other variety and desire. You came forth to live in joy. Anything that is a departure from that is off your path.

Excerpt from the "Secret behind the Secret,"
Last Segment from Episode 3

Resolve Competition And False Loyalties; Embody Cooperation And Healthy Partnerships; Manifest Co-Creative, Supportive Relationships

Acceptance is the key in this endeavor. If we accept ourselves, we can build on that self-esteem to adjust our expectations appropriately. No other part of us knows more about this process than our 6-12 years old because then you had to rely on how you felt about yourself to cope with the rejection or acceptance you felt from your peers.

1. *Being selected to be part of "the team" ...*
2. *Speaking up in front of the class to give reports ...*
3. *Beginning and completing tasks;*
4. *Being judged ... graded on assignments ...*

Each of these activities is an example of how you begin the process of chiseling the clay of your early years into the budding adolescent you are about to become. Your peers become the first set of judges outside of the family. They become the first source of comparison and competition. They become the first externalized barometer for how you are going to fit in with the outside world. Their reflection of you becomes the foundation for your expectations of yourself and others. These expectations become the texture of your partnerships with everything with which you interact—from your body to nature, your friends, family, co-workers ... your pets ... even your Higher Self. They become the foundation of the reciprocal relationship between your inner male and female; your human and spiritual selves; you as the responsible adult; and you and your body.

It also sets the stage for what your Inner Child will expect of you.

Journal Exercise: Giving Form to your Polar Opposites

Take time to reflect on and play with the following pairs; ponder how balanced each of these relationships is with respect to what you give and what you take. Then write a brief paragraph describing your findings. This material later becomes your foundation from which you will build your interactive tapping™ sequences.

Inner Male/Inner Female
Inner Father/Inner Mother
Higher Self/Human Self
Adult Self/Body
Adult Self/Loved One(s)
Adult Self/Coworkers

There is a hierarchy in the relationship between you and your Inner Children; you and your biological children. Yet, it is still important to have a reciprocal respect for each other. With this in mind, what does your Inner Child expect from you as well as others? What is he or she willing to allow … to offer?

Departure from our Path is an Expression of our Inner Child's Wound!

Background: We take everything we learned before the age of six and use it as the foundation upon which we establish equal and satisfying relationships … **with everything** … from our relationship with our bodies to our relationship with Mother Earth, our Higher Power, coworkers, family, friends, and pets.

Our developmental task during the grade-school stage of development which is between the ages of six-to-twelve is to learn how to interact with our peers. We are defining ourselves by how we compete, how we perform; how we produce; how well we are accepted into the popular crowd; and how much we excel at any given assignment or task. Our point of reference moves from family to peers … a group that can often be described as harsh.

What feels even harsher is our inability to focus on the above tasks because our attention is so focused on what is happening at home. We can be so preoccupied with events that are way beyond our control that our ability to address the developmental tasks of this stage can be eclipsed.

Every one of us has a part of us that is loyal to an old, outdated, yet unconscious, contract that governs our interactions with others. It is difficult to attract our heart's desires when the hidden "tail-enders" *(sabotaging self-talk)* that follow our intentions are embedded in false loyalties formed in childhood.

When we begin to set our intentions for reciprocal and supportive partnerships, any dysfunctional patterns related to these unresolved issues will be revealed.

As you enter into the exploration of issues from your grade-school self, you will be invited to explore how these concerns and strengths interface with your peers, coworkers, friends, acquaintances, and family. You will be visiting potential issues involving feeling left out—your discomfort or pride related to your inclusion or exclusion in the "in-crowd." Competition with self and others will also emerge for examination.

You will compare your progress to others in the past and identify when you felt either superior or inferior. Although either experience can bring stress, bringing awareness to these feelings will give you the opportunity to confront how you deal with feeling *better than* or *lesser than* someone else. This comparison with others can result in tension irrespective of which side of the teeter-totter you may slide. Much to your surprise, you may find that feeling superior to others brings about just as much fear as feeling inferior.

Some of us may confront memories of being chosen first on the baseball team—or being first in a spelling contest. Yet others will revisit feeling left out—feeling inept and less than our peers.

You will also begin to build on your experience with what I refer to as your co-dependent bargain™. Again the co-dependent bargain™ is the unconscious agreement you made in childhood with your caretaker. It was an attempt to be perfect with the hope that your perfection would result in your feeling safe. It did not work and with each stage of development, the impact of that perceived failure becomes evident.

In this stage of development, you begin to identify and work with the part of you that may be remaining loyal to your antiquated family system. This pattern is perhaps the most profound remnant left from this stage of development. There were many social tasks to be completed at this stage of your life. In order to succeed, you would have had to have ample emotional energy to concentrate on their mastery. If there was stress in your family—if your emotional energy was tied up with survival rather than progression—your mastery of these tasks would have been thwarted. To understand this dynamic more fully, let's examine these developmental tasks with a little more depth. The focus questions are woven into the body of this discussion because they will be easier to relate to if they are presented in context.

Developmental Tasks During The Six-to-Twelve-Year-Old Stage Of Development

How well you fit into your social groups; the degree of comfort you feel with your coworkers and close friends; the degree of success you experience when you have to perform or compete; the success you experience in a career; when you start and complete projects—these are all related to how well you mastered these tasks when you were between the ages of six and twelve. These years are called the middle years because they span the time between the rapid physical growth of your first six years and the marked changes that arise with puberty. Your attention was more on mastering tasks of a social rather than a psychological nature. Your focus moved from being internally referenced to being externally referenced.

Exclusion versus Inclusion—Around the age of six is perhaps the first time you moved from the safety experienced in your family (or lack thereof) and entered the outside world. You began to focus on issues involving your relationship with peers. "Do I fit in? Am I the same as others or different? Am I accepted by my peers?" Whatever experience you had at this time in your life followed you into adulthood and is now reflected in how well you feel you belong or how much you fear being excluded.

Mastery or Fear of Public Speaking—Another area of exploration that emerges is the degree of comfort you experience when you speak in public. Since this was the time in your life when you were first expected to get up in front of your class and give reports and presentations, your comfort or discomfort will be related back to these childhood experiences. If you are able to do this with ease, then you developed the confidence necessary to feel comfortable with such visibility. This confidence is also evident whenever you are expected to give presentations in your work and other environments. Since—other than death—public speaking is the number one fear, few moved through this task with ease.

Task Completion (Beginning and Completing Projects— Completing tasks and learning the discipline needed to begin and finish projects is also related to what you experienced during this time in your life. Starting and completing tasks is a skill that needs to be learned—it is not innate; you are not considered *lazy* if you did not master it. Many factors influence your success at mastering this ability. It depends on how much assistance you received from your caretakers in following through with your homework. It can be influenced by how secure you felt in your peer groups. It can also be affected by how much emotional energy you had to devote to this lesson. If you were distracted from this focus by family dysfunction— if your energy was directed towards worrying about what was going on at home—whether your mother was drinking or your father had found a job—then you would not have had the emotional energy to focus on such task developments, and your mastery would have been stifled.

You may have grown up having great challenges in completing projects and now interpret this trait as evidence of being lazy or unmotivated. In truth—many adults are unable to begin and complete projects because they simply were never taught how to take the steps necessary to succeed. Those who are able to complete tasks with ease were often forced to focus on this area of their life as a way to survive. They were the *parentified children*, selected as members of the family to hold order. Even though this accomplishment can be experienced as a source of strength in adulthood, it can carry the underpinnings of grief and sadness because of its origin.

*Loyalty to Your Dysfunctional Family System—*Perhaps, however, the most profound pattern that originates from this developmental stage is the pattern of sabotage related to being loyal to your dysfunctional parenting unit. Seldom have I worked with adults on their childhood issues without having to confront this grade-school self that developed a loyalty to one or both parents. This dynamic emerges and sabotages any effort that would result in surpassing their parents' expertise or succeeding in areas where their parents were unable to excel.

The purpose for this is embedded in the fact that, as a child, you needed to think of your parents as *all-knowing.* It is the only way you could survive. You held on to the unconscious belief exhibited in the plea of your co-dependent bargain™ … that if only you could *do what was needed …* then your parents would be able to become the parents you needed them to be in order for you to survive. Breathe. Then read that again because that sentence is loaded.

Many of us remain loyal to this unconscious agreement and sabotage any effort that would result in succeeding in areas our parents had or have been unable to experience success. Why? Because it is too frightening for this part of self to excel and surpass his or her parents—this option brings too much grief and fear of being alone. We would then be expected to be the experts of our own lives, and that fear alone can catapult us into despair, a sense of isolation and/ or a fear of failure. Instead, we become preoccupied with our weight; finances; dysfunctional relationships; or any dysfunction that is not in competition with the areas of accomplishment achieved by one or both of our parents.

How These Patterns May Have Been Carried Into Adulthood

How does all of this material filter into your adult life? The pattern exhibited in adulthood that relates to this stage of development is found in your need to be recognized by your peers and acknowledged for your accomplishments. If you do not have the self-esteem to judge yourself according to your own value system, then you will not feel entitled to expect much from others.

Oddly enough, however, it is common that success can be experienced in other areas of life. As long as the one sacred area that surpasses your parents is left untouched, many proceed without the risk of being disloyal to the parent with whom you long to connect.

The antidote for this pattern in adulthood is to progressively find outside activities and interests that match your own. You slowly begin to develop a support system that matches your inner value system.

You find that you gravitate towards a group that mirrors your specific styles and one in which you feel you belong. You may also find that you begin to develop hobbies or a line of work that gives you the feeling of accomplishment. You may find your psyche can be, and is, drawn to success in at least some areas of your life.

This stage of development and adult pattern reflect the transition made from being a novice to being seasoned. You will see this represented in your present level of achievement in your career or in the manner in which you relate to loved ones and family members. You may see evidence of these threads emerging in the way you attract prosperity; create your life's passion; relate to your sexuality, your body in general, your sense of self, and adult belief systems about success. This transition phase of any endeavor prepares you for entry into your refinement phase of adolescence when true mastery can occur. It will be reflected in the relationship between your inner male and female; your inner father and mother; your Adult Self and your physical form.

Potential Spiritual Lesson

This time in your life and the issues that emerge in this stage of the pursuit of your mastery offer the opportunity to look at the moments in your Soul's history when you perhaps joined a group that led you away from your Source or perhaps a time when you displaced your loyalty onto a false source. It will also dictate the level of reciprocity and give and take you allow and expect in your relationship with your Higher Self. Take a moment to ponder the following questions. Record your thoughts in your journal.

1. What is the relationship between your Spiritual and Earthly selves?

2. How equal do these two aspects of you feel?

3. How much give and take is there between your personality and Soul?

Exercise: Healthy, Reciprocal Actions

The following statements represent the manifestation of healthy actions with respect to mature reciprocity. Take a moment to read the following statements then rate your response to them on a scale from 1–5. 1 = *No* and 5 = *Yes*.

1. _____ I feel connected to my Source.

2. _____ I have more than one vital, intimate relationship in my life.

3. _____ I know what my body needs and am able to respond.

4. _____ I have pets and consider myself a good provider.

5. _____ I am able to decipher and communicate what I like and don't t like.

6. _____ I am able to say *no* when necessary.

7. _____ Likewise I can say *yes* without resentment and *no* without guilt.

8. _____ I can adequately assess the degree to which my body needs exercise.

9. _____ I have come to understand the pros and cons of my key relationships.

10. _____ I am comfortable with the person I am … good and bad traits.

11. _____ I like to be in nature and I am aware of all of Mother Earth's glory.

12. _____ I feel I have a nurturing relationship with my Inner Children.

13. _____ I am able to give form to an idea and execute it.

14. _____ I am a self-starter.

15. _____ I feel I have a reciprocal relationship with my Higher Self.

16. _____ I have good relationships with my coworkers.

17. _____ I feel a balance between my masculine and feminine sides.

18. _____ I have a good idea of what *give and take* means in my relationships.

19. _____ I hold myself accountable for how I feel and how I respond.

20. _____ I accept my human qualities and can, therefore, accept others.

Review your responses. For those for which you checked three or below come up with a statement that reflects the truth of the situation at the present moment. The contrast between your two statements illustrates the ambivalence you feel with respect to this issue. Ambivalence represents the two sides of a concern.

RESOLVING YOUR AMBIVALENCE WITH INTERACTIVE TAPPING™

The tapping process begins with the setup phrases which automatically sets the stage for resolving your ambivalence because it takes the challenge or that thought/behavior you want to change and positions it against a positive affirmation which promotes an acceptance of yourself despite that that behavior. Acceptance is the key. As you teeter-totter between the challenge and the affirmation while tapping on the karate point you send the electrical charge through your body which neutralizes the challenge and reinforces the affirmation. This very act alone rewires the brain and takes the edge off of the polarized position you may be experiencing. As you move through the reminder phrases you progressively take the edge off of the challenging feelings and move into an acceptance of something new.

The following sequence provides a method for you to take these opposing feelings and begin to neutralize the challenging feeling you now exhibit. It will assist you in determining how you want to respond.

I also recommend that you refer back to the "Formula for Designing your own Sequences" in Section Two and practice developing your own unique tapping script that addresses this disparity. For instance, let's take #20 as an example. Imagine you rated this statement as a 2. This rating is based on the fact that you know yourself to be somewhat judgmental. If you are judgmental of yourself, it is likely you are judgmental of others. When you realize this to be the case, you determine how you want to be is nonjudgmental. The application of tapping sequences would, therefore, look something like this.

State the following while tapping on the **k**arate point:

Even though I am very judgmental of myself and often feel critical of others, I love myself completely and profoundly enough to begin to dissolve this reaction, so I can be compassionate and accepting of others as well as myself.

So even though I can be quite critical and often project that out onto others, I care enough about myself to begin to use this technique to heal.

And even though I can judge myself ruthlessly about many situations and often do the same with others, I love myself completely and profoundly and am sincere about wanting to dissolve this pattern so I can work it through.

The Setup Phrase establishes where you are and where you want to go. It sets up the polarization and determines the course of action that will systematically move you from the disturbance to the resolution and conviction to try something new. The actual neutralization process occurs as you move around tapping the respective meridian endpoints. Each time you state the phrase and tap, an electrical pulse is triggered. It is that energetic reaction that neutralizes the energy attached to the negative or challenging stance.

Interactive tapping™ divides the sequences into three sections. You first neutralize the negative thoughts and feelings, then introduce the possibility of change, and finish with a strong infusion of your conviction to a new way of being. This ensures success in your efforts to attract reciprocal partnerships.

Repeat each statement as you sequentially tap on the different meridian points. Refer to the graphic provided to refresh your memory on where to tap.

Neutralizing Emotions

Eyebrow: Feel so much judgment.

Side of the Eye: So full of shame.

Under the Eye: Insecure …

Upper Lip: Don't feel good enough …

Under the Lip: So unworthy …

Collarbone: Feel less than others …

Under the Arm: Can't imagine feeling equal …

Rib: So tired of so much negativity.

Head: What am I going to do; feeling such a lack of worth?

Introducing Possibility of Change

Eyebrow: Maybe I do not have to be so perfect.

Side of the Eye: Maybe I can move beyond this need to judge.

Under the Eye: Wonder if I can be more accepting?

Upper Lip: Maybe I can try feeling more compassion and be more accepting…

Under the Lip: Maybe I can find reciprocity.

Collarbone: Maybe, just maybe I can let go and allow!

Under the Arm: Maybe I can imagine not feeling judgmental!

Rib: Maybe I am ready to let go of this need to be perfect … let go of all of this judgment and shame.

Head: Wouldn't it be wonderful to let go of this judgment, fear, and shame.

Conviction to Change

Eyebrow: I choose to let go of this doubt, fear, and shame.

Side of the Eye: I am so ready to release this unworthiness; these feelings of not being equal ... so much shame.

Under the Eye: I want to feel compassion. I want to feel the presence of the Divine.

Upper Lip: I am ready to feel acceptance; I am ready to let God dissolve the shame.

Under the Lip: Feel so full of compassion, self-love, and acceptance!

Collarbone: I am ready to respond to others in the same way.

Under the Arm: I am so ready to accept myself and others.

Rib: I can manifest reciprocity.

Head: I now stand in the vibration of compassion and love.

JOURNAL EXERCISE: STEPS TO RECIPROCITY

In the following journal exercise, you will begin to revise the false loyalties and worn out belief systems that frame the dynamics of your primary relationships with friends, loved ones, and coworkers.

Take a look at the pairs you worked within the first part of this material. Explore how you feel in each of these relationships.

Does any theme emerge? Is there any common thread of experience that repeatedly emerges in these relationships? Anything about which you might say, "*No matter what I do, this always happens to me...?*"

1. Ask your grade school self what he or she learned about relating to others?

2. What was his /her experience with respect to competition; speaking in front of the class; beginning and completing assignments and projects?

3. Let him or her tell you the story of what it was like for him or her at that time?

4. What did he or she come to expect from others? Your Inner Child's response will provide you with clarity and insight.

5. Explore how such expectations now get projected onto your adult relationships with your children; your body; your Higher Source; nature; and your pets. *(Issues to focus on are how well you feel connected; how well you can hear and say no; and how you feel in the presence of the other person.)*

6. Do you feel good about yourself, or do you feel like you are not quite enough to deserve respect and affection?

7. Would you call these relationships equal partnerships?

Once you respond to these questions ponder your responses to determine your level of reciprocity.

MEDITATION: RECIPROCITY WITH YOUR HIGHER SELF"

Take a deep breath. Imagine you are standing in the shoes of your most Illuminated Human Self. An expression of your Higher Self emerges before you. This aspect of you holds the key to your higher purpose here— it holds the wisdom of your choices; the foundation of all you charted. Your Higher Self holds the blueprint of experiences your personality or human self encounters—that vibration of you that stands outside of your physical form and exists in the ethereal force field.

Now respond to the following questions:

1. Do you feel equal in this relationship?

2. Do you value what your human, earthly self has to contribute to your life situation as much as your Higher Self has to contribute?

3. Can you envision an equal, reciprocal relationship between the two?

4. How can they partner together and effectively team up to manifest your heart's desires?

5. How can the magic of your 6-to-12-year-old, your adventurous self, sprinkle this endeavor with his or wit, charm, and sense of delight?

Record your experiences in your journal. Now make a list of the issues that emerged.

Each issue is one you will ultimately want to neutralize and resolve with the Interactive tapping™ Sequences.

Begin by Neutralizing the Imbalances of your Adult Self.

Even though I sometimes feel so unequal in this situation, and I am not sure what I can expect, I love myself completely and profoundly.

Even though my lack of self-esteem prohibits me from attracting the reciprocal partnerships I so desire, I love myself completely and profoundly.

Even though I feel unworthy of attracting the equal relationships I want and I sabotage myself because of false loyalties that no longer fit, I love myself completely and profoundly.

The following are the reminder phrases that you repeat after you've cleared your Adult Self. State these while you are sequentially tapping on the different meridian points.

Neutralizing the Negativity

Eyebrow: Feel so much fear.

Side of the Eye: Some shame and judgment about what I have to offer.

Under the Eye: Don't feel entitled to expect my share.

Upper Lip: Feel I always have to do more to be loved.

Under the Lip: Feel unsure of my value; don't know what to do.

Collarbone: Just can't let go of this need to do more.

Under the Arm: Can't imagine what it would be like to feel balanced in body, mind, heart, and Soul.

Rib: Feel so much shame and guilt because I cannot establish equal partnerships!

Head: Would like to think I deserve to attract partnerships that are equal

Introducing the Possibility of Change

Eyebrow: Maybe I do not have to feel so unequal.

Side of the Eye: Maybe I can move beyond this sense of being inferior.

Under the Eye: Wonder if I can move beyond my potential shame!

Upper Lip: Maybe I can manifest a partnership that has a promise of an equal exchange.

Under the Lip: Maybe I do not have to drown in this feeling of being "less than…"

Collarbone: Maybe I am loyal beyond measure.

Rib: Maybe I am ready to let go of this need to be liked.

Under the Arm: Maybe I can imagine being treated equally in my partnerships

Head: Wouldn't it be wonderful to stand side by side with those whom I admire.

Conviction to Change

Eyebrow: I choose to let go of this doubt, fear, loyalty, and shame.

Side of the Eye: I am so ready to release these antiquated loyalties; they are not warranted, and I am ready to claim what is mine by Divine right.

Under the Eye: I can trust God and my Higher Source.

Upper Lip: I am ready to balance my intuition with the action of my masculine self.

Under the Lip: I feel so full of inspiration and action; compassion and purpose; nurturance and protection!

Collarbone: I am ready to claim my heart's desire on equal terms!

Rib: I can manifest the partnerships I deserve!

Head: I now stand in the vibration of reciprocity and feel worthy to claim my heart's desire.

You have been exposed to several methods of dealing with reciprocity between your Adult Self and Higher Self; your Adult Self and others. These sequences can be also applied to your relationships with your pets and with Mother Nature as well. It can even be applied to the relationship you have with your body. Few of us engage in a true partnership with our bodies. However, that is exactly what I am suggesting here. I invite you to customize the questions in the previous exercise to explore your own unique relationship with your body. Remember to record your responses in your journal.

1. How *do* you relate to your body?

2. Do you ignore it … feel at its mercy?

3. Do you honor it? *(I always equate our bodies to the infant stage of development because they are just as dependent on us to meet their needs, as infants are on their caretakers.)*

4. Think about it for a minute. Do you over-stimulate your body?

5. Do you make sure it gets enough rest … feed it nourishing food?

6. If your body were an infant, what kind of a parent would you say you are? That puts it in a different perspective, doesn't it!?

You can also extend this thinking to your relationship to Mother Earth.

1. Do you feel you have a reverent relationship with Her?

2. Are you aware of how much of your physical form is a direct extension of Hers? Do you communicate with Mother Earth? Have you ever hugged a tree … or stroked the rays of sunshine as they gently touch your face?

3. If you see trash lying on the sidewalk, do you retrieve it, or do you contribute by littering?

4. Can you feel the beat of Mother Earth's earth?

5. Can you align your heart beat with Hers?

What about your relationship to your pets.

1. Are they part of the family or do you see them as livestock ... second class creatures ... needing to be seen and not heard?

2. How reciprocal is your relationship with the animals in your home?

Think about these relationships and in the following section you will learn how to apply *The Seven-Layers of Healing* to help your Inner Child dissolve the early patterns that set the stage for the thoughts and feelings that have just been revealed. Try not to judge yourself or berate yourself for what you just discovered. Whatever beliefs emerged, they are a product of what you experienced as a child, and you are now in a position to right all wrongs and heal all patterns that no longer serve you. And the following section will equip you to do just that!

Seven-Layer Healing Process
Applied To Attracting Reciprocal
Partnerships

RECIPROCAL PARTNERSHIPS—Overview

*T*he *Seven-Layers Healing Process* is useful if clearing the Adult Self of a current issue does not bring full resolution. As you read in the introduction, if you cannot clear a situation that is current, it is because the situation has triggered a residual issue from your past. This trigger offers you an opportunity to clear the disturbance in all dimensions of time and consciousness.

This modality invites you to identify the aspect of you that has gotten triggered; then it systematically takes you through the process of healing the unresolved issues, so your wounded one can let go. It provides the method for dealing with this aspect of you that carries your blueprint for establishing equal partnerships.

As you discovered in the introductory material of this Module, this most often originates between the ages of six to twelve because it was during this developmental phase that you engaged in relationships with peers and struggled with issues of competition and *give and take*. The following healing process will assist you in neutralizing relationship imbalances that cripple your sense of self and then assist you in replacing them with empowering convictions aimed to ignite your self-esteem and allow you to participate in relationships on an equal basis.

The Seven Layers Of Healing

The following section reviews the *Seven-Layers of Healing* and then offers tapping setup phrases and sequences to work with them. Feel free to experiment with using one sequence a day, or just pick a time and move through the Layers all at once. I have presented it in a daily fashion for simplicity. For some, working with one aspect a day augments the depth of the work. Others may want to intensify the experience by going through this process at one sitting. There is no right or wrong way to proceed. Honor whichever style appeals to you.

If you *are* doing this on a daily basis, then you will want to begin each day with empowering your Adult Self before you work with the Layer of that day. If you do it in one fell swoop, then once you have cleared the Adult Self, it is unnecessary to repeat this with each Layer unless you feel the need to do so.

1ST LAYER: EMPOWERING AND CLEARING THE ADULT SELF

These first sequences neutralize any disturbance that is currently in the Adult Self. This is not necessarily in reference to reciprocity but just general irritations, so you can enter this work with a clear mindset. You begin this part of the process by neutralizing the Adult Self because it is this part of you that will orchestrate the layered healing. It is therefore essential that he or she is cleared of any current, distracting emotions or thoughts.

The process begins with three setup phrases. I use the setup phrases to identify the ambivalence and contrasting feelings of any issue. In the statements presented in the previous section, you established that you have this sabotaging voice. Again, the setup phrases position this sabotage with a positive affirmation.

The sequences themselves are divided into three sections. You first neutralize the negative thoughts and feelings and then introduce the possibility of change. You finish with a strong infusion of your conviction—a commitment to a new way of relating to the part of you that is sabotaging your efforts to successfully engage in reciprocal partnerships.

Stay with each series of sequences until you feel ready to move to the next one. You will intuitively feel an energetic shift when you are done with the negative and your psyche is ready to consider the possibility of something new.

The second set of sequences introducing the possibility of change usually does not take as long. It just softens the psyche, so it is ready to claim the right to feel convicted about the new approach.

The last set of sequences should leave you feeling strong and energized in your new conviction. You will then be ready to proceed with the *Seven-Layers Healing Process*, which will work with each piece of this dynamic more fully.

Again, the setup phrases position your disturbance with an affirmation, thus preparing your psyche to accept the neutralization process that will follow.

Refer to the graphic attached to refresh your memory on exactly where to tap.

Begin by tapping on the karate point while stating the following:

Even though there may be some things I am not totally in harmony with today ... I choose for this time to suspend those feelings, so I can now focus entirely on the exercises for the Layers of this work.

So even though I may need to neutralize some general irritations ... I am going to do that before I do this work because I love myself fully and completely, and I am committed to clear this up, so I can be empowered enough to engage in the equal partnerships that I choose.

So even though I may not be in total harmony, I am willing to suspend any contrasting feelings I have at this time, so that I can be clear and receptive to do this work because I love myself enough to respond.

Next, you will do the general neutralizing. It involves stating reminder phrases while you tap on the designated endpoints.

Neutralizing the Negative:

Eyebrow: Generally disturbed … A little bit antsy … Clear out any anger.

Side of the Eye: Clear out all distractions.

Under the Eye: Any frustration.

Upper Lip: A little bit fatigued.

Under the Lip: But choose to feel empowered to do this work.

Collarbone: Am excited to do this Layer of work.

Under the Arm: Have committed to showing up to do this work.

Rib: Am getting excited to meet this Inner Child and to help this Inner Child heal.

Head: I ask my Higher Guidance to be of assistance so that I can move forward and clear this disturbance and finally heal.

That completes the sequences. These are just suggestions as to how you would neutralize anything that is currently in your daily life. Continue to tap on each of the endpoints until you move through any resistance that emerges in your efforts to heal the inner saboteur.

Note: Sometimes the Adult Self has antagonistic feelings towards the Inner Child, and these would need to be neutralized before you can be effective. This can be especially true for this Inner Child because it is during this stage of development that we first have to deal with what I refer to as "the judgment of our peers."

If our experiences during this stage of development were challenging, our ability to feel secure enough to be able to discern what feels equal and what does not would be thwarted. We may have had experiences that were embarrassing and those memories haunt us in adulthood. If as adults, we do not develop compassion towards this part of self, he or she cannot heal. It is therefore essential to flush out any judgment you may carry regarding your grade-school self. If identified, customize your tapping sequences to respond and clear. Once you feel ready, move on to this next Layer of Healing.

2ND LAYER: THE SEPARATION STEP

In the exercises in the first section, you were able to put a face to the part within you whose low self-esteem impacts your ability to establish and sustain equal, reciprocal partnerships. Now is the time to begin to separate from him or her and *externalize* these feelings. When you externalize the disturbance, you set up a dyad between the part of you that carries the wound and the part of you that can respond to the wound.

You will be using the pronoun "he or she" to begin the separation process. This is a crucial step because this very separation allows the interaction to occur between the wounded one and the Healer within you; ultimately, it is this interaction that creates the healing.

Then take a moment to draw from what you discovered in the previous sections. Get in touch with one of your contrasting feelings about how well you reciprocally relate to others, your environment, your body, your pets, and/or your Higher Self. Know that these responses are the voices of your wounded ones that hold on to all of your issues with respect to engaging in relationships that exhibit an equal give and take.

Next, you want to introduce the possibility that you can respond to these wounded ones … that you can help heal the pain associated with their co-dependency and their inability to expect a "fair shake." Know that you can invite him or her to partner with you to manifest what you deserve. You will want to externalize these feelings so you can prepare to respond to them.

State the setup phrase while tapping on the karate point.

Even though a part of me feels really unable to expect its fair share and is not sure it can trust me, the Adult Self, to set the appropriate limits that will ensure an equal exchange, I know this is only a part of me, and I love myself and this wounded one enough to be willing to respond to his or her pain.

Even though a part of me really doubts I can hold my own and respond to others with a sense of fairness and equal exchange … I now choose to work with that part of self … to help him or her heal … because I love that part of self and I understand that its sabotage is in response to its fears.

So even though a part of me is trying to distract me from my ultimate goal …. I am ready to respond to his or her needs because I love myself and that part of me enough to heal.

That completes the setup phrases. You are now ready to proceed with the reminder phrases. Continue to repeat the reminder phrases until you move through any resistance that crops up in your efforts to heal the inner saboteur.

Neutralizing the Negativity

Eyebrow: he or she experiences such distrust.

Side of the Eye: So competitive … and unable to feel safe.

Under the Eye: Has so much false loyalty …

Upper Lip: he or she can't compete; does not feel equal enough to step up.

Under the Lip: He or she does not have a clue how to feel equal.

Collarbone: So wounded … so afraid to reach out and invest.

Under the Arm: he or she cannot imagine an equal exchange.

Rib: So much fear … so much suspicion and mistrust.

Head: Wonder if I will ever be able to heal this fear.

Introducing the Possibility of Change

Eyebrow: Maybe he or she doesn't have to feel so bad!

Side of the Eye: Maybe I can help him or her feel trust.

Under the Eye: Maybe I can help restore his or her faith.

Upper Lip: Maybe I can help him or her feel enough to show up.

Under the Lip: Really want to teach him or her about what to expect.

Collarbone: Maybe he or she can begin to trust.

Under the Arm: Maybe he or she can let go and begin to trust; I can set limits and participate in an equal exchange.

Rib: I don't want him or her to feel better or worse than someone else.

Head: I really want to teach this little one how to play fair.

Affirming the Conviction

Eyebrow: I'm going to help ... help him or her let go of this fear ... give up the false loyalties ... learn how to be clear.

Side of the Eye: I am so glad to be able to finally teach this little one how to participate in an equal exchange.

Under the Eye: Help him or her let go, so he or she can feel safe.

Upper Lip: I can feel compassion and want to help him or her grieve.

Under the Lip: I really can feel compassion for him or her ...

Collarbone: Every cell in my body feels the compassion he or she needs. I know how hard it was to feel unequal, but that is no longer the case.

Under the Arm: I have developed the self-esteem to help him or her feel equal and to be able to see others as the same.

Rib: Every cell vibrates with a willingness to feel equal ... every cell now invites him or her to trust.

Head: I can invite him or her to replace this fear with trust.

Continue to work with these sequences until you feel complete with this initial clearing and are prepared to proceed.

3ʳᵈ LAYER: THE INTERACTIVE STEP

This step is really the heart of the Inner Child work. Once you have separated from this part of yourself, you can truly begin to relate to him or her and respond to its fears of not feeling good enough. This trait can be masked as acting superior to others, just as easily as acting inferior. Either response is indicative of feeling low self-esteem.

Coming into the middle where there is neither the need to feel better than or lesser than another is the true essence of building a trusting relationship between your most illuminate, nurturing self and the wounded Inner Child or aspect of your Soul. It is essential to ascertain the issues this Inner Child has with being able to accept him or herself as well as others unconditionally. This extends even to his or her relationship with you. Before you can clear feelings from the past, it is necessary to clear issues he or she may have with **you** with respect to treating him or her fairly.

Check in with this part of you and ask if he or she feels you listen and respond. Again, record your thoughts and feelings in your journal.

1. Does he or she experience you as being willing to take his or her feelings into consideration?

2. Do you override the wishes of your Inner Child and ignore his or her needs?

3. Do you cater to your Inner Child and allow him or her to run the show?

Although it is important in this hierarchy that the Inner Child feels safe enough with you to know you will be in charge … he or she also needs to experience your compassion and ability to take his or her feelings into consideration.

You will also want to explore with this little one how he or she experiences you in other partnerships. Think about these following questions and then record your thoughts and feelings in your journal.

1. Does he or she sense you operate in a fair manner?

2. Do you sell yourself out and allow others to dominate you and override your concerns?

3. Can you stand up for yourself without encroaching?

All of these patterns are what need to be addressed in these sequences, and it will take some exploration to flush them out.

You will be doing what is called *surrogate tapping,* tapping on behalf of another. In this sequence, you are using the pronoun "you."

This gives the inner children the experience of being seen and heard. It invites them to feel valued and nurtured.

Again, this part of you may even feel betrayed by you ... all of these feelings need to be flushed out, so you can be effective in your approach. By responding to his or her pain and operating on your inner child's behalf, you enhance the experience of deservedness and nourish a sense of importance. This is true for the Inner Child as well as for an aspect of your Soul's past.

Again, if you have taken a break, then begin your sequences by doing one round where you get the Adult Self ready to be present for this work. Then take a moment to reconnect with the wounded one from whom you separated in the previous sequence. Invite him or her to sit beside you or even jump up on your lap. Explain you are going to be tapping on your face while you speak certain phrases; and it may look a little silly but you are doing this to help him or her feel better, so he or she does not have to feel so much pain. *(It is necessary to do this step every time because you may be dealing with a different Inner Child.)*

When you feel ready, begin to state the following setup phrases while tapping on the karate point.

Even though the circumstances surrounding my partnerships may trigger your old wounds (substitute any feeling that fits) and sometimes cause you great pain, I love you and myself enough to begin to work with your original wound, so we can work together to manifest partnerships that feel equal and fair.

Even though you experience great discomfort when you have to witness my involvement with my environment and with others, I want you to know I love you and I love myself enough to be willing to monitor my reactions to others and to respond to your pain.

So even though I want to experience reciprocal partnerships with everyone with whom I relate, I realize your issues may reflect my incongruence ... but I am willing to listen to you and respond with love and compassion because I value your reactions and want to listen to you and help you feel safe.

Reword these phrases in whatever way speaks to you. Just make sure you state the setup phrases, so you set your psyche up to do this interactive process.

Once you have done the setup phrases, you are ready to begin the neutralization process. Move into the possibility of change. Complete this Layer by stating with conviction your willingness to resolve this Inner Child's insecurities that result in imbalanced partnerships and leave you feeling unfulfilled.

Use these as an example but you may need to work with this in a little more personal manner … so do not be shy to make up your own reminder phrases that suit your needs more specifically. Again, you will be using the pronoun "you."

Neutralizing the Negativity

Eyebrow: Afraid, so afraid to trust I will listen and respond…

Side of the Eye: So many triggers… you carry so much doubt and mistrust…

Under the Eye: I am here to help you heal… to let go of the false loyalties, so together we can relate in the way we desire.

Upper Lip: I promise to listen to you and to respond …

Under the Lip: I know you are afraid to trust me, but I vow to help you see I can listen and respond…

Collarbone: You witnessed such imbalance… so afraid to step up…

Under the Arm: So afraid to trust I know how to relate…

Rib: All these years … so many triggers for your fear and mistrust…

Head: So much fear … so afraid to trust.

Introducing the Possibility of Change

Eyebrow: But it is safe for you to trust me.

Side of the Eye: Can you let me show you how.

Under the Eye: Maybe you will learn to trust me.

Upper Lip: Just take the risk and see if this works.

Under the Lip: I invite you to come along.

Collarbone: I promise you I will not let you down.

Under the Arm: I just invite you to work with me.

Rib: Please notice… I really have healed.

Head: I do deserve your trust, and I am willing to show up. I am really excited to work with you on this. I won't let you down.

Conviction to Change

Eyebrow: I do feel a connection with you.

Side of the Eye: I guarantee you I am trustworthy and can help you heal.

Under the Eye: I can help you heal. I am willing to come back to your time.

Upper Lip: I can come to you. I can teach you how to neutralize your insecurities and dissolve the false loyalties that bring us down.

Under the Lip: I am so excited that you are willing to try.

Collarbone: I am so excited we get to work on this together.

Under the Arm: I am so excited you have shown up.

Rib: I am so excited that together we can heal.

Head: I am so excited that together you and I can heal. I vow not to let you down.

While repeating your reminder phrases, do sequential rounds on the endpoints until you move through any resistance this wounded one holds. Stay with it until he or she can be responsive in your efforts to help it heal.

Specific memories may emerge where, as a child, you felt bullied or you acted superior to cover up your own inadequacies. When these memories arise, assure your Inner Child that in the next Layer you will be returning to these situations and helping him or her learn how to deal with the circumstances in a fresh manner. You will also guide him or her through the process of neutralizing the feelings, so he or she can heal in that past time period.

As you work with this Inner Child, you will sense him or her moving from doubt, fear, or betrayal, into perhaps even anger that it took you so long, then into a willingness to believe, and finally into an eagerness to try it for him or herself.

Again, as new feelings emerge in response to these reminder phrases, tap on them as well. Customize your sequences until you get completely clear.

4ᵗʰ Layer: The Teaching Step: Healing your Inner Child and Soul

In this next sequence, you shift into a meditative state and begin to teach your Inner Child or wounded one the technique for this neutralizing process. If necessary, remember to begin your work by doing one round where you get the Adult Self clear enough to be fully present for this work.

Meditation: Healing the Wound

When you feel ready to proceed, take a moment to reconnect with the Inner Child with whom you worked in the previous sequence. Always invite him or her to sit beside you or even to jump up on your lap. Then explain how you want to teach him or her how to do this process, so he or she can feel safe enough to trust you. It is this relationship you must heal before you can internalize the self-esteem that is necessary for establishing healthy, equal partnerships.

Now, to begin … in your mind's eye, ask your wounded one to take you back to the place where he or she first experienced lack of reciprocity. Again, be prepared that this little one might even begin by taking you back to an experience in which you were the cause of the mistrust. If that occurs, neutralize that first and end the sequence with an apology. Every time you collapse into the fear and act from this part of you, it is experienced by this Inner Child as abandonment. As you progress in your work, you will be able to recognize this more easily and respond more quickly. Record your responses in your journal.

1. When you feel ready, proceed to inquire about past situations where he or she was being bullied and overpowered; or acted as the bully who tried to overpower another.

2. Who was involved?

3. What are the false loyalties?

4. Where did you give your power away?

5. What did he or she hear or witness that resulted in so much fear, sadness, and pain?

Spend time really exploring this past situation, so you will be able to more effectively respond. When you feel you have enough information, close your eyes and imagine you return to the scene where the wound took place. Observe it for a minute; then freeze the scene, and pull your wounded one to the side. Invite him or her to either sit on your lap or sit cross-legged in front of you. Build on the experience of that last sequence when this little one watched as you tapped and explain that in this round you are going to tap along to show him or her how it is done.

All you want is for your Inner Child to repeat what you say and tap where you tap. Explain this, so your little one understands you are stating these sequences as if you are him or her (using the pronoun "I"); you are asking that he or she repeats the phrases after you speak them while tapping where you tap.

In this first round, imagine that both you and your Inner Child are tapping on the karate point as you state the setup phrase on his/her behalf. Then envision him or her tapping with you and repeating after you. Again, determine if these statements need to be tweaked to customize them to your specific needs.

Even though I do not trust myself to know how to establish partnerships that express a fair exchange ... and I know this is what I witnessed as a child ... I know you love me and I love myself enough to trust you to help me heal.

Even though attempting to establish healthy, reciprocal partnerships brings up a lot of doubt for me and causes great fear, I am willing to experiment with this because I trust you, my Adult Self, enough to keep me safe.

So even though this issue triggers many feelings from the past, I am so grateful you are guiding me through it ... and I believe, in response to this, I will be able to trust and heal.

These are only examples of your setup statements. Again, customize them to your needs and, when you feel complete, move into the neutralization sequences. I provide suggestions, but you are going to want to experiment with this because this Layer really is the healing agent of this entire process.

As you will see, the sequencing gradually helps you identify the origin of the disturbance and then assists you in moving into the possibility of letting that go ... the possibility that something really can be different ... that this wound really can be healed. The sequences then end with the conviction that it is safe to trust that reciprocity can be attracted and sustained. Follow this to get a feel for it, but I encourage you to experiment with your own words as well.

Neutralizing the Negative

Eyebrow: So much pain in this scene ... just remember feeling so bullied and overpowered. ... so hard for me to feel trust.

Side of the Eye: Seldom felt safe. Never felt equal.

Under the Eye: Always feared being dominated ... afraid I would not measure up.

Upper Lip: I remember the pain ... the pain of not knowing how to say no.

Under the Lip: Seldom felt safe ... so always gave in.

Collarbone: Now I don't even entertain an equal relationship with someone else.

Under the Arm: Wish I could compete ... wish I could match up...

Rib: So much fear ... will I ever compare?

Head: Wish I didn't feel so inferior ... don't think I can match up.

Another round ... this time from the state of superiority ...

Eyebrow: I know no one else can compare.

Side of the Eye: I always have to be the best ... can never let down my need to win.

Under the Eye: Where did this need to be first come from?

Upper Lip: Always have to compete ... always have to be the best.

Under the Lip: That's how I feel ... when I look back.

Collarbone: Just wish I felt secure enough to let down my guard.

Under the Arm: I get so afraid of being the best.

Rib: So afraid of what will happen ...

Head: ... if I don't compete and win...

Introducing the Possibility of Change

Eyebrow: Maybe this can change...

Side of the Eye: Maybe I can finally let my guard down...

Under the Eye: Maybe this Adult Self will make sure I am safe.

Upper Lip: Maybe it is time to accept myself and others as well.

Under the Lip: Maybe I can let this tension go and trust my Adult Self.

Collarbone: Maybe my Adult Self is really here to help me heal this need to always be the best.

Under the Arm: Maybe I can let go of my need for Mom and Dad's love.

Rib: Maybe I don't have to carry this old belief that I did not deserve.

Head: Maybe I can let go. Maybe it is safe to trust.

Conviction to Change

Eyebrow: I am going to let go and let my Adult Self in…

Side of the Eye: I am going to let go … let go of the past.

Under the Eye: I am willing to let this go and trust my Adult Self.

Upper Lip: I am willing to let go and let God.

Under the Lip: I know I have carried this for so very long.

Collarbone: But I am willing to let it go.

Under the Arm: I am willing to trust my Adult Self might be different than my parents.

Rib: I am willing to give it a try.

Top Head: I feel really good about joining forces with the Adult Self … I am ready to let it go. I am ready to trust.

Again, this gives you an example of how to move through the underlying feelings that resulted in having to compete, compare, and always come out on top. It addresses the opposite fear that you would not be good enough. Both positions cripple you when it comes to establishing and sustaining equal partnerships.

I really encourage you to continue to work with this and keep going through the sequences until you have approached it from every angle that emerges. Keep in mind there is no right or wrong way with this. Continue to work with this Inner Child until he or she is ready to let go and can completely give up the need to be the best or the fear of not being good enough. When this part of self finally feels competent and secure within, it is possible to form partnerships based on mutual respect and appreciation. Your self-esteem will be solid enough to know how to discern what feels fair to you and what does not. It is this base of self-knowledge that invites integrity, the ability to give and take, and the confidence to know how to negotiate.

You will sense this part moving through the stages of grief, the tension, and fear. He or she will eventually acknowledge how badly he or she wanted to feel good enough to compete fairly and to win and lose with honor. You may encounter his or her anger when this did not take place and witness a collapse into total despair in response to the effort it takes to stay on top or to avoid being last.

The ideal situation is to take this part of you through all of its feelings until he or she feels confident enough within and safe enough with you, the Adult, to know that equal partnerships can be attained. He or she really does want to trust that you will be mindful of his/her needs when you engage in a partnership with someone else. He or she needs to experience you will not abandon your own needs when you enter into a relationship. He or she needs to believe you can set limits and reach agreements that benefit both parties equally.

Continue to explore what your Inner Child's experience is around this issue. Tap and neutralize those feelings from every angle, and eventually, you will win back his or her trust. But it is important to be patient. This often takes more than one sequence and more than one day. But this will give you a start.

When you feel you have healed this part enough to proceed to the next Layer, then do so. If you cannot get past the need to compete or the fear of being equal, consider setting up a one-to-one session, and we will see what we can do. You may be inspired to access the Divine and assess if this issue is anchored in a past life. If so, approach the first Four Layers from that angle. The Fifth Layer continues this process for the Inner Child only. If you do discover this is past-life oriented, the process is not to merge but rather to send that past part of your Soul back to its original source.

5ᵗ LAYER: THE STEP OF INTEGRATION AND MERGER

This Layer is perhaps one of the most empowering Layers. As mentioned above, the following process is used only for the integration of an Inner Child. With an aspect of your Soul, you want to just send it back into the Light to free energy. But with an aspect of your personality from this lifetime (the Inner Child), you want to partner with him or her and build a bonding, cooperative relationship.

Combining the neutralization process (with the pronoun "we") enables you to begin to set up the merger and integration. Partnering with the Inner Child in this manner empowers him or her to return to your force field in a healed state and empowers you and your Inner Child to reclaim the magic that was lost in the wounding experience.

This merger, however, can be between you and whatever partner you are addressing. If you have been healing your partnership with your Higher Self, and it is the Inner Child who has thwarted that union, you now merge from all three levels.

When you bring this magic back, the essence of the believability and trust you have as a child returns as well. If you then infuse your desire to attract partnerships of reciprocity with this vibration, you experience magic ten-fold!

If you have taken a break, then begin your Fifth Layer of exercises by doing one round where you get the Adult Self clear enough to be present for this work. You may also want to add another round to make sure your Inner Child has remained clear. When you feel ready to proceed, the sequence will go something like the example below.

For this Layer, you will be using the pronoun "we" because you are stating the sequences as if whoever you are partnering with, be it the Inner Child or anyone else, you are stating this in unison. When you feel ready, begin.

State the setup phrase while tapping on the karate point.

Even though we have both experienced a lot of disappointment and imbalance in our relationships in the past, we are so excited we have found each other again and we love ourselves and each other enough to trust and to manifest the equal partnerships we deserve...

Even though we both have experienced so many disappointments, betrayals, and reasons not to trust, we are so excited we have come together and are now able to feel safe enough with each other, so we can heal.

So even though we have so many experiences with not being equal and have not felt equal to others for the reasons we have discussed ... we are so excited we have found each other ... we have come home to each other and are now ready to heal.

This is an example of the setup phrases; please feel free to customize them, and make them fit your particular situation. The following is an example of the sequences you could use to augment this Layer. It is really not as much of a process of neutralization as an infusion of what you have affirmed. But just to be on the safe side, I have provided one round to help you clear any resistance that crops up in your effort to come together in this fashion. Add more if you feel it would be useful.

Again, prepare to tap by beginning with the corner of your eyebrow.

Tapping in the Merger

Eyebrow: We are so excited to come together and heal.

Side of the Eye: We are just buzzing with enthusiasm and trust for each other.

Under the Eye: So excited we are going to finally manifest relationships that feel equal and mutually satisfying to us both.

Upper Lip: Through our love for each other and with the love of God, we know we can participate in partnerships that will serve us all.

Under the Lip: We are so excited to come together to heal.

Collarbone: So excited we feel safe enough to negotiate and establish partnerships based on trust.

Under the Arm: We are so full of energy, love, and Light … we send this vibration out to the entire world.

Rib: We are so excited we have done such good work.

Head: We are so proud of each other and love each other so much that we are ready to attract others who mirror our love.

Now just keep going with that until you are really, really buzzing and when you feel ready to proceed, move on to Layer Six where you address the partnership with your body.

6ᴛʜ Layer: Rewiring your Brain; Reprogramming your DNA; Reconfiguring the Electromagnetic Field

Discussion: The implementation of this Layer was inspired by the New Brain Science, most specifically the work of Dr. Richard Hanson, and Margaret Ruby's work on reprogramming the DNA. www.possibilitiesdna.com/margaret.html

You use meditations and interactive tapping™ sequences to first rewire the brain by building new neuro-pathways between the amygdala and the prefrontal cortex. You then clear the energetic disturbance from your electrical system in your body, ask your body for its forgiveness, and then give it permission to release. This reprograms the DNA in every cell so it can hold your new vibration and enables you to reconfigure the electromagnetic field around you.

Addressing this Layer of DNA reprogramming in this manner establishes a unique aspect of reciprocity. Seldom do we consider the need to be in a reciprocal relationship with our physical forms. Some of us do not even track our bodies. We are so unaware of them that we treat them as if they were our servants. Actually, quite the opposite is true.

To demonstrate this, I want to include an excerpt from one of my other books that feels especially appropriate for this topic as well.

Excerpt from *Soul Steps … the art of conscious aerobic exercise…* page 119.

Our Bodies and Our Need to Respect Them as Sacred

One of the issues many of us need to heal is our relationship with our bodies. We have spent many years, and perhaps lifetimes, de-valuing our bodies and their needs, believing the physical form is too dense and of such a low vibration that we need to tend to our spiritual path instead of our bodily needs. I have found that, since I am in body and must do my spiritual work from this vibrational reality, it is absolutely essential for me to hold sacred this physical form that enables me to do this work. In exploring this for myself, I realized that the "I" who I identify as my human and physical self had a right to be in an equal partnership with my connection to the God-Source or my Higher or God-Self. This thought inspired me to begin to explore how I became disconnected from respecting my body as well.

I came to realize that as children, we are taught to be shy about our bodies, that our curiosity about our bodies is not acceptable and that, at best, the body is an object to be taken care of but not to be taken too seriously. However, since every mineral and cell found in our bodies is also found in the makeup of Mother Earth, wouldn't it be wonderful if, as children, we were taught to respect our bodies as a gift from Mother Earth. To learn that she has given of herself to give us a physical form that can house the Gift of Spirit we have received from God.

If, in childhood, we could learn to respect the land and the trees as our relatives, the rocks and the rivers as the libraries of the earth; if we could be taught to listen to the land, to say good morning to Grandfather Sun and to bid Grandmother Moon good-night; if as children, we were taught that it is from Mother Earth and her animal and mineral creatures from which our food comes; if we were taught that we too come of the earth, we would be so much more connected to ourselves, to the earth, and to the God-source around us.

Being taught to relate to one's body in this way would allow us, as children, to stay connected to our physical forms, to accept our curious nature, to expect to be respected for our physical boundaries and needs.

Relating to your Inner Children in this manner can at least be a beginning to facilitate your own connection to your physical form and could undo some of this disconnection that took place in your own life. It can restore your trust in your body to tell you what it needs so you can make the appropriate choices.

One of the ways I have tried to reinstate my connection to Mother Earth and my physical form is that at mealtime, I not only thank God for the meal, but I also thank the food, the farmers, the grocery store clerks—every person or element that has been involved in getting this food from its source to my table. It reeducates my Inner Child regarding the sequence of nourishment and sets the stage for her not to be so disconnected from her origin. It also

serves as a metaphor for my Inner Child and facilitates a recon-
nection to appreciate the gifts of Mother Earth as well as those from
God-Source.

Although I feel the relationship we have with our bodies deserves
to have a book dedicated just solely to it, I wanted to at least include
this tidbit because it feels so relevant to not only to reprogramming
your DNA but also to establishing a reciprocal *partnership* with your
body. Few of us think of our bodies in this fashion. I invite you to
entertain this thought as you work through this Layer of healing.

This process begins by first clearing the disturbance of imbalance
and lack of reciprocity from every cell in your body. It involves asking
your body to forgive you and then giving it permission to release
whatever energy it holds around not feeling good enough to ask for
what you deserved or reacting in a superior manner because deep
inside you felt insecure. However your body held this issue for you, it
is now time to reprogram the DNA in every cell, so it can release and
be open to your new vibration.

I have included a suggestion. Please experiment and try it on
every feeling you think you have stored in your body in response to
your wanting to establish equal partnerships with yourself and others
but not having the skills to do so for so many years.

State the setup phrase while tapping on the karate point. Imagine
you are speaking directly to your body.

Even though I have needed you to store my pain, I am now strong
enough to process my pain myself … I can honestly invite you to release
the tension and the stress … invite you to truly let it go.

And even though you, my dear body, have held so many feelings of
tension related to feeling insecure and not even good enough to expect a
fair shake, I now forgive myself and love myself enough to ask for your
forgiveness because I really did not know what else to do.

So even though you have carried so much for me over the years I am
now strong enough to do for myself what you have so gallantly done on
my behalf that I respectfully give you permission to release and let go.

Now sequentially tap around on all of the endpoints while you repeat the following reminder phrases.

Eyebrow: So in turn,

Side of Eye: dear body …

Corner of the eye: I ask you to forgive me as well.

Under the Eye: I humbly apologize …

Upper Lip: …for needing you to hold this disturbance for me …

Under the Lip: … and now give you total permission to release it.

Collarbone: I firmly commit to you …

Under the Arm: … that I will now neutralize and dissolve

Rib: … all disturbances related to my lack of trust and feeling safe.

Head: Thank you. Thank you. Thank you.

Repeat this sequence until you feel you have moved through all the resistance your body is holding for you. Give your body permission to release what it has held. Reassure it that you are now completely willing to deal with what comes your way with the tools you have acquired. When replenishing your body with a new vibration, you are acknowledging that the DNA has been reprogrammed. You infuse every cell with the new vibration of your intention.

Now begin to tap on the two sore spots right on your chest (near the collarbone but not on the collarbone) to infuse your body with this new vibration of energy. State your new intention much like an affirmation. Imagine attracting  reciprocity in your relations with all people, pets, and things. Once you have this image firmly in your mind's eye, hold this vibration for 68 seconds. As has been discussed, according to the *Teachings of Abraham,* this length of focus is enough for your intention to take form and begin attracting reciprocity from the Universe. It will match it and begin the process of materializing your intent. The following is an example of how the narrative of your infusion might flow. Repeat it while tapping on the sore spots.

In a narrative fashion, you will want to say something like this:

I now envision harmony and reciprocity in all of my partnerships. I am free to attract the relationships that feel equal in their exchange. All my needs and wants are fully realized in the presence of the Light. I am so fortunate to experience such reciprocity in my partnerships from my Higher Power to Mother Earth to all those I love! Every area of my life is enriched with this sense of trust and reciprocity. I know how to give and take fairly. I experience trust and equality in my relationships with all those in my life. I experience reciprocity in my career and my livelihood. I experience reciprocity with my body. I engage in equal relationships with everything in the universe. I experience reciprocity in mind, body, heart, and Soul!

7ᵀᴴ LAYER: GIVING BACK TO THE WORLD

Now it is time to share with the world what you have healed. It too needs an infusion of compassionate, unconditional regard. Take all you have neutralized and realigned, and send this energy into the Universe as an offering for planetary healing. It dissolves isolation and contributes not only to the increasing of the Light on the planet but also to the healing of Mother Earth. It reinforces the fact that you are part of something bigger than yourself and a valuable agent of change for mankind. You have shared the gift with your Inner Child and aspect of your Soul. You now have an opportunity to share it with the world.

Again, I encourage you to experiment with the wording as much as your imagination will allow. Just keep tapping and saying affirming statements. I have included a sample, but please experiment and try it on everything. Make sure, however, you use this only after you have moved to a low intensity on the scale from 1–10 or have neutralized your way up Abraham's *Emotional Guidance Scale* because you want the energy you send out into the world to be as pure as possible.

Before you begin, I suggest you do one round as always to clear any current trigger in your body, mind, heart, and Soul! Begin to tap as you enter into a meditative state. When you feel ready, tap again on your sore spots while you say something like this:

I feel so fortunate to have done this work and to have cleared the way for satisfying partnerships. I now envision a cylinder of Light running from the center of Mother Earth to the grid of unconditional love about 60 feet above my head. I am so full of Light and expansive energy and, from this highest place within myself, I now offer 10% or more of this healing back to be used to heal the planet and the universe. I feel so fortunate I have been able to complete this work and am so grateful I am now in a position to share this gift. Thank you, God, Goddess, Higher Power, Angels, Masters, and all above for your support and direction. Thank you Soul fragments for having the courage and fortitude to call me back and thank you my dear little ones for having the patience to await my return. I love that we are healed and can now hold the Light that allows us to claim our right to equal and fair partnerships and to attract our heart's desires. Thank you. Thank you. Thank you.

This is again an example. As you work in this fashion, the inspiration will come to you … the words will come to you, and this last sequence will simply augment your ability to attract the partnerships of your choice–relationships that offer a fair give and take.

ABOUT THE AUTHOR

athryn Taylor is the author of, The Inner Child Workbook-What To Do With Your Past When It Just Won't Go Away, which was published by Jeremy P. Tarcher, Inc. in 1991. Since that time it has been translated into Dutch, Spanish, Czech, and Korean, is in its 40th printing and can still be found on Cathryn's website, the bookshelves of Barnes and Noble, and amazon.com

The Inner Child Workbook was one of five books released in the 1990's which popularized the concept of the inner child. It is considered a classic in the inner child field and has positioned Cathryn as one of the field's leading experts. Of those five authors, Cathryn is the only one who has continued to develop and apply this concept. She does so because she finds it to be invaluable both in her personal growth and in her professional work with others. She has been conducting workshops, lectures, and classes for over thirty years and has authored and recorded a series of lectures which cover topics on the different stages of recovery, issues of the children within, and holistic healing.

Cathryn's approach is an ever-evolving ... her quest for transformation–never-ending.

BACKGROUND–Cathryn was licensed in the state of California in 1979 as a Marriage and Family Therapist was certified in Chemical Dependency in 1985 and is now licensed in the state of Minnesota as an Alcohol and Drug Counselor and as a Marriage and Family Therapist. She has been trained as a Personal Life Coach, an EMDR Practitioner, an Akashic Records Consultant, a catalyst for Dr. Eric Pearl's Reconnective Healing, is a Certified Practitioner of Lindsay Kenny's Pro-EFT energy tapping techniques and is currently receiving training in Dr. David Berceli's Trauma Release Exercises (TRE©). Cathryn weaves these modalities with her expertise of the inner child in a very dynamic and expansive way. Her approach incorporates consultation and facilitation-assisting you in building the relationship between your Higher Self, your Adult Self, and your Children Within.

Having obtained a BA in Sociology from Texas Christian University at Ft. Worth, Texas in 1970 and an MA in Psychology from John F. Kennedy University at Orinda, California in 1979, Cathryn has worked in the mental health field since 1971. In addition to having a successful private practice, she has also worked as a Family Therapist in Residential Treatment Centers, Inpatient and Outpatient Chemical Dependency Units and an Eating Disorders Clinic, and was the Director of the Salvation Army Meth Clinic. She currently has a private practice in both the Twin Cities area and in San Rafael, California.

Cathryn continues to be interviewed on the areas of her expertise in newspapers as well as on radio and television and presents at numerous Expositions around the country. Her most recent interview can be found by clicking on this link: CTV NEWS spotlights Cathryn Taylor. Featured as a columnist in *The EDGE*, a mid-western, metaphysical, monthly newspaper for over eighteen months. Cathryn continues her affiliation with the Edge Newspaper as coordinator of the Edge Talk Radio Blog Talk Network. She also hosts her own monthly show on the Edge network entitled Edge EFT Happy Half Hour. as well as hosting her own show on EFT Radio called, EFT for Your Inner Child and Soul, and on BBM Radio entitled, EFT for Spiritual Fitness. A seasoned lecturer and facilitator, Cathryn is well known in the mental health community for her expertise. Please visit her website which is www.EFTForYourInnerChild.com or her YouTube channel, https://www.youtube.com/user/ctinnerchildwork which has over 100 educational videos demonstrating her unique style of energy therapy she calls, Interactive Tapping™.

I would like to thank Cathy Jacobsen and Tim Miejan, the editors and owners of *Edge Magazine*, (a mid-western metaphysical magazine which, since 1992, has been exploring the evolution of consciousness) for making me a part of the Edge family, and for believing in me as the coordinator, as well as host, of *Edge Inner Views*, and *EFT Happy Half Hour* on the *Edge Talk Radio*; Eleanore Duyndam, the coordinator of EFT Radio—one of the most successful self-help networks on Blog Talk Radio—for inviting me to host of my own EFT show in which, over the last eight years, I have been able to introduce my signature brand of Interactive Tapping to a well-groomed audience. And last but not least, I want to thank Eddie, Tom, and Perry of Bold Brave Media (a world-class producer, distributor and online broadcaster of original live, on-demand talk radio programming), for their unwavering support on my radio show, entitled, *EFT for Spiritual Fitness*. With these broadcasts, I have been able to reach an audience that was before unaware of the gifts of the fantastic method to heal.

If you are interested in pursuing your inner child work please check out the mother book of all of my publications, ***The Inner Child Workbook***.

If you are suffering a personal loss of a loved one then I invite you to read ***Beyond Compassion***. If that loved one is a pet then you might also enjoy reading my shamanic tale called, ***Maximized.***

Soul Steps takes this work into integrating your body, mind, heart, and Soul through "conscious aerobic exercise™".

Which Lifetime Is This Anyway? which you just read guides you through the multiple dimensions of your personality and Soul; and **_Life Beyond Confusion and Fear_** gives you a Four Stage model for multidimensionally dealing your _addictions_, compulsions, manifestations. Each of these can be found at www.EFTForYourInnerChild.com or purchased through Amazon.com in printed form or as a Kindle book.

Made in the USA
Middletown, DE
04 October 2020